INFORMATION TECHNOLOGY

Textbook for Class X
(As per CBSE Syllabus Code 402)

Komalpreet Kaur
Yogesh Kumar

www.bpbonline.com

FIRST EDITION 2022
REPRINT 2025

ISBN: 978-93-91392-71-0

LIMITS OF LIABILITY AND DISCLAIMER OF WARRANTY

The information contained in this book is true to correct and the best of author's and publisher's knowledge. The author has made every effort to ensure the accuracy of these publications, but publisher cannot be held responsible for any loss or damage arising from any information in this book.

All trademarks referred to in the book are acknowledged as properties of their respective owners but BPB Publications cannot guarantee the accuracy of this information.

CBSE is in no way connected with this book. This Book is written solely for the benefit and guidance of students appearing of CBSE Examination.

Distributors:

BPB PUBLICATIONS
20, Ansari Road, Darya Ganj
New Delhi-110002
Ph: 23254990/23254991

DECCAN AGENCIES
4-3-329, Bank Street,
Hyderabad-500195
Ph: 24756967/24756400

MICRO MEDIA
Shop No. 5, Mahendra Chambers,
150 DN Rd. Next to Capital Cinema,
V.T. (C.S.T.) Station, MUMBAI-400 001
Ph: 22078296/22078297

BPB BOOK CENTRE
376 Old Lajpat Rai Market,
Delhi-110006
Ph: 23861747

Published by Manish Jain for BPB Publications, 20 Ansari Road, Darya Ganj, New Delhi-110002 and Printed by him at Manipal Technologies Limited, Manipal

www.bpbonline.com

Dedicated to

My Family

About the Author(s)

- **Komalpreet Kaur** has good experience in writing research documents on computers and Electronics. She has done her Masters in Technology in Electronics and Communication and has more than three years of experience in the Research and IT field. She is pursuing her Ph.D. from Punjabi University, Patiala. Her research areas include Artificial Intelligence, Machine Learning, Natural Language Processing, Wireless Sensor Network, IoT and Communication.
- **Dr. Yogesh Kumar** is working as an Associate Professor in the Department of Computer Engineering, Indus institute of technology and engineering, Indus University, Ahmedabad Gujarat. He has done his Ph.D. in CSE from Punjabi University, Patiala. Prior to this, he has done his M.Tech in CSE from Punjabi University, Patiala. He is having a total of fourteen years of experience in teaching and research. His research areas include Artificial Intelligence, Computer Vision, Machine Learning and Data Science.

Acknowledgements

There are a few people I want to thank for the continued and ongoing support they have given me during the writing of this book. First and foremost, I would like to thank my family for putting up with me while I was spending many weekends and evenings on writing—I could have never completed this book without their support.

This book wouldn't have happened if I hadn't had the support from some of the key vendors and partners in the EUC space. My gratitude goes to the team at BPB Publications for providing valuable insights into some of the new features.

— KomalPreet Kaur

Preface

Book is as per the latest curriculum under NSQF Scheme prescribed by Central Board of Secondary Education, New Delhi; and helps students to:

- ✓ Apply effective oral and written communication skills to interact with people and customers;
- ✓ Identify the principal components of a computer system; Demonstrate the basic skills of using computer;
- ✓ Demonstrate self-management skills;
- ✓ Demonstrate the ability to provide a self-analysis in the context of entrepreneurial skills and abilities;
- ✓ Demonstrate the knowledge of the importance of green skills in meeting the challenges of sustainable development and environmental protection;
- ✓ Work safely on the computer.
- ✓ Use the computer for the data entry process.
- ✓ Collect all necessary information about the query.
- ✓ Log any decision about the query on the data entry tracking form.
- ✓ Follow Rules and guidelines for data entry.
- ✓ Identify and control hazards in the workplace that pose a danger or threat to their safety or health, or that of others.

The objective of this book is to develop a readiness for understanding Computers and its application in our lives. The book is designed to teach Information Technology to the students of class 10th under the aegis of CBSE Subject Code: 402.

The book is divided into two parts, Part-A is related to Employability Skills and Part-B contains Vocational Skills. The first part starts with Communication skills- II, Self-Management skills-II, Basic ICT skills-II, Entrepreneurship skills – II, Green skills –II. Communication skills help students to learn to interact with people and customers in their daily lives. It also demonstrates self-management skills. Afterward, the Information and communication technology skills help to identify the principle components of a computer system along with the demonstration of the basic skills of using the computer. The Entrepreneurial Skills gives an ability to provide self-analysis in the context of entrepreneurial skills and abilities and knowledge of the importance of green skills in meeting the challenges of suitable development and environment protection is demonstrated in the Green Skills chapter of this book. The Part-B of the book covers the Introduction of Digital documentation (Advanced), Electronic spreadsheet (Advanced), Database Management System, Web Applications and Security.

Downloading the coloured images:

Please follow the link to download the *Coloured Images* of the book:

https://rebrand.ly/2d0ffe

Errata

We take immense pride in our work at BPB Publications and follow best practices to ensure the accuracy of our content to provide with an indulging reading experience to our subscribers. Our readers are our mirrors, and we use their inputs to reflect and improve upon human errors, if any, that may have occurred during the publishing processes involved. To let us maintain the quality and help us reach out to any readers who might be having difficulties due to any unforeseen errors, please write to us at:

errata@bpbonline.com

Your support, suggestions and feedbacks are highly appreciated by the BPB Publications' Family.

BPB is searching for authors like you

If you're interested in becoming an author for BPB, please visit **www.bpbonline.com** and apply today. We have worked with thousands of developers and tech professionals, just like you, to help them share their insight with the global tech community. You can make a general application, apply for a specific hot topic that we are recruiting an author for, or submit your own idea.

The code bundle for the book is also hosted on GitHub at **https://github.com/bpbpublications/INFORMATION-TECHNOLOGY-TEXTBOOK-FOR-CLASS-X-**. In case there's an update to the code, it will be updated on the existing GitHub repository.
We also have other code bundles from our rich catalog of books and videos available at **https://github.com/bpbpublications**. Check them out!

PIRACY

If you come across any illegal copies of our works in any form on the internet, we would be grateful if you would provide us with the location address or website name. Please contact us at **business@bpbonline.com** with a link to the material.

If you are interested in becoming an author

If there is a topic that you have expertise in, and you are interested in either writing or contributing to a book, please visit **www.bpbonline.com**.

REVIEWS

Please leave a review. Once you have read and used this book, why not leave a review on the site that you purchased it from? Potential readers can then see and use your unbiased opinion to make purchase decisions, we at BPB can understand what you think about our products, and our authors can see your feedback on their book. Thank you!

For more information about BPB, please visit **www.bpbonline.com**.

Table of Contents

SECTION – A

SECTION – B

1 Communication Skills – II

Learning Outcomes

After this chapter, you will have the knowledge of:

- Communication process
- Various methods of communication
- Elements of Communication Cycle
- Importance of Feedback
- Types of Feedback
- Barriers of Effective communication
- Measures to overcome Barriers to Effective Communication
- 7 C's of Effective Communication
- Define Writing Skills, Phrase, Sentence
- Parts of Sentence
- Parts of Speech
- Articles and its Use
- Paragraph Writing

INTRODUCTION

Communication is the process of sharing information between two or more people. The art of communication involves art of communicating that involves ability to listen, understand and give right message to other person. It is must for speaking and writing in proper way. While working in IT-field all these communication aspects play an important role as it helps them in understanding the needs of client. One should be able to properly write and speak in any situation.

SESSION 1: VARIOUS METHODS OF COMMUNICATION

There are number of ways to communicate like written, visually, vocally and non-verbally. Communication involves both transmission and understanding it. There is need of sender and receiver where sender sends the message and in response get feedback from receiver. In figure given below a sender will send a message through any source of communication and in response receiver will give feedback.

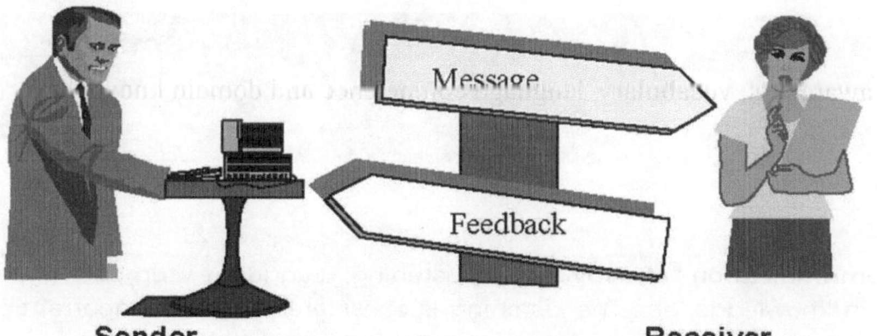

Figure 1.1: Communication process

Knowledge Box

Communication is a process of sharing information between two or multiple persons.

Fact Box

The word communication is derived from Latin word communis that means to impart, to share, to participate or to make common. Communication has become a basic need for interacting with each other's.

Memory Box

A resolution comes in field of communication by invention of computer technology and satellite through which one can communicate throughout the world.

When the sent messages is successfully delivered to receiver and understood by them then a communication is said to be effective communication.

Communication is the way process of exchanging information, data, and ideas among various people throughout the world. There are various methods for expressing the message and these methods are selected by considering various factors. These factors can be type of receiver, like whether they are painter, graphic designers, sculptors, artist and other factors are availability of time, length of message, expenditure involved, urgency of message and emotional level between both sender and receiver.

Practice Box

1. Communication involves both __________ and understanding it.
2. When the sent messages is successfully delivered to receiver and understood by them then a communication is said to be __________.

Methods of Communication

As mentioned above different methods of communication are used by people according to their needs and other various factors. Broadly they are classified into following three types:

1. Verbal Communication
2. Non-Verbal Communication
3. Visual Communication

1. **Verbal Communication:** In this type of communication, message is delivered using words as it is the most powerful and accurate tools in expressing and sharing ideas. While communicating a mutually understanding language like Hindu, Chinese, English, Punjabi, Spanish, etc language is used. Verbal communication can be done orally or by writing. The two primary forms of verbal communication are:

Figure 1.2: Verbal communication

Memory Box

Verbal communication involves general awareness, vocabulary, language competence and domain knowledge to get effective verbal communication.

Knowledge Box

Components that make verbal communication effective are: Listening, Language competency, Vocabulary, General awareness, Domain knowledge, etc. The Listening is considered as most important component that makes verbal communication more effective. Language competency includes grammar that indicates the comfort level with the language use for expressing thoughts. Vocabulary reflects your comfortless that helps in using suitable words in different contexts.

- **Oral Communication:** Oral communication is the way of expressing ideas and information through spoken words and considered as more natural form of communication as compared to written form due to immediate clarification and feedback is involved in it.

  The effectiveness of oral communication depends on:

  o Pace i.e., how fast or slow person is speaking,

- o Clarity in Pronunciation (speaking correct and clear words),
- o Pitch or Volume (how loud or soft is voice of sender and receiver),
- o Fluency (How fluent or ease and accuracy you are speaking),
- o Length of communication (The message should be concise and short as interest is loose by listener when message become long), etc.

Figure 1.3: Oral communication

Advantages of Oral communication:

- o Prompt feedback is provided by it
- o Cost efficient
- o Help in interpersonal and building relationships
- o It is preferred in confidential or private matters

Disadvantages of Oral communication:

- o No legal validity
- o Sometimes message is not understandable due to different accents and pace of voice
- o It can lead to miscommunication due to involvement of emotions
- o Not suitable for exchange of lengthy messages

✦ **Written Communication:** In this form a written messages are used to convey message and is considered as most formal way. While using written communication people should have to choice words carefully and its placement should be in order.

Examples of Written Communication are:

o Letters,	o Emails,	o Notices,
o Memorandums,	o Resumes,	o Reports, etc.

Some standard medium of written communication as messengers and SMS are WhatsApp, Social media, E-mails, etc. The message should be complete, concise and meaningful to have effective written communication.

Figure 1.4: Written communication

Advantages of Written Communication:

- o Written content has legal validity
- o It helps user to draft comprehensive message
- o In case of lengthy messages it is consider as suitable mode.

Disadvantages of Written Communication:

- o Postage cost is involved in it
- o For message drafting need long time
- o It have delays issues in decision making due to feedback

2. **Non-Verbal Communication:** In this communication method information is exchanged using all other things except word. As it includes gestures, postures, eye contact, facial expressions, fingers, etc of your body and oral communication is supported in it.

Fact Box

According to **Albert Mehrabian** a more impact is given by non-verbal communication (93%) as compared to verbal communication which count (7%).

Knowledge Box

In oral communication, to make the whole process powerful, there is the involvement of both sender and receiver who listen and respond accordingly.

The various elements involved in non-verbal communication are:

- o **Facial expression** (Even before hearing we first see on person face that is most noticeable aspect of non-verbal communication,
- o **Gestures** (In the absence of words a gestures that includes pointing fingers, waving, etc like body and hand movement are involved in it).
- o **Voice** (The other person than speaker read its voice and listen to words through which they judge weather speaker is in anger, confidence, affection, sarcasm).
- o **Body Language** (user communicate various messages through body language that includes eye movements, postures, hand gestures, facial expressions, etc),
- o **Eye Gaze** (This includes movement of eyes like staring, looking and blinking that helps in determining whether person is honest or not).
- o Physical Contact, Dress and appearance are other factors of non-verbal communication.

Memory Box

In the absence of verbal communication, feelings and thoughts are convey using non-verbal signs.

Figure 1.5: Non-verbal communication

Advantages:

- o It compliments verbal communication
- o It helps handicapped people

Disadvantages:

- o Not easy to recognize non-verbal messages that can results in miss-communication
- o Necessary explanation and long conversation is not possible

Knowledge Box

Components that make non-verbal communication effective are: Body language, Olfactics, Chronemics, Proxemics, Chromatics, Kinesics, Haptics and Silence & Pause. The Body language is a mixture of movement, tone of voice, gesture and posture you use while using non-verbal way of communication.

Fact Box

- Olfactics define the sense of smell and our brain gets effected in different manner by different smells. Chromatics refer to the use of colours, Proxemics refer to how we are physically space in our day to day interaction with others.
- Chronemics refer to the usage of time in a disciplined manner,
- Haptics refers to communication of our emotions through touch like formal handshake, angry slap, affectionate hug, etc.

3. **Visual Communication:** A sense of sight used in any verbal and non-verbal communication is a visual communication. Any method that relies on pictures, illusions, graphics for sharing messages are comes under graphic or visual communication. These are used to put lasting and penetrative impact on receivers mind through:

   - PowerPoint presentation,
   - Charts,
   - Graphs,
   - Maps,
   - White and black boards,
   - Paper handouts,
   - Models, etc.

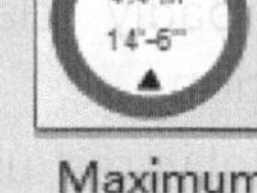

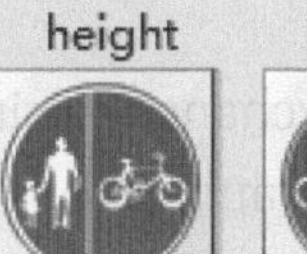

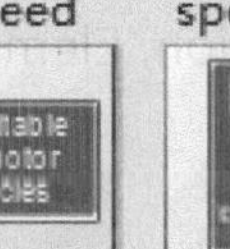

Figure 1.6 Various sign of Visual Communication

Creative minds create visual images using textures, colours, shapes that communicate messages along with emotions, experiences, concepts, textures and lifestyles. This is commonly used method of communication in education field.

Figure 1.7: Visual communication

Advantages:

- o Oral communication becomes more meaningful by addition of models, diagrams and graphs visual aids
- o Communication becomes more interesting
- o Complex data becomes easy to understand

Disadvantages:

- o Aids used in it are costly
- o Sometimes information becomes complex that's why it becomes difficult to understand.
- o Take large time to communicate
- o Limited scope as all topics can't be presented through visual communication.

Practice Box

1. Which of the following is not used in visual communication for putting lasting and penetrative impact on receivers mind?
   a. PowerPoint Presentation b. Maps c. Paper handouts d. Graphs
2. _____________ is not an elements of non-verbal communication.
   a. Facial expression b. Gestures c. Body Language d. Eye Gaze
3. Which of the following is an example of written communication?
   a. Emails b. Resumes c. Reports d. Letters

Summary

- ⊙ Communication is the way process of exchanging information, data, and ideas among various people throughout the world.
- ⊙ Methods of communication are broadly classified into verbal communication, non-verbal communication and Visual communication
- ⊙ In Verbal communication message is delivered using words as it is the most powerful and accurate tools in expressing and sharing ideas.
- ⊙ In non-verbal communication information is exchanged using all other things except word.
- ⊙ Any method that relies on pictures, illusions, graphics for sharing messages are comes under graphic or visual communication.

Keywords: Communication process, Methods of communication, Verbal communication, Non-verbal communication, Visual communication, Oral Communication, Written Communication, Elements of non-verbal communication.

Self-Assessment

A. MULTIPLE CHOICE QUESTIONS.

1. In verbal communication message is delivered using:
   a. Spoken or written message b. Message that uses words of any language
   c. both (a) and (b) d. None
2. Which of the following is not a primary form of verbal communication?
   a. Oral communication b. Written communication
   c. Body language d. None
3. Which of the following is not an example of written communication?
   a. Emails b. Reports c. body language d. Letters

B. FILL IN THE BLANKS

1. The written form of communication is __________ than oral communication.
2. Prompt/ Immediate __________ is the most significant advantage of using Oral communication
3. __________ communication method helps handicapped people
4. Any method that relies on illusions, pictures, graphics, etc for sharing messages are ________ communication

C. TRUE FALSE

1. Written communication is not suitable for lengthy messages (T/F)
2. According to Albert Mehrabian a more impact is given by non-verbal communication as compared to verbal communication. (T/F)
3. Necessary explanation and long conversation is possible in non-verbal communication (T/F)
4. Complex data becomes easy to understand through visual communication (T/F)

D. ANSWER THE FOLLOWING QUESTIONS:

1. Name three methods of communication.
2. Explain Verbal communication.
3. Differentiate Oral and Written communication.
4. What is non-verbal communication? Give advantages and disadvantages of it.
5. Give the significance of Visual communication.
6. Give disadvantage of written communication.

E. PRACTICAL WORK

1. Make a presentation on common body language errors that must be avoided while communicating.
2. Try all three methods of communication in your class for communicating and conveying message to your friends. Then make a chart on various pros and cons of each methods.
3. Do group discussion on how a communication cycle is disrupted by Non-verbal communication.
4. Play dumb Charades by following its rules to observe the non verbal method of communication.

Answers

A. Multiple choice question.

1. c 2. c 3. c

B. Fill in the blanks.

1. More formal and less flexible 2. Feedback
3. Non-verbal 4. Visual

C. True False answers.

1. False 2. True 3. False 4. True

SESSION 2: FEEDBACK IN COMMUNICATION

Feedback is the response given to sender information. To complete the communication cycle a response should be feedback by receiver. The communication cycle will broke down when feedback is missing. In this session we will learn about feedback in communication along with types of feedback: Descriptive and Specific feedback.

Elements of Communication Cycle

Various elements of communication cycle are:

Message: The actual information to be conveyed

Sender: Sender is the source who sends information or message. Sender can be a single person or a group who send information and message through appropriate channel

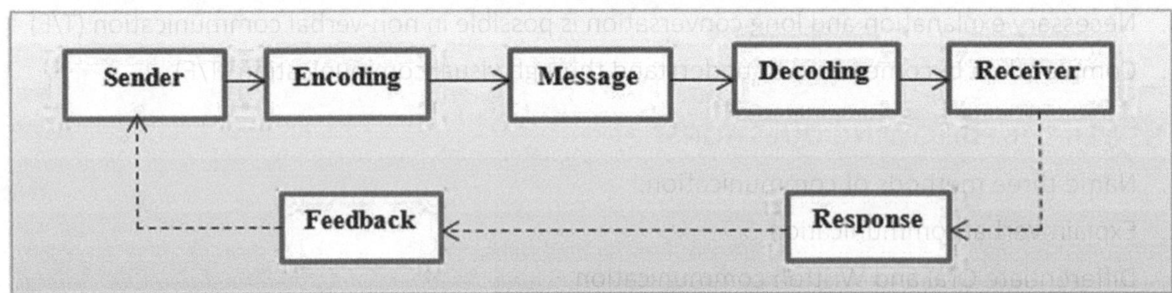

Figure 1.8: Communication Cycle

Encoding: Encoding or converting data or information into the coded language that is not understood by any other person. It can be encoded by selecting specific alphabet, words or symbols that is clear to both sender and receiver. While encoding a message or information sender must have to consider the content include in it, how to interpret it at receiver side. Various encoding schemes available are Hamming code, ASCII codes, etc.

Receiver: Receiver is the person or group who will receive the sent information or message by sender and understand it by decoding. A miss communication may take place if receiver interprets the wrong message.

Communication Channel: An appropriate channel or medium is selected by sender to send message. The communication channel can be faxes, electronic mail, letters, face to face, telephone calls, etc.

Decoding: The encoded information is decoded at receiver side to understand the sent message or information. The messages should be decoded according to the pattern use by receiver while encoding it that helps in having correct information.

Feedback: Feedback is the response given to sender information. To complete the communication cycle a response should be feedback by receiver. The communication cycle will broke down when feedback is missing.

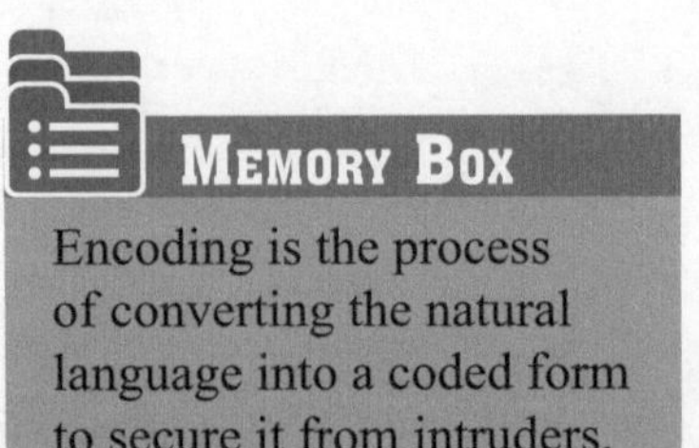

Memory Box

Encoding is the process of converting the natural language into a coded form to secure it from intruders.

Knowledge Box

Sender is the one who initiates the communication
Encoding is the structure of the message
Communication channel is a medium of communication that vary from type of communication.
Decoding is for understanding the meaning from the message received through a certain medium.
Feedback indicates the information about successful delivery of message.

Practice Box

1. What is the purpose of the receiver in communication?
   a. Understand the message and respond to it   b. Send message
   c. Take response   d. None
2. Which of the following is not a type of encoding scheme?
   a. ASCII   b. ABCD   c. Hamming   d. None

Importance of Feedback

The feedback is helpful information about prior action or behaviour from an individual and communicated to another individual who use that information for adjusting and improving the current or future actions and behaviours. The feedback occurs when there is reaction of environment to an action or behaviour. Some of the important points of feedback are:

- Feedback is done regularly that keeps everything on track. This is prove to be beneficial for everyone who are involved in either preparing for an event, working on a project, studying, etc.
- Feedback is the response given to sender by receiver. This helps sender to decide whether the communication is effective or not.
- By feed one have clear communication flow during any kind of teamwork that helps their tem in avoiding major mistakes. This results in saving of time for correcting someone's work and also reduces errors that mainly cause due to miscommunication.
- Honest feedback encourages better relationships with team members
- Personal as well as professional growth is promoted by feedback that includes listening actively, taking time for analysis and also thinking for best possible solution for performing better. It creates healthy communication
- Feedback paves way for new idea generation
- Feedback promotes personal and professional growth by actively listening, taking time for analysis and then to perform better think for best possible solution. It creates a healthy communication flow by bringing people together.
- The feedback tells about whether the message is received successfully or not, whether the used channel or medium was appropriate and whether it is liked by receiver or not.
- Feedback makes communication meaningful
- It is a tool for continuous learning

Types of Feedback

Feedback can be of various types. In this section we will discuss about feedback used in communication.

Formal and Informal Feedback

Formal Feedback is a planned and systematically schedules into the process. It has a specific blueprint and according to this blueprint a feedback is framed by receiver then sent it. Usually it is associated with formal feedback that includes competencies or achievement of standards, likes of marketing criteria. It takes time to construct.

Informal Feedback can occur at any time as it is something that emerges spontaneously in the moment or during action. Due to it, the informal feedback need to build the report with students for effectively encouraging, coach or guide them in daily management and decision making for learning. The information feedback can take place in the classroom, in virtual classroom or over the phone. It doesn't take time to convey as it is instantly conveyed.

Descriptive and Non-descriptive Feedback

Descriptive Feedback provides meaningful information in a detailed and expressive manner. The specific information in the form of written comments or conversations help learner in understanding the needs of improving.

Non-descriptive Feedback provides some specific information but doesn't give detailed description. It is also known as perspective feedback that provides advice on communication. This type of feedback conveys meaningful specific response but does not come with descriptive analysis or suggestions.

Specific and Non-Specific Feedback

Specific Feedback provides detailed or specific information on what the employee did well or poorly. It helps in modifying the behaviour and thinking for the purpose of learning by influencing the thought processes.

Non-Specific Feedback talks about entire thing while giving a general interview. It doesn't particularly pinpoint a specific feature or things. In most of the cases it is not prove to be helpful.

Knowledge Box

Feedback is important as it ensures the success and effectiveness of communication. Without feedback, the sender cannot find if the message intended has been successfully delivered with the same intent.

Practice Box

Name the type of Feedback:

1. Congratulations on scoring A+ in your final test performance. You are promoted to your next class.
2. In your article, conclusion needs rework.
3. I like your story. It's good.

Effective feedback need to be:

- Specific
- Well-timed
- Truly Representative
- Clear
- Informative
- Bearing Right Attitude
- Impersonal

Summary

- Feedback is the response given to sender information. To complete the communication cycle a response should be feedback by receiver.
- Encoding or converting data or information into the coded language that is not understood by any other person.
- When the sent messages is successfully delivered to receiver and understood by them then a communication is said to be effective communication.
- An appropriate channel or medium is selected by sender to send message. The communication channel can be faxes, electronic mail, letters, face to face, telephone calls, etc.
- The feedback is helpful information about prior action or behaviour from an individual and communicated to another individual who use that information for adjusting and improving the current or future actions and behaviours.

- Types of feedback are Formal and Informal, Descriptive and Non-descriptive, Specific and Non-specific
- Effective feedback need to be specific, Well-timed, truly representative, clear, informative, impersonal, etc.

Keywords: Feedback in Communication cycle, Elements of communication cycle, Message, Sender, Encoding, Decoding, Receiver, Feedback, Communication channel, Importance of Feedback, Types of feedback, Formal and Informal feedback, Descriptive Feedback, Non-descriptive feedback, Specific feedback, Non-Specific Feedback.

Self-Assessment

A. MULTIPLE CHOICE QUESTIONS.

1. What is the purpose of receiver in communication:

   a. Understand the message and respond to it   b. Send message

   c. Take response   d. None

2. Which of the following is not a type of feedback:

   a. Formal feedback   b. Non- formal feedback

   c. Descriptive feedback   d. Non- descriptive feedback

3. Which of the following cannot be totally absent in a communication process:

   a. Light   b. Air   c. Noise   d. Sound

B. FILL IN THE BLANKS

1. ____________ is necessary for sender to get confirmation about receiver received message successfully.
2. Message is travel from sender to receiver side through ___________
3. The message is encoded by ____________.
4. Two-way communication involves both ____________ and ____________.

C. TRUE AND FALSE:

1. Sender sends a message and in response gets feedback from receiver. (T/F)
2. Communication channel is not a element of communication cycle (T/F)
3. Decoding is the process of converting coded information into original form (T/F)

D. ANSWER THE FOLLOWING QUESTIONS:

1. What is communication?
2. What are the characteristics of communication?
3. Name various elements of communication cycle with explanation.
4. Define encoding and decoding with its purpose.
5. Name various types of feedback in communication. Explain any two types in detail.
6. Write a short note of importance of feedback.
7. Give any 5 elements of effective communication.

E. PRACTICAL WORK

1. Communication is important in each and every field of life. Prepare a chart of communication cycle and explain it in the class.
2. Observe your best friend for week and write a points on feedback of his/her written and spoken assignment in the class.

Answers

A. Multiple choice question.

1. c 2. b 3. c

B. Fill in the blanks.

1. Feedback 2. Channel 3. Sender 4. Sender and receiver

C. True and False.

1. True 2. False 3. True

SESSION 3: BARRIERS IN COMMUNICATION

Barrier to communication is anything that prevent the smooth sending or receiving of message at either sender side or receiver ends. This results in failure of communication as it can occur at any stage and creates ambiguity and misunderstanding.

Barriers to Effective Communication

Effective communication is one of the most valuable skills you can possess. Without proficient communication skills, there will be no staff members who are not aware about the roles and responsibilities in the organisation. There are several barriers that are responsible for the people view our messages. Some of those barriers are:

Linguistic Barriers: Language can be a barrier that limits the effective communication. As, language is consider as most commonly employed tool of communication as each region have their own language such as Spanish person will not be able to interact with Indian person who is only familiar with Hindi language.

Psychological Barriers: There are various psychological or mental issues that can cause a barrier in effective communication. As you must have seen that some people around you have speech disorders, depression, stage fear, phobia, speech disorders, etc., and sometimes these conditions becomes difficult to manage and also limits the communication.

Physical Barriers: Communication is a two way process and distance between message sender and receiver can become a barrier to communication.

Emotional Barriers: The emotional IQ of any person helps in determining the easiness and comfort for communicating with another person. As an emotionally mature person will be able to communicate effectively on other hand a difficulty is faced by person who easily let their emotions take over.

Perception Barriers: As we know same thing is perceive differently by different people. In communication process this fact need to be consider that makes all messages clear.

Cultural Barriers: Sometimes cultural differences hinder us from communicating properly. As due to globalisation, companies may have people from several parts of the world and for several basic values of society there is different meaning of different cultures.

Attitude Barriers: There are some introverts or not very social people that want to be lifted alone. Some people have attitude issues like ego and inconsiderate behaviours that can be barrier to communication. These employees can cause strains in the communication channels in which they are present.

Feelings: Sometimes our feelings don't let us to have an effective communication. As, we avoid conversation when we are upset and that remind us of the thing that make us angry.

Noise: Noise word is used to define any unwanted information that make difficult for useful information to be clearly understood.

A skilled communicator must be aware of these barriers and try to reduce their impact by continually checking understanding and by offering appropriate feedback.

Fact Box

In communication noise is consider as one of the major barrier that also includes any kinds of physical interference like blemished copies of typewriters, slow internet connections, handwriting, poor telephone connections, etc.

Knowledge Box

The process of communication has multiple barriers. The intended communique will often be disturbed and distorted leading to a condition of misunderstanding and failure of communication.

Practice Box

Select the appropriate option:

1. Which of these is the external sounds present in the channels of communication?
   a. Noise b. Semantic problems
   c. Cultural barriers d. Over communication
2. In which of these problems, is the actual message lost in the abundance of transmitted information?
   a. Selecting perception b. Over communication
   c. Under communication d. Filtering

Measures to overcome Barriers to Effective Communication

Clarify the Ideas before communication: Any issue to be communicated to a subordinate should be clearly and completely studied and analysed by the superior. Moreover, it should be stated in such a manner that subordinate can easily understand it in the same sense in which the supervisor wants him to receive it.

Communicate according to the need of Receiver: The level of understanding and education of the subordinates must be very clear to the manager. Manager should try to communicate according to their level.

Consult others before Communicating: It is desirable to involve others in developing a plan for communication. Consulting the subordinates before communicating the message helps to gain their ready acceptance and willing cooperation.

Be aware of Language, Tone and Content of Message: The language, tone and content of a message to be communicated are very important aspects of an effective communication. The language should be clear, simple and easily understandable. Similarly, the tone & content of the message should not provide any harm to the sentiments of listeners rather it should stimulate them to give response.

Convey Things of help and value to Listeners: It is always better to know the needs and interests of the listeners before communicating the message. The response from the listeners is surely obtained if the message is related directly or indirectly to their needs or interests.

Ensure proper Feedback: Proper feedback helps in improving the communication process. The sender should ask questions regarding the message conveyed and the receiver should be encouraged to respond to communication.

Communicate for Present and Future: In order to maintain consistency, the communication should aim at meeting both present as well as future requirements of an organisation.

Follow up Communications: Regular follow up and review of the instruction given to the subordinates help in removing difficulties in implementing the instructions.

Be a Good Listener: It has been well established that listening attentively solves more than half the problems in any organisation. Hence, to overcome all likely communication barriers a manager should try to be a good listener too.

Knowledge Box

Throughout our lives, we face both negative and positive experience but you don't let it affect the way you respond with other people.

Practice Box

1. Explain any three types of barriers to effective communication.
2. There are some barriers in communication which are concerned with encoding and decoding of message. State any three such barriers.

Summary

- Barrier to communication is anything that prevent the smooth sending or receiving of message at either sender side or receiver ends.
- Effective communication is one of the most valuable skills you can possess.
- Factors that cause communication barriers are: Linguistic barriers, Psychological barriers, Physical barriers, Emotional barrier, perception barriers, cultural barriers, Attitude barriers, fillings and Noise
- Various measures to overcome barriers to Effective communication are: Clarify the ideas before communication, Communicate according to the need of receiver, consult others before communicating, be aware of language, tone and content of message, Convey things of help and value of listener, Ensure proper feedback, communicate for present and future, follow up communications and Be a good listener.

Keywords: Barriers in communication, Linguistic barriers, Physical barriers, Psychological barriers, Emotional Barriers, Perception Barriers, Cultural Barriers, Noise, Measures to overcome barriers to Effective communication.

Self-Assessment

A. MULTIPLE CHOICE QUESTIONS.

1. Communication barrier is
   a. Anything that prevent the smooth sending or receiving of message
   b. Elements that cause communication failure
   c. Both (a) and (b) d. None
2. Linguistic barrier is related to:
   a. Grammar b. Language c. Words d. All

B. ANSWER THE FOLLOWING QUESTIONS:

1. What do you understand by communication barriers
2. Name and define any 5 barriers to effective Communication.
3. Write a short note on measures to overcome barriers to effective communication?

C. PRACTICAL WORK

1. Odd roll number students make an innovative collage on communication barriers and even roll number students make presentation on various measures to overcome the communication barriers.
2. **Blindfold Game**

   Blindfold Game builds trust, listening and instructional skills.

   What you'll need:

   - Four or more people
   - Blindfolds
   - Private room or recreational area
   - Various "obstacles" such as boxes, chairs or books

   How to play:

   Construct an obstacle course with your various items. Divide your players into teams of two. Tie a blindfold on one member and have them stand at the "start" of the obstacle course. The second member must then guide the blindfolded member through the course by calling out directions. This game encourages cooperation, successful teamwork and trust, which is crucial for effective communication. When there is a lack of trust, it builds suspicion and prevents buy-in.

   Clarity in giving instructions is a must for effective customer service, especially in technical fields. When customers have a difficult time understanding technical directions, it's tempting to use more words to explain, which just further confuses customers. Brevity and careful word selection is key for better communication.
3. Talk to your friends in school and home area about their beliefs on the politics. Do all of them have the same beliefs? Which factors are influencing their perspectives on it.

Answers

A. Multiple choice question.

1. a 2. b

SESSION 4: PRINCIPLES OF COMMUNICATION

Effective communication is the one in which both parties participate in a constructive way. A liberty to both sender and receiver is provided by an effective communication system for conveying their message in proper way. Effective communication is a two-way communication process where bot the parties have right and convenience for expressing their messages, opinions, facts and other information.

7 C's of Effective Communication

The seven elements of communication are used to improve the professional communication skills and increases the chances of having correct message that deliver right meaning. These 7C's are:

Completeness: The communication must be complete. It should convey all facts required by the audience. The sender of the message must take into consideration the receiver's mind set and convey the message accordingly. A complete communication has following features:

- Complete communication develops and enhances reputation of an organization.
- Moreover, they are cost saving as no crucial information is missing and no additional cost is incurred in conveying extra message if the communication is complete.
- A complete communication always gives additional information wherever required. It leaves no questions in the mind of receiver.
- Complete communication helps in better decision-making by the audience/readers/receivers of message as they get all desired and crucial information.
- It persuades the audience.

Conciseness: Conciseness means wordiness, i.e, communicating what you want to convey in least possible words without forgoing the other C's of communication. Conciseness is a necessity for effective communication. Concise communication has following features:

- It is both time-saving as well as cost-saving.
- It underlines and highlights the main message as it avoids using excessive and needless words.
- Concise communication provides short and essential message in limited words to the audience.
- Concise message is more appealing and comprehensible to the audience.
- Concise message is non-repetitive in nature.

Consideration: Consideration implies "stepping into the shoes of others". Effective communication must take the audience into consideration, i.e, the audience's view points, background, mind-set, education level, etc. Make an attempt to envisage your audience, their requirements, emotions as well as problems. Features of considerate communication are as follows:

- Emphasize on "you" approach.
- Empathize with the audience and exhibit interest in the audience. This will stimulate a positive reaction from the audience.
- Show optimism towards your audience. Emphasize on "what is possible" rather than "what is impossible". Lay stress on positive words such as jovial, committed, thanks, warm, healthy, help, etc.

Clarity: Clarity implies emphasizing on a specific message or goal at a time, rather than trying to achieve too much at once. Clarity in communication has following features:

- It makes understanding easier.
- Complete clarity of thoughts and ideas enhances the meaning of message.
- Clear message makes use of exact, appropriate and concrete words.

Concreteness: Concrete communication implies being particular and clear rather than fuzzy and general. Concreteness strengthens the confidence. Concrete message has following features:

- It is supported with specific facts and figures.
- It makes use of words that are clear and that build the reputation.
- Concrete messages are not misinterpreted.

Courtesy: Courtesy in message implies the message should show the sender's expression as well as should respect the receiver. The sender of the message should be sincerely polite, judicious, reflective and enthusiastic. Courteous message has following features:

- Courtesy implies taking into consideration both viewpoints as well as feelings of the receiver of the message.

✦ Courteous message is positive and focused at the audience.

✦ It makes use of terms showing respect for the receiver of message.

✦ It is not at all biased.

Correctness: Correctness in communication implies that there are no grammatical errors in communication. Correct communication has following features:

✦ The message is exact, correct and well-timed.

✦ If the communication is correct, it boosts up the confidence level.

✦ Correct message has greater impact on the audience/readers.

✦ It checks for the precision and accurateness of facts and figures used in the message.

✦ It makes use of appropriate and correct language in the message.

Memory Box

Ensure that the self-respect of the audience is maintained and their emotions are not at harm. Modify your words in message to suit the audience's needs while making your message complete.

Practice Box

Find single word substitutes for the phrases:

- At this time
- During the time of the day
- For a price of
- Date of policy
- Consensus of opinion
- Few and far between
- During the year of
- Along the same lines

Summary

- Effective communication is the one in which both parties participate in a constructive way.
- The seven elements of communication are used to improve the professional communication skills and increases the chances of having correct message that deliver right meaning.
- The 7 C's of effective communication are Completeness, Conciseness, Consideration, Clarity, Concreteness, Courtesy, Correctness.
- The communication must be complete. It should convey all facts required by the audience.
- Conciseness means wordiness, i.e, communicating what you want to convey in least possible words without forgoing the other C's of communication.
- Consideration implies "stepping into the shoes of others". Effective communication must take the audience into consideration, i.e, the audience's view points, background, mind-set, education level, etc.
- Clarity implies emphasizing on a specific message or goal at a time, rather than trying to achieve too much at once.
- Concrete communication implies being particular and clear rather than fuzzy and general
- Courtesy in message implies the message should show the sender's expression as well as should respect the receiver.
- Correctness in communication implies that there are no grammatical errors in communication.

Self-Assessment

A. MULTIPLE CHOICE QUESTIONS.

1. Which of the following is not the 7C's or elements of communication?

   a. Clear b. Complete c. Concentrate d. Concise

2. ____________ in message implies the message should show the sender's expression and respect the receiver:

   a. Correctness b. Concreteness c. Courtesy d. Clarity

B. FILL IN THE BLANKS

1. ____________ in communication implies that there are no grammatical errors in communication.
2. ____________ is one of the 7 C's of communication that implies "stepping into the shoes of others".

C. TRUE AND FALSE:

1. In effective communication out of two, one party participate in a constructive way. (T/F)
2. Concise message is more appealing and comprehensible to the audience (T/F)

D. ANSWER THE FOLLOWING QUESTIONS:

1. Name 7 C's of effective communication?
2. Define each 7 C's of effective communication.
3. Give features of any 3 C's out of 7 C's of effective communication.

E. PRACTICAL WORK

1. Make a presentation on 7 C's of effective communication.
2. You are the president of an industry association and have received the following inquiry from an out of town member, "I think I would like to attend my first meeting of the association, even though I am not acquainted with your city. Will you please tell me where the next meeting is being held?

   To this: How would you reply to this letter kepping in mind Completeness of the message.

Answers

A. Multiple choice question.

   1. c 2. c

B. Fill in the blanks answers:

   1. Correctness 2. Consideration

C. True and False:

   1. False 2. True

SESSION 5: BASIC OF WRITING SKILLS

Writing Skills

To have an effective written communication both sender and receiver should be able to easily share their message without any confusion, grammatical errors. Any laps at with sender or receiver side lead to miss communication. Use of correct grammar, selection of right words and easy sentence structure making are important aspects of writing skills. By correct grammar it means a correct grammar is used along with sentence structure, time, gender and tense. Avoid using too technical, difficult words as it will be difficult for receiver to understand it if he/she belongs from non-technical background. Try to using sentences for expressing messages instead or words.

Phrase

Words are used to express our ideas and thoughts while communicating with each other. A sentence is a group of words that make complete sense. For example I am going, behind the table, etc These group of words are not known as sentence as they are not making complete sense and known as phrases. Phrase is a group of words that gives only hint about the message sender want to communicate. It doesn't have object and subject.

For example: Phrase: I am sitting Sentence: I am sitting on the table

By adding finite verbs or objects in the phrase it become a sentence. For example: early in the morning, difficult task, hard work, etc.

These all are phrases and in sentence it will be: I daily wake up early in the morning, It is difficult task to do, We all must have to do hard work.

Noun, Verb, Adjective, Adverbial and prepositional are five types of phrases.

1. Noun phrase act like noun in a sentence. *Example:* The yellow house is for sale. Where yellow house is a noun phrase
2. Verb phrase is a group of helping and main verbs within a sentence. *Example:* She was walking quickly to the mall. Where was walking is a verb
3. Adjective phrase is built around an adjective and consist of articles and adjectives. *Example:* The woman on board is my aunty Dolli. Where on the boat is a adjective
4. Adverbial phrase is built around adverb by adding words before or after it. *Example:* I will sit in silence. Where in silence is a adverbial phrase.
5. Prepositional phrase always begins with a preposition followed by noun. *Example:* The store at the corner sells patties. Where at the corner is a prepositional phrase.

Practice Box

Identify the type of phrases in the following given in bold:

1. She was looking at the painting of Horse-riding.
2. I love to go Near the sea.

Sentence

As mentioned in last section a group of words that make complete sense is called a sentence. It must consist of predicate and subject.

Examples: Not a sentence: Understand too much is there

Sentence: There is too much to understand

The first one is not a sentence as it don't make any sense and second one is consider as sentence.

There are mainly four kind of sentences as given below:

1. **Asserted or declarative sentence:** The sentence that report events, describe things and state facts. It is a simple sentence that indicates, declares or asserts which gives positive or negative meaning.

   Example: This is my favourite movie

   My husband love eating cake in the morning

2. **Interrogative sentence:** These sentences are used to make enquiries and asking for information. In the end question mark is used and it starts with words like Why, What, When, How, etc.

   Example: What do you mean by sentence?

   How often do you use Internet?

3. **Imperative sentence:** These are the sentences that express an order, advice, request, suggestion, direction, etc. It ends with full stop or explanation sign.

   Example: Never speak to me like this again.

   Do not argue!

4. **Exclamatory sentence:** These sentences express wonder, surprise, happiness, sorrow, sympathy or gratitude like strong and sudden feelings. It can form by either selecting how, what like words or oh, ah, hurrah, alas, oops like interjections.

   Example: I can't believe how fast that train was moving.

   Bravo! Well done!

Parts of Sentence

Subject and predicate are two parts of every complete sentence. Where subject is a word or group of words that convey the name of things or persons about whom we are speaking. On other hand predicate is a part of sentence that contains verbs and state something about the subject. Some of the examples to understand these two parts of sentence are:

Simran runs: In this simran is a subject

Simran and his dog Stella run on a beach: In this simran and his dog stella is a subject (multiple subject)

She is nice: She is a subject

Samar is a good boy: Here Samar is subject and is a good boy is predicate

She was hit by a ball: Here hit by a ball is a predicate

Stand up! : Stand up is a predicate

While writing the sentence keep is short, limit sentence contents, arrange sentence in proper sequence, economise on words and design sentence that emphasize the topics.

Parts of Speech

According to the functions in a sentence it is classified into eight types are given below:

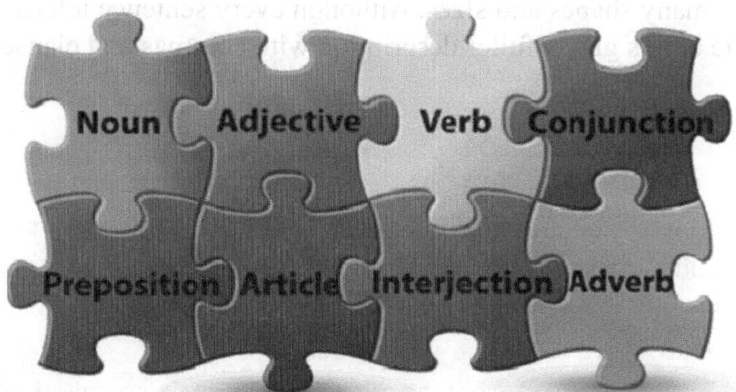

Figure 1.9: Parts of Speech

Part of speech	Function of word	Example words	Example sentences
Noun	It refers to the words used to name person, animals. Things, ideas, places, events.	Komal, Cat, Table, Music, Patiala, cocktail	Her name is Komal. Cutes can be extremely innocent. We live in Patiala.
Pronoun	It is used in replacement of noun	She, I, He, We, you, some, their, ours	We are number one. My dog name is Stella.
Adjective	Used to describe noun or pronoun. It specify quality, size and number	Some, like, sing, must, have, work, cold, happy	I have two soft toys. She is feeling Cold.
Verb	It shows an state or action	Speaking, been, go, must, can, lived	As usual, the Simran missed their train. They are always prepared in emergency. India is a country.
Adverb	Describe a verb, adjectives or another adverb	Very slowly, too, well, later, really, soon	She came yesterday. Komal dance well. The child is very talented.
Preposition	It refers to the word that specify location and shows the relation of noun, noun phrase, sentence with another word	Above, below, after, but, yet, from, with, throughout, under	Sam is hiding under the bed. The dog is under the chair
Conjunction	Joins words, clauses, phrases, sentences together,	And, but, while, because, if	This colour is very beautiful and soothing. I like garlic bread, but I don't like pasta.
Interjection	Used to convey strong emotion and usually put exclamatory sign in the end	Hey! Wow! Ouch! Hi!	Hey! I said enough. Well! I don't know. Ouch! It hurts

MEMORY BOX

Complete sentences come in many shapes and sizes. Although every sentence tells a story, some only require a scant number of words while others give a fuller description with commas and clauses.

Knowledge Box

- A new sentence begins with a capital letter.
- A sentence ends with punctuation (a period, a question mark, or an exclamation point).
- A sentence contains a subject that is only given once.
- A sentence contains a verb or a verb phrase.
- A sentence follows Subject + Verb + Object word order.
- A sentence must have a complete idea that stands alone. This is also called an independent clause

Practice Box

Find the verb, subject, object or key from given sentences:

1. She reads many books
2. I like spring roll
3. He reads many books in the library

Articles and its Use

An article is a word used before noun (person, object, place or idea). In English language there are definite and indefinite article. 'A' and 'an' are Indefinite articles 'the' is a definite article. 'A' is used before the words starting with constants and 'an' is used before words starting with vowels (A, E, I, O, U). It is mainly used to refer to a noun or group of nouns.

Indefinite Articles

As mentioned above indefinite articles are 'A' and 'An'. These articles are used before Singular Countable Nouns (SCN) that indicates a noun is not refer to any particular thing or person. Various rules for using indefinite articles are:

'A' and 'An' is used before the singular countable noun when it is mentioned for the first time

Example: I saw a good film yesterday

An orange

'A' can be used before Mr/Miss/Mrs and first name or surname

Example: A certain Miss Komal called me to ask about her medicine

'A' is used before a singular countable noun or adjective beginning with a constant sound

Example: A beautiful flower

She ate a banana

'A' is used to express quantity or numbers

Example: A dozen

I felt a bit depressed

'A' and 'An' is used after the words like rather, many, quite, such in certain structures

Example: Many a friend of mine are not coming to school

'An' and 'a' perform a same function but 'an' is used before vowels sound singular countable noun.

Example: She wants to eat an Orange

She works as an Engineer

While applying article focus on sound rather than words as sometimes it gives sound of another word while pronouncing it.

Definite Articles

'The' is a definite article used with plural uncountable noun and singular countable noun. It mainly used in specifying thing, place, person.

'The' is used to indicate a noun that is definite or has been previously specified in the context

Example: I like the clothes you gave me

'The' is used to indicate a unique noun

Example: I Bhakra River is near to me

'The' is used to designate a natural phenomenon

Example: The wind is blowing so hard

'The' is used to refer to a time period

Example: I was very active in the past

'The' is used to indicate all the members of a family

Example: I invited my friends for dinner

Knowledge Box

English has two articles: **the** and **a/an. The** is used to refer to specific or particular nouns; **a/an** is used to modify non-specific or non-particular nouns. We call **the** the definite article and **a/an** the indefinite article.

Make sure you don't use 'The' before proper noun, colours, meals, names of materials, plural nouns, names of games used in general sense.

Practice Box

Add the appropriate article:

1. __________ is wind blowing so hard.
2. Komal speaks ____________ Hindi.
3. I want ___________ orange from tha basket.

Paragraph writing

Paragraph is a number of related sentences focused on an idea. It forms a part of a larger piece of writing such as a composition. The communication of idea in efficient and clear way is the basic aim of paragraph that mainly discuss one aspect of the topic or subject.

Before writing the paragraph writer should be clear about the topic and what contents have to add in it. As there will be lack of unity, clarity and focus without having the definite idea about topic. According to the complexity or simplicity of main idea a paragraph length may vary. As it should not be very short that idea is explained inadequately and it should not be too long that it covers not intended data.

Before writing paragraphs thinks about it and consider all relevant issues or ideas about it. While writing it consider only relevant data related to topic to make it short and fruitful. Some of the essential sections of paragraph are:

Paragraph topic: The first and foremost important thing before writing a paragraph is its subject or topic

Introduction: Start paragraph with one or two sentence introduction about topic that will be feature in complete paragraph. It is also known as topic sentence

Explanation: To clarify more about topic give information about topic sentence in 7-8 sentences.

Conclusion: In this section summarizes the whole sentences written about the topic.

Proofread: It is the last and most important step to avoid mistakes and delivering good paragraph. In this writer should check the paragraph for grammatical mistakes and sentence making.

Regardless of information contain in paragraph there are some rules or characteristics. Some of them are:

Unity: Give paragraph unity or it should concern with a single focus.

Length: Keep short and concise length of paragraph by avoiding unnecessary details

Introduction/Topic sentence: Make use of topic sentences

Coherence: It makes the paragraph easily understand to a reader as in this each sentence will be related to the topic.

Conclusion: Add conclusion in the end that conclude about all the sentences written in the paragraph.

Use transition words or phrases like but, because, in fact, etc.

Tips: Paragraph should not be very short that idea is explained inadequately and it should not be too long that it covers not intended data.

Summary

- To express ourselves a sentences are written that should be correct otherwise its meaning gets changed.
- The seven elements of communication are used to improve the professional communication skills and increases the chances of having correct message that deliver right meaning
- 7 C's of communication are clear, correct, complete, concrete, concise, consideration, courteous
- To have an effective written communication both sender and receiver should be able to easily share their message without any confusion, grammatical errors. Any laps at with sender or receiver side lead to miss communication.
- Words are used to express our ideas and thoughts while communicating with each other.
- A sentence is a group of words that make complete sense
- Phrase is a group of words that gives only hint about the message sender want to communicate.
- There are four kind of sentences are asserted, interrogative, imperative and exclamatory
- Subject and predicate are two parts of every complete sentence.
- Eight parts of speech are noun, adjective, verb, conjunction, preposition, article, interjection and adverb
- An article is a word used before noun (person, object, place or idea). In English language there are definite and indefinite article. 'A' and 'an' are Indefinite articles 'the' is a definite article.
- Paragraph is a number of related sentences focused on an idea. It forms a part of a larger piece of writing such as a composition.

Self-Assessment

A. MULTIPLE CHOICE QUESTIONS.

1. Which of the following is not the 7C's or elements of communication?

   a. Clear b. Complete c. Concentrate d. Concise

2. Group of words that make complete sense are

   a. Phrase b. Sentence c. Both (a) and (b) d. None

3. Which of the following is not a type of phrase?

   a. Noun b. Adjective c. Adverbial d. Pronoun

4. Which of the following is not a type of speech?

   a. Noun b. Pronoun c. Adverb d. Adjective

5. ____________ article is used before words starting with vowels.

   a. A b. An c. The d. definite article

B. FILL IN THE BLANKS

1. ____________ is a group of words that gives only hint about the message sender want to communicate
2. ____________ Type of phrase built around an adjective and consist of articles and adjectives.
3. ____________ Sentence type is used to make enquiries and asking for information.
4. Two parts of every complete sentence are ____________ and ____________.
5. ____________ is a definite article

C. TRUE FALSE

1. Phrase doesn't have object and subject (T/F)
2. A sentence must consist of predicate and subject (T/F)
3. Exclamatory sentence report events, describe things and state facts. (T/F)
4. Predicate part of sentence contains words or group of words that convey the name of things or persons. (T/F)
5. Pronoun is used in replacement of noun (T/F)

D. ANSWER THE FOLLOWING QUESTIONS:

1. What is phrase? Name different kind of phrases.
2. Give 7C's or element of communication.
3. List some of the elements that make effective written content.
4. Differentiate phrase and sentence with example.
5. Describe four types of sentences with example of each.
6. Name various parts of speech with explanation of any five.
7. Write a short note of effective paragraph writing.
8. What do you mean by article, its usage. Give their types with one example.

E. PRACTICAL WORK

1. Develop a paragraph on any of your favourite topics considering all essential sections of paragraphs.
2. Do group discuss on essential sections of paragraph

Answers

A. Multiple choice question answers:

1. c 2. b 3. d 4. b 5. b

B. Fill in the blanks answers:

1. Phrase 2. Adjective phrase 3. Interrogative sentence
4. Subject and predicate 5. The

C. True False answers

1. True 2. True 3. False 4. False 5. True

Exercise for Assessment

A. MULTIPLE CHOICE QUESTIONS

1. Which of the following is not a characteristic of Communication?
   a. Continuous process b. Two-way process
   c. Mutual understanding d. one-way process
2. Verbal communication involves:
   a. Any message that uses words of different languages
   b. A written message
   c. A Spoken message
   d. Both b) and c)
3. Sender sends a message and in response gets _________ from receiver?
   a. Nothing b. Result c. Feedback d. All
4. _______________ is the process of converting coded information into original form
   a. Communication b. Encoding c. Feedback d. Decoding
5. One way communication is ___________ due to absence of receiver response.
   a. Difficult b. Steady and slow c. Fast d. Effective
6. In verbal communication message is delivered using:
   a. Spoken or written message b. Message that uses words of any language
   c. both a) and b) d. None
7. Which of the following is not a primary form of verbal communication?
   a. Oral communication b. Written communication
   c. Body language d. None

8. Which of the following is not an example of written communication?

   a. Emails b. Reports c. body language d. Letters

9. Which of the following is the negative attitude especially when it is related to hatred for some people?

   a. Feelings b. Attitude c. Prejudices d. Language

10. Group of words that make complete sense are

    a. Phrase b. Sentence c. Both a) and b) d. None

11. Which of the following is not a type of phrase?

    a. Noun b. Adjective c. Adverbial d. Pronoun

12. Which of the following is not a type of speech?

    a. Noun b. Pronoun c. Adverb d. Adjective

Answer

1. d	2. d	3. c	4. d	5. b	6. c
7. c	8. c	9. c	10. b	11. d	12. b

B. VERY SHORT QUESTIONS:

1. What is communication?
2. Define Encoding and Decoding?
3. Name the methods of Communication.
4. What is the significance of Visual communication?
5. Give any two disadvantage of written communication.
6. Name the part of sentence.
7. Define Linguistic Barriers.

C. SHORT QUESTIONS:

1. What are various characteristics of communication?
2. Define Effective communication.
3. What do you understand by barriers to effective communication?
4. Define Non-verbal communication. List the main elements of Non-verbal communication.
5. What is Visual Communication? Give its any two advantages and disadvantages.
6. Enlist the factors affecting the Perspective in communication.
7. Name various barriers to Effective Communication.
8. Differentiate Phrase and Sentence with example.

D. LONG QUESTIONS:

1. State the importance of effective communication?
2. Briefly explain the various elements of communication cycle.
3. Write a short note on various methods of communication.

4. Define verbal communication? Give two primary forms of verbal communication.
5. What is barrier in communication? Explain any five factors affecting the barriers to effective communication.
6. Give various parts of speech?
7. Explain the meaning of Phrases with example.
8. Write a short note on Paragraph writing.

E. APPLICATION BASED QUESTIONS:

1. When you want to take permission from your parents for going out with your friends, do you have analysed their response when they are in good and bad mood. How it effects on their response for your permission to go out with your friends.
2. Write any one instance where your prospective has influenced your behaviour towards your school best friend.
3. Komal is preparing for a declamation contest, Help her in preparing a list of all the elements of non-verbal communication that she should have to consider while giving her speech.
4. Simran is a new principle of your school, and he want to share his idea with his teaching staff. Compare the advantages and disadvantages of both oral and written communication and suggest him which form of communication is more effective.
5. Jass has to write a paragraph for a debate held in school, tell him all the essential sections of paragraph that helps him in preparing a good paragraph.

F. GROUP DISCUSSION

1. Do a group discussion on importance of feedback in day to day professional and personal life.
2. Conduct a group discussion on various barriers that affects the effective communication.
3. Arrange a group discussion in the class on various elements of different types of communication.

PROJECT WORK

1. Role play with your friend on communication process related to barriers of communication process
2. Role play in class to give introduction of yourself that includes your name, class, school name, hobbies, qualities and aim in life
3. Do group discussion of various characteristics of communication and what are the barriers affecting it
4. Make a presentation on common body language errors that must be avoided while communicating
5. Try all three methods of communication in your class for communicating and conveying message to your friends. Then make a chart on various pros and cons of each methods.
6. Do group discussion on how a communication cycle is disrupted by Non-verbal communication.
7. Play dumb Charades by following its rules to observe the non-verbal method of communication.
8. There are various methods for expressing the message, and these methods are selected by considering various factors. Make a collage of various methods by considering those factors and enlist the pros and cons of each.

LISTEN AND DRAW

This game is easy to play but not so easy to "win." It requires participants' full attention and active listening. Gather your group of participants together and hand out a piece of paper and a pen or pencil to each player. Tell them you will give them verbal instructions on drawing an object, one step at a time.

For example, you might give them instructions like:

- Draw a square, measuring 5 inches on each side.
- Draw a circle within the square, such that it fits exactly in the middle of the square.
- Intersect 2 lines through the circle, dividing the circle into 4 equal parts.

TEACHER NOTES:

1. Give practical examples of various types of communication.
2. Make a list of importance of feedback other than given in the chapter.
3. Arrange a paragraph writing competition in class and give feedback to students according to the paragraph written by them.

EXAM TIPS:

1. Relate everything with your day to day life to keep things in mind for long time.
2. More Workout on practical work.

2 Self-Management Skills – II

Learning Outcomes

After this chapter, you will have the knowledge of:

- Self-Management
- Stress Management Techniques
- Self-management skills
- Importance of Self-Management
- SMART Strategy
- Important things about independent working
- Ability to work independently
- Skills to work independently
- Self-Awareness
- Types of Self-awareness
- Self-Motivation
- Types of Self-Motivation
- Self-Regulation
- The Psychology of Self-Regulation

INTRODUCTION

Self-management refers to self-regulation or self-control is the ability to regulate one's thought, emotions, behaviour effectively in various situations. Self-management is about organizing your time, regulating actions, etc to achieve a predetermine goals. By having strong self-management skills a student is able to do different activities effectively by cooperating with others in school, focusing on their tasks, managing time and performing better in studies. This helps in facing any situation with confidence either related to school, college, home or office in day to day life.

Take **example** of your class teacher. She manages her home along with her work of teaching students, etc. To do all these tasks in effective way she plans and delegates the responsibility and then organizes the resources like time, money, etc. Then according to the priorities she recognizes the resources. In these whole tasks nobody is directing her in setting and achieving all the goals she is self-managing it all.

So, this self-management skills help in both personal and professional life. Self-management skills include:

- Self-awareness,
- Self-control,
- Self-confidence,
- Problem solving,
- Self-motivation,
- Positive thinking,
- Managing our emotions,
- Anger,
- Openness to learning new ideas and team work.

SESSION 1: STRESS MANAGEMENT TECHNIQUES

Self-management is a key to manage everything around us. Various factors that includes in self-management are making you more organised, instils discipline, helps in achieving goals, helps in completing all work on time and effectively, Enhances self-confidence, get problem solving skills, etc.

These all achieve by learning:

- Time management,
- Settings goals and priorities,
- Accepting people from different cultures,
- Managing your emotions, mood, anger, team working ability, etc.

MEMORY BOX

Self-management: Self-management is a key to manage everything around us.

SELF-MANAGEMENT SKILLS

The three key skills of self-management are:

Initiative: It is the ability to work without always getting instructions for what to do. This requires believe on their own capabilities even in case of worst situations. It means using your mind and drives to achieve. How to grow your Initiative skills:

- Always look for various ways to simplify tasks
- Help the team members and colleagues when they need it
- Keep yourself organized and stay on top of activities
- Keep you plans and ambitions clear.

Organization: You can plan your time, energy and resources effectively then when you are organized in work and life. Being organized will save your energy and time and help in completing task effectively and gets more productive results. The most important thing you should know is what should be done firstly and in what longest time is taken.

This includes preparation and availability of things when needed and must follow:

- Defining and identification of specific tasks
- Break down goals into smaller and fruitful tasks: To achieve a bigger tasks or goals make sure divide it into smaller parts and define your targets using **SMART** strategy.
- Management of time so that right time is given to right activity and assigning specific time slots to activities as per their importance. It includes:
    - o **Planning** (learn to plan each day, week, month and year to control workload).
    - o **Give time slot** (before setting time slot estimate the time required for completion of specific tasks).
    - o **Prioritise and schedule** (Accommodate the planned tasks according to their priority or importance).
    - o **Spend right time on right activity** (This includes setting time to complete the task).

Accountability: Both accountability and responsibility are similar but have different meaning. As one can share responsibility but accountability is specific to oneself. In case of responsibility one can blame other for any wrong actions but in accountability only you will be responsible and have to answer for your actions.

Some of the characteristics of accountability are:

- Avoid procrastination that means avoiding the important tasks that need to be completed. This includes choosing a easy task rather than doing the important difficult task.
- Adopting problem solving Attitude is required in every area of work. Sometimes there can be situation come when people have to face difficult situation even after planning or prioritizing everything.
- Managing your own Emotions: As emotions prevent us from working towards best or most having constructive solutions.
- Coping with Distress: As there can be situation of injuries, accidents, illness and death in a family that impact on your physical and emotional well-being. In those situations surround yourself with people who can provide you required practical and emotional support.

Knowledge Box

If you say to yourself that you are accountable then it means you take ownership of responsibilities that come to your way.

Memory Box

In **SMART** strategy, S stands for specific,

M stands for Measurable like divide your tasks whose completion gives measurable outcome,

A stands for Achievable that means set a task that can be achieved,

R stands for Realistic,

T stands for Time bound.

Fact Box

A self believe is must in initiative as then only you will be able to go out of your way to solve problems without being instructed from other person.

Practice Box

1. S in SMART strategy stands for ____________.
2. In ____________ one can't blame other for any wrong action.

Importance of Self-Management

Self-management is important in every field of file as it teaches to be productive and efficiently achieving all the goals. It also helps in managing the time and completing task with less effort, managing stress, prioritising the things.

Figure 2.1: Self-management

Some of the other importance of self-management is:

- **Organised:** By self-management one get skills of organizing and allocating all their resources while planning or setting time, resources and other essential activities.
- **Teaches discipline:** When one make a schedule in organized way and committed oneself to do it on time then he/she will not do other unimportant tasks as one know that doing the unimportant task.
- **Attain Goals:** If you have organised all the tasks and time for everything than it selects in attaining goal on right time.
- **Self-confidence enhancement:** If you set goals and achieve them then it will give you self-confidence in achieving more challenging tasks.
- **Respects from others:** If you are doing well and achieving good results than you will get appreciated or respect from people surrounding you either in school, officer or at home.

Knowledge Box

It also gives you courage to take initiatives when any opportunity comes.

Fact Box

By self-management one know that unimportant activities will result in delay or failing to achieve the target.

Memory Box

They know that unimportant activities will result in delay or failing to achieve the target.

Stress Management Techniques

Stress is a very powerful force and is a part of life that involves awareness, attention and energy. Stress can't be avoided irrespective of location and work you are doing. You can empower yourself by managing it. There are numbers of techniques available that can be used and followed for reducing the levels of stress. Some of the stress management techniques are:

Physical exercise: Healthy life style is necessary for managing stress. So, do plenty of exercise that is good for your body and for managing stress levels. The production of your brains boost up by physical exercises and starts brain's feeling good neurotransmitters known as endorphins.

Sports: Sports are also physical activities that help our body in releasing endorphins that helps in releasing tensions from our mind and body. One built their self-esteem by being a part of sport team. The quality of sleep is also gets improves with sports that is linked with our well-being.

Yoga: Yoga brings body, spirit and mind together. Yoga is an effective way to deal with stress that allow yourself from inhalation of a breath full of oxygen that brings the good supply of it to your brain. This is consider as an effective way of dealing with stress.

Meditation: Our mindfulness gets enhanced by meditation that is cleaning of our mind from all thoughts by sitting in a relaxed position. Our mind stops following every new thoughts that come across and reduces our emotional and physical stress by learning to calm our mind and body.

Vacations or holidays: Taking break from daily routine and when for a holidays or vacations have various health benefits. As our stress level gets reduces by vacation and holidays that also control cortisol in our body. It also releases feel good hormones in our body that make us feel relaxed and stress free.

Practice facing stressful moments: Think about those situations that make your mind stressed. After that find ways to deal with these challenges. For example if you know that speaking in front of someone frightens you then do practise by standing in your class and speaking about any topic.

Nature Walks: Going for a walk in natural surroundings have also proven therapeutic. By taking even a quick walk can give yourself a change of scenery and a little exercise.

Fact Box

Stress management techniques are used in everyday life for handling and minimising the physical and emotion effects.

Knowledge Box

The contract of muscles is one of the common sign of getting stressed that discomfort us with back pain, high blood pressure, muscle pull and headache. Regular exercises will makes us less reactive to stress and provides a useful technique for refocusing your attention and also let out our frustrations. By deep breathing muscles gets relaxed and to deal with stress one has to closed their eyes or sit with a firm head support.

Practice Box

1. ____________ is a very powerful force and is a part of life that involves awareness, attention and energy.
2. Our mindfulness gets enhanced by ____________ that is cleaning of our mind from all thoughts by sitting in a relaxed position.

Summary

- Self-management refers to self-regulation or self-control is the ability to regulate one's thought, emotions, behaviour effectively in various situations

- Various factors that includes in self-management are making you more organised, instils discipline, helps in achieving goals, helps in completing all work on time and effectively, Enhances self-confidence, get problem solving skills, etc.
- To achieve a bigger tasks or goals make sure divide it into smaller parts and define your targets using SMART strategy.
- Stress is a very powerful force and is a part of life that involves awareness, attention and energy. Stress can't be avoided irrespective of location and work you are doing. You can empower yourself by managing it.
- Stress management techniques are physical exercise, yoga, sports, meditation, vacations or holidays, practice facing stressful moments and nature walks.

Keywords: Self-management skills, SMART, Organization, Accountability, Importance of self-management, Self-confidence enhancement, Stress Management Techniques.

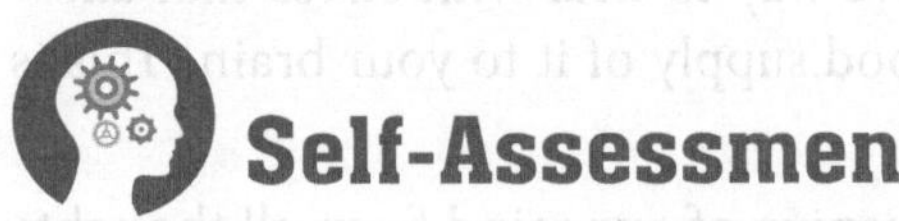

A. MULTIPLE CHOICE QUESTIONS

1. Which of the following shows the ability to participate as a team member?

    a. Interpersonal skills   b. Communication skills

    c. Entrepreneur skills   d. None

2. Self-management skills do not involve:

    a. Initiative   b. Organization   c. Management   d. Accountability

3. ____________ is the ability to work without always getting instructions of doing things.

    a. Self-confidence   b. Organization   c. Initiative   d. Accountability

4. R in SMART strategy stands for __________?

    a. Real   b. Rate   c. Realistic   d. Required

B. FILL IN THE BLANKS

1. ____________ of tasks and time helps in attaining goal in right time.
2. A ____________ attitude helps one to focus on the possible solutions.

C. TRUE FALSE

1. S in SMART strategy stands for Specific (T/F)
2. To grow your initiative skill you plan and ambition should be clear (T/F)
3. Self-management helps in completing all work on time but doesn't enhance self-confidence (T/F)

D. ANSWER THE FOLLOWING QUESTIONS:

1. What do you mean by self-management? How it is different from management.
2. Name three key skills of self-management.
3. What do you mean by Organization skills of self-management? Explain SMART strategy used in it.
4. How accountability is dissimilar to responsibility?
5. Gives 3 characteristics of accountability.

6. What is the importance of self-management?
7. Name 6 techniques of stress management. Explain any 5 in details.

E. PROJECT WORK

List out your strengths and weaknesses, make 2 week plan using SMART strategy to work on your weakness and tract your progress and then repeat it for next week.

Answers

A. Multiple choice question answers:

1. b 2. c 3. c 4. c

B. Fill in the blanks answers:

1. Organization 2. Time-bound

C. True False answers

1. True 2. True 3. False

SESSION 2: ABILITY TO WORK INDEPENDENTLY

One of the abilities that most faculty mentors (and employers, folks!) desire to cultivate in their undergraduate charges is independence. In this section, we'll discuss some strategies that will help you learn how to become a self-motivated, self-regulating independent scientist. You will find that the principles you learn here are foundational to lifelong learning, professional growth, development, and long term career satisfaction. They will stand you in good stead in your life no matter your specific choice of career or career path.

Knowledge Box

Important things about independent working are:

- You take full responsibility of work
- You are ready to do unsupervised work that means you don't need constant supervision.
- You take the ownership of it that means you take yourself accountable for it.
- You know what to do and when
- You do what is asked to the best of your ability without any external or internal fear.
- You don't let your self-doubt or negative emotions hamper your present or future actions.
- You are capable of completing work within stipulated time and budget
- You have ownership of your mistakes and not looking for excuses or blame-game

Skills to work independently

The seven necessary skills to work independently are:

- **Communication skills:** Communication skills help in connecting with yourself and with others for the support and cooperation required for finishing the work at hand.
- **Organizational skills:** Organisational skills are necessary for knowing what to do, when to do and where to start for finishing everything on time.
- **Adaptability or flexibility:** Adaptability or flexibility is your quality for adapting your working style to suit other people working with you.
- **Negotiating skills:** Negotiating skills is the ability to see the bigger picture. It is related to willingness for doing any work for the benefits of all.

- **Multitasking ability:** Multitasking ability is your ability for doing work on more than one thing at a time and complete each of them with required proficiency and in given time.
- **Ability to deal with rejection and not to take it personally:** This is a never say no attitude and open mindedness for facing failure and not get dishearten and start afresh after any failure.
- **Discipline:** Discipline is most important skill for keeping you and your actions in track for the successful completion of the task at hand.

Self-Awareness

Self-aware people know about themselves without any bias. They have a full understanding of their personality traits and flaws, their attitudes, strengths and weaknesses, interests and abilities, emotions, assumptions, beliefs and their shortcomings.

Types of Self-awareness:

Self-awareness of your strengths: You can only lead in ways that god has designed you to lead. Take time to discover your strengths by paying attention to the work that you do or want to do. Discover where do you feel energized, where do others comment on how good your work is and what types of projects are you naturally drawn toward.

Self-awareness of your weaknesses: Discovering your weaknesses helps you to know what types of projects to avoid. It guides you in selecting the right work and it builds humility and acknowledge you to work on that particular things that you can't do. You can find your weaknesses by asking your co-workers, friends and family.

Self-awareness of your dark side: You dark side includes your sin patterns and character flaws along with your hidden weaknesses. Avoid to hide them and start facing it to overcome them with the help of your family and friends. It is not fun to think about your dark side, but not only will your dark side will infect you, it will also affect everyone influence by you.

Self-awareness of your emotional triggers: Your anxiety will create anxiety in your team, family and friends. You need to discover the situations that trigger anxiety in you. There are your trigger points and keeping yourself calm and composure in worst situations is the best way of dealing with them. As if you know your emotional triggers then you can develop a strategy for remaining calm in those situations.

Memory Box

Self-awareness refers to your knowledge and understanding of yourself - your emotions, beliefs, assumptions, biases, knowledge base, abilities, motivations, interests, etc. As you carry out your undergraduate research project, make a conscious effort to learn about yourself - your abilities, beliefs, likes and dislikes.

Knowledge Box

- Knowledge of your strengths also gets increased by an assessment that includes standout and strengths Finder.
- As you anxiety will makes everyone around you anxious, your habit of twisting truth creates a culture of deceit, your shame causes everyone to feel ashamed.

Self-Motivation

Self-motivation refers to your ability to identify effective methods of getting yourself to move from thought to action. Everyone is different. Some individuals are highly self-motivated while others require the imposition of external deadlines or some type of reward or penalty in order to move from thought to action. Identifying your specific needs in this area is the first step.

Types of Self-motivation:

There are two types of self-motivation:

- **Intrinsic:** Intrinsic self-motivation is performing the task for just having the satisfaction of doing it. This is usually something fun and personally challenging for interaction.
- **Extrinsic:** Extrinsic self-motivation is performing a task for a reward. Whether that is money, power, praise or fame.

Knowledge Box

A common barrier to action is often the perception that a task is too large or too complex to accomplish. If that is an issue for you, then a useful practice is to break down the job into several smaller, more "doable" tasks each of which you can envision accomplishing in a set time period.

Practice Box

1. How do you motivate yourself to get work done after trying many things and failing over and over again?
2. What moved you to first start the change into the Leo we know today? What was your very first step?

Self-Regulation

Self-regulation focuses on your ability to affect personal and professional growth based on your self-awareness and motivation. It can also be defined in another ways.

- In most of the basic sense, it involves controlling one's behaviour, thoughts and emotions in the pursuit of long term goals. This is emotional self-regulation.
- On other hand Behavioral self-regulation is "the ability to act in your long-term best interest, consistent with your deepest values". It is what allows us to feel one way but act another.

Useful questions you should ask yourself in an effort to self-regulate are the following:

- Who will provide direct supervision or oversight on my project? With what frequency (daily, weekly, etc.)?
- What are the deadlines, if any, relevant to my research project?
- What are the formal requirements, if any, for my research? These might include progress reports, oral presentations, a final written report or thesis?
- What are the outcomes that I desire from my participation in this project? What, if anything, do I need to do in order to achieve these outcomes?

The Psychology of Self-Regulation

According to Albert Bandura, an expert on self-efficacy and a leading researcher of SRT, self-regulation is a continuously active process in which we:

- Monitor our own behavior, the influences on our behavior, and the consequences of our behavior;
- Judge our behavior in relation to our own personal standards and broader, more contextual standards;
- React to our own behavior (i.e., what we think and how we feel about our behavior) (1991).

Fact Box

Andrea Bell from **GoodTherapy.org** has a straightforward definition of self-regulation: It's "control [of oneself] by oneself"

Practice Box

Activity to improve self-regulation:

Musical chairs. Set out enough chairs in a row, alternating facing front and back, for every player—minus one. Play music and have kids walk or dance around the chairs. When the music stops, they must make a beeline for the closest chair. Each round, the player who doesn't manage to grab a seat is eliminated, until just one winning player remains.

Summary

- One of the abilities that most faculty mentors (and employers, folks!) desire to cultivate in their undergraduate charges is independence
- Important things about independent working are you take full responsibility of work, You are ready to do unsupervised work that means you don't need constant supervision, You take the ownership of it that means you take yourself accountable for it, You know what to do and when, You do what is asked to the best of your ability without any external or internal fear, etc.
- Skills to work independently are communication skills, organizational skills, adaptability or flexibility, negotiating skills, multitasking ability, ability to deal with rejection and not to take it personally, discipline.
- Self-awareness refers to your knowledge and understanding of yourself - your emotions, beliefs, assumptions, biases, knowledge base, abilities, motivations, interests, etc.
- Types of self-awareness are self-awareness of your strengths, self-awareness of your weaknesses, self-awareness of your dark side and self-awareness to your emotional triggers.
- Self-motivation refers to your ability to identify effective methods of getting yourself to move from thought to action.
- Types of self-motivation are intrinsic and extrinsic.
- Self-regulation focuses on your ability to affect personal and professional growth based on your self-awareness and motivation.

Self-Assessment

A. MULTIPLE CHOICE QUESTIONS

1. Self-regulation is controlling:

   a. Behaviour b. Emotions c. Thoughts d. All

2. Which of the following is a systematic effects to direct thoughts, actions and feelings towards the attainment of one's goals:

   a. Self-motivation b. Self-regulations c. Self-awareness d. All

3. ________ is your ability to identify effective methods of getting yourself to move from thoughts to action.

   a. Self-motivation b. Self-regulations c. Self-awareness d. All

4.

a. Real b. Rate c. Realistic d. Required

B. FILL IN THE BLANKS

1. ____________ is having a clear perception of your personality, including strengths, etc.
2. ____________ is what pushes us to achieve our goals.
3. ____________ involves controlling one's behaviour in the pursuit of long-term goals.

C. TRUE FALSE

1. Motivation is what pushes us to achieve our goals, feel more fulfilled abd improve overall quality of life (T/F)

D. ANSWER THE FOLLOWING QUESTIONS:

1. What do you mean by work independently? Give important things about independent working.
2. What skills are required to work independently?
3. What is Self-awareness?
4. Give four types of self-awareness.
5. Why self-regulation is important in your life?
6. Write a short note on self-motivation.

E. PROJECT WORK

1. Make a chart on seven skills required to work independently and also make a presentation on self-awareness.

For self-Control:

Play Blurt. Blurt is a set of cards with definitions for vocabulary words. A leader will read the card and students "blurt" out the answer. For this tell students of different sections to make cards and use them for playing with different section of class.

To play this, have two students stand next to each other for a duel. Read the card and allow only those two students to shout out the answer. All other students in the room have to use self-control and not shout out, even if they know the answer when no one else does! This can be a big challenge for those students who struggle with shouting out when it is not their turn. Note that if you don't have blurt, you can always make up your very own cards with content area questions!

Answers

A. Multiple choice question answers:

1. d 2. b 3. a

B. Fill in the blanks answers:

1. Self-awareness 2. Self-motivation 3. Self-regulation

C. True False answers

1. True

Do group discussion on importance of self-management and techniques of self-management

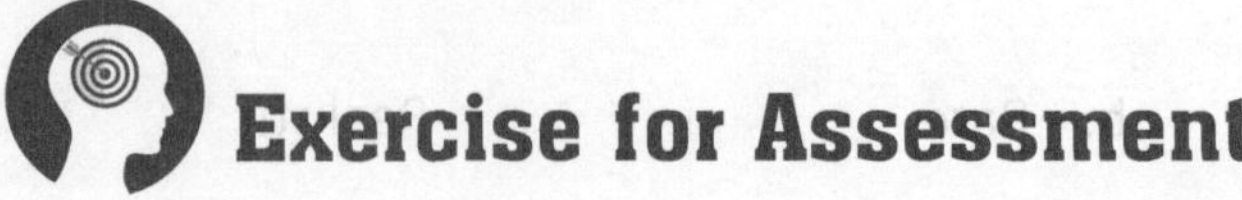

Exercise for Assessment

A. MULTIPLE CHOICE QUESTIONS

1. _________ is the ability to work without always getting instructions of doing things.
   a. Self-confidence b. Organization c. Initiative d. Accountability
2. R in SMART strategy stands for_________?
   a. Real b. Rate c. Realistic d. Required
3. Self-management skills do not involve:
   a. Initiative b. Organization c. Management d. Accountability
4. _________ is your ability to participate as a team member.
   a. Rational Abilities b. Personal qualities c. Interpersonal skill d. Communication skill
5. O in SWOT stands for __________
   a. Operation b. Organization c. Opportunity d. Openly
6. People with low self-esteem are more affected by:
   a. Personal matters b. others thinking about them
   c. Work load d. None
7. People with self-confidence have a__________ outlook:
   a. Negative b. Arrogant c. Outward d. Positive
8. Which of the following refers to a belief about your own ability to deal with events and challenges?
   a. Self-esteem b. Self Confidence c. Self-monitoring d. Self-efficacy

Answer

1. c 2. c 3. c 4. c 5. c 6. b 7. d 8. d

B. VERY SHORT QUESTIONS:

1. What is Self-management?
2. Write down the full form of SMART strategy.
3. Give two characteristics of accountability.
4. Name the three factors influencing self-confidence.
5. What do you mean by self-esteem?
6. How positive thinking helps in achieving the self-confidence.

C. SHORT QUESTIONS:

1. What do you mean by Self-management? Explain in brief.
2. Explain SMART strategy.
3. How being organised is one of the importance of self-management?
4. Differentiate accountability and responsibility.
5. Define Self-confidence
6. Explain SWOT technique for improving self-confidence.

D. LONG QUESTIONS:

1. Give three key skills of self-management.

2. What is the importance of Self-management? Explain five points of importance of self-management.
3. What do you mean by Organization skills of self-management? Explain SMART strategy used in it.
4. Give in detail any five factors for building Self-confidence.
5. Write a

E. APPLICATION BASED QUESTIONS:

1. You are organising an foundation day function in your school, Use SWOT analysis to find out your classmates strengths and weakness and assign a task to them according to their specifications.
2. Arrange a press conference in your class and tell students to take interview of class top 3 toppers, how he/she work or manage to get highest score in the class.
3. Devinder focus on playing and always unable to finish his homework, suggest him few things for managing his time effectively and completing his homework on time and also get time for playing.

F. GROUP DISCUSSION:

Divide the class into two groups one with even roll number and other with odd roll number. Then have a group discussion on key-skills of self-management.

Arrange a group discussion in the class room on the topic of how self-management prove to be helpful in different work.

Do discussion on various ways of managing stress.

What are the main skills that is necessary in working independently. Do group discussion on it in the classroom.

PROJECT WORKS

1. **Freeze:** This game incorporates movement, play, and self-control all in one. Just play some music and let kids dance, wiggle, and walk around. Have one person be the leader (a teacher to start) and yell "Freeze!" at any time. As soon as someone shouts it, everyone should freeze in place, with the music still playing. This can be challenging with the music still going, because you might have the urge to keep dancing. This is a great game to practice at the end of the week for some added fun.
2. **Simon Says:** This game focuses on attention skills, but self-control, too! Kids have to be focused to listen for what Simon says to do, while using self-control to stop themselves if "Simon" doesn't say it! Stand in front of the class and shout out commands like "Simon says put your hands on your head" and "Simon says stand on one foot." Then, throw one in there that doesn't say "Simon says" and see who can follow along. Afterwards, you can switch it up and have students be the leader as well.
3. Inculcate positive thoughts by repeating it to yourself for one month and observe how it has affects you.
4. List out your strengths and weaknesses, make 2 week plan using SMART strategy to work on your weakness and tract your progress and then repeat it for next week.
5. **For self-awareness: Write a personal manifesto.**

   A personal manifesto describes your core values and beliefs, the specific ideas and priorities that you stand for, and how you plan to live your life. This acts as both a statement of personal principles and a call to action. A personal manifesto can help frame your life, point you in the right direction to help achieve your goals, and act as a tool to remind you of your primary concerns.

TEACHER NOTES:

1. Give practical examples of using SMART strategy for preparation and availability of things
2. Clear the difference of self-awareness, self-regulation and self-motivation to students.

3 Basic ICT Skills – II

Learning Outcomes

After this chapter, you will have the knowledge of:

- Define Information and communication technology
- Introduction to Word processor
- Word processing Applications
- Opening MS Word 2010
- Closing a Document
- Saving a Document
- Setting Text fonts
- Applying Bullets and Numbering
- Printing the document
- Creating a Table using Grid option and Dialog box
- Creating a New workbook
- Saving a workbook
- Renaming, Deleting, moving a Worksheet
- Closing of opened workbook
- Use of basic formulas for calculation
- Use of Simple functions for calculation
- Creating a presentation
- Adding Text and New slide in a presentation
- Saving or closing a presentation
- Exiting the PowerPoint Application
- Adding, Formatting a Text
- Inserting pictures from files, Clip Art
- Adding a Slides
- Presenting a Presentation

INTRODUCTION

ICT stands for Information and communication Technology that includes a set of technological resources and tools used for communication, creation, storing, managing and disseminating information. ICT includes Internet, computers, telephony and broadcasting technologies that take the knowledge about how computer works and how different computers communicate with each other.

Knowledge Box

In digital technology, the information is translated into a binary format where each bit represents two distinct amplitudes; on the other hand, information is translated into varying amplitude electric pulses in case of analog technology.

SESSION 1: DOCUEMTATION PREPARATION USING WORD PROCESSING APPLICATION

The purpose of this session is to aware user about word processor and its various applications. Word processor and its various features are explained which will help user to creates different types of documents.

INTRODUCTION TO WORD PROCESSOR

Through word processing programs user is able to manipulate the text and images. Word processor allows us to create, save, edit and print a document. The notepad and other text editor are not same as word processor. As notepad allow user to only create and edit the plain text. On other hand text can be illustrated and changed using word processor. It also allows to use images in the documents.

Definition Box

According to *Vangie Beal*, A word processor is software or a device that allows users to create, edit, and print documents. It enables you to write, store, display text on a screen, modify it by entering commands and characters from the keyboard, and prints it.

Knowledge Box

The first version of Microsoft Word was developed by Charles Simonyi and Richard Brodie, former Xerox programmers hired by Bill Gates and Paul Allen in 1981.

WORD PROCESSING APPLICATIONS

By the use of word processing any kind of text document can be written and its overall performance can be further enhance using various features of word processor. In short, by use of it one can able to create a professional projects for office or other document as per their requirements.

Various word processing applications are:

Some of the below give application of word processing are desktop based and some are based on utility

- WordPad
- Microsoft Word
- Google Docs
- Notepad
- OpenOffice Writer
- LibreOffice Writter

Notepad and Wordpad are basic text editors and they are desktop based application that comes with windows. On other hand advanced word processing applications are Microsoft word, LibreOffice Writer and Open Office and all these three are different packages. These three are also desktop based utility. OpenOffice is available online on www.openoffice.org website and it is a part of OpenOffice suite. Microsoft office is a part of Microsoft Office suite.

Definition Box

Notepad: Notepad is a generic text editor included with all versions of the file contains special formatting or is not a plaintext file, it cannot be read in Microsoft Notepad. The image is a small example of what the Microsoft Notepad may look like while running.

WordPad: WordPad is a basic word processor available in every version of Microsoft's operating systems since Windows 95. It can be used to create and modify documents. Although slower to load than Notepad, it can handle graphics and rich formatting, unlike notepad, along with handling larger files. WordPad is well preferred for taking quick notes and text-based writing.

Opening MS Word 2010

Launch a Document: To open a MS Word 2010 step are given below:

Click on Start > Click on all programs > Microsoft Office > Microsoft Word

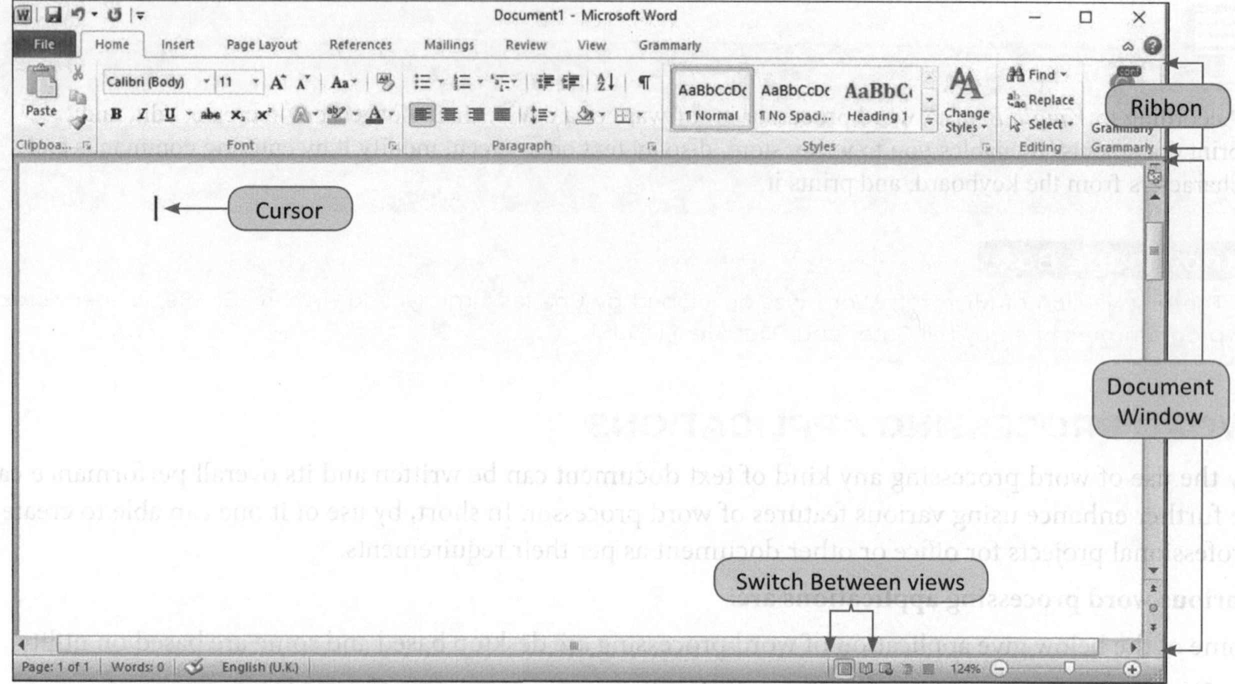

Figure 3.1: Opening MS Word 2010

The above figure or blank document comes on screen after opening MS Word 2010. The temporary name of this blank document is Documnet1. One small blinking cursor is appears on the screen and it is also known as insertion point. The component are shown in the figure. The open application of MS Word displays document window, Ribbon bar, Cursor and switch between views icon. The formatting, editing, typing part is done in document window. The typing part is start from cursor and ribbon bar contains various functionality buttons that can be used.

Memory Box

In case if above shown blank document is not visible in MS Word. Then you can open it by: Clicking on File > New > Blank Document.

Knowledge Box

It is estimated that more than 10 million people worldwide use the MS Office Suite on either Windows or macOS X, and 15 million use it on Linux.

Creating a Document

In above step we have open a document either by default when we open MS Word or by creating it using the instructions given in note.

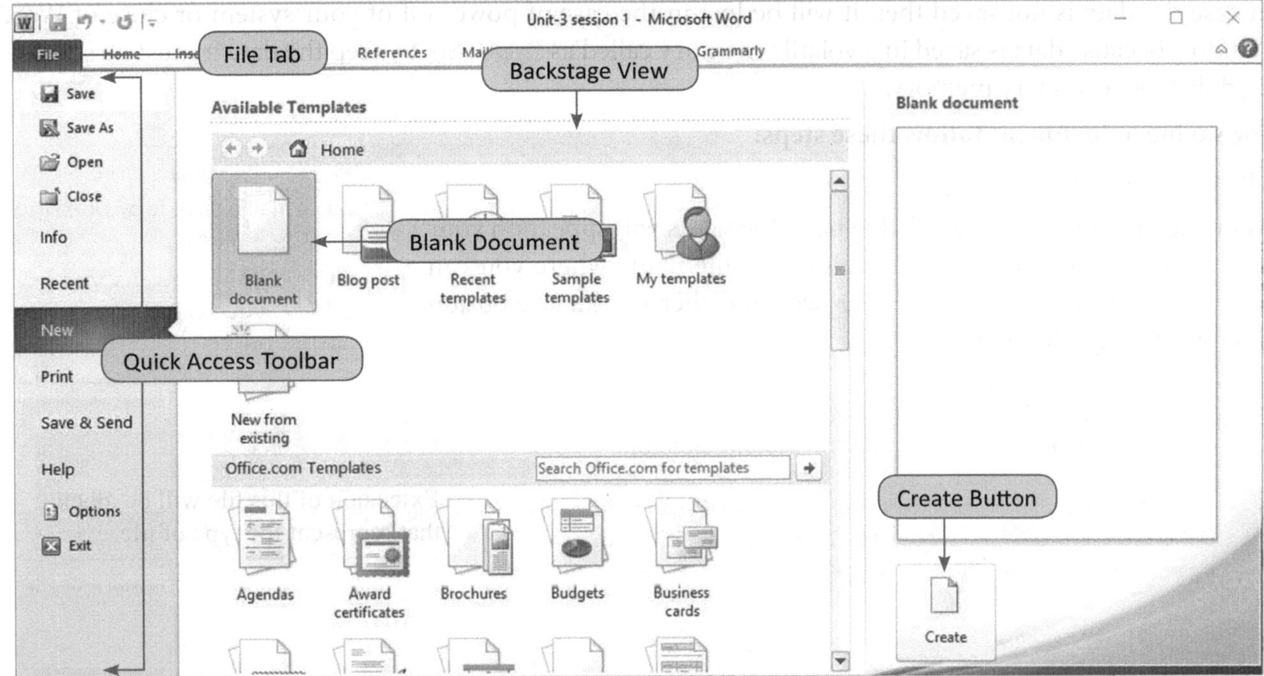

Figure 3.2: Creating a document

Once you are done with creating a new document then you can type the data you want to enter in it. The typing will start from cursor position. The cursor will move horizontally from left to right while typing a text.

Saving a Document

The written data in the document is temporarily available in the **Random Access Memory (RAM)** or internal memory of your system. This can be saved permanently on the hard disk for future use. (Figure 3.3)

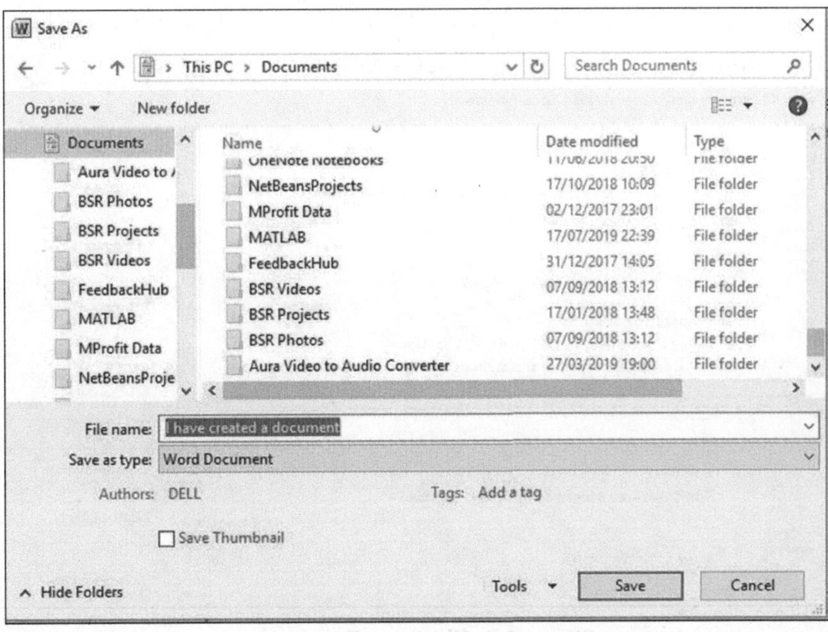

Figure 3.3: Saving a document

In case the data is not saved then it will be lost in the case of power off of your system or close of Word Window because data is saved in a volatile memory called as **RAM**. So, to keep the data it must be saved in hard disk or secondary memory.

For saving a document follow these steps:

Click on **File** tab > **Save.**

After clicking on **Save**, a new dialog box of **Save As** will appear on your screen. (Figure 3.3) There is one column of file name where you can write the name of the file as per your need and click on the save button given in the right bottom.

Shortcut

You can also save it by pressing both Ctrl + S keys.

By Clicking on Save As, you can save your existing file with another name.

Knowledge Box

The Save As dialog box will give the default location, further it can change by creating a folder and put name in the file name dialog box and click on save button to save it. Now document is saved with the name given by you and in the location chosen by you.

MEMORY BOX

Extension of this file will be .docx that represent the type of file.

Fact Box

Google Docs, Office 365 Word, and Microsoft OneDrive Word are Web-based word processor.

Closing a Document

Once you are done with your work, you can close the document by following the step:

Click on **File** > **Close** (Figure 3.4)

After clicking on close icon your document will be close or one new Window will be pop up for asking to save the document if you have not saved in before. (Figure 3.5)

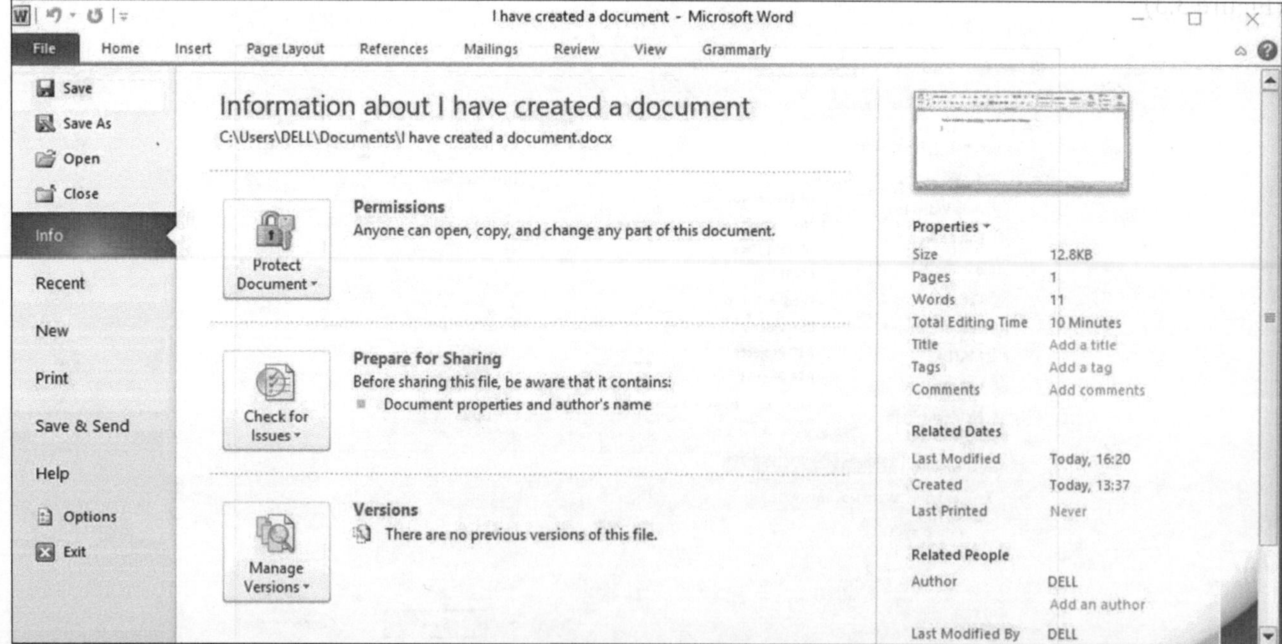

Figure 3.4: Closing a Document

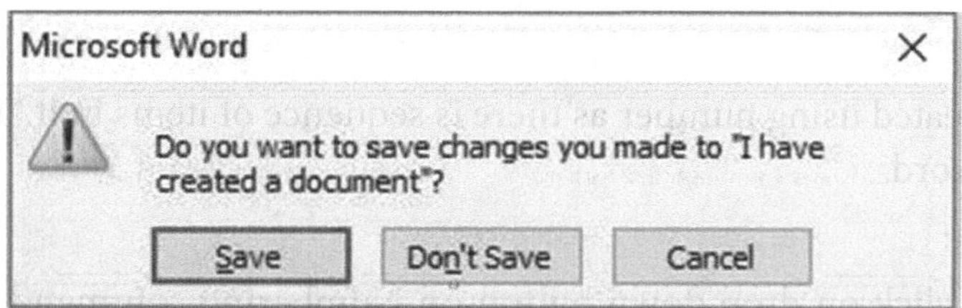

Figure 3.5: New pop up window for saving the alteration before closing the document

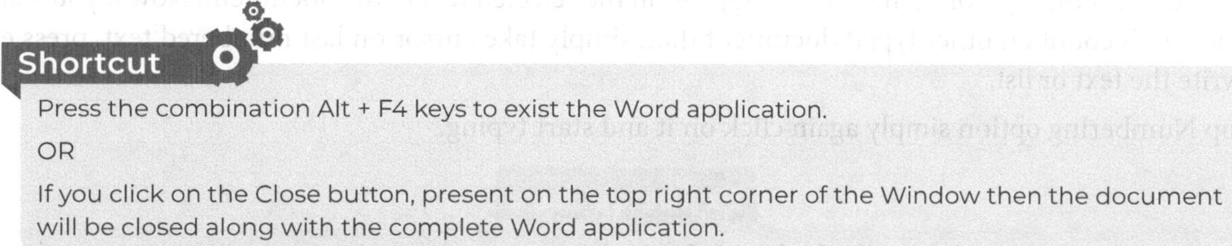
Shortcut

Press the combination Alt + F4 keys to exist the Word application.

OR

If you click on the Close button, present on the top right corner of the Window then the document will be closed along with the complete Word application.

SETTING TEXT FONTS

How to set text font and its size is covered in this section. There are various types of fonts available in MS Word 2010 along with various sizes. Mainly it is used while giving heading, etc., that differentiates it with other text available in that document.

Change the type and size of font

This can be performed using keyboard, Home tab and shortcut menu. The font type of below given document in figure is Calibri and its size is 11. The font changing function is available in font group of home tab.

To perform the change in font types follow the following steps:

Click on home tab > click on font type drop down arrow > select the font type

You can apply this on whole document by selecting it or on specific paragraph or line of the document. Same is applicable for changing the font size of document.

OR

Another option to change font type and size is by clicking on font dialog box launcher. After clicking on font dialog box a new dialog box will come where, you can select the font type, style, size, color and other functionality.

BULLETS

Mainly unordered list are created using bullet as there is no sequence of items in it. There are various styles of bullets available in Word.

Steps to create a bullet list:

Create a list > select it > click on drop down button on Bullets command from paragraph group > select the style

When you select the style of bullet it will appear on the selected text in the document. Now if you want to bullet on other typed document then simply take cursor on last text with bullet, press enter and write the text or list.

To stop bullet option simply again click on it and start typing.

NUMBERING:

Mainly ordered list are created using number as there is sequence of items in it. There are various styles of numbering available in Word.

Steps to create a bullet list:

Create a list > select it > click on drop down button on Numbering command from paragraph group > select the style

When you select the style of number it will appear on the selected text in the document. Now if you want to continue with count on other typed document then simply take cursor on last numbered text, press enter and write the text or list.

To stop Numbering option simply again click on it and start typing.

Practice Box

Write the correct answer in the blank given below:

1. To put a list of items in a good manner format, there is an option of ____________.

Printing the document:

The word processor will allow to access the copy of saved document. But for the person who is not using computer need its printed copy to read it. The printout option is available in MS Word that brings the document in printed pages or hard copy. We can set the document in print preview before taking its hard copy.

Steps to print a document are:

Open the required document > click on File tab > Print

There are various options available on print dialog box.

Click on file tab > print > enter the number of copies > choose printer from printer drop down button > Print All pages or other options

MEMORY BOX

Shortcut key to print a document is Ctrl + P.

CREATING A TABLE

There are two methods to create or insert a table in the document. One is using a grid option and other is using a dialog box.

Method 1: Using Grid option

To create a table using grid option follow the following steps:

Click on Insert Tab > Table command Drop down arrow > Drag the mouse pointer over the grid on number of rows and columns required by you

Once you have selected the number of rows and columns from grid a table will appear on your document. There is 10 x 8 block of table out of which user can select the count according to their requirements.

Method 2: Using Dialog box

Another option to create a table in word document is using a dialog box. To create a table using dialog box perform the following steps:

Click on Insert Tab > Select the table drop down arrow > Select Insert Table option

Knowledge Box

Example: In the case of datasheet made for a survey done on the type of house people are living in particular village will contain the row of the name of a person, contact number or numeric data, Number of persons in house and type of house. In Word processor, we have a tool to create and manage tables.

MEMORY BOX

1. On a display screen in character mode, a column is a vertical line of characters extending from the top to the bottom of the screen. The size of a text display is usually measured in rows and columns.
2. In spreadsheets, a column is a vertical row of cells. Spreadsheet columns are usually identified by letters.
3. In database management systems, column is another name for field.
4. In documents, a column is a vertical area reserved for text. Most newspapers, for example, contain four or more columns per page. Modern word processors and desktop publishing systems enable you to automatically divide a page into columns.

Practice Box

Check whether the given statement is true or false:

1. Once you have added rows in a Table, you can't edit the count.
2. One can add number of tables in a document.

Summary

- ICT stands for Information and communication Technology that includes a set of technological resources and tools used for communication, creation, storing, managing and disseminating information.
- Word processor allow user to organize and present to a text on a page or several pages. The text organized in this way is referred to as a document.
- Formatting, graphic, ease and speed, printing, storage, mail merge, Vocabulary and spell check are basic features of Microsoft word 2010.
- Notepad and Wordpad are desktop based applications
- LibreOffice Writer, OpenOffice writer and Microsoft word are desktop based applications of word processing
- To open MS word 2010, Click on Start > Click on all programs > Microsoft Office > Microsoft Word 2010
- To save a Document, Click on file tab > Save Or press both Cntl + S keys
- To close a Document, Click on File > Close
- To create a bullet list, Create a list > select it > click on drop down button on Bullets command from paragraph group > select the style
- Steps to print a document, Open the required document > click on File tab > Print
- There are two methods to create or insert a table in the document. One is using a grid option and other is using a dialog box.

Keywords: Word processor, Word processing applications, Notepad, Wordpad, Opening MS Word 2010, Creating a document, Saving a document, Closing a document, Setting Text Fonts, Change the type and size of font, Bullets, Numbering, Printing the document, Creating a Table, using Grid option, Using dialog box.

Self-Assessment

A. MULTIPLE CHOICE QUESTIONS

1. What is the extension of Word document:

   a. .doc b. .dob c. .docx

2. Which of these is not a application of Word Processor

   a. Notepad b. Paint c. Open Office

3. Shortcut key used to Save a document

   a. Cntl + A b. Cntl + C c. Cntl + S d. Cntl + C

4. Shortcut key to Open an existing document?

   a. Cntl + E b. Cntl + S c. Cntl + C d. Cntl + O

5. Which of the following button will reduce the size of window from its standard size?

   a. Maximize b. Reduce c. Minimize

6. The default tab of word?

   a. Home b. View c. File d. Page Layout

7. Shortcut key to Open an existing document?

   a. Cntl + E b. Cntl + S c. Cntl + C d. Cntl + O

8. Which of the following is a not a default buttons present in quick access toolbar?

   a. Undo b. Open c. Redo d. Save

9. Font type, Font size, Font color is the commands of

   a. Clipboard group b. Styles group c. Font group d. Editing group

10. Which of the following is the group of Bullet and Numbering?

    a. Clipboard b. Font c. Paragraph d. Editing

B. FILL IN THE BLANKS

1. ____________ is the Shortcut key used to Save a document
2. Notepad is a ____________ application of Microsoft processing.
3. MS Word is a ____________ application of Microsoft programming
4. ____________ is used to save the existing file with another name
5. Title bar contains ____________ and ____________.
6. To cancel the last editing ____________ button is used
7. The text is set according to the margins using ____________.
8. User type in ____________ area

C. TRUE AND FALSE:

1. Whether you can open existing file (T/F)
2. Save and Save As perform same task (T/F)
3. Whether we can do changes in existing document (T/F)

4. Whether you can open existing file (T/F)
5. Save and Save As perform same task (T/F)
6. Whether we can do changes in existing document (T/F)
7. This key is used to create a number list (T/F)
8. Thus key is used to create a bullet list (T/F)

D. ANSWER THE FOLLOWING QUESTIONS:

1. What is a Word processor?
2. Name the various applications of word processor?
3. Name and explain various features of word processor?
4. What are the four major operations of MS Word?
5. Write down the steps to open a MS Word 2010?
6. How to create a new document in MS Word 2010?
7. What are the steps to save a file in MS Word 2010?
8. How to close a document in MS Word 2010?
9. What are the steps to open an existing document?
10. What are the steps to save an existing file with different name?
11. What is the difference between Save and Save As?

E. PRACTICAL WORK

1. Create a new document and write one paragraph in it, then save it with your name, close the document and reopen it.
2. Open a existing document from its location, edit the text, Use Undo and Redo, then Save it with different name
3. Open a word, check the functioning of each tabs in the toolbar, write a document, perform undo and redo, use various view options given in it.
4. Open a word, write a text, change its font size and type, Write more data select half of it and use font color button, and in other half of text select it and use text highlight color. Use subscript and superscript effect to check its output.
5. Open a word, write two list, select first one and apply bullet on it, then select second one and apply numbering on it.

Answers

A. Multiple choice question answers:

1. a	2. b	3. c	4. d	5. c
6. a	7. d	8. b	9. c	10. b

B. Fill in the blanks answers:

1. Ctrl + s	2. desktop based	3. desktop based utility
4. Name and type of document	5. Undo	6. MAX
7. Cntl + U	8. Change case	

C. True False answers:

1. True	2. False	3. True	4. True
5. True	6. False	7. True	8. False

SESSION 2: PERFORM TABULATION USING SPREADSHEET APPLICATION

The spreadsheet is an electronic way of doing the same work which your grandparents used to do in dairy. In case of maintaining the long list of budgets, data, sales figures and other data, spreadsheets are used and Microsoft Excel is considered as one of the very useful spreadsheet. In the field of business and accounting part spreadsheets are used that is derived from the word 'Spread'. The bills you get from shopkeepers can be in handwritten form or printed from computer that contains the list and total amount of things you have buy from them including all taxes, discount, Vat part in it. These all tasks can be done using spreadsheet that organise the data in the form of rows and columns.

Definition Box

A spreadsheet or worksheet is a file made of numerical data. What makes a spreadsheet software program unique is its ability to calculate values using mathematical cells.

Knowledge Box

In case of maintaining the long list of budgets, data, sales figures and other data, spreadsheets are used and Microsoft Excel is considered as one of the very useful spreadsheet.

CREATING A NEW WORKBOOK

A blank spreadsheet or workbook is appears on starting the MS Excel that contains by default three worksheets. But sometimes there is requirement of creating a new workbook for this follow the steps:

Click on File tab > New > Blank Workbook > Create

Or

Click on drop down arrow of Customize quick access Toolbars > New

MEMORY BOX

Shortcut key to create a workbook: Press Ctrl +N

SAVING A WORKBOOK

We have created a workbook and worksheet in previous section now next part is to save it. To save a worksheet or workbook follows the steps:

Click on File > Save > Select the location from given list in the left of Save As dialog box > Enter name in file name text box

MEMORY BOX

Shortcut key to save a workbook: Press Ctrl +S

RENAMING A WORKSHEET

In last section we have learned to save a workbook or worksheet and renaming it while saving. In Excel 2010 we can also rename the worksheet by simply following the steps:

Double click on the sheet tab given in bottom left side > Type a name > Press Enter button given on keyboard

Or

Right click on sheet tab > select rename option > Assign new name by typing on it

DELETING A WORKSHEET

The unwanted worksheet can be deleted from workbook by following the simple steps.

Right click on desired worksheet > Select Delete option

Select the sheet tab given below in left side of worksheet > Click on delete option given in Cells group of Home tab

MOVE A WORKSHEET

The worksheet can be copy or move within a workbook or between workbooks. To copy or move a worksheet performs the following steps:

Right click on desired sheet tab > Select Move or Copy option

CLOSING OF OPENED WORKBOOK OR WORKSHEET

When user is done with the entire task on worksheet or workbook and saved all data then next step will be close the workbook. In order to close the workbook performs the following steps:

Click on File Tab > Close

Or

Click on cross button given on the right upper corner of title bar. This will exist the MS Excel 2010.

Memory Box

The shortcut key to Close an existing worksheet, Press both Ctrl + W

Definition Box

A Worksheet is a collection of cells organized in rows and columns. It is the working surface you interact with to enter data. Each worksheet contains 1048576 rows and 16384 columns and serves as a giant table that allows you to organize information. Typically, a workbook contains several worksheets with related content and only one of the worksheets is active at a time.

Knowledge Box

Users can enter data, text, formulas, and numbers in each cell, and up to 32767 characters can become single cells.

Formulae: The mathematical or symbolic expression can enter in the cell to perform the calculation on it. Cell addresses, parenthesis, numbers and arithmetic operators come under it.

For example to perform addition between B1, C2, C5 and D6 cell and put result in E7 cell, write =B1+C2+C5+C6 in E7 cell.

Like same way subtraction, multiplication and other operation can be perform on it by replacing + with -, * respectively. Every formulae in MS Excel is begin with '=' symbol.

USING BASIC FORMULAS

As mentioned above there are two ways to perform calculation one is either use formulas or functions. Formulas are simply equations that perform calculations on values in our sheet. This can include numbers, parenthesis, cell address and arithmetic operators and result will be displayed on the cell where user has entered the formula. In this section we deal with performing various operations using formulas.

Operation	Symbol Name	Symbol	Example
Addition	Plus sign	+	B2 + C2, B3 + 6
Subtraction	Minus sign	-	B2 - C2
Multiplication	Asterisk	*	C2 * D2
Division	Forward slash	/	C2 / D2

USING SIMPLE FUNCTIONS

In Excel there are predefined formulas that can be used to perform the required calculations. In above method where we type formulas to perform the various calculations there will be more chances of error. Arguments are accepted by it and in return it will give values. Arguments and Structure are two parts that make a complete function.

The input values to function is known as arguments that can be a text, numbers, logical values, formulas or range of a cell written in between the parenthesis.

On other hand basic skeleton is defined by structure part that makes the basis of writing a general function or its syntax. The syntax is:

=FUNCTION NAME(argument1, argument2, ……)

SUM( )

Just like + sign in basic formulas a SUM() function will add all the numbers given in the arguments between the parenthesis of sum function. Basic steps need to perform are:

Click on cell where you want to enter the result > Type =SUM(B2:B6) or =SUM(B2,B6)

These both function will give you the sum of data in cell B2 to B6. User can also enter the direct value in parenthesis instead of entering the cell name. For example =SUM(2,4,6)

AVERAGE( )

The arithmetic mean and average of the arguments is return by AVERAGE function. In arguments user can enter the range of cells, direct numbers, both numbers and cell reference. For example:

AVERAGE(B2:B6)

Or

AVERGAE(B2,B6)

Or

AVERAGE(1,4,3)

Or

AVERAGE(B2:D2,B3:D3) : In this we have given two ranges of cells. It will return the average for cell B2 to D2 and B3 to D3

MAX( )

The MAX function will return the largest value from specified arguments in parenthesis of MAX function. It accept only numeric data and logical values as arguments and return zero 0 in other cases. Steps to find the largest value from range of value is:

Open the document > Enter the required data > Type =MAX(starting range: Ending range)

This will return the largest value from the range given in MAX parenthesis.

Same like MAX function a lowest value in the cell can be obtained using MIN function.

TODAY( )

The current date of particular cell can be display using the function TODAY( ).

Example type =TODAY() function in cell E3 it will display the date of E3 cell.

This today function can also be using with other functions to get the current month, day and year. For example:

=DAY(TODAY()) function will return the current date in number form. To get the result in text form write =TEXT

Practice Box

Choose the correct option from following options given under questions:

1. The Sum ( ) function and addition gives the same.

   a. True b. False

2. The Average ( ) function do the same operation as Division.

   a. True b. False

3. The Today( ) function will give the current date.

   a. True b. False

Summary

- The spreadsheet is an electronic way of doing the same work which your grandparents used to do in dairy.
- To create a new workbook, Click on File tab > New > Blank Workbook > Create
- To save a workbook, Click on File > Save > Select the location from given list in the left of Save As dialog box > Enter name in file name text box
- To rename a worksheet, Double click on the sheet tab given in bottom left side > Type a name > Press Enter button given on keyboard
- To delete a worksheet, Right click on desired worksheet > Select Delete option
- The worksheet can be copy or move within a workbook or between workbooks.
- When user is done with the entire task on worksheet or workbook and saved all data then next step will be close the workbook.
- The mathematical or symbolic expression can be enter in the cell to perform the calculation on it.
- In Excel there are predefined formulas that can be used to perform the required calculations. For sum it is SUM(argument1, argument2,.....).
- The arithmetic mean and average of the arguments is return by AVERAGE function.
- The MAX function will return the largest value from specified arguments in parenthesis of MAX function.
- The current date of particular cell can be display using the function TODAY( ).

Keywords: Spreadsheet, Creating a new workbook, MS Excel, Saving a workbook, Renaming a worksheet, Deleting a worksheet, Move a worksheet, Closing of opened workbook, Formulae, Calculation using basic formulas, Calculation using Simple functions.

A. MULTIPLE CHOICE QUESTIONS

1. Extension of MS Excel file is:
   a. .xcl b. .doc c. .xlxs d. .xlsx
2. What is the shortcut key to create a new workbook:
   a. Ctrl + C b. Ctrl + N c. Ctrl + P d. Ctrl + W
3. Shortcut key to save the file?
   a. Ctrl + A b. Ctrl + C c. Ctrl + S d. Ctrl + N
4. Which of the following is the correct way of using addition formula:
   a. B2+C2 b. (B2+C2) c. =B2+C2 d. £B2+C2
5. The Autosum command available in which group of Home tab:
   a. Clipboard b. Data c. Styles d. Editing
6. The name given to predefined formulas to Excel is ?
   a. Basic formula b. Formulas c. Formulae d. None
7. The output of MAX(3, 2, 4, 8) will be:
   a. 3 b. 2 c. 4 d. 8

B. FILL IN THE BLANKS

1. A cell can be activate by ____________.
2. ____________ is the shortcut key to open a workbook
3. You can close the file by clicking on File > ____________ option
4. Output of A2-B2-C2, where A2= 7, B2=2 and C2=1 will be ____________.
5. The output of SUM(A1:A3),Where A1, A2 and A3 is 2, 3 and 5 respectively.
6. The formula to find the largest value for range of value between A2 to D2.
7. The AVERAGE(1,2,3) function will give ____________ of three numbers in parenthesis.
8. In Excel user can measure the day, ____________ and date of particular cell

C. TRUE AND FALSE:

1. Theme is a Tab in Excel (T/F)
2. A cell consists of single row and multiple columns (T/F)
3. By default there are three number of worksheets available in MS Excel 2010 (T/F)
4. Cell can be identified with unique row number and column number (T/F)
5. A new worksheet can be added in the workbook (T/F)
6. The calculation can be perform on any type of data in Excel (T/F)
7. In Excel we can perform calculation on data given in range of cells using single instruction (T/F)
8. The output of C2/D2 is 2.5. Where C2 is 4 and D2 is 2 (T/F)
9. TODAY() function written in particular cell will give the time of it (T/F)

D. ANSWER THE FOLLOWING QUESTIONS:

1. How to create a new workbook and add worksheet in it.
2. How formula bar can be used to enter the data in Active cell?
3. Write down the steps of various methods to add a worksheet in workbook?
4. Gives the various option of renaming the worksheet?
5. Describe the process of saving a workbook and what happen when user close the workbook without saving it?
6. Name the four basic mathematical operations supported by Excel.
7. Give example of using SUM function for addition of range of values.
8. Write down the steps to perform addition, subtraction, multiplication and division in Excel using formulas.
9. Explain the usage of DAY(TODAY()) function in MS excel 2010.
10. How result of current day or month can be obtained in text form.

E. PRACTICAL WORK

1. Open a MS Excel, Insert new worksheet, add data given below in table, Save it with your name, Close it, Reopen it, delete the worksheet then again close it using shortcut key

Student name	Roll No.	Age
Komal	12	13
Simran	13	12
Gurutek	14	13
Harshan	15	13

2. Open a MS Excel, and type the given data in it, Calculate sum using addition formula and SUM function and subtraction and put result of subtraction in output after discount column

Student name	Fees	Discount	Output after discount
Komal	5500	500	
Simran	5000	450	
Gurutek	5500	500	
Harshan	5500	500	
Total			

3. Perform Multiplication using formula and put date and day on their column

Product name	Cost	Quantity	Total Cost	Date	Day
Sethi candles	5500	3			
Diya	5000	4			
Twist candle	5500	10			
Elephant Diya	5500	25			

Answers

A. Multiple choice question answers:

1. d   2. b   3. c   4. c   5. d   6. c   7. d

B. Fill in the blanks answers:

1. Clicking on Cell   2. Ctrl + O   3. Close   4. 4
5. 10   6. MAX(A2:D2)   7. Average   8. Time

C. True and False:

1. False   2. False   3. True   4. True   5. True   6. False
7. True   8. False   9. False

SESSION 3: PREPARE PRESENTATION USING PRESENTATION APPLICATION

Presentation software is used to display information in a sequence of slides or slide show that is used in colleges, schools, organizations, etc for various purpose. Microsoft PowerPoint 2010 is one of the presentation software that allow to make dynamic slide presentations that can include images, videos, animation and text. It is a part of Microsoft Office 2010 that provides various templates, layouts, wizards, themes and tools.

Definition Box

A presentation is a means of communication that can be adapted to various speaking situations, such as talking to a group, addressing a meeting or briefing a team.

Knowledge Box

Presentation skills include the content and flow of the presentation. There are number of advantages to using a presentation prepared by computer. Such as organization, educational field, entertainment, conferences, and seminars.

Creating a Presentation

When user launch the MS PowerPoint 2010 a blank presentation with default name of Presentation1 is appear on screen. In this you can either start working on that presentation or create new presentation. The steps need to follow to create a new presentation are:

Click on File tab > Select New option > Select template or blank presentation as per your requirements > Click on create button

Memory Box

Shortcut to create a presentation is: Press Ctrl +N keys

Adding Text and New slide in a Presentation

By default there is single slide in the presentation for blank presentation and 12 slides for Project status inbuilt template and rest number of slides will depend on type of in-built template sample chosen by user.

To add new slide perform the following steps:

Click on drop down menu of New Slide given in Slides group of Home tab > Select the layout as per your requirements

This will add a new selected layout type of slide in your presentation.

Saving a Presentation

Once you are done with creating a presentation either using blank presentation or in built presentation, the next step is to save it. This step is done to avoid the loss of data. The steps need to follow to save the presentation are:

Click on File tab > Select Save option given in the drop down menu > Save As dialog box appears > Specify the name in File name Text box > Click on Save button given in the bottom right side of dialog box

MEMORY BOX

Shortcut to Save a presentation is: Press Shift + Ctrl +S keys

Or

Click on Save given in the Quick Access Toolbar then rest of the steps will be same

Closing a Presentation

Till now we have learnt to create and save a presentation with or without password. Now, next step is to close the presentation. To close presentation performs the following steps:

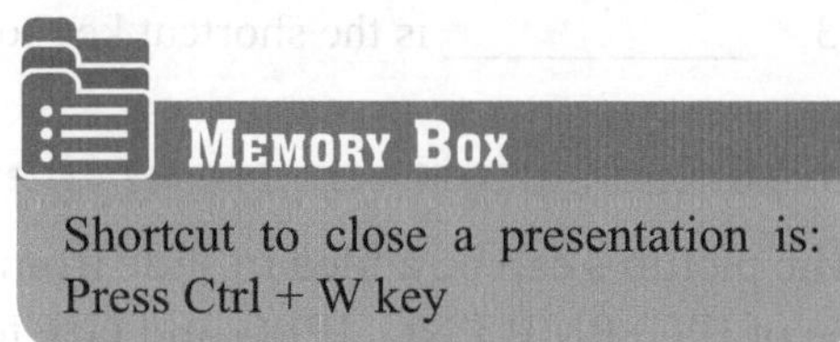

Click on File tab > Select Close option from drop down menu

Exiting the PowerPoint Application

To exist or close the PowerPoint user can use one of the two ways given below:

In first way, simply click on Close button present on the top right side of the application

In second way, Click on File tab > Select Exit option from drop down menu

Adding Text

The text can be added in slide by simply clicking on it and start typing. In case to add more text than the area provided for entering text user can insert a text box. To add a text box in a slide perform the following steps:

Create a new presentation > Write text in given space > Click on Insert Tab > Select Text Box command from Text group > Create a text box by dragging the mouse on the slide then release it > Now simply take mouse and click in it to start typing a text

Formatting Text

User can also edit text in presentation like changing the alignment, highlighting the text by making it bold, italic and underline and changing the color of textbox.

Align Text: It is related to the position of text in the slide. There can be four ways or option to align a text.
Align Text left: The left text alignment is a default type of alignment. In this case there is little space in the right side. Click on Align Text left command given in Paragraph group of Home tab

Center: This will align the text in the center of document and leave little space from both the ends. Mainly its use has been found in writing the title. Click on Center command given in Paragraph group of Home tab

Align Text Right: This is the opposite case of left text alignment as in this the text is align towards right side and leave little space in the left. Mainly used to put sign and date option or sometimes giving the chapter heading. Click on Align Text right command given in Paragraph group of Home tab

Justify: In this case text is evenly aligned between the left and right side. Click on Justify command given in Paragraph group of Home tab

Knowledge Box

Shortcut keys to:

- Align text left: Ctrl + L
- Align Text right: Ctrl + R
- Align Text center: Ctrl + E
- Justify Text: Ctrl + J

Practice Box

Select the option from following options:

1. To make the text center align one can use ____________ as shortcut key.
2. ____________ shortcut key to align the text left.
3. ____________ is the shortcut key to align the text in right.

Inserting pictures from files

The pictures can be added in slide from saved pictures in your system of different formats. The pictures can be of JPG, BMP, PNG, JPEG and GIF format. The steps need to perform for inserting pictures from file:

Place the cursor on the location of adding picture > Click on Picture command from Images group of Insert tab or apply the slide layout that contains picture > Insert dialog box will appear, select the picture from the folder and double click on it or select picture and click on Insert button given in bottom right side

Inserting pictures from Clip Art

Another option is adding pictures in slide from clip art. To add pictures in slide from clip art perform the following steps:

Click on Insert tab > Clip Art command present in Images group of Insert Tab > At right side of window a Clip Art task pane is displayed > Here you can enter the name of the required clip art in search text box > Click on Go button > Click on desired clip art

Adding a Slides

In last section we have learnt to Copy and paste a slide. In this section will learn to add a new slide in presentation. User can insert number of slides in presentation as per their requirements. To add new slide perform the following steps:

Launch the PowerPoint > Select the type of slide from add a new slide command drop down arrow

Or

Right click on any of the slide given in presentation > Select New slide option for Context menu

This will create a new slide of same style.

PRINTING A PRESENTATION

Mainly presentation is made for showing on big projector, computer in front of students or audience. But in some cases print copy of presentation is provided by presenters. The steps need to perform for printing a presentation are:

Click on File tab > Select Print option from menu

Summary

- Presentation software is used to display information in a sequence of slides or slide show that is used in colleges, schools, organizations, etc for various purpose.
- When user launch the MS PowerPoint 2010 a blank presentation with default name of Presentation1 is appear on screen
- To create a presentation, Click on File tab > Select New option > Select template or blank presentation as per your requirements > Click on create button
- By default there is single slide in the presentation for blank presentation and 12 slides for Project status inbuilt template and rest number of slides will depend on type of in-built template sample chosen by user.
- Once you are done with creating a presentation either using blank presentation or in built presentation, the next step is to save it. This step is done to avoid the loss of data.
- To close a presentation, Click on File tab > Select Close option from drop down menu
- To exist the presentation, click on Close button present on the top right side of the application
- The text can be added in slide by simply clicking on it and start typing. In case to add more text than the area provided for entering text user can insert a text box.
- User can also edit text in presentation like changing the alignment, highlighting the text by making it bold, italic and underline and changing the color of textbox.
- Text can be align in left, center, right and justify.
- The pictures can be added in slide from saved pictures in your system of different formats. The pictures can be of JPG, BMP, PNG, JPEG and GIF format.
- Another option is adding pictures in slide is from clip art.
- To add new slide, Right click on any of the slide given in presentation > Select New slide option for Context menu
- To print a presentation, Click on File tab > Select Print option from menu

Keywords: Presentation, Creating a presentation, Adding Text and New slide a presentation, Saving a presentation, Closing a presentation, Exiting the PowerPoint application, Adding text, Formatting Text, Inserting pictures from files, clip Arts, Adding a slides, Printing a presentation.

Self-Assessment

A. MULTIPLE CHOICE QUESTIONS

1. What is the shortcut key to open an existing presentation?

   a. Ctrl + A b. Ctrl + C c. Ctrl + O d. Ctrl + P

2. Which of the following option not come after closing the presentation without saving it?

   a. Save b. Save As c. Cancel d. Don't Save

3. Which of the following is the extension of presentation file?

   a. .jpg b. .doc c. .pptx d. .xlsx

4. Which of the following is not the source of adding images in presentation?

   a. Saved pictures in system b. Clip Art

   c. Sand Art d. Internet

5. Which of the following Tab contain commands to add images in presentation?

a. Home Tab b. Insert Tab c. Design Tab d. Animation Tab

6. Shortcut key to print a presentation is?

a. Ctrl + A b. Ctrl + V c. Ctrl + P d. Ctrl + C

7. Standard size of printout is?

a. A2 b. A4 c. A5 d. A6

B. FILL IN THE BLANKS

1. ____________ command of File tab is used to exit the PowerPoint.
2. ____________ command is used to save the existing presentation with different name
3. The Clip Art command is available in ____________ Group.
4. ____________ is the shortcut key to paste image in slide copied from Internet.
5. The print command is available in ____________ tab.
6. In ____________ box user specify the number of copies to print.

C. TRUE AND FALSE:

1. The presentation can be saved using password protection (T/F)
2. Modification by other in presentation can be restricted in PowerPoint (T/F)
3. In PowerPoint we cannot add image of .gif format (T/F)
4. User can add image directly from Internet (T/F)
5. The printout of range of slides can be taken in PowerPoint (T/F)
6. In Print dialog box there is option to specify the color scheme (T/F)

D. ANSWER THE FOLLOWING QUESTIONS:

1. Write down the steps to create a presentation using in-built layout?
2. How to add a new slide and text in a presentation
3. What are the steps to save the presentation with password protection?
4. How user can open the existing presentation using open option of File tab.
5. What is different between closing a presentation and PowerPoint software with their methods.
6. Write down the three common types of image files that can be inserted in presentation?
7. Name the commands or options available in Images group of Insert tab.
8. What are the steps to Insert images from Internet?
9. Write down the steps to Insert images in slide from saved images in system?
10. Write down the steps to print a single slide in PowerPoint?

E. PRACTICAL WORK

1. Open a Microsoft PowerPoint 2010, Create a new presentation, save it with password protection as Pass and name of Practise, Close it and then open the file saved with the name of practise

2. Open a Microsoft PowerPoint 2010, Create a new presentation with name types of candles, In first slide add logo of any candle company taken from Internet, in second slide add clip art and add all sample images of candles from saved images.
3. Open a Microsoft PowerPoint 2010, open the existing presentation, take printout of 1-3 and 5th slide of presentation

Answers

A. Multiple choice question answers:

1. c 2. b 3. c 4. c 5. b 6. c 7. b

B. Fill in the blanks answers:

1. Exit 2. Save As 3. Images 4. Ctrl + V
5. File 6. Copies Box

C. True False answers:

1. True 2. True 3. False 4. True 5. True 6. True

Exercise for Assessment

A. MULTIPLE CHOICE QUESTIONS

1. ____________ enables drawing text in a MS-Word document.
   a. Word Art b. Macros c. Templates d. None of these
2. The tool used to find a similar word in a document is called:
   a. Finder b. Thesaurus c. Dictionary d. Find and Replace
3. ____________ is a rule of pattern that specifies how a certain input sequence should be mapped to an output sequence according to defined process.
   a. Word Art b. Macros c. Templates d. None of these
4. ____________ is a spreadsheet developed by Microsoft.
   a. Excel b. Word c. Access d. PowerPoint
5. Which type of program the Microsoft PowerPoint is?
   a. Calculating b. Presentation c. Graphical d. None of these
6. In MS-Excel, all formulas must begin with:
   a. / b. (c. = d. %
7. Extension of a PowerPoint template is:
   a. .pptx b. .potx c. .ppsx d. .ppsm
8. Extension of an excel template is:
   a. .xlsx b. .xltm c. .xltx d. .xlsm
9. Which tab is not available on left panel when you open a presentation?
   a. Outline b. Slides
   c. Notes d. All of above are available
10. Which of the following statements is not true?
    a. You can type text directly into a PowerPoint slide but typing in text box is more convenient.
    b. From Insert menu choose Picture and then File to insert your images into slides.

c. You can view a PowerPoint presentation in Normal, Slide Sorter or Slide Show view.

d. You can show or hide task pane from View >> Toolbars

11. What does Ctrl + = key effect?

a. Superscript b. Subscript c. All Caps d. Shadow

12. Which of following is Not one of Excel's what-if function?

a. Goal seek b. Solver c. Scenario manager d. Auto Outline

13. When you insert an excel file into a word document. The data are

a. Hyperlinked placed in a word table b. Linked

c. Embedded d. Use the word menu bar and toolbars

14. Clear the contents by pressing "DELETE" key from a keyboard will clear

a. Text Only b. Format Only

c. Contents Only d. Both Contents and Format

15. Which of the following shortcuts can be used to insert a new line in the same cell?

a. Enter b. Alt + Enter c. Ctrl + Enter d. Shift + Enter

Answers

1. a	2. b	3. b	4. a	5. b	6. c	7. b	8. c
9. c	10. a	11. b	12. d	13. b	14. c	15. b	

B. VERY SHORT QUESTIONS:

1. Name the basic features of Word processor?
2. Name applications of word processing?
3. How to close a document?
4. Name various types of Toolbar?
5. Define workspace?
6. Define scrollbar?
7. Name various elements of presentation?
8. Define simplicity in terms of good quality presentation?

C. SHORT QUESTIONS:

1. What does WordPad mean?
2. How to close a document?
3. What is a worksheet? How one can insert more worksheet?
4. Define the usage of Average in Excel? Give example?
5. What is the purpose of using MAX function in Excel? Write diwn the steps to use it?
6. Give various characteristics of good quality presentation?
7. Write down the steps to cut and paste a slide in presentation?

D. LONG QUESTIONS:

1. What do you mean by formatting text? Give various option for formatting a text in Word processor?
2. Define a spreadsheet? Name various existing popular spreadsheet software? Define in detail about MS Excel along with the steps to start it.
3. What is worksheet? How one can insert more worksheet and Define various terms related to it.
4. Give formulas of various commonly used basic functions with example?

5. What is PowerPoint? Write down the steps to start PowerPoint in various window software?
6. Give the steps of copying and moving slides?

E. APPLICATION BASED QUESTIONS:

1. Komal has created a document that he want to secure from other persons who are using that same computer. Which feature of Word processor should he use for the same.
2. Ma'am has given assignment to Jasspreet to count the students with age of 12. Is there any easy way to perform the task.
3. Devinder has to make a spreadsheet, in some of the cells the data is hiding. How she can solve this problem.
4. The document Harsaroop has made is not properly visible to people sitting far from him. Which feature he can use for showing it to far distance?
5. Simran has to make a presentation on the topic given to her by her teacher. She don't know how to open the PowerPoint in her window OS.

PROJECT WORK

1. Open a MS Word, create a document and give it heading 1, then create a second heading name as heading 2 and insert the same text in it without rewriting it, Then create one more heading with the name of heading 3, change the location of data from heading 2 to heading 3.
2. Open an existing document from its location, edit the text, Use Undo and Redo, then Save it with different name.
3. Install or check for MS Word 2010 in the system of every students so that they can practically work on it.
4. Open a MS Excel, Insert new worksheet, add data given below in table, Save it with your name, Close it, Reopen it, delete the worksheet then again close it using shortcut key.

Name of the employee	Age	Designation	Contact number
Komal	25	Software engineer	1234567890
Simran	25	Web developer	0123456789
Jasspreet	27	Web designer	9012345678
Harsaroop	26	Senior Software tester	8901234567

TEACHER NOTES

1. Install or check for MS Word 2010 in the system of every students so that they can practically work on it.
2. Arrange a practical class to start MS Excel and performing various basic functions in it that help students to understand it more thoroughly.
3. Tell students to make presentation in the class on particular topic in which they have to make table and insert images.

EXAM TIPS

1. Do all the things practically on computer to know exactly about various parts of Word Processor, Excel and PowerPoint.
2. Make a document and presentation then apply all the formatting functions on it such as adding border, inserting image, adding color, etc.
3. Make list in Excel then add more row and column. After that try splitting and merging function.

4 Entrepreneurship Skills – II

INTRODUCTION

Everyone process an inherent attitude and there is need to identify our area of interest and inner strengths then according to it develop our skills. We have to face various challenges and competition in every sphere of life and we should have different and optimistic thinking to have a winning attitude.

We should be clear that after completion of our education what carrier we want to opt for:

- ✦ Either you want to explore various job opportunities,
- ✦ Preparing for further competition
- ✦ Want to appear for interviews or
- ✦ Want to start something your own and become an entrepreneur.

In this unit will learn about various types of Business activities, Types of business enterprises and characteristics of Entrepreneur.

SESSION 1: CHARACTERISTICS OF A SUCCESSFUL ENTREPRENEUR

Entrepreneur Skills

In above section we have defined what is entrepreneur. An entrepreneur can be an educator, businessman, artist, restaurateur, inventor or professional. An employment opportunities are created in society and goods and services is provided by entrepreneur that plays an important role in it. It can be from any socio-economic background. Some of the very famous entrepreneurs are:

- Mark Zuckerberg who has becomes one of the youngest billionaires with his skills and talent in computers. He first launched his website Facebook whilst attending Harvard University, the website was launched from his dormitory room, on 4 February 2004.
- A William bill gate who is a second richest man on the planet, one of the most recognized names in the world, as much a celebrity as the pop stars and movie stars due to his highly public profile.
- Larry Page who is a Co-Founder of one of the most recognized search engines in the world, Google
- Ariana Huffington, who was born in 1950 in Athens has got to be the most influential and professional as well as successful female within the blogging industry.

Definition Box

Entrepreneur is a self-employed person who is willing to take a risk and start a business with a new idea. All self-employed persons, like shopkeepers, are not entrepreneurs until a new idea or method is not introduced by them in business.

Entrepreneurship and Society

Entrepreneurship has a major contribution in the growth of national economy. So, it is very important to acknowledge the motivational features spurring people to become entrepreneurs and explaining why some are more successful than others. An enterprise lives in a society that's why they get affected by economic opportunities and gains affect. The entrepreneurship ventures results in innovative services, innovative products and solutions for many problems of people. Entrepreneurs create organizations and creates job that results in increase of their own living standards and others too.

Fact Box

According to studies a growth of the society is very much linked to the growth of entrepreneurship in a country.

Qualities of good Entrepreneur

Successful business people have many traits in common with one another. They are confident and optimistic. They are disciplined self starters. They are open to any new ideas which cross their path Successful entrepreneurs want to see what the view is like at the top of the business mountain. Once they see it, they want to go further. They know how to talk to their employees, and their businesses soar as a result. Here are some of the qualities of the successful entrepreneur.

Disciplined: These individuals are focused on making their businesses work, and eliminate any hindrances or distractions to their goals. They have overarching strategies and outline the tactics to accomplish them. Successful entrepreneurs are disciplined enough to take steps every day toward the achievement of their objectives.

Confidence: The entrepreneur does not ask questions about whether they can succeed or whether they are worthy of success. They are confident with the knowledge that they will make their businesses succeed. They exude that confidence in everything they do.

Open Minded: Entrepreneurs realize that every event and situation is a business opportunity. Ideas are constantly being generated about workflows and efficiency, people skills and potential new businesses. They have the ability to look at everything around them and focus it toward their goals.

Self Starter: Entrepreneurs know that if something needs to be done, they should start it themselves. They set the parameters and make sure that projects follow that path. They are proactive, not waiting for someone to give them permission.

Competitive: Many companies are formed because an entrepreneur knows that they can do a job better than another. They need to win at the sports they play and need to win at the businesses that they create. An entrepreneur will highlight their own company's track record of success.

Creativity: One facet of creativity is being able to make connections between seemingly unrelated events or situations. Entrepreneurs often come up with solutions which are the synthesis of other items. They will repurpose products to market them to new industries.

Determination: Entrepreneurs are not thwarted by their defeats. They look at defeat as an opportunity for success. They are determined to make all of their endeavors succeed, so will try and try again until it does. Successful entrepreneurs do not believe that something cannot be done.

Strong people skills: The entrepreneur has strong communication skills to sell the product and motivate employees. Most successful entrepreneurs know how to motivate their employees so the business grows overall. They are very good at highlighting the benefits of any situation and coaching others to their success.

Strong work ethic: The successful entrepreneur will often be the first person to arrive at the office and the last one to leave. They will come in on their days off to make sure that an outcome meets their expectations. Their mind is constantly on their work, whether they are in or out of the workplace.

Passion: Passion is the most important trait of the successful entrepreneur. They genuinely love their work. They are willing to put in those extra hours to make the business succeed because there is a joy their business gives which goes beyond the money. The successful entrepreneur will always be reading and researching ways to make the business better.

Functions of good Entrepreneur

The various functions of good entrepreneurs are:

Taking Initiative: Entrepreneurship is a pro-active activity that takes such actions. This unique function of entrepreneurship provides our civilization with a wide variety of products, ways of actions, production techniques, etc. Therefore, taking initiative with such end and qualification is the prime function of entrepreneurship in every economy.

Organizing Resources: Organizing entails identifying those resources that are required to transform a particular idea into reality. The resources include human and nonhuman resources. Organizing in entrepreneurship will increase productivity, promote new ventures, distribute and supervise work and responsibility, and will remove barriers to work.

Identifying Opportunities and Prospects: Entrepreneurship searches those activities of value that have an economic and social contribution. It identifies new opportunities in the socio-economic arena which have got profitable prospects therefore, entrepreneurs are called searchers of hopes into blind spots and this function enormously indebted our society to entrepreneurship.

Risk Taking: Entrepreneurship takes the risk for the new venture. For innovative actions in the field of production technology for new products in a volatile market and new raw materials used in production. Moreover, it also takes the risk for theft, robbery, snatching market fall and hooliganism that may be involved with new entrepreneurship This is a major function of entrepreneurship in developing countries.

Decision Making: Entrepreneurship is a new initiative therefore, it has to decide multivariate issues that affect new ventures. Entrepreneurship has to decide upon equipment to be used quality, price and its variation, deficiency, capital structure, the feasibility of the project, organizational structure, philosophy of management, etc. that will guide, run and prosper the new venture or distinct attempt for entrepreneurship. We know that decision making is the process and entrepreneurship to make in a success, goes through this process.

Technology transfer and adaptation: Entrepreneurship throughout the world brings invented technology from different comers of the world and makes it appropriate by making required adjustments for local conditions. This function of entrepreneurship involves identifying appropriate technology with market potentials and adapts it into the local environment.

Innovation: Under the context of the changing environment, the entrepreneur locates the most feasible opportunity for the venture as well as improved or distinct technology that gives competitive advantages or a new opportunity to prosperity. Innovation is a creative means to add new utilities to existing situations or products. Entrepreneurship through innovation creates innovative products or operations for human society.

Fostering Autonomy: Entrepreneurship is an exposure of creative faculty that provides personal satisfaction and independence. The unique freedom to think differently is the impetus for entrepreneurship. Thus, entrepreneurship Fosters autonomy to advent something new of value by the application of devoted efforts and time.

Social Responsibility: Entrepreneurship with its innovative technology somehow promotes human efforts. It restarts closed industries with innovative managerial strategies and techniques. It also motivates new entrepreneurs and attracts them to engage into an entrepreneurial venture.

Public Relations: Entrepreneurship is a new venture that requires social acceptance by the regulatory bodies and the public at large. The government, as well as the persons' who will be subject to entrepreneurship, would be convinced through public relations to accept and to allow the entrepreneur to execute an entrepreneurial venture. History tells that many entrepreneurs were disregarded, coerced and even eliminated for their entrepreneurial activities. Failure is costly and therefore, public relation is a significant function of entrepreneurship.

Experience Sharing: Entrepreneurship may spread in society through publishing and sharing its success stories. Thus, entrepreneurship holds workshops, industrial visits through which the entrepreneurial experience in different counties may be shared with a widespread adaptation of success. This function will benefit the economies of the countries as well as the world bodies.

Managerial Roles: Entrepreneurs perform several managerial roles to keep their venture functioning with success. The roles are interpersonal roles that consist of a figurehead role, leadership role, and liaison role; informational roles that include recipient role, disseminator role, and the spokesperson role; decisional roles that consist of an entrepreneurial role, disturbance-handler role, resource allocator role, and the negotiator role. The entrepreneur also does the associated managerial functions such as planning, organizing, leading and controlling.

Balanced Economic Development: Sustainable economic development requires a balanced development among various regions and sectors of a country. Every country tries to ensure such a situation that makes industrialization throughout the country "possible. Entrepreneurs make it possible by establishing business ventures in various parts of the country in various sectors of the industry.

Fact Box

Entrepreneurship, thus, is the taping tool fur assuming indigenous skills and resources for the productive purpose.

Memory Box

Sometimes, the technology uses indigenous materials that reduce cost and wastage of resources. This entrepreneurial function virtually makes the world united in terms of homogeneous technology.

Entrepreneurship provides new products or ideas that give momentum and diversity into society. Therefore, entrepreneurship performs social responsibility that protects the welfare, benefit and economic gain of the society. It also promotes the community standard by providing jobs and amenities.

Knowledge Box

Entrepreneurship innovates a new production process or technology, market, sources of new materials, management, strategy or technique, investment opportunity, etc. that Schumpeter (1934) calls as the fundamental characteristics of entrepreneurship.

Role and Significance or Importance of Entrepreneurs

Entrepreneurship is the dynamic process of creating incremental wealth and innovating things of value that have a bearing on the welfare of an entrepreneur. It provides civilization with an enormous amount of goods and services and enhances the growth of social welfare.

Growth of Entrepreneurship: Entrepreneurship the advent of new venture particularly small ventures to materialize the innovative ideas of the entrepreneurs. Thus, the growth or establishment of small enterprises is the specific contribution of entrepreneurship in every economy of the world.

Creates job opportunities: Entrepreneurship firms contributed a large share of new jobs. It provides entry-level jobs so necessary for training or gaining experience for unskilled workers.

Innovation: Entrepreneurship is the incubator of innovation. Innovation creates disequilibria in the present state of order. It goes beyond discovery and does implementation and commercialization, of innovations. "Leapfrog" innovation, research, and development are being contributed by entrepreneurship.

Impact on community development: A community is better off if its employment base is diversified among many small entrepreneurial firms. It promotes abundant retail facilities, a higher level of homeownership, fewer slums, better, sanitation standards and higher expenditure on education, recreation, and religious activities. Thus, entrepreneurship leads to more stability and a higher quality of community life.

Consequence of business failure: The collapse of the large industry almost has irresistible damage to the development of the state and the state of the economy and the financial condition of the relevant persons. The incumbents lost their jobs: suppliers and financial institutions face a crisis of recovery.

Political and economic integration of outsiders: Entrepreneurship is the most effective way of integrating those who feel disposed of and alienated into the economy. Minorities, migrants, and women are safely integrated into entrepreneurship that will help to develop a well-composed plural society.

Spawns entrepreneurship: Entrepreneurship is the nursing ground for new inexperienced adventurists. It is the field where a person can start his/her idea of the venture, which may be ended up in a giant enterprise. All the large industrial ventures started as a small entrepreneurial enterprise.

Enhances the living standard: The standard of living is a concept built on an increase in the amount of consumption of a variety of goods and services over a particular period by a household. So, it depends on the availability of diversified products in the market. Entrepreneurship provides enormous kinds of a product of various natures by their innovation. Besides, it increases the income of the people who are employed in entrepreneurial enterprises. Those also capable employed persons to consume more goods and services. In effect, entrepreneurship enhances the standard of living of the people of a country.

Promotes research and development: Entrepreneurship is innovation and hence the innovated ideas of goods and services have to be tested by experimentation. Therefore, entrepreneurship provides funds for research and development with universities and research institutions. This promotes the general development, research, and development in the economy. Entrepreneurship is the pioneering zeal that provides events in our civilization.

Knowledge Box

The main importance of entrepreneurship is the creation of job opportunities, innovation, and improves the economy.

The small enterprises are the only sector that generates a large portion of total employment every year. Moreover, entrepreneurial ventures prepare and supply experienced labor to large industries.

Memory Box

Customers are deprived of goods, services, and government losses taxes. This could not happen in the case of failure of entrepreneurship. There shall be no measurable effect upon the economy and no political repercussions too.

Fact Box

Entrepreneurship nurses innovation provides new ventures, products, technology, market, quality of good, etc. to the economy that increases Gross Domestic Products and standard of living of the people. Therefore, entrepreneurship provides a wide spectrum of ventures and entrepreneurs in every economy. The vast open arena of entrepreneurship thus acts as an incubator to entrepreneurs.

Myths of Entrepreneurship

Entrepreneurship is a dream of almost 83% of working people that want to be an entrepreneur but in reality only 5% are able to do it. These days everyone wants to be an entrepreneur. Everyone love the idea of being their own boss and working when and where they like. But most of the peoples are doing away their enterprising ideas due to several myths as given below:

Entrepreneurs are born, not made: This is the same as saying that you can't teach entrepreneurship. According to management guru Peter Drucker, entrepreneurship is a discipline that can be learned. Passion and persistence may be in your genes, but it takes work to develop the skills that entrepreneurs have.

A lot of money is require to start a business: Not true! In fact, every year *Inc* magazine profiles businesses that have started on $1,000 or less. And among *Inc*'s annual list of the 5000 fastest-growing private companies, there is no direct relationship between the amount of start-up capital invested and ultimate business success.

There is need of business plan to get succeed: Sure, investors and lenders want to see a business plan before handing you a wad of cash, but if you don't need these resources at start up, you may be able to launch your business based on the results of a feasibility analysis and then get some traction with customers. Some Internet entrepreneurs, like Richard Rosenblatt of Demand Media, know how to get a website up and making money within a couple weeks. These savvy entrepreneurs know that testing the market is more important than spending the time to write a business plan.

Entrepreneurs are in it for the money: Some entrepreneurs do think that making money is what it's all about, but the #1 reason that most entrepreneurs start businesses is independence -- the ability to create something they can call their own instead of working for someone else. Entrepreneurs want to control their destiny.

You have to be young and restless to be an entrepreneur: You definitely do not have to be young to be a successful entrepreneur. In fact, a Global Entrepreneurship Monitor report found that the number of older adults who are self employed outweighs that of young adults. Entrepreneurship is for all ages

Most start-ups are successful: Most or maximum of start-ups fail. An average profit of an managed firm owner is only 20,000 rupees per month. And very few of them are able to earn more than their employees.

Entrepreneurship as a carrier option

Entrepreneurship are independent-minded, innovative business people who have skill sets, which make them self-starters. An entrepreneur can be an artist, educator, professional, homemaker, restaurateur, businessman, service sector worker or an inventor. Entrepreneurial careers can be found (or created) in just about every field, industry and organization.

Skills required being an Entrepreneur

- Desire and courage to strike out on one's own in the world of business rather than work for someone else
- Work experience in sales, retail, customer service and management
- Ability to promote yourself and develop a positive self-image
- Leadership skills
- Ability to work in teams
- Ability to train and coach in the desired skills
- Ability to multitask
- Good training and qualifications in the field of entrepreneurship
- Ability to write an effective business plan to sell an idea to co-founders, investors, customers and business partners
- Confidence to execute the plan
- Ability to make the right connections and maintain good business relationships
- Good listening skills
- Tolerance for risk taking

Advantages of Entrepreneurship as a Career

Flexible schedule: One of the best things and biggest advantages of being an entrepreneur is you can work from home, work from the office and work from virtually any destination with a great view. You can also choose when you work.

You learn a lot: Not just about your field, but about accounting, marketing, public speaking, website design, search engine optimization, how to delegate, how to take risks, how to be more creative and think about problems in other ways. And, importantly, how to fail, how to be rejected, and how to get back up on your feet anyway.

It's exciting and fulfilling: It is exciting to build something from the ground up. Especially, when you love what you do. It is such a cool feeling to make something out of nothing. And it is so fun to hire awesome people to work for the company. And to have amazing clients, many of whom are not only paying customers, but also friends! The ups and downs are never ending. It is never boring.

The salary makes sense: When you make money, you get paid more. It is not an arbitrary number that you are being paid each year. And you don't have to wait for someone to give you a raise. You get to keep the profits. You pay the expenses. And if you are doing it right, this will end up being a good deal.

You are viewed as a leader: This increases confidence. People say "you have a brilliant business model" and all sorts of other compliments that are very nice. And to be honest, ones I am not sure I have truly earned. But it is a very nice side benefit!

Knowledge Box

The flexibility of having your own business cannot be beat! It remains, in my opinion, as one of the best advantages of being an entrepreneur. It is hard to come by this amount of flexibility in any other job!

Disadvantages of Entrepreneurship as a Career

For every advantage, there is a disadvantage and most of the disadvantages of being an Entrepreneur are:

- **You wear a lot of hats:** You are not just the owner of the company. You are the CEO, secretary, website designer, accountant, head of marketing, and janitor. That is, until you can afford to delegate this to contractors and employees. And then you take on the title of "employer" which, true, replaces some of these other titles, but also brings a whole new set of benefits and challenges to the table. So true, while you learn a lot as an entrepreneur, it is because you do a lot. There is a lot to juggle at once.
- **You are always at work:** It is true you can work from anywhere and at any time. But really that is because you are working everywhere at all times! I have heard it said that entrepreneurs "beat 9-5 to work 9-9." There some truth to that. You are always on call and always doing something for the company. It is one of the exhausting parts of entrepreneurship that others may not readily see.
- **Work-life balance becomes tricky and is sometimes non-existent:** Work-life balance becomes tricky. It is hard to draw a line between "work" and "life" when you work from home. When your office is not that-place-a-few-miles-away but is instead your bedroom, your living room, your room, your home office. Your personal phone is your work phone (even if you have a work phone). Same with personal email. And personal time as well. This doesn't mean you can't place limits on work-life balance. Or draw a line. Or not check your emails after 7:00. Or not work on Sunday mornings. And it is not to say it is not a challenge for other professions.
- **A non-regular paycheck can be scary:** If your company doesn't make money, you don't make money. So in some ways while the salary is "rationale" – you get what you bring in – in other ways, it is not. Because you can work 50 hours a week and make nothing. This is both liberating and terrifying.
- **You will feel a new kind of stress:** Entrepreneurial ventures can bring about a new kind of stress. Instead of an employee, you are responsible for all decisions. If you fail or succeed, customers, vendors, employees, and others are looking at *you*. So, just as you can be looked at as a "leader", you can also be looked as a fool. Stress can be heightened if you do not make a consistent income. Or if you don't have health insurance. Or if you don't feel your self-employment is especially "secure."

Summary

- An entrepreneur can be an educator, businessman, artist, restaurateur, inventor or professional.
- Entrepreneurship has a major contribution in the growth of national economy.
- Qualities of good Entrepreneur: Disciplined, Confidence, Open minded, Self starter, Competitive, Creativity, Determination, Strong people skills, Strong work ethic, Passion

- Functions of good Entrepreneur: Taking Initiative, Organizing resources, Identifying Opportunities and Prospects, Risk taking, Decision making, Technology transfer and adaptation, Innovation, Fostering autonomy, Social responsibility, Public relations, Experience sharing, Managerial roles, Balanced economic development.
- Roles and significance of Entrepreneurs: Growth of Entrepreneurship, Creates job opportunities, Innovation, Impact on community development, Consequence of business failure, Political and economic integration of outsiders, Spawns entrepreneurship, Enhances the living of standard, Promotes research and development.
- Entrepreneurship are independent-minded, innovative business people who have skill sets, which make them self-starters.
- Advantages of Entrepreneurship as a career: Flexible schedule, You learn a lot, It's exciting and fulfilling, the salary makes sense, You are viewed as a leader
- Disadvantages of Entrepreneurship as a Career: You wear a lot of hats, You are always at work, Work-life balance becomes tricky and is sometimes non-existent, A non-regular paycheck can be scary, You will feel a new kind of stress.

A. MULTIPLE CHOICE QUESTIONS

1. Which of the following quality should be present in successful entrepreneur?
   a. Confidence b. Open minded c. Disciplined d. All
2. ___________ is one of the disadvantages of entrepreneurship as a career.
   a. Flexible schedule b. Learn a lot c. Stress d. None
3. To be a successful in an entrepreneurial venture, you need:
   a. Money b. Innovative idea c. Hard work d. All
4. ___________ is one of the most important factor in starting a new business.
   a. Marketing b. Finance c. Govt. support d. Friends support

B. FILL IN THE BLANKS

1. A ___________ must be innovative, hardworking, confidence, etc.
2. ___________ is the ability to start a new business for earning profits.
3. ___________ entails identifying those resources that are required to transform a particular idea into reality.
4. Entrepreneurship takes the ___________ for the new venture.

C. STATE WHETHER THE FOLLOWING STATEMENTS ARE TRUE OR FALSE

1. Entrepreneurs are generally less educated than the general population (T/F)
2. An entrepreneur must be innovative (T/F)
3. There is need a lot of money to start a business is a myth of Entrepreneur (T/F)
4. Stress is one of the advantage of choosing Entrepreneur as a career (T/F)

D. ANSWER THE FOLLOWING QUESTIONS:

1. Define Entrepreneur?
2. Write a short note on Entrepreneurship?
3. Give any five qualities of successful Entrepreneurs.
4. What do you mean by Self- starter?
5. Differentiate between Entrepreneur and Entrepreneurship?
6. What are the functions of good Entrepreneur?
7. Give myths about Entrepreneurship?
8. Write a short note on Entrepreneurship as career?
9. Describe four advantages and disadvantages of entrepreneurship as a career.

E. PRACTICAL WORK

1. Collect related information for a business of your interest and prepare a team for setting up the business.
2. The teacher brings in a cake to celebrate the end of a successful session. Participants cannot eat it until they have cut it. They cannot make more than three cuts and they must divide the cake into eight pieces.
3. Discuss the roles and importance of entrepreneur and make a presentation on entrepreneurship as a career option.
4. Tell students they are going to create a new product and then try to convince the class to buy it.

Answers

A. Multiple choice question:

1. d 2. c 3. d 4. b

B. Fill in the blanks:

1. Entrepreneur 2. Entrepreneurship 3. Organizing 4. Risk

C. State whether the following statements are True or False

1. False 2. True 3. True 4. False

Exercise for Assessment

A. MULTIPLE CHOICE QUESTIONS

1. Which of the following shows the process of creating something new?

   a. Business model b. Modeling c. Creative flexibility d. Innovation

2. Which one of the following gives suggestions for new product and also helps to market new products?

   a. Existing products and services b. Federal government

   c. Distribution Channels d. Consumers

3. Which of the following is used by entrepreneurs to acquire experience in an international market before making a major commitment?
   a. Merger b. Minority Interest c. Joint venture d. Majority interest
4. Which of the following is alternatively called corporate venturing?
   a. Entrepreneurship
   b. Intrapreneurship
   c. Act of stating a new venture
   d. Offering new products by an existing company
5. Individuals influencing an entrepreneur's career choice and style are known as which of the following?
   a. Moral-support network b. Role model
   c. Professional support network d. Support system
6. EDP (Entrepreneurship Development Programmes) is required to help:
   a. Existing entrepreneurs b. First generation entrepreneurs
   c. Future generations entrepreneurs d. None of the above
7. Entrepreneurs attributes includes:
   a. Preservence b. Hard working c. Determination d. All of above
8. From the following which one is factor affecting entrepreneurial growth:
   a. Social b. Economic c. Psychological d. All of above
9. What is the need of entrepreneurship:
   a. For new innovation b. To fill gap in growth
   c. For healthy competition d. All of above

Answers

1. d 2. c 3. b 4. b 5. b 6. b 7. d 8. d 9. b

B. VERY SHORT QUESTIONS:

1. What do you mean by Entrepreneur?
2. Define Confident entrepreneur?
3. Define Service as business activity?
4. What are the myths of entrepreneurship?
5. Name various methods that can be used to provide training?

C. SHORT QUESTIONS:

1. What are the qualities of good entrepreneur?
2. What is the role of passion in entrepreneur?
3. How taking initiative is a function of good entrepreneur?
4. Define the term managerial roles in entrepreneur?
5. What is the role of entrepreneurship in economic development?

D. LONG QUESTIONS:

1. What are the functions of good entrepreneurs? Give some of it in detail.
2. Define Role or importance of entrepreneurship? Give various significance of it.
3. Give various advantages of Entrepreneurship as a career?
4. Give various disadvantages of Entrepreneurship as a career?
5. Give various rewards of entrepreneur?

E. APPLICATION BASED QUESTIONS:

1. Komal is thinking to start a new business. Before starting it what things should she has to keep in mind to be a successful entrepreneur.
2. Everyone can be an entrepreneur in their life. Jaspreet want to start his own IT organization. Before starting it
3. Entrepreneurship is a new venture that requires social acceptance by the regulatory bodies and the public at large. The government, as well as the persons' who will be subject to entrepreneurship, would be convinced through what to accept and to allow the entrepreneur to execute an entrepreneurial venture.

PROJECT WORK

1. Make groups of two students and discuss Myths of Entrepreneurship.
2. Have a group discussion on quality of good Entrepreneur.
3. Prepare a chart on Advantages and Disadvantages of Entrepreneurship as a Career.
4. Organize a group discussion on topic: Role and Significance or Importance of Entrepreneur

TEACHER NOTES:

1. Make a presentation on various Myths of Entrepreneurship.
2. Tell your students to make a report on various skills required being an Entrepreneur.

EXAM TIPS:

1. Read the Stories of great entrepreneurs to know more about entrepreneurs and important skills required to be a successful entrepreneurs.
2. Make a list of different qualities of being a good entrepreneur. For this, check those qualities in entrepreneur you know personally.
3. Make a presentation on different skills required to be an entrepreneur.
4. Check for advantages and disadvantages that one can have being an entrepreneur.

5 Green Skills – II

INTRODUCTION

All aspects of our life gets affected by environment around us and environment gets affected by our day to day activities. People who live in cities get their food from surrounding villages and in turn are dependent on forest, rivers, grasslands, seashores for fodder, fuel word and water like resources. Environment is made by everything around us and our lives depend on the flora and fauna around us.

Knowledge Box

Similarly our school environment is made of socio-culture and physical environment and physical environment includes the school building and the library, toilet, classrooms, kitchen, laboratories and playground.

SESSION 1: IMPORTANCE, PROBLEMS AND SOLUTIONS OF SUSTAINABLE DEVELOPMENT

Definition of Sustainable Development

Sustainable development is the development that meets the needs of the present without comprising the ability of future generations for meeting their own needs. The overall goal of sustainability development is to achieve sustainability or gaining the long term stability of the economy and protection of natural environment while driving innovation, development and growth of natural environment. There is need of efforts in building a sustainable, resilient and inclusive future for people as well as whole planet.

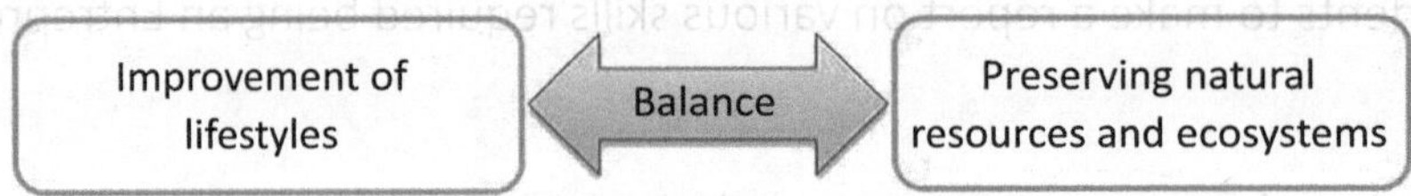

Figure 5.1 Sustainable development

The concept of sustainable development can be interpreted in many different ways, but at its core is an approach to development that looks to balance different, and often competing, needs against an awareness of the environmental, social and economic limitations we face as a society.

According to Brundtland Commission in its 1987 report "Our Common Future",

"Sustainable development is development that meets the needs of the present, without compromising the ability of future generations to meet their own needs."

The definition emphasis two important things:

- The natural resources are vital not only for us but also for future generations.
- It is a long term concept and not only focus on the present economic growth but it also takes into account the future economic growth.

There are 3 components of sustainable development:

- ✦ Economic growth,
- ✦ Environmental stewardship,
- ✦ Social inclusion

Countries are recognizing the importance of conserving natural resources, people are switching to cycling instead of driving that will improve their health, farmers are practicing climate smart agriculture and industries are realizing as to how much they can save through energy efficiency.

Definition Box

Sustainability is the ability to be maintained at a certain rate or level or you can also say it is a avoidance of the depletion of natural resources for maintaining an ecological balance.

Knowledge Box

The word sustainable development is comprise of two words as sustainable and development that means if you sustain something then there will be development because one will be able to continuously use or maintain it for long time.

Memory Box

The main idea behind it to create a system that is suitable that's means it can be kept indefinitely in future. The existing air, minerals, water, etc., are enough to meet our mainly required for fulfilling our needs. But if we deplete the natural gas, petroleum, coal like natural resources and pollute water and air then future generation would suffer. So, the concept of sustainable development emphasises that we don't have right to deny the right to live in future generations.

Importance of Sustainable Development

Sustainable development is important for the environment development and also a hard thing to achieve due to wide range of things. Some of the main points of sustainable development that shows its importance are:

- **Provides essential needs of human:** The explosion of population means people will have to scramble for the limited life essentials like food, shelter, and water. Adequate provision of these basic needs almost entirely hinges on infrastructure capable of sustaining them for a long time.
- **Agricultural requirement:** Growing population means agriculture must catch up. Finding ways to feed more than 3 billion people can be staggering. If same unsustainable cultivation, planting, irrigation, spraying, and harvesting techniques are utilized in the future, they might prove to be financially burdening considering fossil fuel resources are projected to run out.
- **Manage the change in climate:** Climate change can be mitigated by sustainable development practices. Sustainable development practices seek to reduce the use of fossil-based sources of fuel like oil, natural gas, and coal. Fossil fuel sources of energy are unsustainable since they will deplete in the future and are responsible for the emission of greenhouse gasses.
- **Financial stability:** Sustainable development practices have the ability to create more financially sustainable economies across the globe. Developing countries that can't access fossil fuels can leverage

renewable forms of energy to power their economies. From the development of renewable energy technologies, these countries can create sustainable jobs as opposed to finite jobs based on fossil fuel technologies.

- **Sustain Biodiversity:** Biodiversity is greatly impacted by overconsumption and unsustainable development. Life ecosystem is designed in such a way that each species depends on one another for their survival. For example, a plants produce oxygen that is taken by humans for respiration. On other hand the carbon dioxide exhale by humans is used by plants for their production and growth.

Knowledge Box

Brandt Commission is one of the earliest international commissions that deals with environment and ecology. The earth's vital signs reveal that a patient health is getting declined. So, there is need to realise our ethical and moral obligations to the mother Earth. We as Human beings are caretakers of planet and also responsible for future generation legacy.

Fact Box

If governments insist on utilizing fossil fuel based sources of energy instead of renewable and sustainable options, the cost and environmental effects of supplying these basic needs would become a tall order.

Memory Box

Sustainable development focuses on sustainable agricultural methods such as effective seeding techniques and crop rotation to promote high yields while maintaining the integrity of the soil, which produces food for a large population.

Number of plant species gets killed by emission of greenhouse gases due to unsustainable development practices that results in reduction of amount of atmospheric oxygen. This is not good for humans. The use of renewable energy is encouraged by sustainable development practices and no greenhouse gas is emitted to the atmosphere by adapting the practices of organic farming.

Problems related to Sustainable Development

Having highlighted the importance of sustainable development, it is also important to understand that it does need a lot of concentrated effort and, like many things in life, it does have many challenges ahead of itself. It is also important to note that sustainable development is equally valid in developing and developed countries, despite them dealing with polarly opposite sides of the spectrum. Developed countries may be developed but that doesn't necessarily imply that they are sustainable and for these countries, the main goal is to rid their society of issues such as social inequalities, waste management, and environmental responsibility.

- Lack of financial resources to carry out and plan sustainable development
- Sustainable development is often not possible in war-torn countries as there are other priorities on hand.
- Natural occurrences, such as earthquakes and tsunamis, can pose a threat to sustainability as they can shift the flow of water and destroy certain elements of infrastructure. (*In the village of* Ramche in Nepal, the only source of water was shaken off course by the earthquake of 2015 and as a result of the difficulty of access to the village, it has been undergoing a water crisis. Expenditure on bottled water in the village has in turn grown and in many other areas in Nepal undergoing a water crisis, people resort

to drinking and cooking with E-Coli infected water *as an act of desperation. Meanwhile tsunamis in Southeast and East Asia may pose a threat to the already existing sustainable infrastructure, such as the destruction of means of public transport in Japan.*)

- The governmental conflict between immediate profit and investment towards sustainable technologies. (In Poland, the government has even increased financing towards the mining sector *instead of moving full steam ahead towards adopting sustainable energy sources, with coal amounting towards* 80% of total energy generation *in Poland. These measures are thought to have been implemented as a move to win miners' votes in the south of Poland.*)
- Corruption. (Funding to developing countries is usually provided through foreign grants, in the case of Nepal foreign grants constitute the majority coming from the UK. Nevertheless, due to bureaucracy and corruption in Nepal, in order to pass certain development projects a stipend needs to be paid to ministers as well as service fees to the Nepal government which significantly slow down NGO processes.)
- Lack of efforts at a municipal level

Solutions related to Sustainable Development

Sustainable development is the way to reach development without causing damage to the surrounding environment that contains three dimensions namely ecological, economical and social. The main principles of sustainable development are respecting and caring for all forms of life, improving the quality of human life, minimising the depletion of natural resources, enabling communities to care for their own environment, conserving the earths vitality and diversity and changing personal attitude and practices towards the environment. Further there can be short term or long term solutions.

Short term solutions:

- Stop the illegal smuggling and deforestation of forest resources and minerals
- Compensate the loss of forest cover by encouraging people to regenerate forest, quantitatively and qualitatively
- Maintain proper balance between deforestation and afforestation
- One of the main cause of pollution is the discharge of sewage and waste into water bodies. So, proper treatment system along with waste recycling and proper disposal of waste should be undertaken
- To manage and process all types of wastes a planning and building exclusive industrial zones should be made
- Industries causing pollution should be relocate to outside of cities and residential areas
- Adopt drip/sprinkler irrigation, rainwater harvesting and alternative sources of energy
- Prohibit the use of toxic chemical consumption that improves the quality of arable land. Instead use environment friendly weedicides and pesticides or less chemical fertilizer

Long term solutions:

- Organise awareness and responsibility campaigns for industrialists and farmers
- The resources should be taken to legal framework and privacy making by governments for stopping the illegal activities which are not environment friendly.
- Put more emphasis on developing sustainable agriculture that include agroforestry, permaculture, mixed farming, crop rotation and multiple cropping.

- Ensure the access of reliable, affordable and modern energy for everyone.
- Introduce taxes and fines for protecting ecology
- Take action to combat the change in climate and its impacts
- Conserve and sustainable use of seas, oceans and marine resources.

Summary

- All aspects of our life gets affected by environment around us and environment gets affected by our day to day activities
- Sustainable development is the development that meets the needs of the present without comprising the ability of future generations for meeting their own needs.
- The concept of sustainable development can be interpreted in many different ways, but at its core is an approach to development that looks to balance different, and often competing, needs against an awareness of the environmental, social and economic limitations we face as a society.
- There are 3 components of sustainable development: Economic growth, Environmental stewardship and Social inclusion.
- Sustainable development is important for the environment development and also a hard thing to achieve due to wide range of things.
- Developed countries may be developed but that doesn't necessarily imply that they are sustainable and for these countries, the main goal is to rid their society of issues such as social inequalities, waste management, and environmental responsibility.
- Sustainable development is the way to reach development without causing damage to the surrounding environment that contains three dimensions namely ecological, economical and social.
- The main principles of sustainable development are respecting and caring for all forms of life, improving the quality of human life, minimising the depletion of natural resources, enabling communities to care for their own environment, conserving the earths vitality and diversity and changing personal attitude and practices towards the environment.

Keywords: Green skills, sustainable development, Importance, Economic growth, Environmental stewardship, Social inclusion, Problems, Solutions, Short term solutions, Long term solutions

Self-Assessment

A. MULTIPLE CHOICE QUESTIONS.

1. What is sustainable development?
   a. The development that meets the needs of the present without compromising the ability of future generations to meet their own needs.
   b. To conserve natural resources and to develop alternate sources of power while reducing pollution and harm to the environment.
   c. It is the practice of developing land and construction projects in a manner that reduces their impact on the environment by allowing them to create energy efficient models of self-sufficiency.
   d. All of the above

2. What are the Primary Goals of Sustainability?
   I. The end of poverty and hunger
   II. Better standards of education and healthcare- particularly as it pertains to water quality and better sanitation
   III. To achieve gender equality
   IV. Sustainable economic growth while promoting jobs and stronger economies

   Code:

   a. I, II & III b. I, III & IV c. I & III d. I, II, III & IV
3. Any adulterated elements leak into the ground, filtration, and are carried into groundwater reservoir is known as
   a. Land Contamination b. Noise Pollution
   c. Water Pollution d. Air pollution
4. Which of the following are the primary causes of water pollution?
   a. Plants b. Animals c. Human activities d. None of these

B. FILL IN THE BLANKS

1. We should ___________ drink polluted water.
2. Energy _____________ in an Ecosystem.
3. Herbivores are __________ consumers.
4. Sustainable development is the way to reach development without causing damage to the surrounding _________.

C. TRUE FALSE

1. Carnivores are primary consumers (T/F)
2. Conservation of the environment aims at keeping it safe and healthy (T/F)
3. Green Economy is defined as an economy that aims at enhancing environmental risks (T/F)

D. ANSWER THE FOLLOWING QUESTIONS:

1. What is sustainable development?
2. What are the measures for overcoming the challenges of sustainable development goals?
3. What are he challenges in the attainment of sustainable development?
4. List all the short term solutions for sustainable development?

E. PRACTICAL WORK

Identify the problems related to sustainable development and make a flowchart.

Prepare a Solar energy, Solar cooker and Rainwater harvesting model by dividing the class into 3 or multiple groups

Answers

A. Multiple choice question answers:

1. d 2. d 3. c 4. c

B. Fill in the blanks answers:

1. Not 2. Flows 3. Primary 4. Environment

C. True False answers

1. False 2. True 3. False

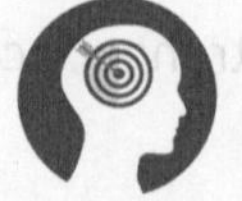

Exercise for Assessment

A. MULTIPLE CHOICE QUESTIONS

1. Which of the following is correct, if we only achieve two out of three pillars of Sustainable Development?
   a. Social + Economic Sustainability = Equitable
   b. Social + Environmental Sustainability = Bearable
   c. Economic + Environmental Sustainability = Viable
   d. All of the above
2. Consider the following statement (s) related to the Sustainability.
   I. It refers to a process or state that can be maintained indefinitely.
   II. Natural resources must use in ways that do not create ecological debts by over exploiting the carrying and productive capacity of the earth.
   III. A minimum necessary condition for sustainability is the maintenance of the total natural capital stock at or above the current level.

   Code:

   a. Only I b. Only II c. Only II & III d. I, II & III
3. Which of the following is/are not an objective (s) of sustainable development?
   a. Continue to implement the family planning program.
   b. Maintain a dynamic balance of arable land (not less than 123 million hectares) and implement an agricultural development strategy
   c. Maintain a dynamic balance of water resources by reducing water consumption for every unit of gross development product growth and agricultural value added
   d. To bring about a gradual and sometime catastrophic transformation of environment
4. When was the term 'Sustainable Development' came into existence?
   a. 1987 b. 1980 c. 1978 d. 1992
5. The United Nations Commission on Sustainable Development (CSD) was established by the UN General Assembly in December-------.
   a. 1992 b. 1993 c. 1994 d. 1995
6. Which option is correct, when we only accomplish two out of three pillars of Sustainable Development?
   a. Economic + Environmental Sustainability = Viable
   b. Social + Environmental Sustainability = Bearable

c. Social + Economic Sustainability = Equitable

d. None of the above

7. After mining the huge holes left behind is used for

a. Wastewater storage b. Waste and water storage

c. Waste Disposal d. Waste Storage

8. Mercury and lead are toxic elements, which causes

a. Noise Pollution b. Air Pollution

c. Water Pollution d. Land contamination

9. The other word of Landscaping is

a. Reduction b. Restoration c. Removing topsoil d. Restore

10. Whenever the price of the mineral remains high, the firm seeks for

a. New countries b. Remains the same c. New miners d. New deposits

11. Which of the following is the first National Park of India?

a. Periyar b. Raja ji c. Jim Corbett d. Bandipur

12. Name the forests in which teak is the most dominant species?

a. Tropical Evergreen forests b. Tropical Thorn forests and scrubs

c. Tropical Deciduous forests d. Mangrove forests

13. In which type of forests does Sundari tree belong?

a. Tropical Evergreen forests b. Tropical Thorn forests and scrubs

c. Tropical Deciduous forests d. Mangrove forests

14. A very large ecosystem on land having distinct type of vegetation and wildlife is called?

a. Ecology b. Biome c. Biodiversity d. Biosphere reserve

15. Which of the following country has the highest biodiversity?

a. India b. Brazil c. Russia d. South Africa

16. In which of the following areas we will find pitcher plant?

a. Sunderban Deltas b. Thar desert

c. Western Ghats d. Rain forests of North-East India

17. The environment includes:

a. Aboitic factors b. Biotic factors

c. Both (a) and (b) d. Oxygen and Carbon

18. Pollution is increasing due to:

a. Increase in trees b. Increasing population

c. Increasing forest area d. None of the above

Answers

1. d	2. d	3. d	4. b	5. a	6. d	7. c	8. d	9. b
10. d	11. c	12. c	13. d	14. b	15. b	16. d	17. c	18. b

B. VERY SHORT QUESTIONS:

1. What do you mean by sustainable development?
2. What do you mean by environment?
3. Name various components of environment?
4. What do you mean by challenges for obtaining sustainable development?

C. SHORT QUESTIONS:

1. Give any two examples of recycling of products for sustainable development of environment?
2. Name and explain the various components of environment?
3. What are the problems related to sustainable developments?
4. What is the importance of sustainable development?
5. Explain various biotic components?

D. LONG QUESTIONS:

1. Describe in detail the meaning and importance of sustainable development?
2. Explain both short term and long term solutions for obtaining sustainable development?
3. Explain in detail the ways of reducing the pollution.
4. What are the various factors that is effecting the environment?

E. APPLICATION BASED QUESTIONS:

1. Tell Komal about the importance of conserving sustainable development. Also give her various tips related to it.
2. Explain how you are contributing towards sustainable development
3. Tell Rahul about the challenges faced in your surrounding about sustainable development

F. GROUP DISCUSSION

1. Organise a group discussion on the responsibilities and benefits of environmental citizenship including the conservation and protection of environmental values.
2. Hold a group discussion on whether the sustainable development is actually possible or not.
3. Conduct a group discussion on the importance of conserving indigenous knowledge and culture heritage.

PROJECT WORK:

1. Prepare a poster on sustainable development giving popular quotations by famous ecologists and environmentalists.
2. Prepare a presentation on problems related to sustainable development in your surroundings
3. Make a model on various approaches that can be used for keeping environment healthy and pollution free.

TEACHER NOTES:

1. Observe the city you are living in then make a list of biotic and abiotic components in environment.
2. Ecosystems are balanced when species coexist with other species. If something happens in an ecosystem it becomes imbalance. Make a list of things that imbalanced the ecosystem.
3. Learn the benefits of green economy by checking its importance in your surroundings.

SECTION-B

1 Digital Documentation (Advanced)

Learning Outcomes

After this chapter, you will have the knowledge of:

- Various Styles in Word Processor
- Styles and Formatting Window
- Creating and updating new style from selection
- Load style from template
- Applying Styles
- Insert and use images in document
- Modify, crop and delete an image
- Creating drawing objects and changing its properties
- Positioning image in the text
- Creating and using templates
- Changing template
- Creating and customize table of contents
- Character styles
- Implement Mail Merge
- Creating Main document, Data source
- Edit Individual documents
- Entering data in the fields
- Merging data source and main document
- Printing letter and address label

INTRODUCTION

This unit covers the topics of word processors. As you know word processing application allows us to create text documents and also provides great flexibility in checking written text and performs formatting to enhance the appearance of text or documents. This chapter covers word processing application to understand the utilities and various advance features of it. These advance features help in creation of professional documents.

SESSION 1: CREATE AND APPLY STYLES IN THE DOCUMENT

A style is a predefined combination of font style, color, and size that can be applied to any text in your document. Styles can help your documents achieve a more professional look and feel. You can also use styles to quickly change several things in your document at the same time.

1.1 Styles/ categories in Word Processor

Style is a set of formatting characteristics that can be applied to text, lists and tables in your document for changing the appearance of it. By applying a style, one can apply it on whole group of formats in one simple task. The style helps in formatting the document quickly when someone is working on long documents.

There are basically two types of styles in MS word that are character and paragraph. Mainly paragraph style is used for frequently than character styles due to easiness to use it. There is one more type that is linked styles a blending of both type of styles.

So, various categories in styles are:

- ✦ Paragraph style
- ✦ Character style
- ✦ Linked style

Paragraph style: It consists of both paragraph and font formatting that makes it more flexible to use as compared to character style. While applying paragraph style the entire paragraph gets affecting by formatting. For instance: Use of Center text will centered the entire paragraph instead of single word. Other formatting options come under paragraph styles are line spacing, bullets, numbers, tabs, text alignment, borders and frames.

Character style: It can be applied to individual words or characters. It is built from the formatting options available from the Format menu by:

Select Font > Setting from the Tools menu > select language > Select Set language

Or in some cases it is selected from the format menu by selecting Border and shading and look on the Borders and Shading tabs of the Borders and Shading dialog box.

1.2 Styles and Formatting window

Various available text styles in formatting window are:

Text Style (B, I, U)

To make a character Regular, Bold, Italic.

Select the text > mini toolbar appears > click the corresponding button on the mini toolbar (Figure 1).

These are toggle buttons and clicking on them once switches on the option and clicking them the second time will switches off the option.

To Apply Character Formatting by using Keyboard

To format text by using shortcut keys:

Select the text which you want to format > Use the shortcut key combinations for the desired formatting effect or select it from commands given in various groups

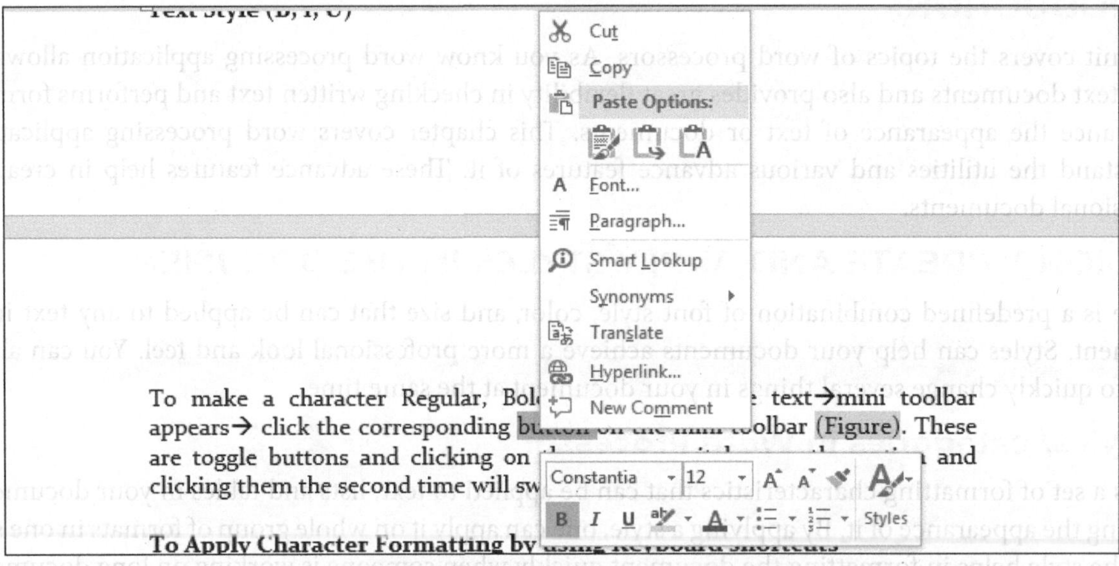

Figure 1.1: Applying text style

LETS KNOW MORE

- Bold: Ctrl + B
- Italic: Ctrl + I
- Single underline: Ctrl + U
- Word underline: Ctrl + Shift + W
- Double underline: Ctrl + Shift + D
- SMALL CAPS: Ctrl + Shift + K
- ALL CAPS: Ctrl + Shift + A
- Hidden text: Ctrl + Shift + H
- Superscript: Ctrl + Shift + =
- Subscript: Ctrl + =
- Copy formatting: Ctrl + Shift + C
- Paste formatting: Ctrl + Shift + V
- Remove formatting: Ctrl + Spacebar
- Change case of letters: Ctrl + F3

- Font: Ctrl + Shift + F
- Symbol font: Ctrl + Shift + Q
- Point size: Ctrl + Shift + P
- Next larger point size available for selected fonts: Ctrl + Shift + >
- Next smaller point size available for selected fonts: Ctrl + Shift + <
- Up one point size: Ctrl +]
- Down one point size: Ctrl + [

1.4 Creating and updating new style from selection

Changing color

To change the color of the character, one can either use the commands in Ribbon or a mini toolbar which appears when you select a text

To change the font color by using Ribbon:

- Select the text of which you want to change the color.
- On Home tab under the Font group, click on the down arrow of font color (Figure 1.2).

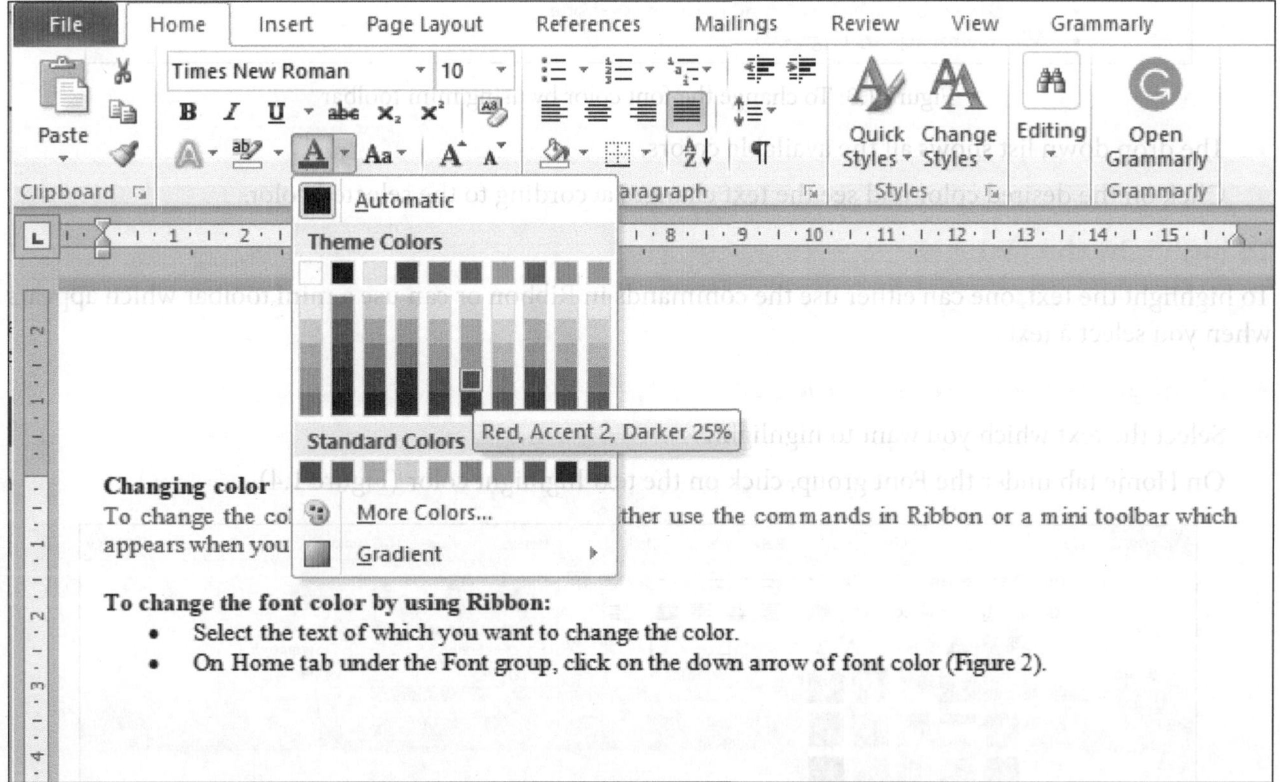

Figure 1.2: To change the font color by using Ribbon

- The drop down list shows all the available colors.
- Click on the desired color and see the text changes according to the selected color.

To change the font color by using mini toolbar:

- Select the text of which you want to change the color.
- Mini toolbar appears (Figure 1.3).

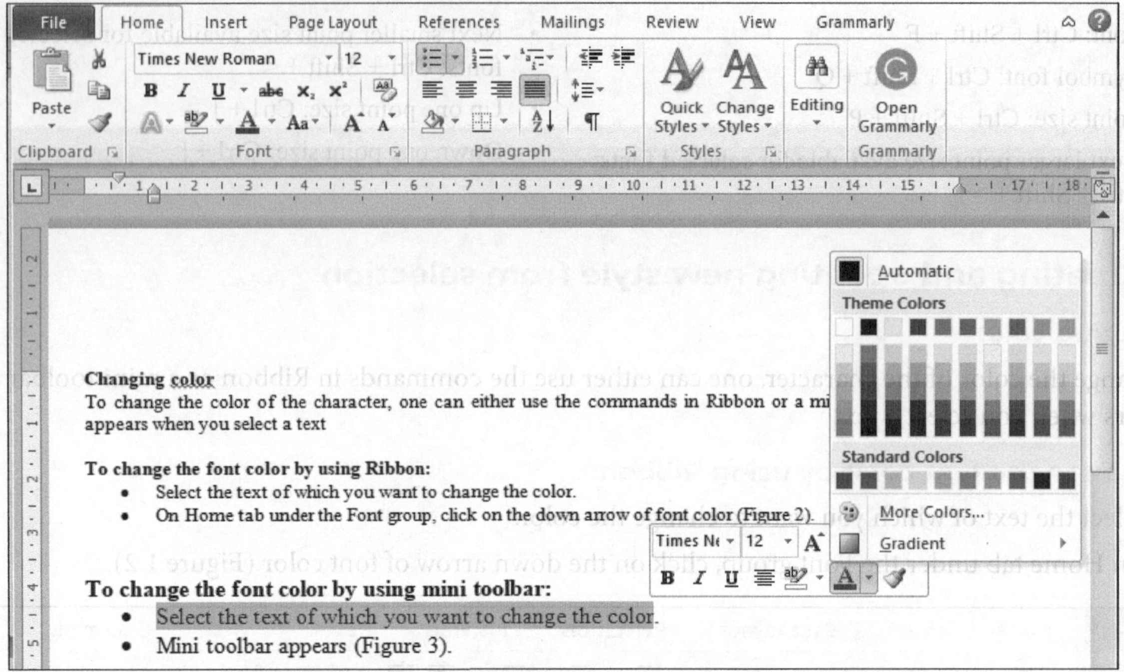

Figure 1.3: To change the font color by using mini toolbar

- The drop down list shows all the available colors.
- Click on the desired color and see the text changes according to the selected color.

To highlight the text

To highlight the text, one can either use the commands in Ribbon or can use a mini toolbar which appears when you select a text

To highlight the text by using Ribbon:

- Select the text which you want to highlight.
- On Home tab under the Font group, click on the text highlight color (Figure 1.4).

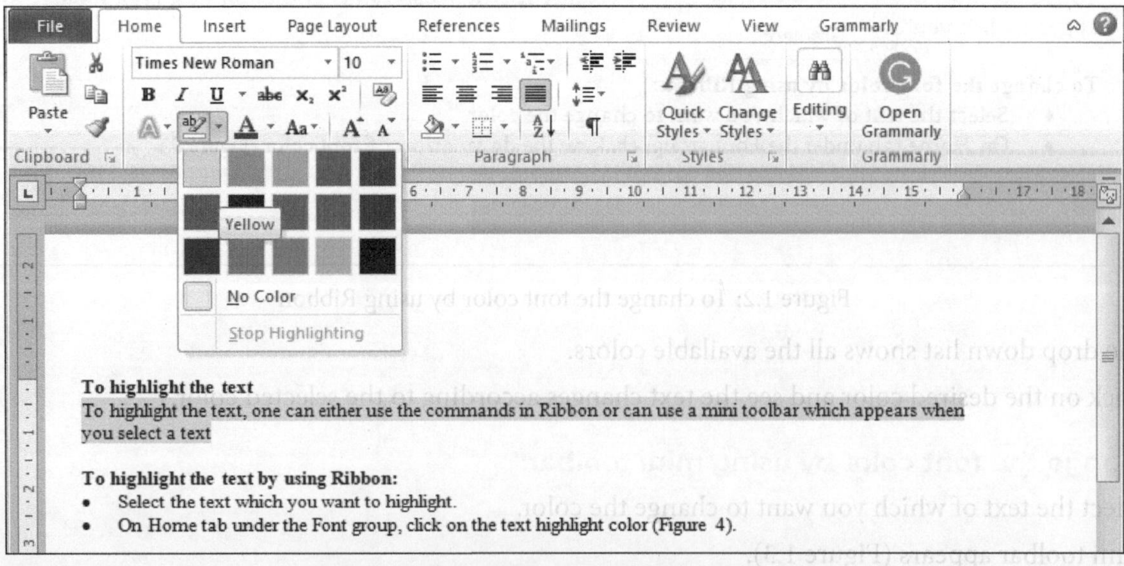

Figure 1.4: To highlight the text by using Ribbon

- The text will get highlighted by default color (yellow color).

If you want to highlight the text with different color:

- Click the drop down arrow of text highlight color.
- List showing all the available colors appears.
- Click on the desired color and see the text will get highlighted according to the selected color. (Figure 1.5)

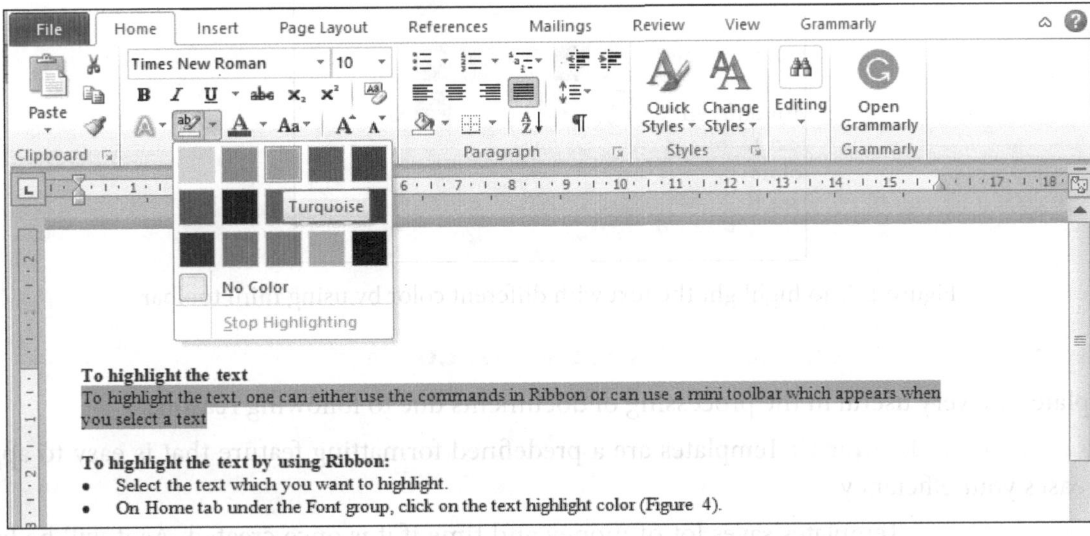

Figure 1.5: To highlight the text with different color

To change the font color by using mini toolbar:

- Select the text which you want to highlight.
- Mini toolbar appears (Figure 1.6).
- Click on the text highlight color

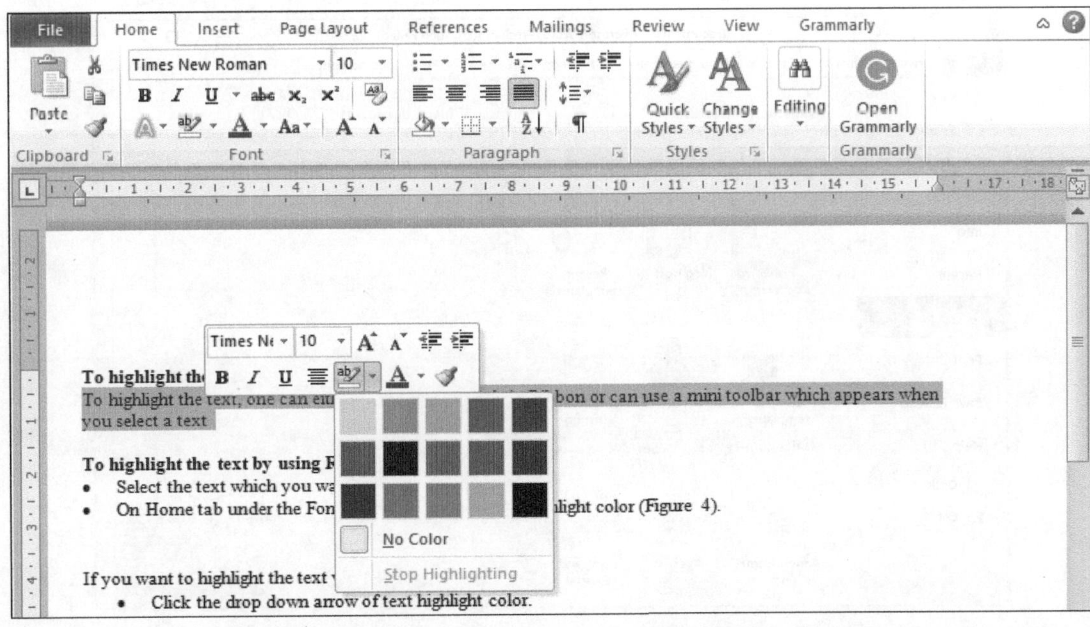

Figure 1.6: To change the font color by using mini toolbar

- The text will get highlighted by default color (yellow color).

If you want to highlight the text with different color by using mini toolbar:

- Click the drop down arrow of text highlight color.
- List showing all the available colors appears.
- Click on the desired color and see the text will get highlighted according to the selected color. (Figure 1.7)

Figure 1.7: To highlight the text with different color by using mini toolbar

1.5 Load style from template or another document.

The templates are very useful in the processing of documents due to following reasons:

Simplify creation of document: Templates are a predefined formatting feature that is easy to apply and also increases your efficiency

Save money and time: Templates saves lot of money and time if it is once created. As it will be less time consuming to use pre-defined samples rather than creating it for each document.

Clarity and consistency: Templates also ensures all the documents have a standard layout, look and feel.

Inserting or Creating a Template

To insert a template perform the following steps:

Click the Command **File** > New > Templates and Documents

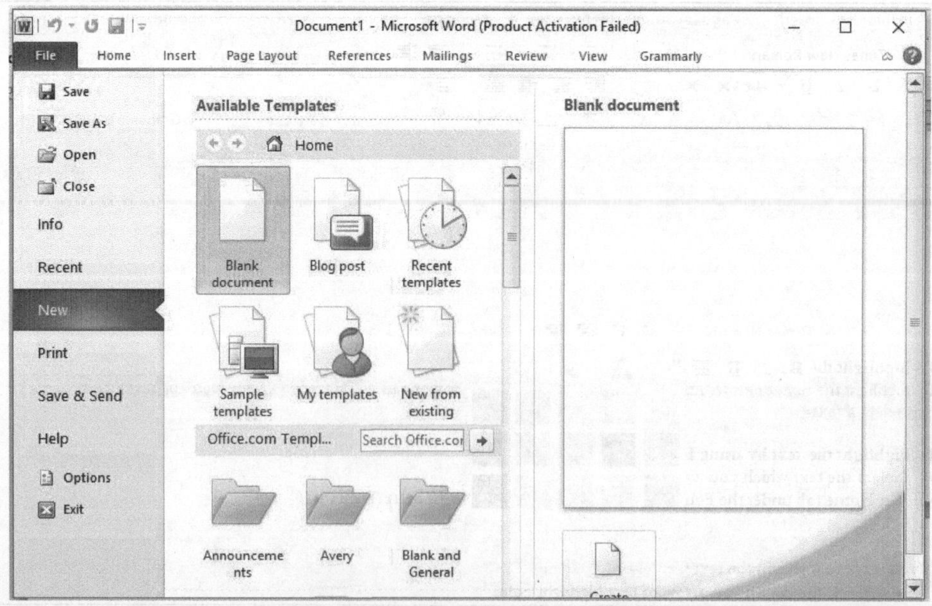

Figure 1.8: New Document Pane

To choose the built in template, click on Sample Templates given in figure 1.8 > A Window will appear that consists of different types of templates

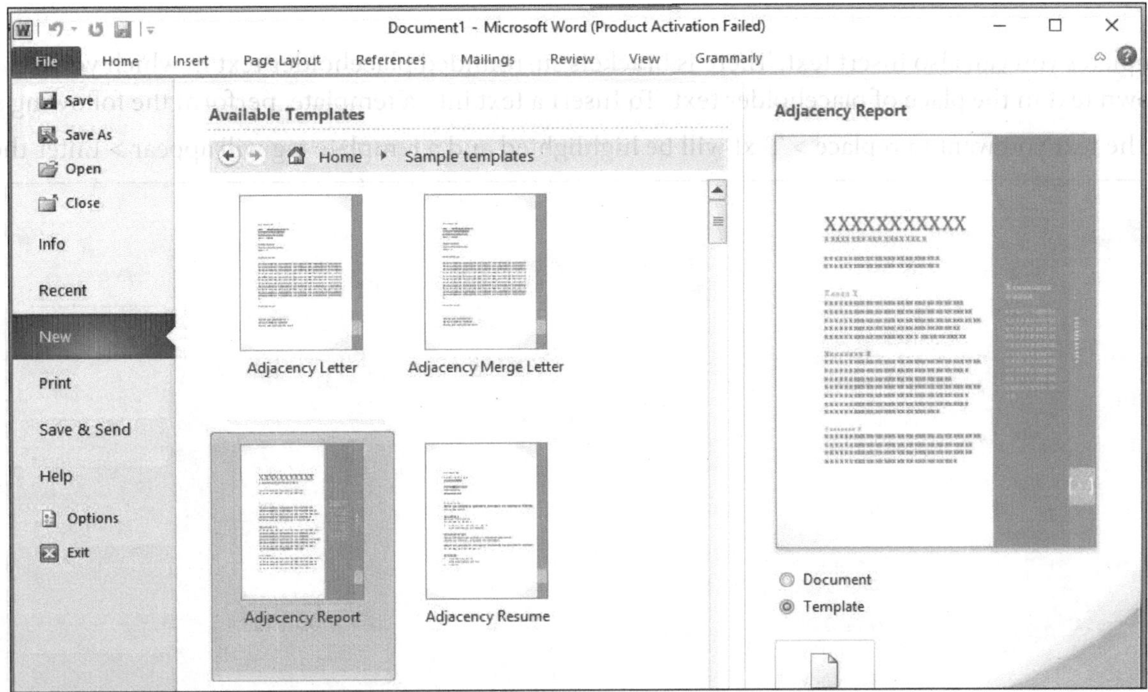

Figure 1.9: Various Sample Templates

Select template option and click on Create button given on the right bottom side of figure 9. After clicking on it a template will be created in a new document.

Saving and Reusing a Templates

You can make changes in downloaded template and save it on your computer for further use. In New Document dialog box there is **My templates** in which all customized templated are save. To save template in **My templates** folder, perform the following steps:

Click the **File** tab > **Save As** by which **Save As** dialog box will appear

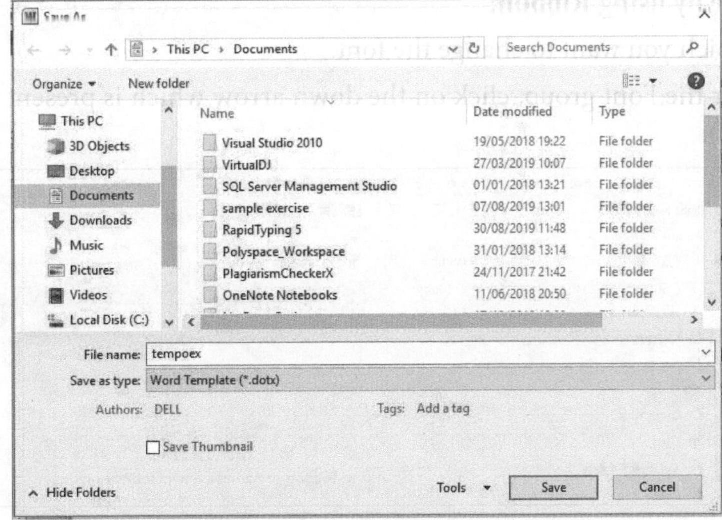

Figure 1.10: Save As dialog box

In Save As dialog box there is one option of Save as type in which select the Word template > Type a name in File name box > Click on **Save** button given in the bottom right side of **Save As** dialog box

Inserting a Text into a Templates

In templates you can also insert text. There is brackets surrounded placeholder text in which you can enter your own text in the place of placeholder text. To Insert a text into a template, perform the following steps:

Click the text you want to replace > Text will be highlighted and a template tag will appear > Enter the text

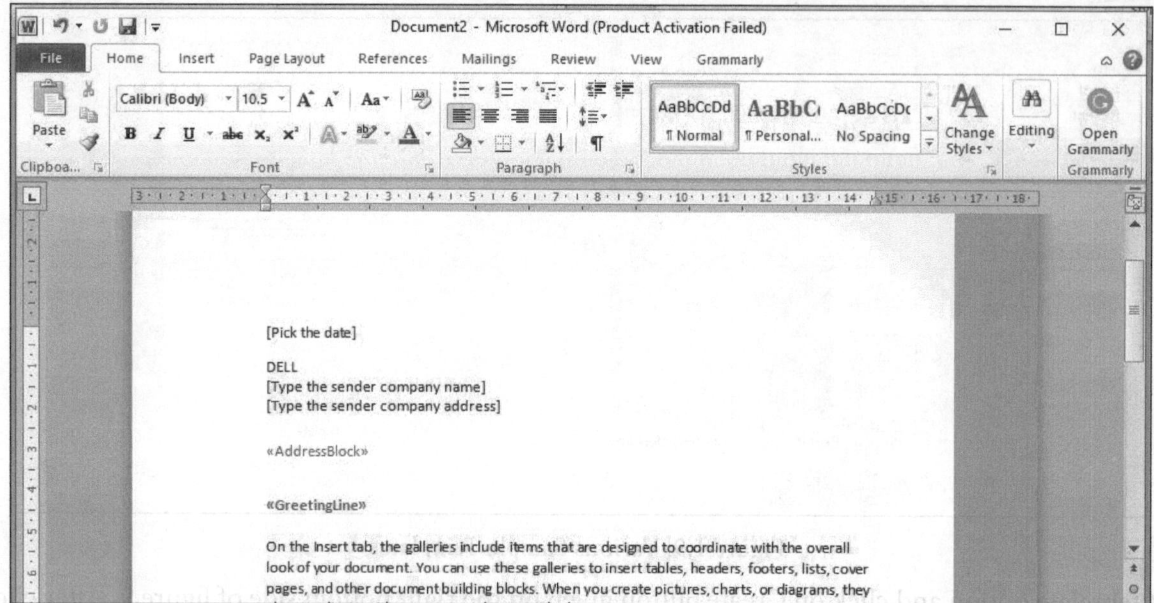

Figure 1.11: Showing placeholder with square brackets

1.7 Applying styles

Font Type

To modify the appearance of the character, one can either use the commands in Ribbon or a mini toolbar which appears when you select a text

To change the font type by using Ribbon:

- Select the text of which you want to change the font.
- On Home tab under the Font group, click on the down arrow which is present to the right of the font list box (Figure 1.12).

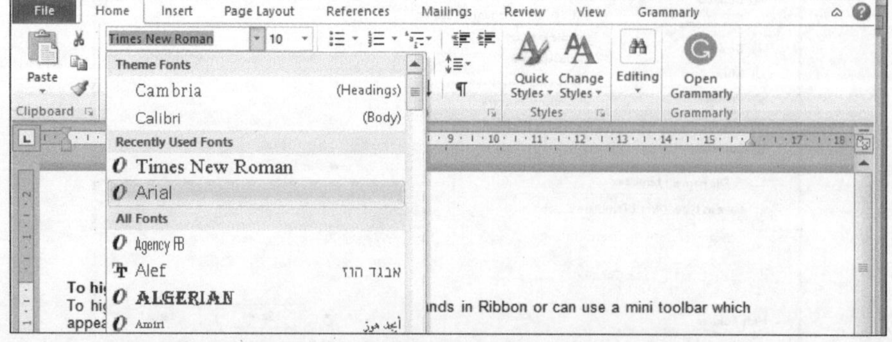

Figure 1.12: To change the font type by using Ribbon

- The drop down list shows all the available fonts.
- Use the scroll arrow on the right of the drop down list to scroll through the list.
- Appearance of the text will change when you move the cursor over the font list.
- Click on the desired font and see the text changes according to the selected font.

To change the Font type by using mini toolbar:

- Select the text of which you want to change the font.
- Mini toolbar appears (Figure 1.13).

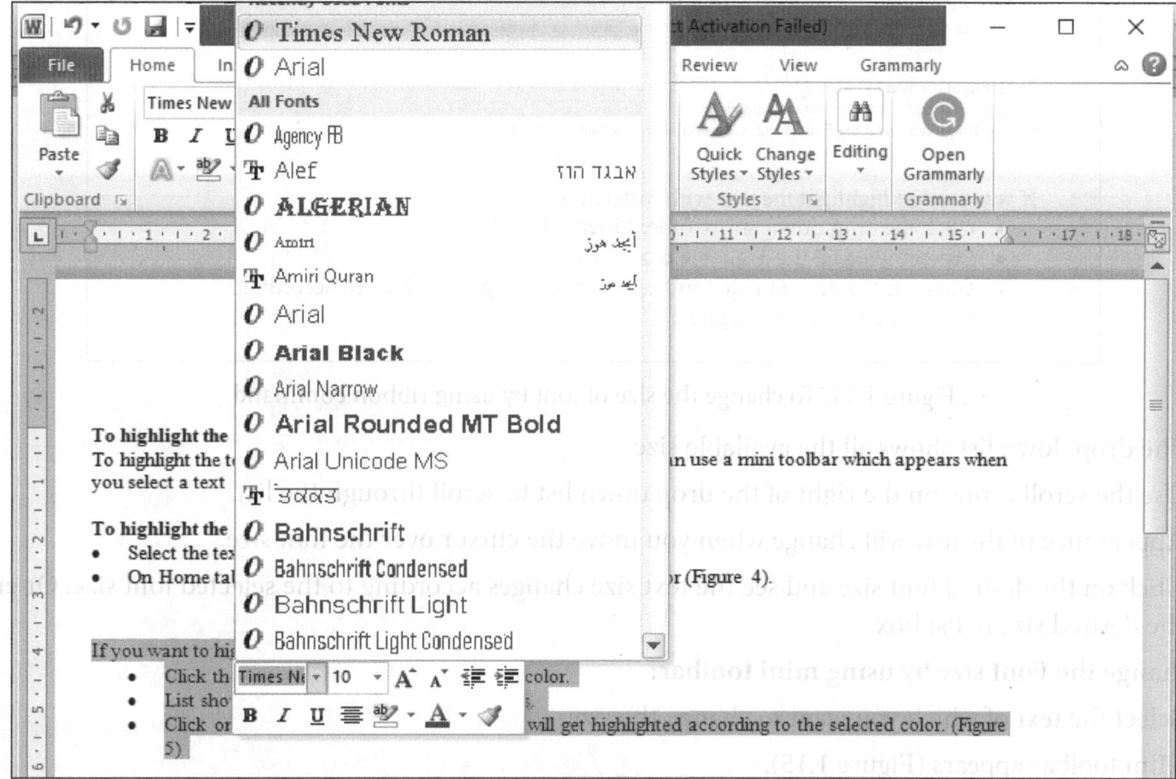

Figure 1.13: To change the Font type by using mini toolbar

- Click on the down arrow which is present to the right of the font list box
- The drop down list shows all the available fonts.
- Use the scroll arrow on the right of the drop down list to scroll through the list.
- Appearance of the text will change when you move the cursor over the font list.
- Click on the desired font and see the text changes according to the selected font.

Font Size

To change the size of font by using ribbon command:

1. Select the text of which you want to change the size.
2. On Home tab under the Font group, click on the down arrow which is present to the right of the font size list box (Figure 1.14).

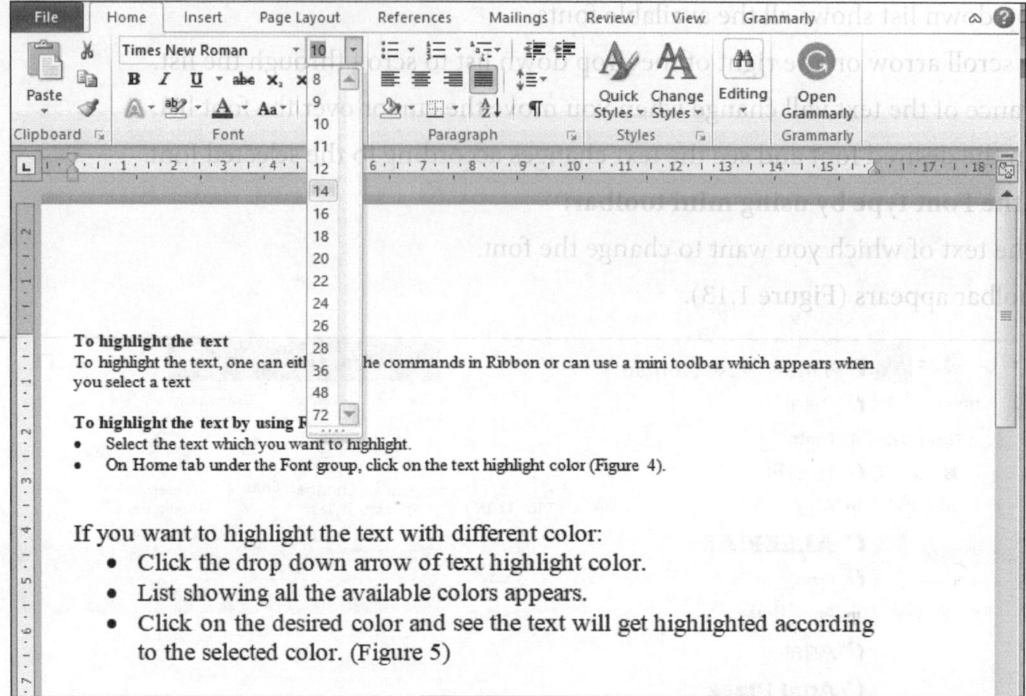

Figure 1.14: To change the size of font by using ribbon command

- The drop down list shows all the available size.
- Use the scroll arrow on the right of the drop down list to scroll through the list.
- Appearance of the text will change when you move the cursor over the font size.
- Click on the desired font size and see the text size changes according to the selected font size. Or enter the desired size in list box.

To change the Font size by using mini toolbar:

- Select the text of which you want to change the size.
- Mini toolbar appears (Figure 1.15).

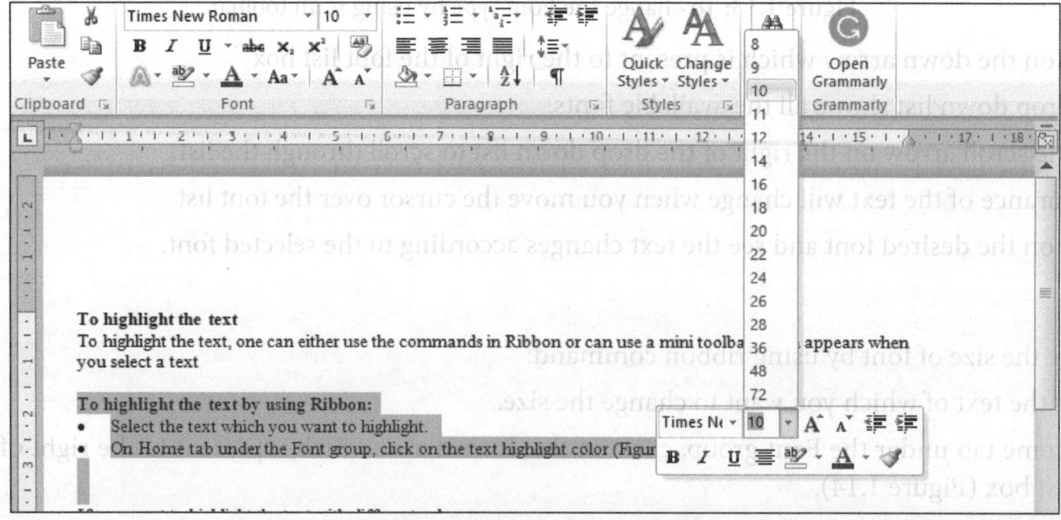

Figure 1.15. To change the size of Font by using mini toolbar

- The drop down list shows all the available size.
- Use the scroll arrow on the right of the drop down list to scroll through the list.
- Appearance of the text will change when you move the cursor over the font size.
- Click on the desired font size and see the text size changes according to the selected font size. Or enter the desired size in list box.

Summary

- A style is a predefined combination of font style, color, and size that can be applied to any text in your document.
- Style is a set of formatting characteristics that can be applied to text, lists and tables in your document for changing the appearance of it.
- There are basically two types of styles in MS word that are character and paragraph.
- Paragraph consists of both paragraph and font formatting that makes it more flexible to use as compared to character style.
- Character style can be applied to individual words or characters.
- To format text by using shortcut keys, Select the text which you want to format > Use the shortcut key combinations for the desired formatting effect or select it from commands given in various groups.
- To change the color of the character, one can either use the commands in Ribbon or a mini toolbar which appears when you select a text.
- To highlight the text, one can either use the commands in Ribbon or can use a mini toolbar which appears when you select a text.
- The templates are very useful in the processing of documents due to Simplify creation of document, Save money and time, Charity and consistency.
- To insert a template, Click the Command File > New > Templates and Documents
- You can make changes in downloaded template and save it on your computer for further use.
- In Save As dialog box there is one option of Save as type in which select the Word template > Type a name in File name box > Click on Save button given in the bottom right side of Save As dialog box
- In templates you can also insert text.
- To modify the appearance of the character, one can either use the commands in Ribbon or a mini toolbar which appears when you select a text
- To highlight the text, one can either use the commands in Ribbon or can use a mini toolbar which appears when you select a text

Keywords: MS Word, Styles, Character Formatting, Changing Font Type, Font Size, Changing Color, Highlight text, Template

Self-Assessment

A. MULTIPLE CHOICE QUESTIONS

1. Shortcut key of single underline is ______________.
   a. Ctrl + B b. Ctrl + I c. Ctrl + U
2. AutoFit title text to placeholder ______________ the font size of the title text so that the text fits in the defined title text placeholder:
   a. decreases b. increases c. either a or b d. neither a nor b

B. FILL IN THE BLANKS

1. ______________ is a set of formatting characteristics that can be applied to text, lists and tables in your document for changing the appearance of it
2. ______________ are a predefined formatting feature that is easy to apply and also increases your efficiency

C. TRUE FALSE

1. Pressing Ctrl +I keys together will make the selected text Italic. (T/F)
2. The maximum Font size available in Word is 72. (T/F)

D. ANSWER THE FOLLOWING QUESTIONS:

1. Define Styles and name various categories of styles in Word Processor?
2. Write down the steps to highlight the text by using Ribbon.
3. How to insert or create a Template in Word 2016.

E. PRACTICAL WORK

Divide class into two groups one with even roll numbers and other with odd roll numbers. Then even roll number students will write a paragraph and apply Paragraph style. Odd roll number students will write a paragraph and Linked Style and observe the difference between two.

Answers

A. Multiple choice question answers:

1. c 2. a

B. Fill in the blanks answers:

1. Style 2. Template

C. True False answers

1. True 2. True

SESSION 2: INSERT AND USE IMAGES IN DOCUMENT

Document can be made more interesting by including some graphics in it. In a technical report there is need to add graph of corporate performing or a technical illustration. While in letters to family and friends you can share memorable events that are presented by photos. There are various ways to insert them. For every topic there are built-in Clip Art images. In case if you don't find any images then you can also insert a picture from files.

2.1 Options to insert image to document from various sources.

Pictures can be inserted from various places, including a computer, an online source or a Web page into an Office 2016 document.

To Insert a picture from your computer

- Find the location in your document where you want to insert a picture.
- Click on the Insert tab.
- Choose Pictures. (Figure 1.16)

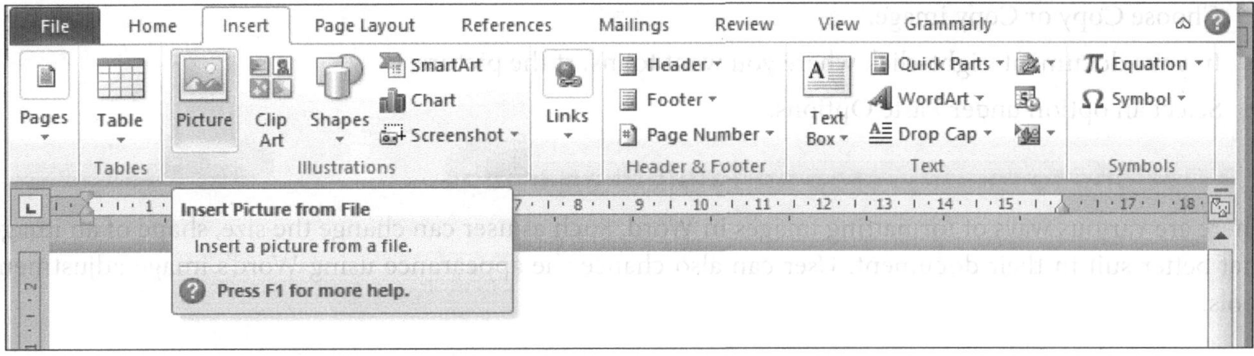

Figure 1.16: Inserting pictures

- Browse to the picture which you want to insert.
- Select the picture.
- Choose Insert.
- Once the picture get added to the document, you can move the picture, resize the picture or wrap text around the picture.

To Insert a picture from an online source

- Find the place in your document where you want to insert a picture.
- Click on the Insert tab.
- Choose Online Pictures in Word 2013. (Figure 1.17)

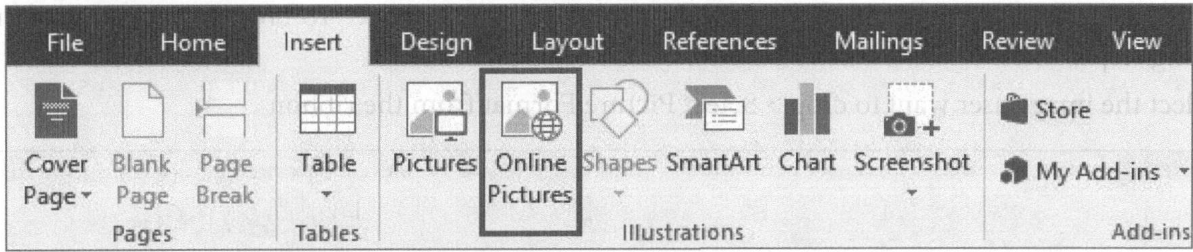

Figure 1.17: Inserting pictures from an online source

- Type a word or phrase in the search box which describes the image you want.(Figure 1.18)
- Press Enter.

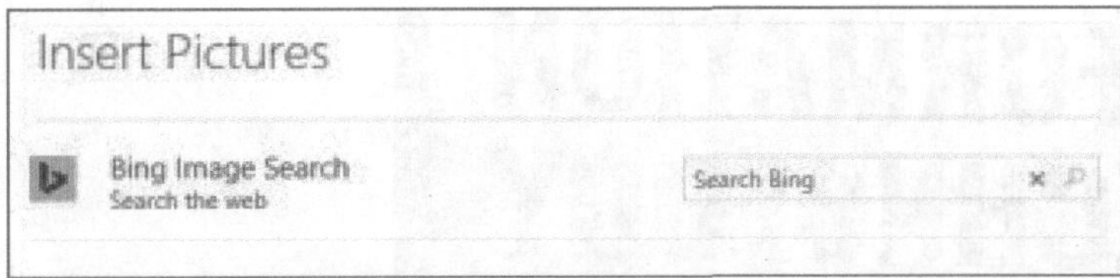

Figure 1.18: Searching pictures from an online source

- In the list of results, select the picture which you want to insert.
- Choose Insert.

To Insert a picture from a webpage

- Open the document.
- From a webpage, Right-click on the picture which you want.

✦ Choose Copy or Copy image.

✦ In your document, right-click where you want to insert the picture,

✦ Select an option under Paste Options.

2.2 Options to modify, crop and delete an image.

There are various ways of formatting images in Word. Such as user can change the size, shape of an image that better suit in their document. User can also chance the appearance using Word's image adjustment tools.

Resize the Image

Resizing of an image is linked with shrinking it to fit in a tight spot in a document or making it larger for filling the extra space in a document. Any type of object such as SmartArt, charts, shapes, text boxes, WordArt and images can be resized. To resize an Image using clicking and dragging option, perform the following steps:

✦ Select the object user want to resize in a Word document

✦ Select and drag a Sizing handle by using the mouse or touchpad. The sizing handles are located on each corner and top, bottom, right and left of the object.

✦ To keep the proportions of the object same, press and hold the Shift key while selecting and dragging it. Press and hold the Ctrl key to keep the object centered in its current location.

Crop an Image

In Word, user can crop or remove the unwanted portion in an image. To crop an image, perform the following steps:

✦ Select the image user want to crop > Select Picture Format from the ribbon

Figure 1.19: Crop Command

✦ Select Crop from Size group. The crop handles start appearing around the outside border.

Figure 1.20: Dragging

✦ Crop the image by selecting and dragging a handle

✦ To confirm, again click on Crop command and the image will be cropped.

Figure 1.21: Crop Image

2.3 Creating drawing objects and changing its properties. Resizing and grouping drawing objects.

Sometime, user wants to group number of objects into single object to keep them together. This is easier than selecting objects individually and it also allow the resizing and moving of all the objects at the same time. To group objects, perform the following steps:

- Hold the Shift or Ctrl key and click on the objects user want to group
- Click on Group command on the Format tab > Select Group

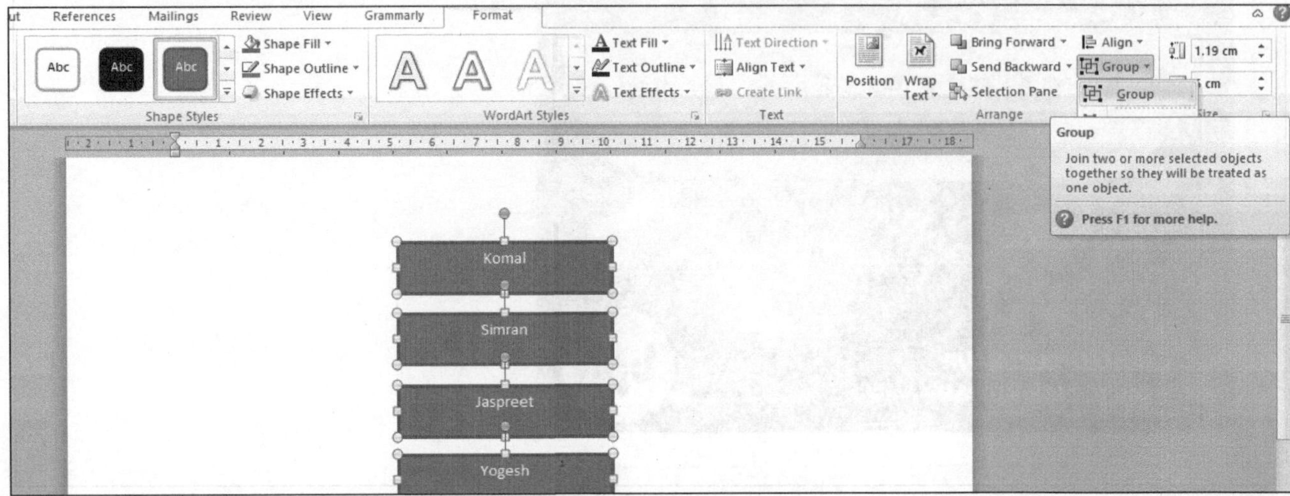

Figure 1.22: Group Command

- Now, the selected objects will be grouped and appear as single box with sizing handles around the entire group. This enable user to move and resize all of the objects at the same time.

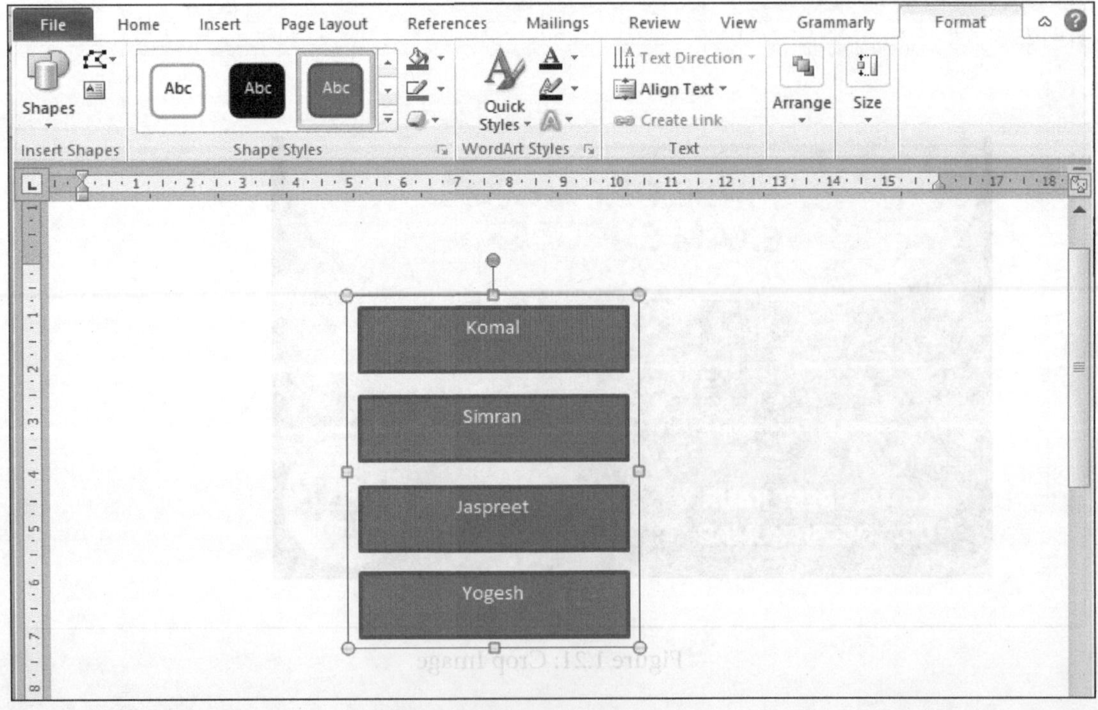

Figure 1.23: Grouped Object

2.4 Positioning image in the text.

Adding images to document is a good of illustrating the important information and make document look more attractive. The addition of image improves the overall appearance of the document. To wrap text around an image, perform the following steps:

- Select the image user want to wrap text around and Format tab will start appearing on the right side of the Ribbon

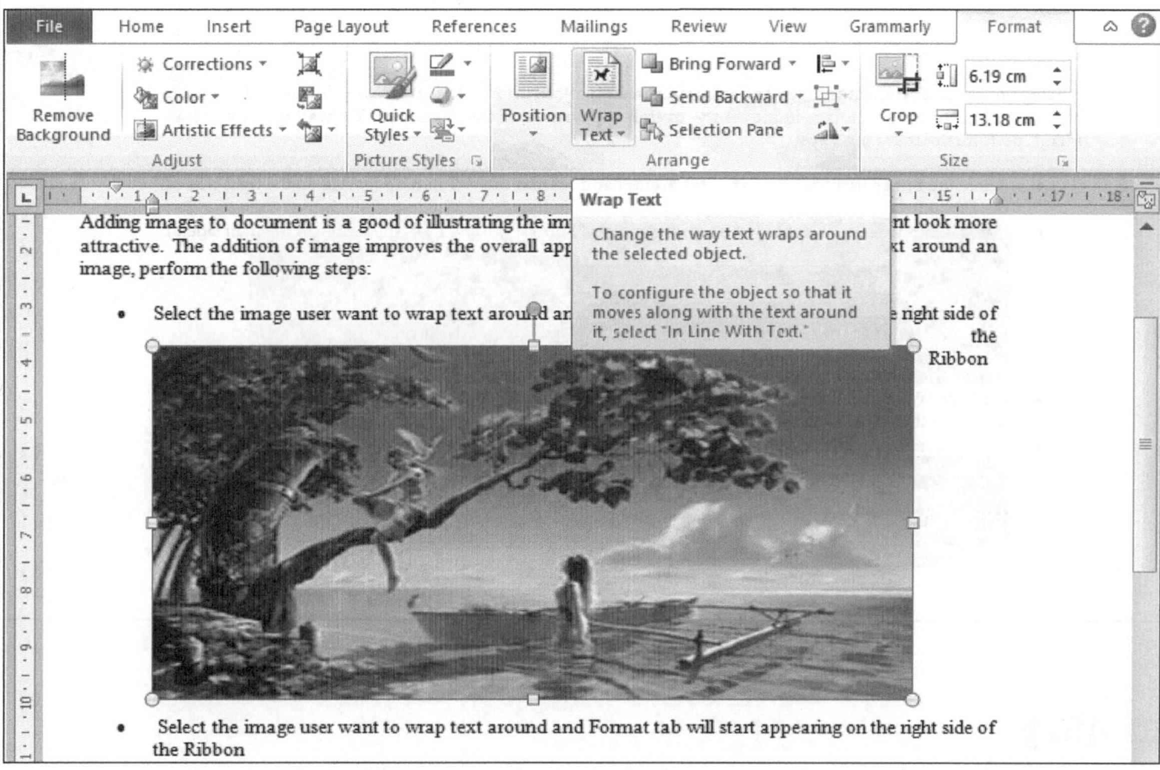

Figure 1.24: Selecting Wrap Text command

- Click on Wrap Text command in the Arrange group of Format tab. After that select the desired text that user want to wrap.
- Select More Layout Options to fine tune the layout

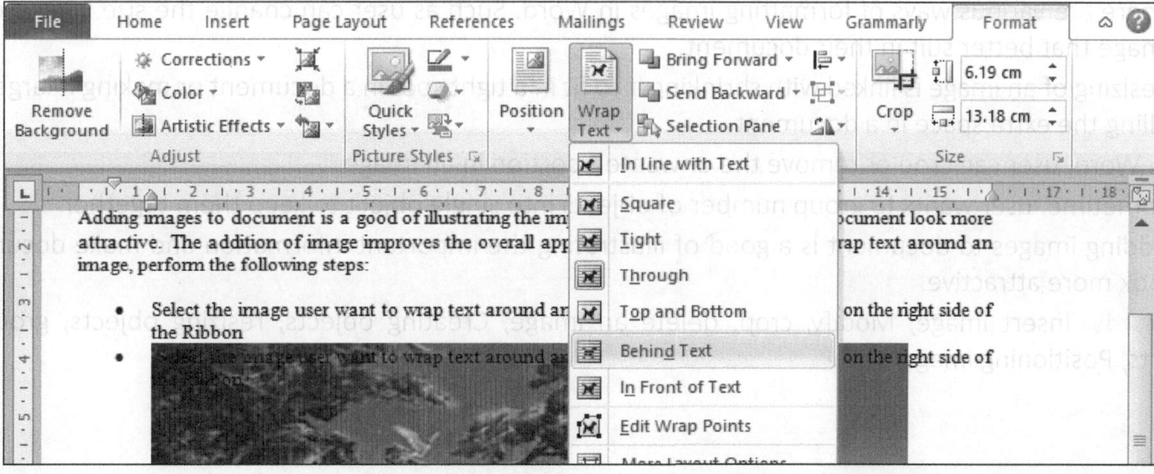

Figure 1.25: Selecting Format of Text

- Now the text will wrap around the image. Now, user can move the image by just clicking and dragging it to desired location. By moving it an alignment guides will appear to help user aligning the image on the page.

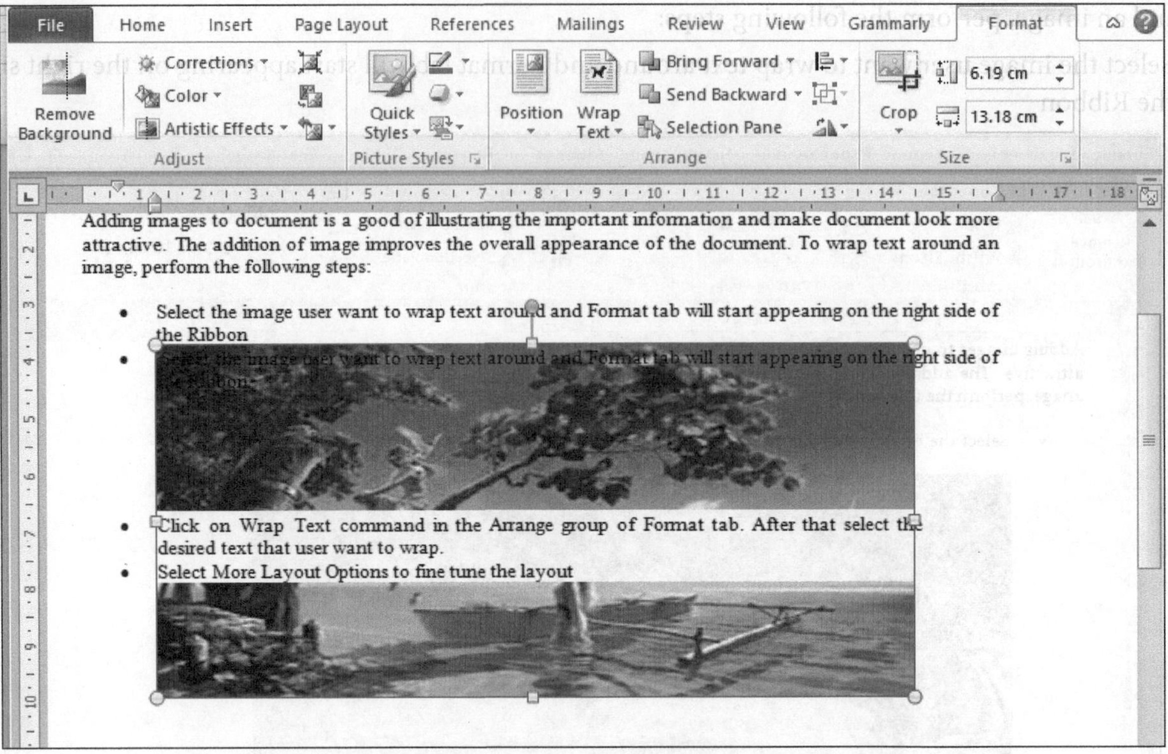

Figure 1.26: Text wrap image

Summary

- Document can be made more interesting by including some graphics in it.
- There are various ways to insert them. For every topic there are built-in Clip Art images. In case if you don't find any images then you can also insert a picture from files.
- Pictures can be inserted from various places, including a computer, an online source or a Web page into an Office 2016 document.
- There are various ways of formatting images in Word. Such as user can change the size, shape of an image that better suit in their document.
- Resizing of an image is linked with shrinking it to fit in a tight spot in a document or making it larger for filling the extra space in a document.
- In Word, user can crop or remove the unwanted portion in an image.
- Sometime, user wants to group number of objects into single object to keep them together.
- Adding images to document is a good of illustrating the important information and make document look more attractive.

Keywords: Insert image, Modify, crop, delete an image, Creating objects, resizing objects, grouping objects, Positioning image

Self-Assessment

A. MULTIPLE CHOICE QUESTIONS.

1. To add a shape to your document first:

   a. click shapes b. click insert

   c. select shapes d. click and drag to draw the shape

2. You can change and enhance drawing objects with:

   a. colors b. patterns c. borders d. all of these

3. Picture command is available in _______ group

   a. Tables b. Links c. Illustration d. Text

B. FILL IN THE BLANKS

1. Clip Art can help in making a document look _____________
2. Clip Art command is available in _____ group of Insert tab.

C. TRUE FALSE

1. In Word, user can't crop or remove the unwanted portion in an image. (T/F)
2. Resizing of an image is linked with shrinking it to fit in a tight spot in a document or making it larger for filling the extra space in a document. (T/F)

D. ANSWER THE FOLLOWING QUESTIONS:

1. Why there is need to crop an Image?
2. How to group various drawing objects and resize it.
3. Is it possible to position the image in the text? If yes, then write down the steps to do it.
4. How do you insert picture from a file?

E. PRACTICAL WORK

Open a word, insert any existing picture from a file and then write text about it and wrap the text in the middle of the picture

Answers

A. Multiple choice question answers:

   1. b 2. d 3. c

B. Fill in the blanks answers:

   1. More attractive 2. Illustration

C. True False answers

   1. False 2. True

SESSION 3: CREATE AND USE TEMPLATE

In MS Word, templates are a pre-defined document that is created for using as a pattern for a project. The template can be presentation, brochure, business card, resume, etc. The design consistency is provided by templates irrespective of the purpose that is needed by any organization to look professional.

A template consists of specific layout, design, style or text and fields that are very common. Some templates are so complete that user only has to change the individual phone number, name and email address.

3.1 Templates.

Using Word 2016, one can create document such as memo, letter, report, Brochures, Calendars, etc.

To create a new document:

- Click on File tab.
- A backstage view appears.
- Click on New tab in the backstage view.
- A list of documents appears which consist of blank documents and templates.
- Click on the Blank document option which is present under Available templates
- The new blank document appears (Figure 1.27)

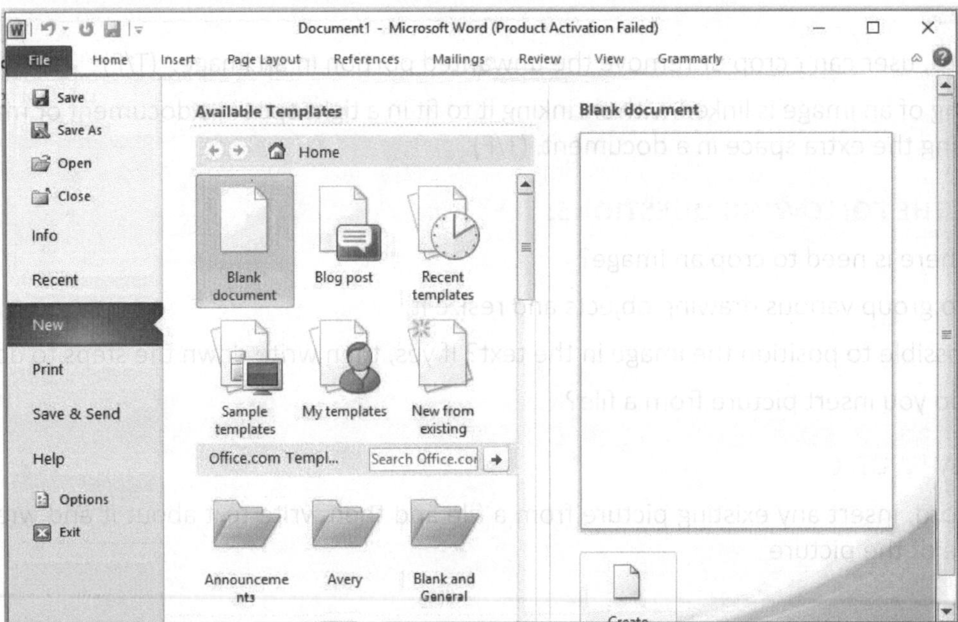

Figure 1.27: Creating a document

Note: One can also create a blank document from the blank template of Word 2016. The blank template will offer you the flexibility of creating and editing documents according to your requirements.

3.2 Using predefined templates.

To Create a New document from a Template:

Word includes a number of in-built pre-designed document templates which you can use to create a new document by quickly.

To create a new document by using template:

- Click the File tab to access Backstage view, then select New.

- The New backstage view there are several templates will appear.
- In the Search box at the top of the page, enter a term related to the template content.
- Word displays templates matching the category, click the desire template to preview it.
- In the Category list, click any categories to further filter the templates.
- A Preview of the template will appear.
- Click Create to use the selected template
- A new document will appear with the selected template

3.3 Creating a template

One of the easiest ways of creating a new template in Word 2016 is to base the template on an existing document. For instance, an already written document is formatted to perfection. The document formatting and styles are retains by template so that user can instantly create a new document using the same settings. To make a template based on an already created document, perform the following steps:

- Open or create a document contains styles or formats or text that user want to use repeatedly.
- Remove the text that doesn't need to be in every document
- Click on File tab and file screen will appear, Choose the Save As command from it
- Click on Browse button and Save As dialog box will appear
- Type the name for the template then from the Save As drop down list, choose word template
- Click on Save button
- Close the Template

LETS KNOW MORE

All Word templates are saved in a predefined folder, and Word automatically chooses that location for you.

3.4 Set up a custom default template

In Word 2016, the Normal.dotm template or default Word template can be changed. This enable the opening of new document that has the settings prefer by user every time when they open it. To do it, perform the following steps:

- To access Normal.dotm template file, Click on File tab and select Open > Click on C: drive and browse **users/yourID/appdata/roaming/microsoft/templates/Normal.dotm.**
- Click "Open."

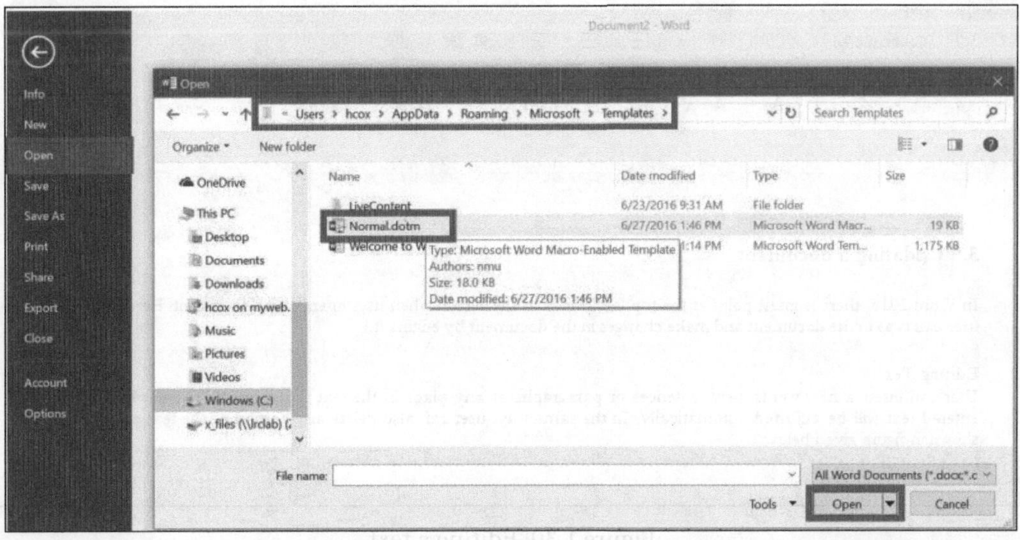

Figure 1.28: Opening Normal.dotm

- This will open what appears to be a blank Word document that is a template file. Here, user can set their preferred font, header, page margins, tabs and other things but don't write anything on it.
- When user is done with all these things, then press on save button present in the upper left and closes the document.
- Open Word and confirm the template that has been saved and open it when required.

3.5 Updating a document

In Word 2010, there is insert point at the top left corner of the screen when user open a new document. Here, user can type in the document and make changes in the document by editing it.

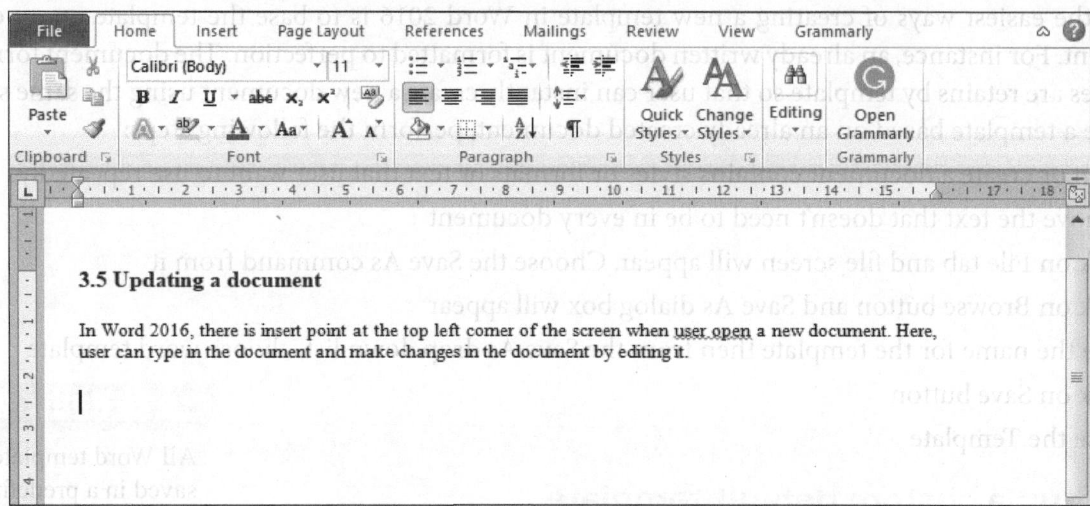

Figure 1.29: Start typing in a document

Editing Text

User can insert a new words, new sentences or paragraphs at any place in the text typed earlier. The newly entered text will be adjusted automatically. In the same way, user can also delete any portion of the text as shown in figure given below:

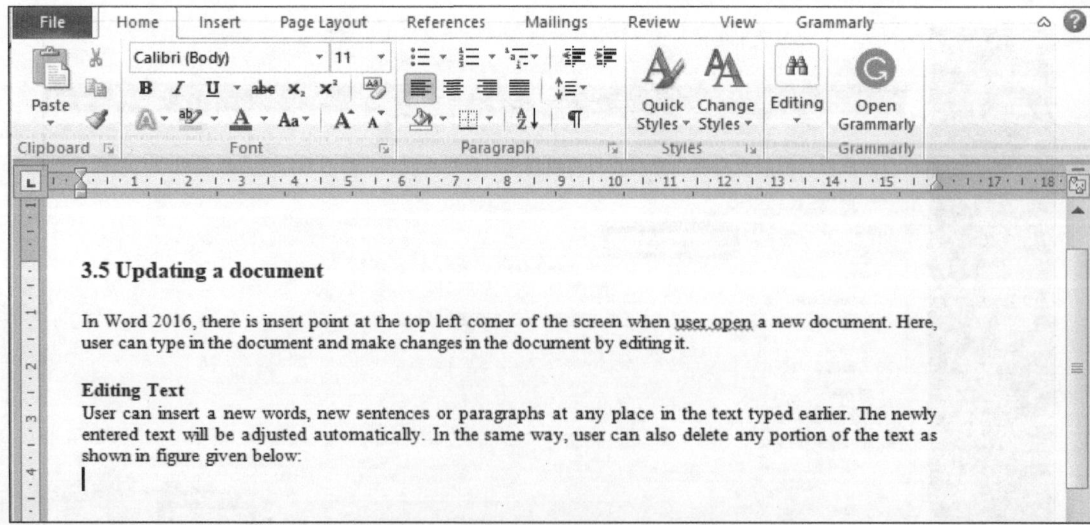

Figure 1.30: Editing a text

Inserting Text

User can move the Insertion pointer to the position where user have not typed the text and then start typing a text after the insertion point.

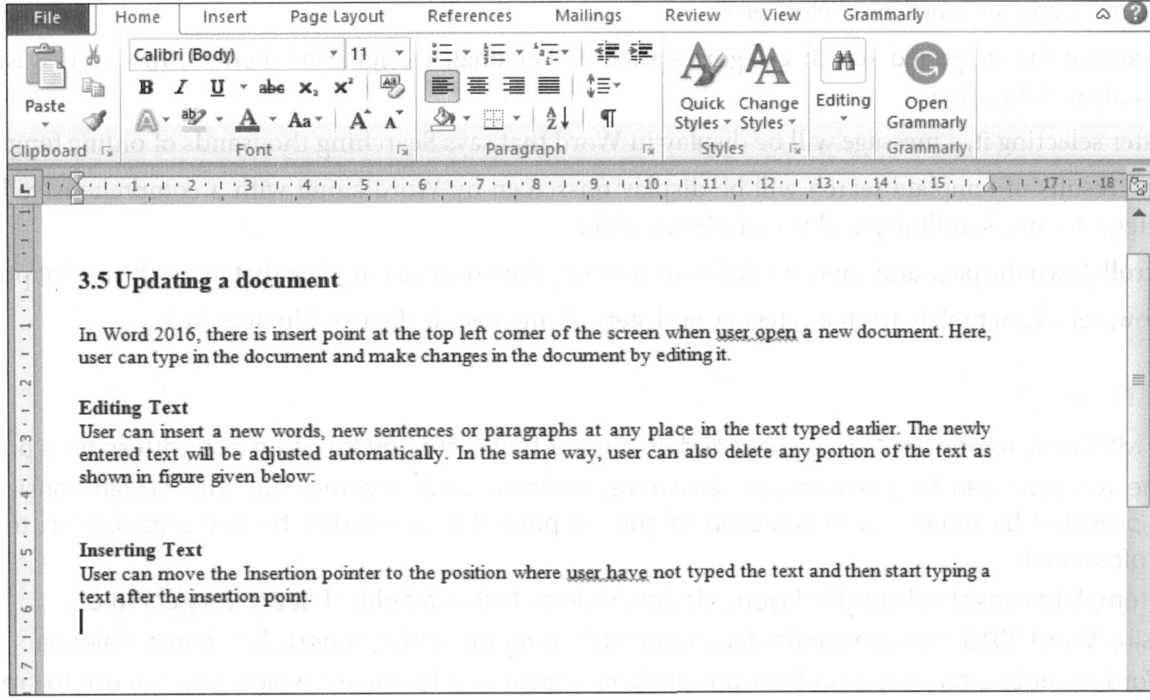

Figure 1.31: Inserting a text

3.6 Changing to a different template.

Word 2016 documents include blank documents in which Normal template is used. In case of reassigning a documents template, perform the following steps:

- Open a document that needs a new template attached
- Click on File tab and choose options command on File screen and Word options dialog box will start appearing
- Here, choose Add-Ins from the left side of the Word Options dialog box
- Choose templates from the Manage drop-down list
- Click on Go button and Templates and Add-ins dialog box will appear in which user can see which template is attached to the document.
- Click on Attach button and Attach Template dialog box start appearing
- From there, select the template that user want to attach
- Click on Open button and template is attached to the document
- Click on Ok button

The styles stored in that template are now available to your document, and the document is now attached to the template.

Knowledge box: Note that attaching a template doesn't merge any text or graphics stored in that template. Only the styles (plus custom toolbar and macros) are merged into your document.

3.7 Using the Template

There are number of templates provided by Microsoft for all of its programs. To open and use the system provided templates in Word, perform the following steps:

- Open Microsoft Word and Select New
- Examine the suggested search categories such as Personal, Design Sets, Letters, Industry, Business, Events or Education.
- After selecting it, a message will be display in Word that says Searching thousands of online templates.
- The results of template search will be display on-screen by Word along with a comprehensive list of categories in a scrolling panel present in the right.
- Scroll down the page and choose a different category then select a template that fits with current project.
- Now, select a template from a category and start filling in your data and images in it.

Summary

- In MS Word, templates are a pre-defined document that is created for using as a pattern for a project.
- The template can be presentation, brochure, business card, resume, etc. The design consistency is provided by templates irrespective of the purpose that is needed by any organization to look professional.
- A template consists of specific layout, design, style or text and fields that are very common.
- Using Word 2016, one can create document such as memo, letter, report, Brochures, Calendars, etc
- Word includes a number of in-built pre-designed document templates which you can use to create a new document by quickly.
- One of the easiest ways of creating a new template in Word 2016 is to base the template on an existing document.
- The document formatting and styles are retains by template so that user can instantly create a new document using the same settings.
- In Word 2016, the Normal.dotm template or default Word template can be changed. This enable the opening of new document that has the settings prefer by user every time when they open it.
- In Word 2016, there is insert point at the top left corner of the screen when user open a new document.
- User can insert a new words, new sentences or paragraphs at any place in the text typed earlier. The newly entered text will be adjusted automatically.
- User can move the Insertion pointer to the position where user have not typed the text and then start typing a text after the insertion point.
- Word 2016 documents include blank documents in which Normal template is used.
- There are number of templates provided by Microsoft for all of its programs.

Keywords: Templates, Predefine templates, Creating template, Setting default template, Editing Text, Changing template, Using the template

Self-Assessment

A. MULTIPLE CHOICE QUESTIONS

1. ____________ is a pre-defined document that is created using as a pattern for a project.

   a. Brochure b. Presentation c. Template

2. All Word templates are saved in a ____________ folder and Word automatically chooses that location for user.

a. New b. Predefined c. Existing d. all of these

B. FILL IN THE BLANKS

1. Template option is available in ____________ tab
2. ____________ is a base used f`or creating documents that contains predefined formatting styles, graphics, tables, objects and other information
3. Template refers to a ____________ document

C. TRUE FALSE

1. You can make changes in downloaded templates and save it on your computer for further use (T/F)

D. ANSWER THE FOLLOWING QUESTIONS:

1. Define the term Template?
2. Write down the steps to create a new document by using template.
3. Write down the various tasks that can be performed to update a document.

E. PRACTICAL WORK

Open Word and insert any of the existing template, do changes in it according to your requirements and save it for further use

Answers

A. Multiple choice question answers:

1. c 2. b

B. Fill in the blanks answers:

1. File 2. Template 3. Sample

C. True False answers

1. True

SESSION 4: CREATE AND CUSTOMIZE TABLE OF CONTENTS

4.1 Table of contents

A table is made of rows and columns of cells which you can fill with text and graphics. (Figure 1.32)

- **Rows: A row is a horizontal block of cells that runs through the entire width of the table.**
- **Column: A column is a vertical block of cells that runs through the table.**
- **Cell: A cell is the intersection of a row and a column.**

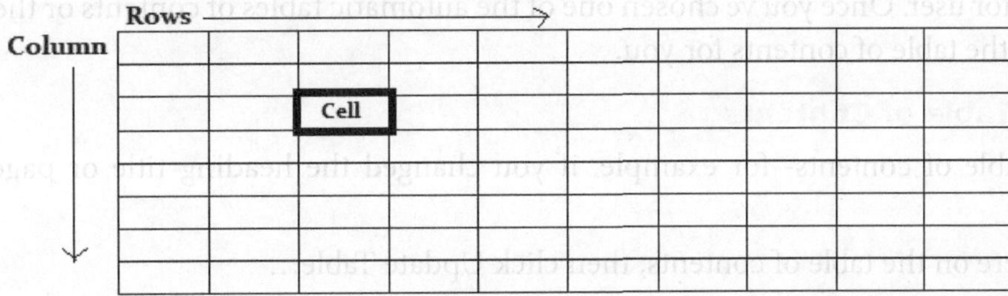

Figure 1.32: Table

Tables are used to create documents such as forms, financial reports, catalogs and biodata. MS Word tables consist of horizontal rows and vertical columns. Text is typed in the areas called cells which is formed by intersection of rows and columns.

4.2 Hierarchy of headings

There are number of schemes for the headings in the document by using multilevel-list templates and built-in heading styles in Word that is Heading 1, Heading 2 and so on. The headings can be numbered so that top level heading 1 are numbered 1, 2, 3 and second level headings that is Heading 2 are numbered 1.1, 1.2, 1.3.

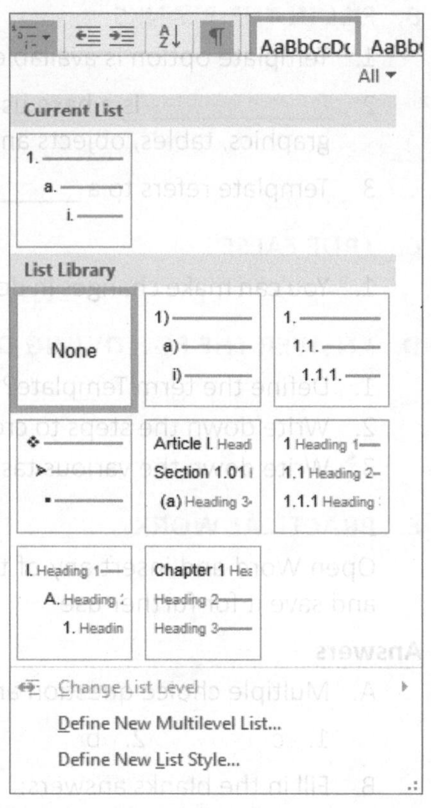

Steps:

- Open the document in which user want to use built-in heading styles and by adding heading style, select the first Heading 1.
- In paragraph group of Home tab, choose Multilevel list
- Choose the numbering style given under List Library

4.3 Customization of table of contents

Adding a table of contents in word document will enable the easy updating if user changes anything in the document. To inset a table of content, perform the following steps:

- Format your document using heading styles found on the Home tab, e.g., Heading 1, Heading 2, and so on. Word will create your table of contents based on these headings, so do this for all of the text you want to show up in the table of contents.
- Place the cursor where you want the table of contents to appear (usually, the beginning of the document)
- Click Table of Contents on the References Tab, and choose one of the types of tables of contents available.

The two automatic tables can be updated when you change the heading text, rearrange the order of your content, or change between heading styles. (They only differ by either saying "Contents" or "Table of Contents" at the top.)

Alternatively, if user clicks the Custom Table of Contents… option, user can format the way the table of contents will look: Choose a different style, hide page numbers, include more heading levels than the default three levels, and more.

If user chooses instead to create a manual table of contents, Word will add dummy text to the table instead of using your headings, you'll have to manually type in each entry, and Word won't be able to update the table of contents for user. Once you've chosen one of the automatic tables of contents or the custom option, Word will create the table of contents for you.

Updating the Table of Contents

To update the table of contents--for example, if you changed the heading title or page numbers have changed:

- Click anywhere on the table of contents, then click Update Table…
- Choose to update either the entire table or just the page numbers.

Remember to do this before user finalize their document so the table of contents will be current. The table of contents is a finishing touch on long documents, such as reports, manuals, or books. Thankfully, you don't have to create and manage one manually, as Word's built-in table of contents tool does the heavy lifting for you.

4.4 Character styles

In Word 2010, a style is a collection of text and paragraph formats. These formats are saved as a collection, given a name, and applied to text just like any other format. The difference is that when you apply a style, you're applying all the formats stored in that style. For heavy-duty formatting, styles save time.

Styles are available in all documents, whether or not you choose to use them. In fact, any text you type has a style automatically applied; it can't be avoided. All text in a blank document uses the Normal style, Word's primary (or default) text style.

The Normal style is defined with the following formats: Calibri font, 11 points tall, left-justified paragraphs, multiple line spacing at 1.08 lines, no indenting, zero margins, and 8 points of space after every paragraph. Word's Style names give you a clue to how to use the style, such as Heading 1 for the document's top-level heading, or Caption, used for figure and table captions.

Styles are also categorized by which part of the document they affect. Five style types are available:

- **Paragraph:** The paragraph style contains both paragraph- and text-formatting attributes: indents, tabs, font, text size — you name it. It's the most common type of style.
- **Character:** The character style applies to characters, not paragraphs. This type of style uses the character-formatting commands.
- **Linked:** The linked style can be applied to both paragraphs and individual characters. The difference depends on which text is selected when the style is applied.
- **Table:** The table style is applied to tables, to add lines and shading to the table cells' contents.
- **List:** The list style is customized for presenting lists of information. The styles can include bullets, numbers, indentation, and other formats typical for the parts of a document that present lists of information.

MEMORY BOX

These types come into play when you create your own styles, as well as when you're perusing styles to apply to your text.

Summary

- A table is made of rows and columns of cells which you can fill with text and graphics.
- A row is a horizontal block of cells that runs through the entire width of the table.
- A column is a vertical block of cells that runs through the table.
- A cell is the intersection of a row and a column.
- Tables are used to create documents such as forms, financial reports, catalogs and biodata. MS Word tables consist of horizontal rows and vertical columns.
- There are number of schemes for the headings in the document by using multilevel-list templates and built-in heading styles in Word that is Heading 1, Heading 2 and so on.

- Adding a table of contents in word document will enable the easy updating if user changes anything in the document.
- Format your document using heading styles found on the Home tab, e.g., Heading 1, Heading 2, and so on. Word will create your table of contents based on these headings, so do this for all of the text you want to show up in the table of contents.
- To update the table of contents--for example, if you changed the heading title or page numbers have changed, Click anywhere on the table of contents, then click Update Table > Choose to update either the entire table or just the page numbers.
- In Word 2016, a style is a collection of text and paragraph formats. These formats are saved as a collection, given a name, and applied to text just like any other format.
- Styles are available in all documents, whether or not you choose to use them.
- The Normal style is defined with the following formats: Calibri font, 11 points tall, left-justified paragraphs, multiple line spacing at 1.08 lines, no indenting, zero margins, and 8 points of space after every paragraph.
- Word's Style names give you a clue to how to use the style, such as Heading 1 for the document's top-level heading, or Caption, used for figure and table captions.
- The paragraph style contains both paragraph- and text-formatting attributes: indents, tabs, font, text size — you name it. It's the most common type of style.
- The character style applies to characters, not paragraphs. This type of style uses the character-formatting commands.
- The linked style can be applied to both paragraphs and individual characters. The difference depends on which text is selected when the style is applied.
- The table style is applied to tables, to add lines and shading to the table cells' contents.
- The list style is customized for presenting lists of information. The styles can include bullets, numbers, indentation, and other formats typical for the parts of a document that present lists of information.

Keywords: Table of contents, Hierarchy of headings, Customization, Updating, Character styles

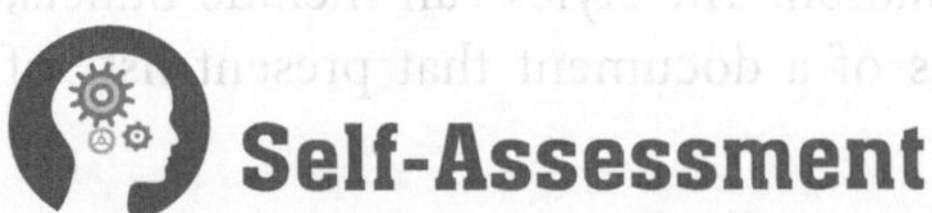

A. MULTIPLE CHOICE QUESTIONS.

1. A row is a ____________ block of cells that runs through the entire width of the table.
   a. Vertical   b. Interaction   c. Horizontal

B. FILL IN THE BLANKS

1. ____________ is a predefined combination of font style, color and size of text that can be applied to selected text.

C. TRUE FALSE

1. Is it possible to make a hierarchy of headings in MS Word (T/F)

D. ANSWER THE FOLLOWING QUESTIONS:

1. Define the term Cell?
2. Write a note on hierarchy of headings.
3. Name various types of styles available in Word 2016. Define Character style in brief.

E. PRACTICAL WORK

Create a Table of content with Name of figure and page number list for around 20 figures

Perform the following:

Create a new style > Apply several different styles to different parts of your document

Answers

A. Multiple choice question answers:

   1. c

B. Fill in the blanks answers:

   1. Style

C. True False answers

   1. True

SESSION 5: IMPLEMENT MAIL MERGE

If you want to send a document to many people via email, but you want it to be personalized then, use Word for an email merge.

5.1 Advance concept of mail merge in word processing

Word makes it fairly simple to send out this invitation to every one of your contortionist cohorts, each of them getting an email message addressed and personalized, just to—and for—them.

Basic steps of sending an e-mail are:

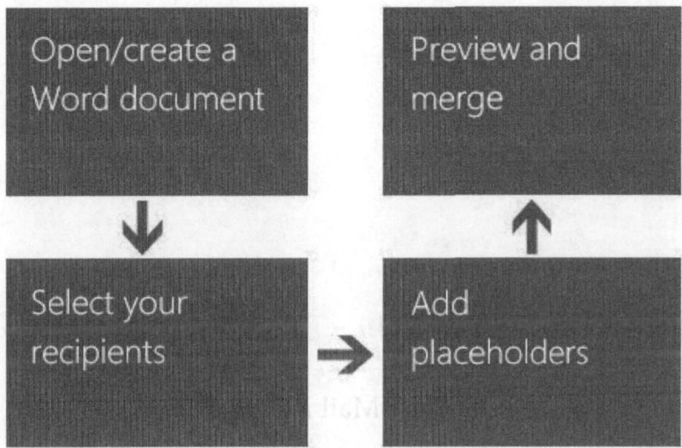

Figure 1.37: Basic steps of sending an e-mail

The mail merge process entails the following overall steps:

- Set up the email message. In this step, you're going to open up Word to either a blank document or one you've already created and get started on the merging part of the process.
- Connect the message to your address list. Your address list is the data source that Word will use in the mail merge. It's a file that contains the email addresses where the messages will be sent.
- Add placeholders, called mail merge fields, to the email message document. When you perform the mail merge, the mail merge fields are filled with information from your address list.
- Preview and complete the merge. You can preview each message before you send the whole set.

LETS KNOW MORE

For example, if you are a manager and want to inform your customers of a meeting, then the meeting purpose is the same in all the documents, but there are changes in the recipient's information such as their first name, last name, and many more.

Definition Box

Mail merge is a feature within most data processing applications that enables users to send a similar letter or document to multiple recipients. It enables connecting a single form template with a data source that contains information about the recipient's name, address and other predefined and supported data.

5.2 Creating a main document

Set up the email message main document

- Start Word and either create your message in the blank document, or start Word and open up something you've already started.
- Click Mailings> Start Mail Merge> E-mail Messages.

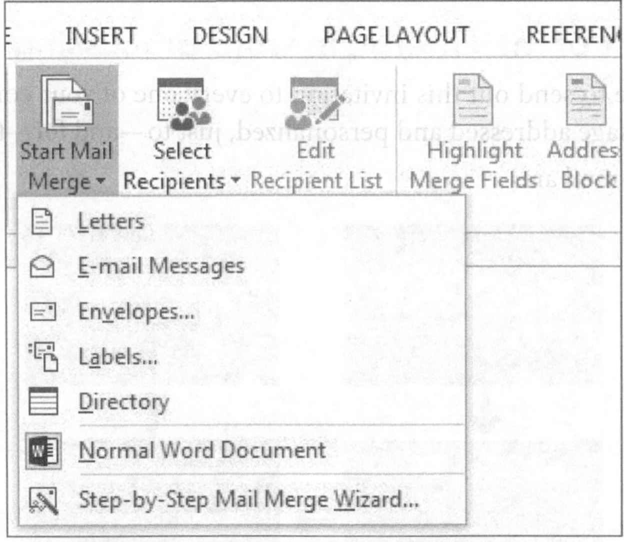

Figure 1.38: Start Mail Merge drop down

5.3 Creating the data source

Corresponding values are kept in data source that is a set of mailing address in multiple rows and columns that is also known as database. In this each row contain the record of each person that have other fields such as name, address, roll no., etc. Best way to create a database is use of spreadsheet as table format is used in this for storing the data. Other option is use of mail wizard for creating an address book during mail merge.

Steps to use Mail Merge are:

Create a new document and add data to be sent to multiple people: To create a new document, perform the following steps:

- Click on Tool

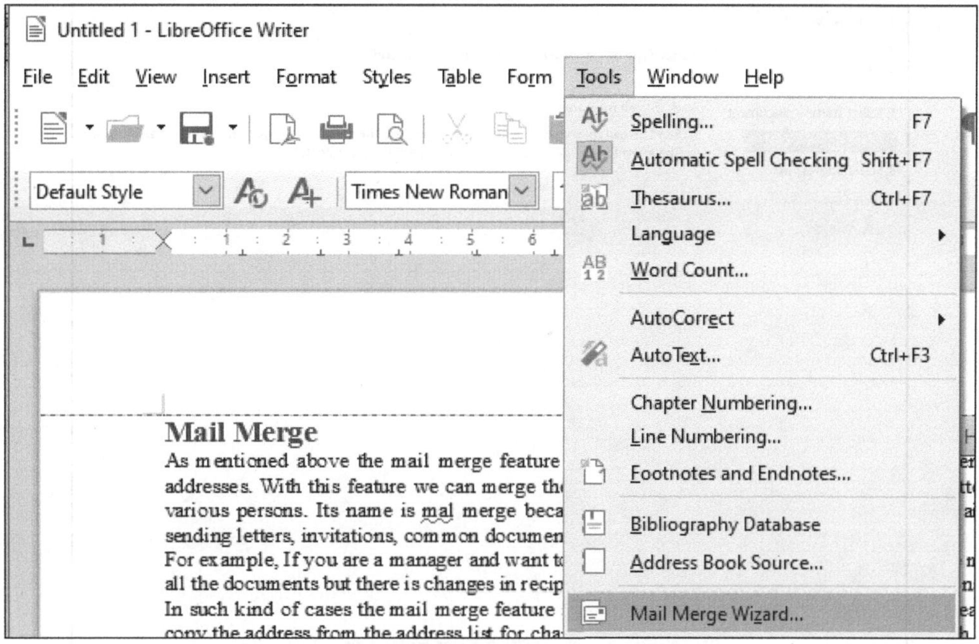

Figure 1.39: Mail Merge Wizard option

✦ Mail Merge Wizard and a new window will appear

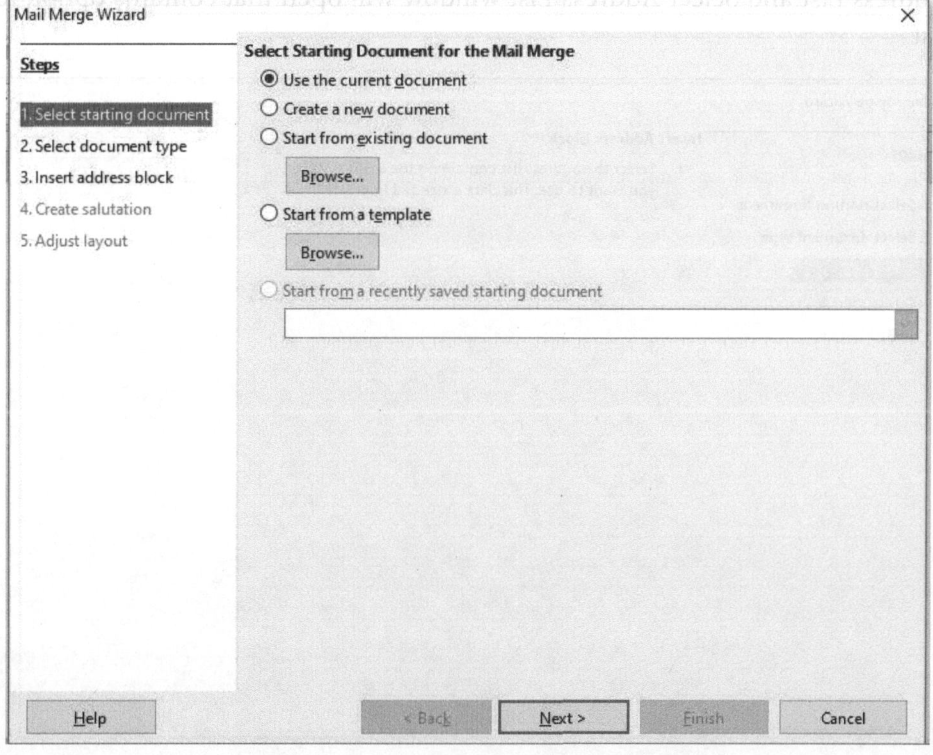

Figure 1.40: Mail Merge Wizard dialog box

✦ Select Starting document from Mail Merge Wizard dialog box > Use the current document > click on Next button given in the bottom of dialog box

✦ Then Click on Document type > E-mail message > Next button

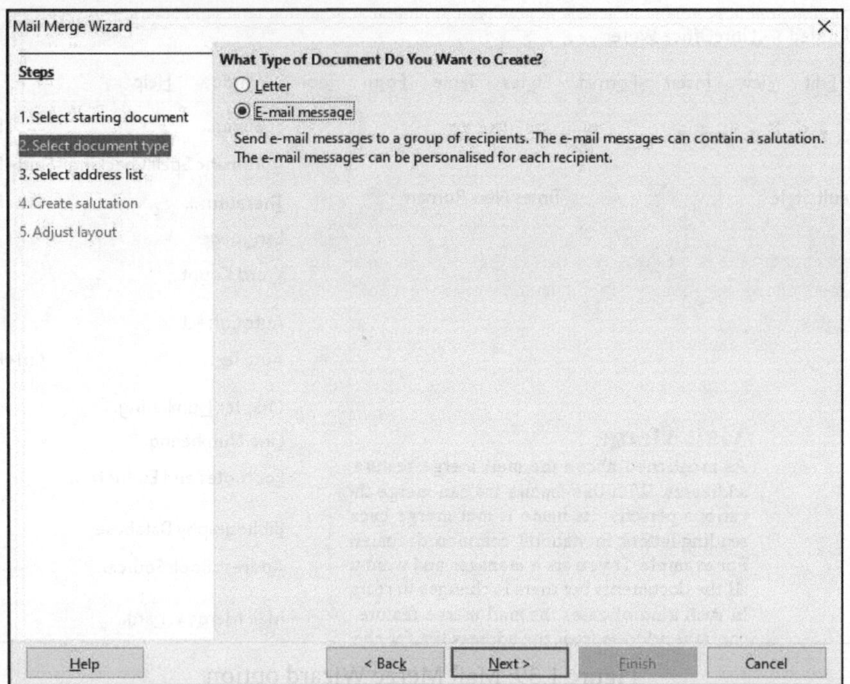

Figure 1.41: Selected document type

- Click on Address List and Select Address List window will open that contains option for creating the recipient list

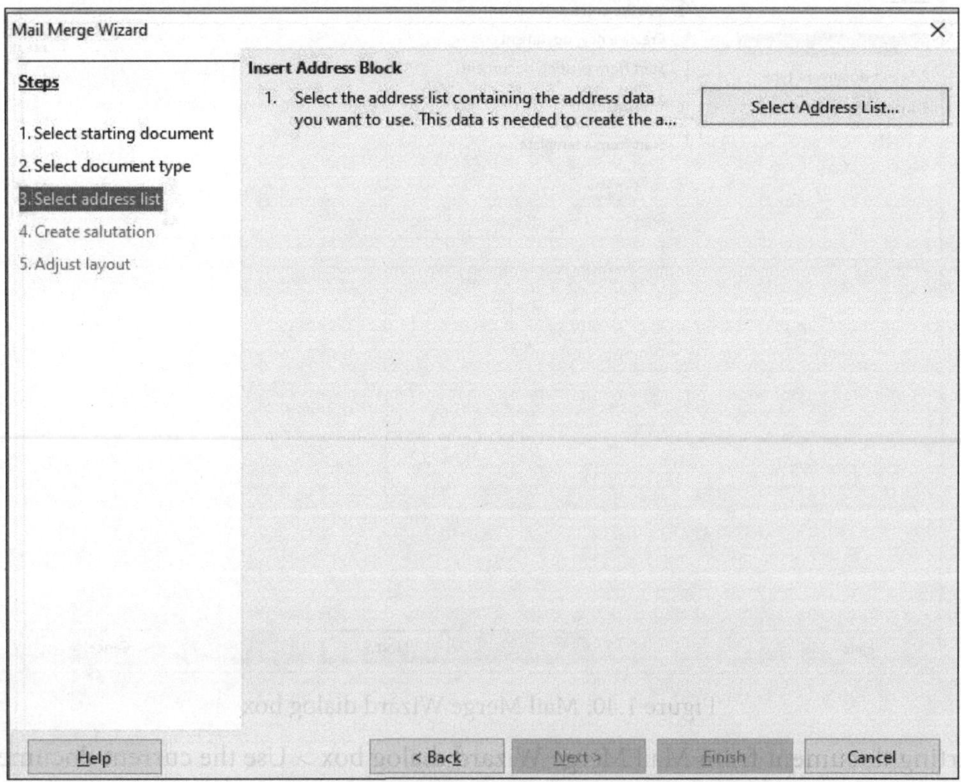

Figure 1.42: Select address list

- In above window, click on Select Address List and a Select Address List will open

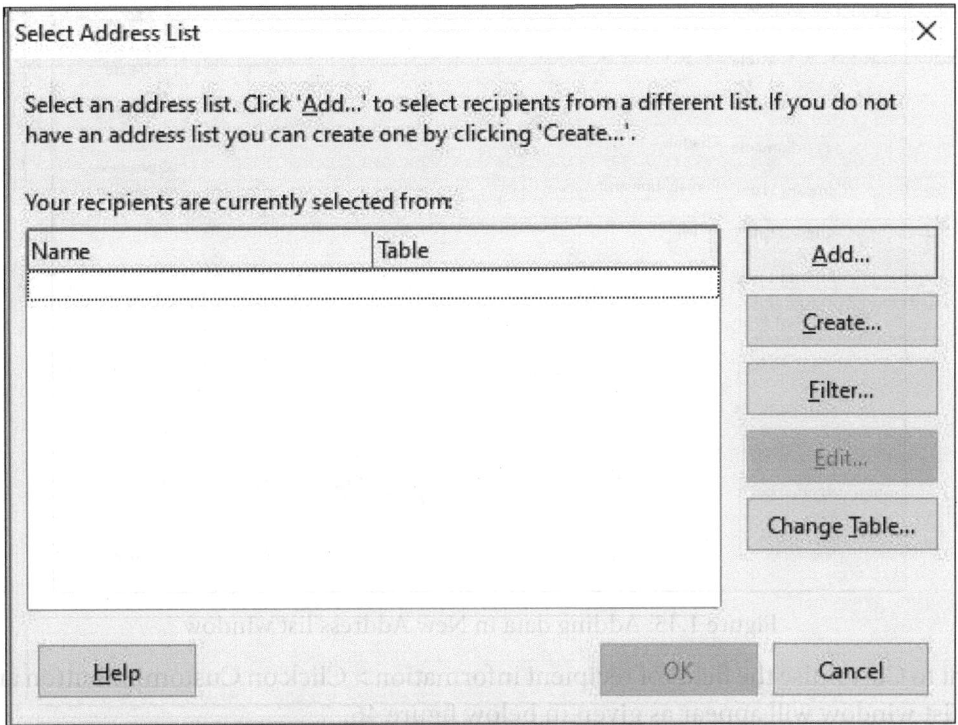

Figure 1.43: Select Address List dialog box

- In above given dialog box, click on Add to add various members address > Click on Create button, this will open a New Address List window

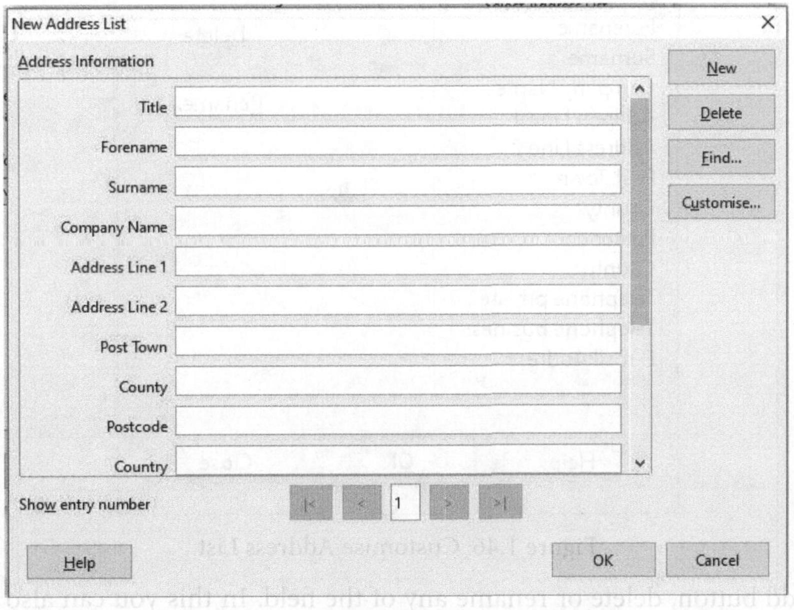

Figure 1.44: New Address list window

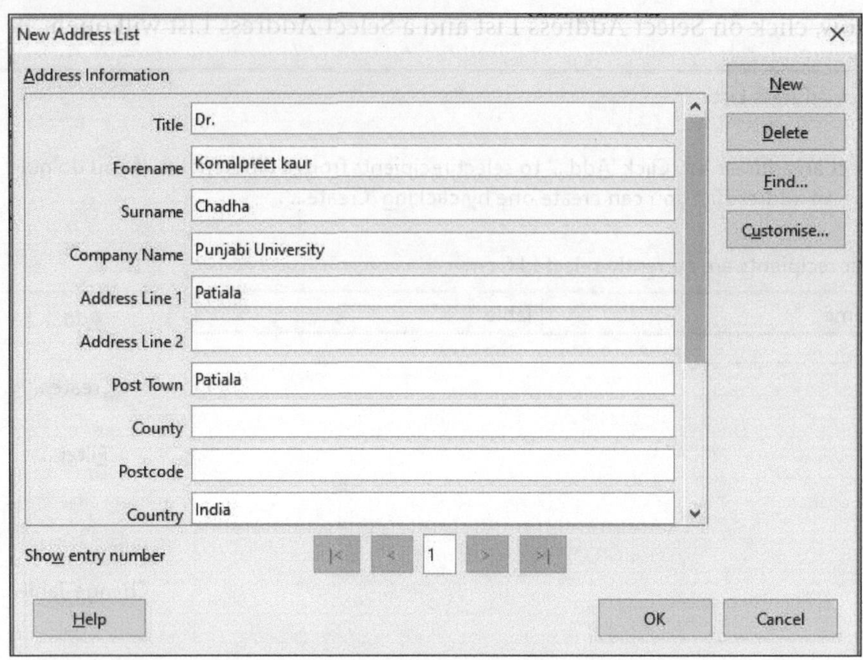

Figure 1.45: Adding data in New Address list window

- If you want to Customise the fields of recipient information > Click on Customize button and Customise Address List window will appear as given in below figure 46.

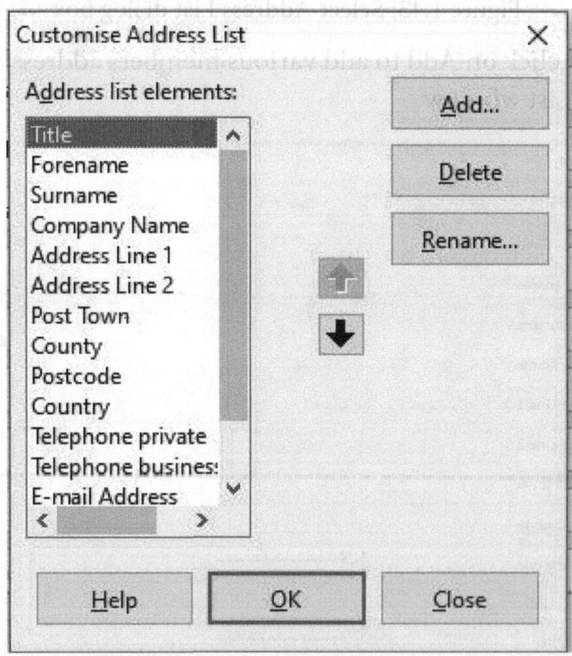

Figure 1.46: Customise Address List

- Now click on Add button, delete or rename any of the field. In this you can also change the order of appearance of the fields using up/down arrow button given on the Customise Address List window.

  The Add option is used for creating a new field, Delete is used to delete an unnecessary field, Rename is used to change the name of the field.

- Then click on Ok button to close the list and this will open a Save As dialog box.

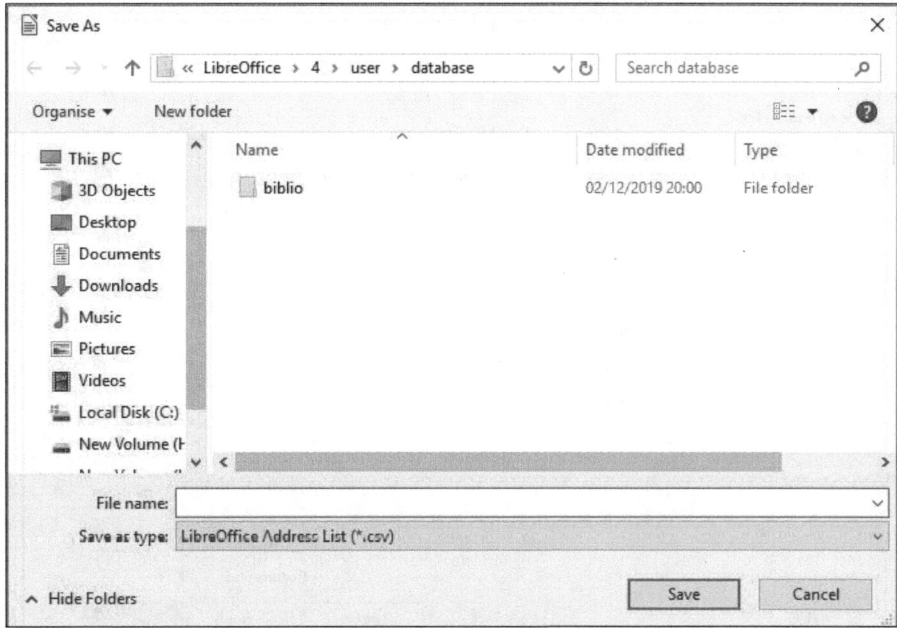

Figure 1.47: Save As dialog box

- In Save As dialog box, add the name in File name text box > Click on Save if you want to save the document in the opened location otherwise Change the location and Save it.
- A list window will appear after saving the list that will display all the recipient list created by you.
- From list you can select any of the created list > Click on Ok button to send the mail to selected list.

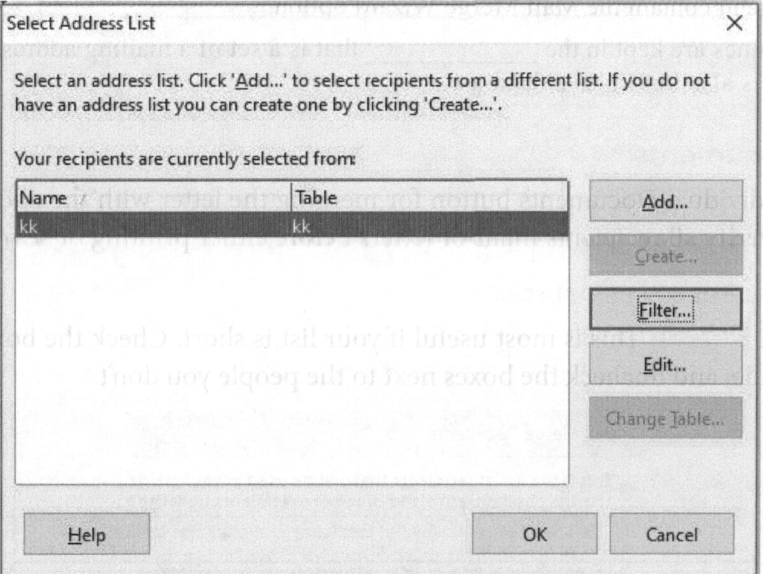

Figure 1.48: Selected Address List dialog box

- After selected the address from list, next step is to click on Create salutation > Add the required information > Click on Next button

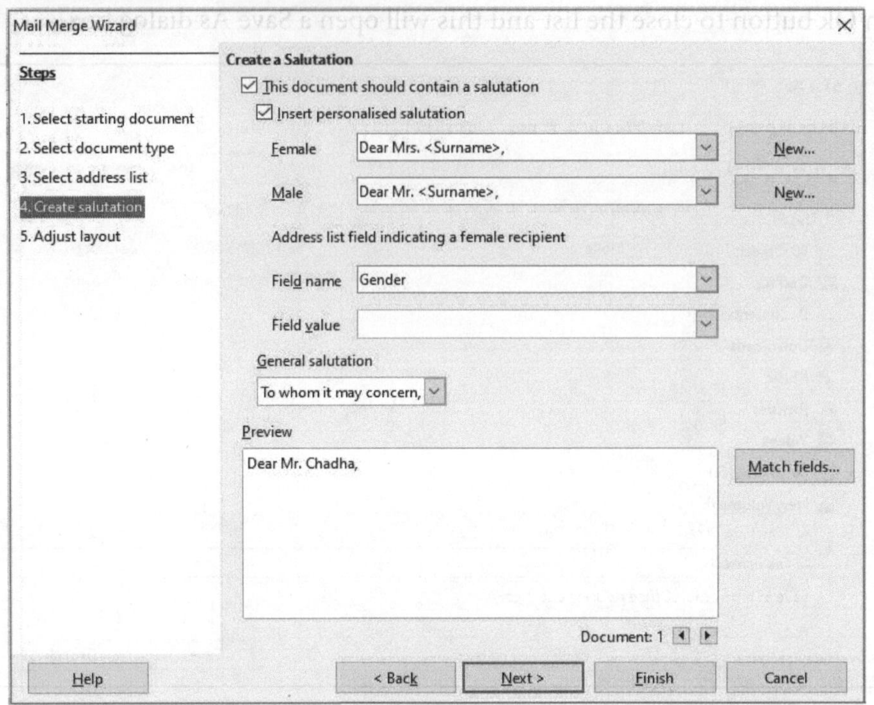

Figure 1.49: Create salutation window

- In the next step, a Writer will display the document with Mail Merge Toolbar

Practice Box

Enter the correct answer in the blanks given below:

1. ____________ Menu contain the Mail Merge Wizard option.
2. Corresponding values are kept in the ____________ that is a set of a mailing address in multiple rows and columns that is also known as a database.

Edit individual documents:

Now click on Edit individual Documents button for merging the letter with the address of the recipients. In this part you can verify all recipients mails or letters before either printing or sending it

To narrow your list, follow the steps:

- **Select individual records:** This is most useful if your list is short. Check the boxes next to the people you want to include, and uncheck the boxes next to the people you don't.

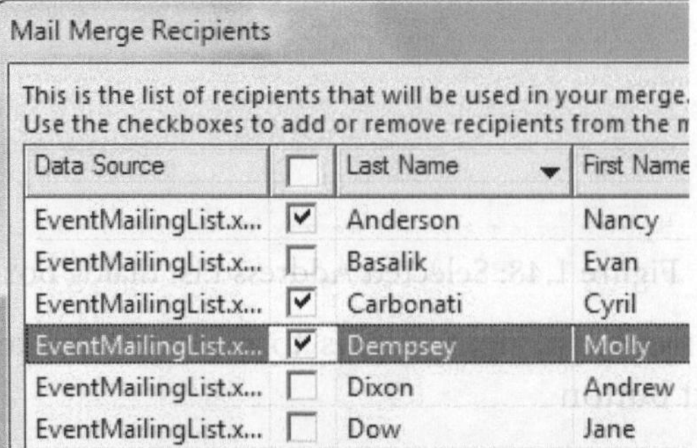

Figure 1.50: Selecting Individual records

- **Sort records:** Click the column heading of the item that you want to sort by. The list sorts in ascending alphabetical order (from A to Z). Click the column heading again to sort the list in descending alphabetical order (Z to A).

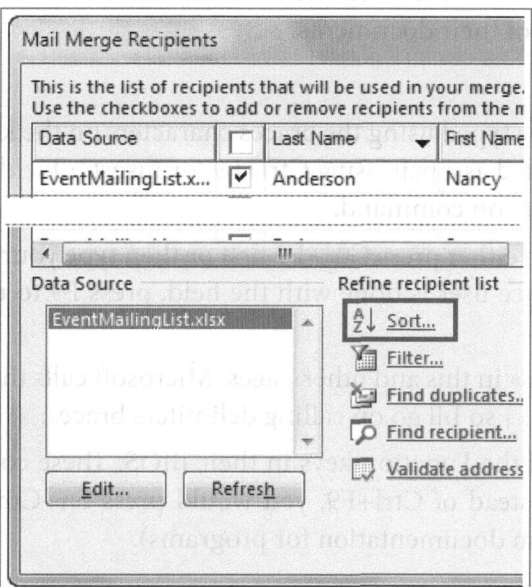

Figure 1.51: Sorting command

- **Filter records:** Under Refine recipient list, click Filter. This is handy when the list contains things that you know you don't want to see or include in the merge. After you filter the list, you can check or uncheck the boxes to include or exclude people.

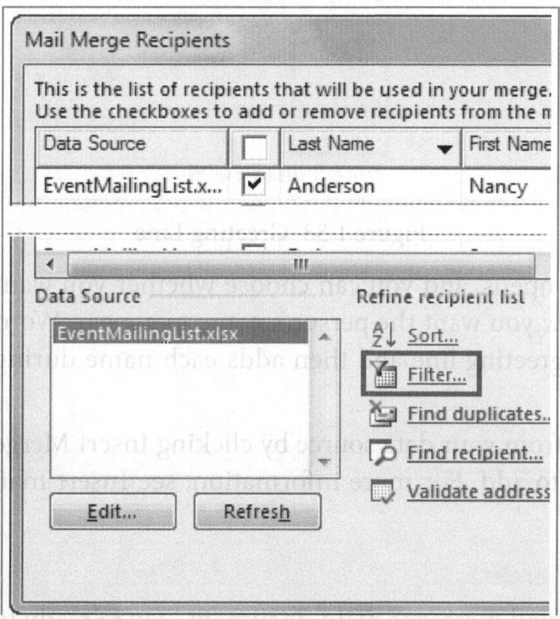

Figure 1.52: Mail Merge Recipients

- **Add recipients:** To add people to the list, under Data source, click the name of your data file. Click Edit > New Entry and type the information for that recipient.

Add placeholders—or fields—to the email message document. After you connect your document to your address list, type the text of the message.

5.4 Entering data in the fields

Field is a one of the basic tools in preparing a document templates that can automatically update themselves to give the information user want in the document. Combination of filed with AutoText will give a easy toolbox that user can use in all of their documents.

Type fields in Word

The { } field delimiters cannot be typed using the braces characters on the keyboard. They are special Word characters that have to be inserted as a pair using Ctrl+F9, or Insert > Field... or Insert > Cross Reference... or some other special field insertion command.

If user is using Ctrl+F9 user can either press Ctrl+F9 first or then type your field or type the field code first, select it, and press Ctrl+F9. Once user is done with the field, press F9 to update the field and display the result.

I call these delimiters { } «braces» in this and other pages. Microsoft calls them brackets, but to me brackets have right angles and look like [ ] so I›ll go on calling delimiters braces.

Some computers have hijacked the Function keys in their BIOS. These computers should have a Fn shift key on their keyboards. So, instead of Ctrl+F9, you would press Fn+Ctrl+F9 (or edit the BIOS so that function keys act as described in documentation for programs).

5.5 Merging the data source with main document

To personalize each message, add mail merge fields from your data source. For example, click Mailings > Write & Insert Fields> Greeting Line to add a line with the person's name.

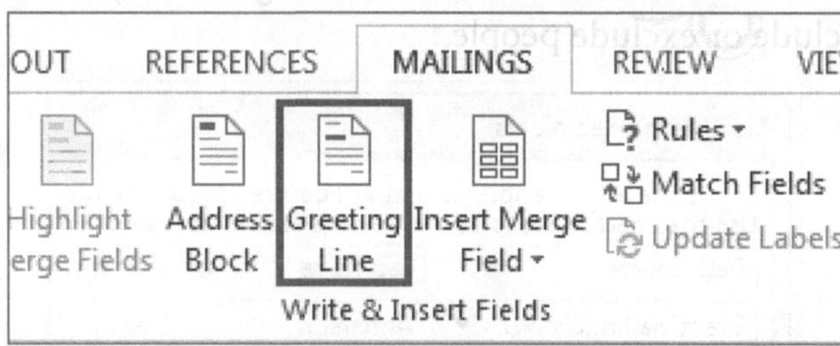

Figure 1.53: Greeting Line

The Insert Greeting Line box opens, and you can choose whether you want to add "Dear" or "To" and how you want the person's name to appear. Word inserts a placeholder for the greeting line and then adds each name during the merge.

You can also add other fields from your data source by clicking Insert Merge Field and the field you want to add. For more information, see Insert mail merge fields.

Preview and finish the merge

After you add fields to your email message's main document, you're ready to preview the merge results. When you're satisfied with the preview, you can complete the merge.

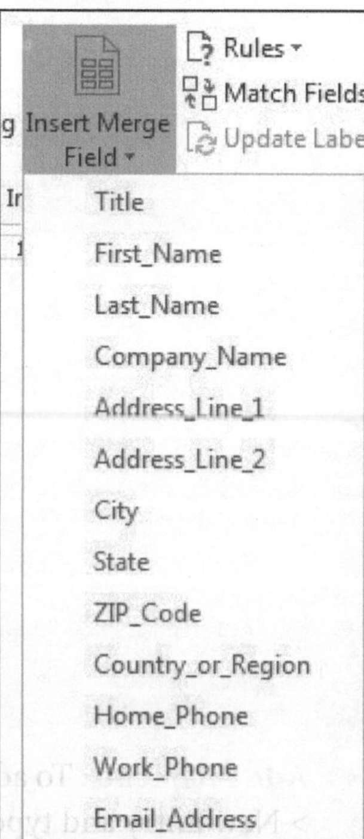

Figure 1.54: Insert Merge Field drop down

Preview the merge

Click Mailings, and a couple of groups to the right, you'll see Preview Results.

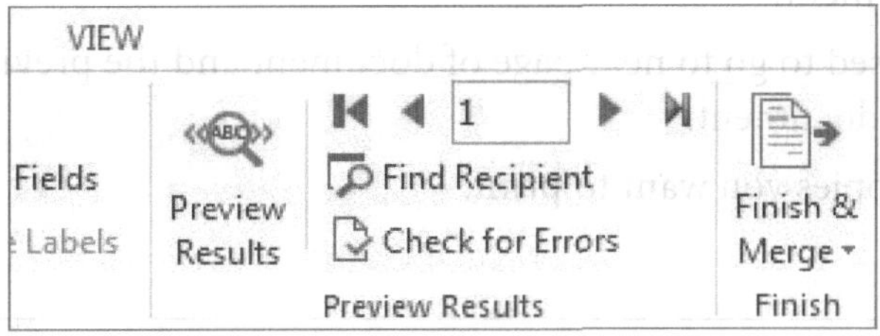

Figure 1.55: Preview Results

Now you can do any or all of the following:

- Click Preview Results. (This option is available only if you chose one or more placeholder fields, such as greeting, name, address, etc.)
- Page through each email message by clicking the blue arrows.
- Preview a specific document by clicking Find Recipient.
- Edit your recipient list—who's getting this message—by clicking Mailings > Edit Recipient List.

Complete the merge and send the messages

1. Click Mailings> Finish & Merge> Send E-mail Messages.
2. In the To box, select the name of the email address column in your list.
3. In the Subject line box, type a subject line for the message.
4. In the Mail format box, click HTML or Plain text to send the document as the body of the email message.

Save the message

Save the message if you plan to use it for another mail merge. When you save the email message's main document, you also save its connection to the data file you chose. The next time you open the email message main document, Word prompts you to choose whether to keep the connection to the data file.

- If you click Yes, the document opens with information from the first record merged in.

If you click No, the connection between the email message main document and the data file is broken. The email message main document becomes a standard Word document

5.6 Printing a letter and its address label

Preview and Print a document

- Open the document of which you want to see print preview.
- Click on the File tab.
- Choose Print option (Figure 1.56)
- The Backstage view consists of three panes.
  a. The left pane consists of several options such as Save, Save As, Open, Close, Info, Recent etc.,
  b. In the middle pane, there are print options and its related printer settings.
  c. In the right pane, you can see the preview document.

d. In the bottom of the right pane, the Zoom control button is available, whose button are:

   i. The + (plus) button is use to increase the document and the (minus) button is use to decrease the preview document.

e. The Next button is used to go to next page of document and the previous button is use to move to the pervious page of document.

✦ Choose the number of copies you want to print.

✦ Click the Print button.

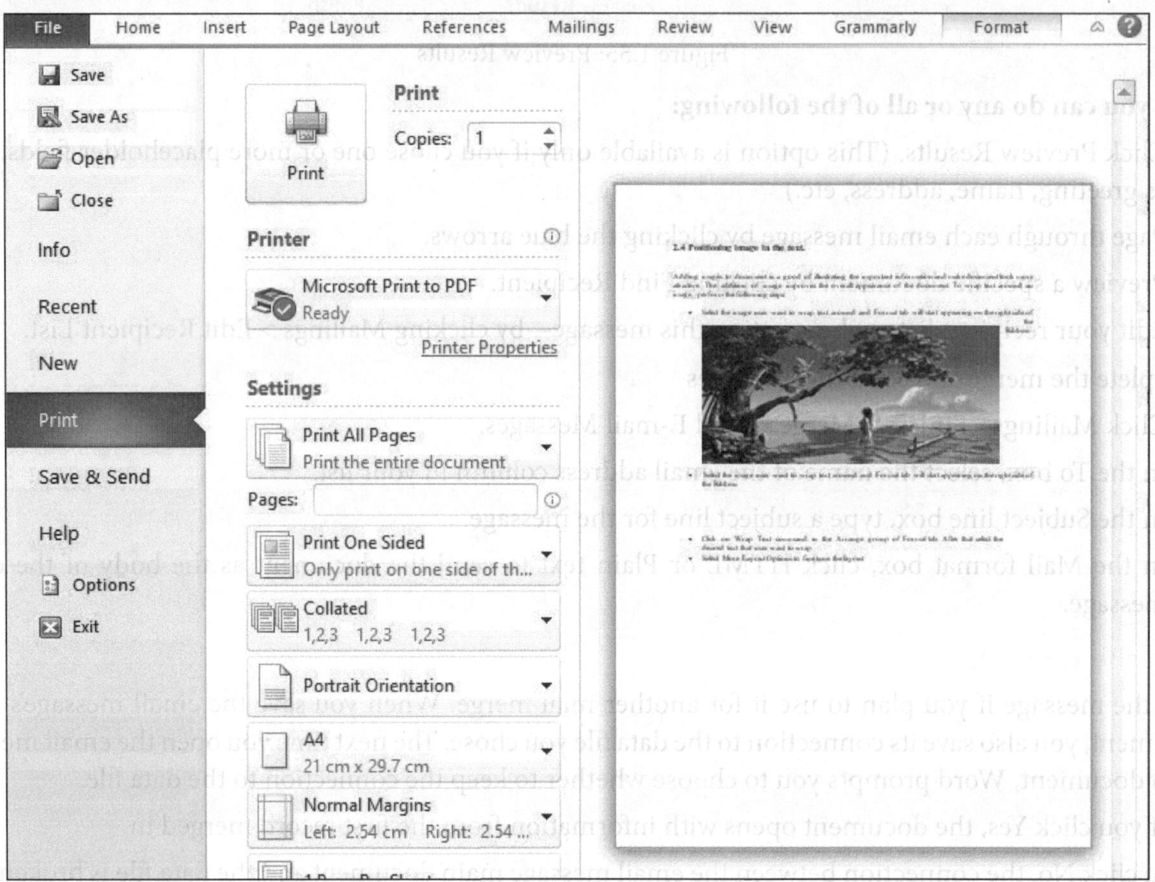

Figure 1.56: Print

To Print specific pages

✦ Click on the File tab.

✦ Choose Print option (Figure 1.57)

✦ To print only certain pages, print some of the document's properties, or print tracked changes and comments, click the arrow under Settings, next to Print All Pages (the default), to see all your options.

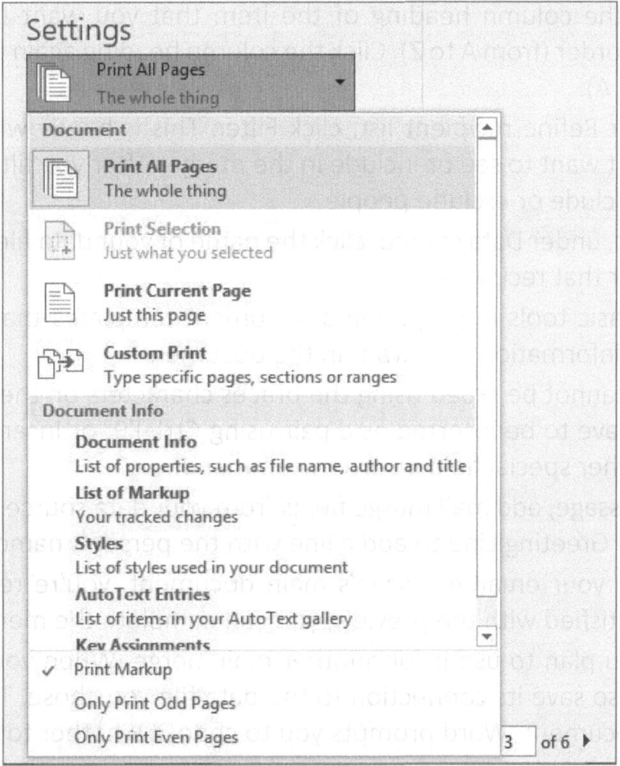

Figure 1.57: To print a specific page

To print only certain pages:

- To print the page shown in preview, select Print Current Page.
- To print consecutive pages like 1-3, select Custom Print and enter the first and last page numbers in the Pages box.
- To print individual pages and a range of pages (like page 3, and pages 4-6) at the same time, select Custom Print, and enter the page numbers and ranges separated by commas (e.g. 3, 4-6).

Summary

- Word makes it fairly simple to send out this invitation to every one of your contortionist cohorts, each of them getting an email message addressed and personalized, just to—and for—them.
- The mail merge process entails the steps: Set up the email message > Connect the message to your address list > Add placeholder, called mail merge fields, to your address list > Add placeholder, called mail merge fields, to the email message document > Preview and complete the merge.
- Start Word and either create your message in the blank document, or start Word and open up something you've already started.
- Choose your recipients from a data source. If you don't already have a data source, you can create one during the mail merge process.
- To use the email addresses from your Outlook contacts, click Choose from Outlook Contacts. If Word prompts you to choose a contact list or and Outlook profile, click the list or profile you want to use in the merge.
- To narrow the list of recipients, select the names you want in the Mail Merge Recipients box. (You can open the Mail Merge Recipients box by clicking Mailings > Edit Recipient List.)

- To Sort records, Click the column heading of the item that you want to sort by. The list sorts in ascending alphabetical order (from A to Z). Click the column heading again to sort the list in descending alphabetical order (Z to A).
- To Filter records, Under Refine recipient list, click Filter. This is handy when the list contains things that you know you don't want to see or include in the merge. After you filter the list, you can check or uncheck the boxes to include or exclude people.
- To add people to the list, under Data source, click the name of your data file. Click Edit > New Entry and type the information for that recipient.
- Field is a one of the basic tools in preparing a document templates that can automatically update themselves to give the information user want in the document.
- The { } field delimiters cannot be typed using the braces characters on the keyboard. They are special Word characters that have to be inserted as a pair using Ctrl+F9, or Insert > Field... or Insert > Cross Reference... or some other special field insertion command.
- To personalize each message, add mail merge fields from your data source. For example, click Mailings > Write & Insert Fields> Greeting Line to add a line with the person's name.
- After you add fields to your email message's main document, you're ready to preview the merge results. When you're satisfied with the preview, you can complete the merge.
- Save the message if you plan to use it for another mail merge. When you save the email message's main document, you also save its connection to the data file you chose. The next time you open the email message main document, Word prompts you to choose whether to keep the connection to the data file.

Keywords: Mail Merge, Creating main document, Data source, Edit documents, Sort records, Filter records, Entering data, Merging data source and main document, Greeting Line, Preview the merge, save message, Printing a letter and address label

Self-Assessment

A. MULTIPLE CHOICE QUESTIONS.

1. In mail merge which of the following is the last step of sending an email:
    a. Preview and complete the merge
    b. Connect the message to your address list
    c. Add placeholders, called mail merge fields, to the email message document
    d. Set up the email message
2. In the last step of mail merge i.e. Preview and complete the merge. You can preview ________ message before you send the whole set:
    a. only one b. two c. any one d. each
3. In mail merge, if you clicked which of the following, Word automatically selects everyone on the list you chose:
    a. use an existing list b. choose from outlook contacts
    c. type a new list d. none of the above

B. FILL IN THE BLANKS

1. In mail merge address list a file that contains ________ where the messages will be sent:

2. In mail merge, if you don't have an address list yet, click ____________ and fill in the form that Word opens.

C. ANSWER THE FOLLOWING QUESTIONS:

1. Write a note on concept of mail merge in word processing.
2. Write down the steps of creating a main document.
3. How to enter data in the fields.
4. Is it possible to merge the data source with main document? If yes, then give the steps to merge it.

D. PRACTICAL WORK

Demonstrate Word to send out invitation of Bonus meeting to every one of your School teachers, each of them getting an email message addressed and personalized using Mail Merge concept.

Answers

A. Multiple choice question answers:

1. a 2. d 3. a

B. Fill in the blanks answers:

1. E-mail addresses
2. Type a new list

Solved Exercise

A. MULTIPLE CHOICE QUESTIONS

1. __________ group consists of Style Dialog Box Launcher Arrow that helps in creating a New Style.
   a. Font group b. Editing Group c. Paragraph group d. Style group
2. Template option is available in ____________ tab
   a. Home b. Insert c. File d. Page Layout
3. Shortcut key to Bold the text?
   a. Cntl + E b. Cntl + B c. Cntl + C d. Cntl + S
4. Shortcut key to Tilt the text?
   a. Cntl + T b. Cntl + O c. Cntl + I d. Cntl + U
5. Shortcut key to use Superscript?
   a. Cntl + + b. Cntl +- c. Cntl + Shift + + d. Cntl + Shift + =
6. Clip Art is available in ____________ tab
   a. Home b. Insert c. Page Layout d. View
7. Picture command is available in ____________ group
   a. Tables b. Links c. Illustration d. Text
8. ____________ objects are used when you don't want to change the copied data when it changes in source file
   a. Linked b. Anchor c. Embedded d. Both (a) and (c)

9. Shape command is available in __________ tab

a. Home b. Insert c. Page Layout d. View

10. By selecting a shape __________ tabs appear on the top of document

a. Design b. Layout c. Format d. Both (a) and (c)

Answers

1. d	2. c	3. b	4. c	5. c
6. b	7. c	8. c	9. b	10. c

B. SOLVED VERY SHORT AND SHORT QUESTION AND ANSWERS:

1. What is Word Processor?

Ans. A word processor is software or a device that allows users to create, edit, and print documents. It enables you to write, store, display text on a screen, modify it by entering commands and characters from the keyboard, and prints it.

2. Name the basic features of Word processor?

Ans. Some of the basic features of word processor are:

- Formatting
- Graphics
- Ease and speed
- Printing
- Storage
- Mail merge
- Vocabulary and Spell check

3. What is the purpose of Copy and Paste function?

Ans. It is used when you want the duplicate copy of the selected text or image.

4. What is the shortcut key to copy the text?

Ans. Press Ctrl + C key

5. What is the shortcut key to paste the text?

Ans. Press Ctrl + V key

6. What is the shortcut to clear direct formatting?

Ans. Press Ctrl + M keys

7. How to remove manual formatting done in the document?

Ans. One can remove the manual formatting done in the document can be done after clicking or selecting the Clear Direct Formatting option, you can observe that default formatting on the text by removing the manual formatting done on it.

8. Name various common text formatting features in Word processor?

Ans. There is various common text formatting features in Word processor. Some of them are:

- Change of font size
- Change of Font style
- Change of font type
- Change of font color

9. Give the shortcut key for making the selected text bold?

Ans. Press Ctrl + B keys

10. Give the shortcut key for making the selected text Italic?

Ans. Press Ctrl + I keys

11. Give the shortcut key for making the selected text Underline?

Ans. Press Ctrl + U keys

12. What changes occur in the text after selecting the subscript option ?

Ans. After selecting subscript, whatever user type will come below the baseline, and it will look smaller than other normal text in the document.

13. What changes occur in the text after selecting the superscript option ?

Ans. The superscript will place the text above the baseline.

14. Name various options of paragraph alignment in Word processor?

Ans. There are mainly four-paragraph alignment styles comes under this category are:

- Align paragraph left
- Center
- Align paragraph right
- Justify

15. What is the keyboard shortcut for aligning the paragraph in left?

Ans. Press Ctrl + L key

16. What is the keyboard shortcut for aligning the paragraph in right?

Ans. Press Ctrl + R key

17. What is the keyboard shortcut for aligning the paragraph in center?

Ans. Press Ctrl + E key

18. What is the keyboard shortcut for aligning the paragraph in justify?

Ans. Press Ctrl + J key

19. Give various options of formatting a page in Word processor?

Ans. In Word processor, there are various options for formatting the page like page layout, inserting a page break, header, and footer, borders, background, inserting images, page size, margins, placement of header and footers, borders and backgrounds, number of columns, page numbers, and more.

20. Define Mail merge feature of Word processor?

Ans. Mail merge is a feature within most data processing applications that enables users to send a similar letter or document to multiple recipients. It enables connecting a single form template with a data source that contains information about the recipient's name, address and other predefined and supported data.

C. LONG SOLVED QUESTION AND ANSWERS:

1. What is a word processor? Give its various features in detail.

Ans. A word processor is software or a device that allows users to create, edit, and print documents. It enables you to write, store, display text on a screen, modify it by entering commands and characters from the keyboard, and prints it.

Various basic features of word processor are:

Feature	Explanation
Formatting	Italic, Font name, Boldface, WordArt, Font Color, etc. are some of the formatting features.
Graphic	Charts, drawing, pictures can be added in your documents. This results in overall document presentation enhancement.
Ease and Speed	For text typing a faster and easier method is provided by word processor
Printing	Printout of documents can be easily taken, and a printed version of document can be seen in word processor.
Storage	All documents can be stored for future use.

Feature	Explanation
Mail merge	Through this feature a piece of text can be sent to multiple addresses. Example: Mail merge feature will change the invited guest names, address and send the same document to multiple guests. This results in time and effort saving
Vocabulary and Spell Check	Spell check feature in word processor that keeps your documents free from errors. There is Vocabulary feature of synonyms that gives multiple alternate to same word.

2. What do you mean by formatting text? Give various option for formatting a text in Word processor?

Ans. The formatting text means the formatting of paragraphs and characters. In case you want to format the particular text in the document, select the text you want to format and apply the required text formatting features.

In Word processor, there is number of options for formatting text that can be chosen according to suitability. Various methods of formatting text are:

- Using the menu options from the menu bar.
- Using the readily available buttons on the formatting toolbar.
- Using the context menu by right-clicking on the selecting text.
- Using a keyboard shortcut.

Some of them are:

- **Change of font-size:** You can change the font size by selecting font size.
- **Change of font style:** You can change the font style by either making it bold, italic, or underline.
- **Change of font type:** You can change the font type by selecting font dropdown.
- **Change of font color:** You can change the font color by selecting the font color icon.

To apply any of the effects, firstly select the text, then press the desired buttons given on the formatting toolbar.

Changing text case: You can change the case of the text. In Word processor Writer, there are 6 change case options. There are six options of text case in Word processor that can be applied to text by selecting

3. What do you mean by Paragraph? Give various paragraph formatting options in Word processor?

Ans. The paragraph can consist of several sentences, a single word, or a single sentence.

There is paragraph style for every paragraph in Word processor Writer such as:

Indenting paragraph

Like text, you can also indent the entire paragraph. To do it, perform the following steps:

- Select the paragraph, click on the **Increase indent** tool.
- This will increase the indent of the currently selected paragraph. Like the same way, you can decrease the indent by clicking on **Decrease indent**.

Aligning paragraph

The position of paragraph between the page margins is known as paragraph alignment. By default, the text is aligned on the left side of the document, and the right margins in the document are known as horizontal text alignment.

There are mainly four-paragraph alignment styles comes under this category are:

- **Align paragraph left:** The left paragraph alignment is a default type of alignment. In this case, there is little space on the right side.

- **Center:** This will align the paragraph in the center of the document and leave little space from both the ends. Mainly its use has been found in writing the title.
- **Align paragraph right:** This is the opposite case of left paragraph alignment as in this, the paragraph is aligned towards the right side and leaves little space in the left. They are mainly used to put sign and date options or sometimes giving the chapter heading.
- **Justify:** In this case, the paragraph is evenly aligned between the left and right sides.

All these alignment options are present in the Paragraph group of Home toolbar.

4. How to insert images, shapes and special characters in a document?

Ans. To make a regular document more attractive and presentable, Word processor gives the option to add various elements like image, shapes, and special characters to the document.

Inserting image: To insert any image or picture in any document, the first, foremost important thing is image or picture should be present either in hard disk or external storage like pen drive, and many more. To insert image in a document, perform the following steps:

- Select the **Insert** tab and click on **Image** option, then go to the desired location and select an image from it. Click on the **Open** button or double click on it.
- Alternatively, click on the **Insert Image** icon available on the formatting toolbar. A file manager will appear, go to the desired location, and select the image. Click on **Open** button or double click on it

Inserting shapes: Like images, you can also insert various shapes in your document. The variety of shapes available in Word processor is a line, arrows, symbols, stars, callouts, flowcharts, and many more. To insert a shape in the document, select the Insert tab, and click on the Shape option. Choose the required shape

Inserting special characters: Sometimes, there is a need to write some equations and adding special characters that can't be typed using the keys of the keyboard. To insert special characters in Word processor, perform the following steps:

- Select the Insert tab and click on the Special Character option.
- A Special Characters dialog box will open from where you can select the required special character by simply selecting it then clicking on the Insert button.

5. Define Mail merge in detail?

Ans. The mail merge feature is used for creating a series of same documents and sent it to multiple addresses. With this feature, we can merge the main document that can be certificates or letters with a mailing address of various persons. Its name is mal merge because in this main document is merged with a mailing address that helps in sending letters, invitations, common documents or certificates for a number of peoples.

For example, if you are a manager and want to inform your customers of a meeting, then the meeting purpose is the same in all the documents, but there are changes in the recipient's information such as their first name, last name, and many more.

In such kind of cases, the mail merge feature saves time and resources. One of the ways is creating a letter in Writer and copy the address from the address list for changing the address or first and last name of each employee. This procedure of copying and changing the name of the employee is very time consuming and tedious. This approach is good when we have to send the letter to a limited number of the person, but it is not possible in case of hundreds or thousands of addresses. In those cases, the use of a mail merge feature is proving to be efficient through this task can be accomplished in one stroke.

Let the common contents is the main document that you want to send to all of your employees or students, and others will be the data source that holds the address list of all employees or students. The actual information is kept in form letter along with the variable names that will be different in every document.

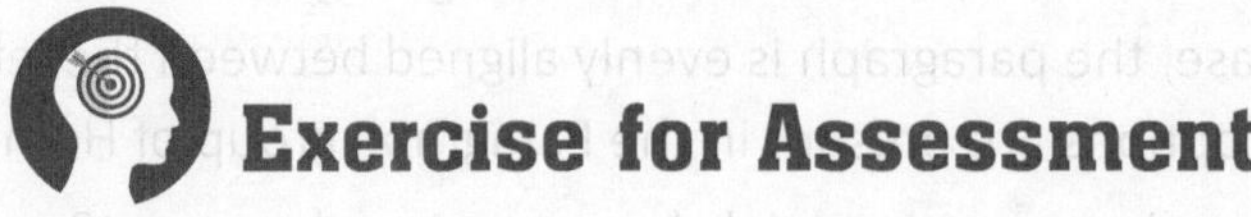

Exercise for Assessment

A. MULTIPLE CHOICE QUESTIONS

1. To format and align your text first:

   a. click home tab b. click file tab
   c. choose options from font or paragraph d. both a and c

2. You can change and enhance drawing objects with:

   a. colors b. patterns c. borders d. all of these

3. The first step to search for a specific comment is to press:

   a. Ctrl + G b. Ctrl + H c. Ctrl + F d. Ctrl + C

4. In track changes, to see the changes, click the line:

   a. above the margin b. below the margin c. near the margin d. all of the above

5. Which is the first step to complete the merge and send the messages:

   a. Click Mailings> Finish & Merge> Send E-mail Messages.
   b. In the To box, select the name of the email address column in your list.
   c. In the Subject line box, type a subject line for the message.
   d. In the Mail format box, click HTML or Plain text to send the document as the body of the email message.

6. You'll see Preview Results when click Mailings, and a couple of groups to the:

   a. left b. right c. either a or b d. neither a nor b

7. AutoFit title text to placeholder ____________ the font size of the title text so that the text fits in the defined title text placeholder:

   a. decreases b. increases c. either a or b d. neither a nor b

8. For Heading 1, type a new line; for Heading 2, precede the new line with a single tab; for Heading 3, precede the new line with how many tabs:

   a. two b. three c. four d. single

9. Define styles based on your formatting applies a built-in style to manually formatted text when the text has the ____________ formatting as a built-in style:

   a. same b. different c. both of these d. none of these

10. Word processing is an application program which allows you to create:

    a. letters b. brochures c. tables d. all of the above

B. VERY SHORT QUESTION AND ANSWER

1. What is Mail Merge?
2. What is Auto correct?
3. Give the shortcut key to Superscript the text.

4. How to change the font color using Mini toolbar.
5. How to save and reuse templates.
6. Write down the steps to group objects.
7. Define Cell in table.
8. What is paragraph style?
9. Give the shortcut key to insert a word characters as a pair.

C. SHORT QUESTION AND ANSWERS

1. Explain Auto format in MS Word 2016.
2. Write the steps to narrow the list in mail merge
3. Give various options come under Styles and Formatting window.
4. How to modify, crop and delete an image in MS Word 2016.
5. Write a note on creating a template.
6. What do you mean by Hierarchy of heading?
7. Give steps to narrow a list in Mail Merge.
8. Define the term Computer network.
9. How to add data in the fields.

D. LONG QUESTION AND ANSWERS

1. What are the options in Auto format in MS Word?
2. What are the basic steps of sending an e-mail?
3. Briefly explain the various categories of styles in Word 2016.
4. How to create and customize the table of contents.
5. Give advanced concept of mail merge in MS Word 2016.
6. Write down the steps to create a data source in mail merge?
7. Write the steps to add a drawing.
8. How to insert shapes?
9. How to connect e- mail message document to list?

E. APPLICATION BASED QUESTIONS:

1. Jasspreet wants to apply a style to individual words or characters. Which type of style should he use for it.
2. Komal is new to Word processor, tell her various shortcuts in Word processor so that she can complete her tasks in less time.
3. Yogesh is working on making an assignment. The teacher asked him to draw a table of content for the assignment. Tell him the steps to make it efficient.
4. Simran Company wants to use a common template for all their employees. Tell him how he can create a new template in MS Word.
5. Gurutek wants to send an invitation to the school annual function to his co-workers that contain the information of their students who are participating in it. It also contains other information concerning performance timing for practice by their students. Tell Him how he can send a single mail with different information to all of them.

F. GROUP DISCUSSION:

1. Conduct a group discussion on whether to load styles from template or create a new one in Word Processor.

2. Divide class into two parts and tell them to do a group discussion on various steps involved in sending a letter using Mail Merge.
3. Arrange a group discussion on various styles available in Word Processor.

PROJECT WORK

Download and Insert an image of Corona virus from internet then modify it by changing the size that fits in A4 sheet.

Make a poster by inserting various shapes, resize it and add text in it. After that, modify the shape style, outline and shadow effects.

Load a style either from a template or another document and also create a new style using drag and drop.

Download any word file and make a table of contents by defining hierarchy of headings in the document. In the end, apply character styles on it.

Demonstrate to print the label using mail merge by performing the following tasks:

- Create a main document
- Create the data source
- Enter data in the fields
- Merge the data source with main document
- Edit individual document
- Print the letter and address label

TEACHER NOTES:

1. Install or check for MS Word 2010 and 2016 in the system of every students so that they can practically work on it.
2. Practically show class to step by step use of Mail merge for merging the main document with mailing address of various students.

EXAM TIPS:

1. Practically apply various styles of Word processor in a new document to know the difference and how to apply it
2. Send invitation to 2-3 Ids using mail merge in one go to keep the steps of it in mind for long time.
3. Make a new template for your assignment that you can use in your all the subjects.
4. Make a table of content for any of your assignment that help you in keeping all the steps in mind while answering question related to it.

2 Electronic Spreadsheet (Advanced)

Learning Outcomes

After this chapter, you will have the knowledge of:

- Various Styles in Word Processor
- Excel or spreadsheet
- Analyse data using scenarios and goal seek
- Creating subtotals using consolidating data
- Use and goal seek in What if scenarios
- Setting up multiple sheets
- Creating reference to other sheets or document using mouse and keyboard
- Relative and absolute hyperlinks
- Linking to external data and registered data sources
- Setting up a spreadsheet for sharing
- Recording and reviewing changes in a shared spreadsheet
- Add, Edit and Format the comments
- Merging and comparing
- Create and use Macros in spreadsheet
- Accessing cells directly
- Sorting the columns using macro

INTRODUCTION

A worksheet / spreadsheet, is an electronic sheet which is made up of rows and columns. It is mostly used for planning a project or checking the financial position of an organization. Excel 2016 is a popular spreadsheet program, by using which user can design worksheets. It uses a workbook-style presentation made up of several worksheets, like pages in a notebook.

SESSION 1: ANALYSE DATA USING SCENARIOS AND GOAL SEEK

Excel is a spreadsheet program that allows you to store, organize, and analyse information. Excel is only used by certain people to process complicated data, anyone can learn how to take advantage of the program's powerful features.

Spreadsheet application accepts the data values and makes relationships among the data values in a tabular format which consist of rows and columns. Spreadsheet allows user to perform either arithmetic or logical calculations on the values. It also manipulates data in a desired format.

Features:

- It has a grid of columns and rows.
- It can perform mathematical or logical calculations and show the results.
- You can plot graphs also by using this.

1.1 Using consolidating data: Creating subtotals

Excel have feature through which user can merge and summarize the values from multiple worksheets. It is a good tool for combining data taken from various users work with different instances of the same file. User can also use it for quickly summarizing the data in a single sheet without sorting the data by:

- The values you're summarizing by must be to the left of the values you're summarizing.

- The data range must have headings for each column.
- You must assign a range name to the columns you're summarizing.

Example: Let take a simple range of data for illustrating the consolidate feature. In this we will find the subtotal for each date but the data must meets the first two conditions given above.

	A	B	C	D
1	Date	Region	Item	Sold
2	11/7/2011	Owenton	A203	33
3	11/7/2011	Lexington	B603	15
4	11/8/2011	Lexington	A203	19
5	11/9/2011	Paris	C214	26
6	11/11/2011	Frankfort	C214	87
7	11/11/2011	Louisville	B603	73
8	11/11/2011	Lexington	B603	5
9	11/12/2011	London	A204	12
10	11/12/2011	Frankfort	A203	75
11	11/13/2011	Lexington	A203	25
12	11/13/2011	London	A203	7
13	11/14/2011	Frankfort	C214	82

Figure 2.1: Excel Sheet

Now, user has to only name the range of data in setup task using favourite technique given below:

- Click anywhere inside the data range and press [Ctrl]+[Shift]+8.
- With the data range selected, enter CByDate (consolidate by date) in the Name Box - that›s the small control above the top-left corner of the sheet and to the left of the Formula Bar (circled above).
- Press Enter.

Now user can use the consolidate feature for subtotal the sold values by date using following steps:

- Position the cursor in the top-left corner of the subtotal range as here the subtotal will be display by consolidate Then select A1 in another sheet which name is ByDate or user can also select any other area of the same sheet.
- Click on Data tab > Consolidate in the Data Tools group. User can select the Consolidate from the Tools menu.
- In the opened dialog box, user can choose several functions by clicking on Function dropdown. Here, our task is to sum the sold values.
- In Reference control, enter CByDate. In case of having any other references in the All References list, Delete them.
- Click on Ok button and Excel will display a summarized version of data in which one row is for each

date and total of sold values for the date.

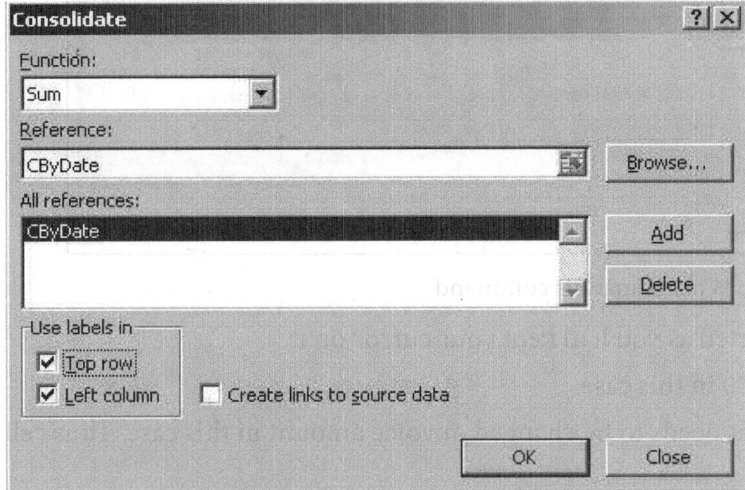

Figure 2.2: Consolidate pop-up window

	A	B	C	D	E
1		Region	Item	Sold	
2	11/7/2011			48	
3	11/8/2011			19	
4	11/9/2011			26	
5	11/11/2011			165	
6	11/12/2011			87	
7	11/13/2011			32	
8	11/14/2011			82	
9					

Figure 2.3: Selected range of data

1.2 Using "what if" scenarios. Using "what if" tools

In Excel, the What-If Analysis tools can be used for several different sets of values in one or more formulas for exploring all the results. For instance, User can do What-If Analysis for building two budgets in which each assumes a certain level of revenue. User can also specify a result that user want a formula to produce and then determine what sets of values will be produced by result. Several different tools are provided by Excel that help in performing the type of analysis that fits the needs of user.

Various parts of What-if analysis in Excel:

- Goal Seek for reverse calculation
- Data Table for Sensitivity analysis
- Scenario Manager for comparison of scenarios

1.3 Goal Seek in What if analysis

Here, we have considered a simple dataset in which the invoice amount is Rs. 10,000 on which there is 9% CGST and 9% SGST that in turn amounts to a total of Rs. 11,800.

	A	B
1	**Invoice Amount**	**10,000**
2	CGST	9%
3	SGST	9%
4	**Total**	**11800**

Figure 2.4: What if analysis

Let, customer have asked to get a discount of Rs. 800 and this shows that the final amount should be Rs. 11,000

Now, the equation in simple terms is, X + 18% = 11000, where X is the invoice amount, 18% is the total GST.

To find out, how much + 18% = 11000, we will use Goal Seek in What if analysis.

- Place your cursor on the 'Total' cell
- Under the 'Data' tab, click on 'What-If-Analysis', then on 'Goal Seek'

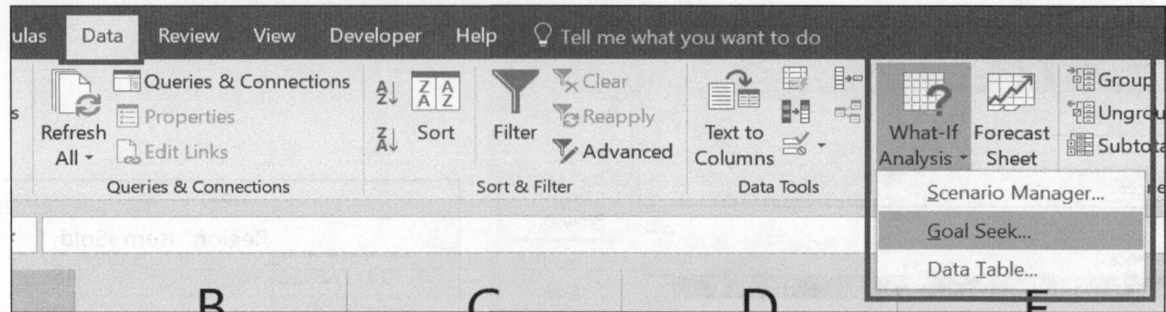

Figure 2.5: What if analysis command

- In 'Set Cell', B4 will automatically be selected as you had kept your cursor on it.
- In 'To value', enter the desired value, 11000 in this case.
- In 'By changing cell', choose the value that needs to be changed, invoice amount in this case. Thus cell B1 is selected.
- Press Ok

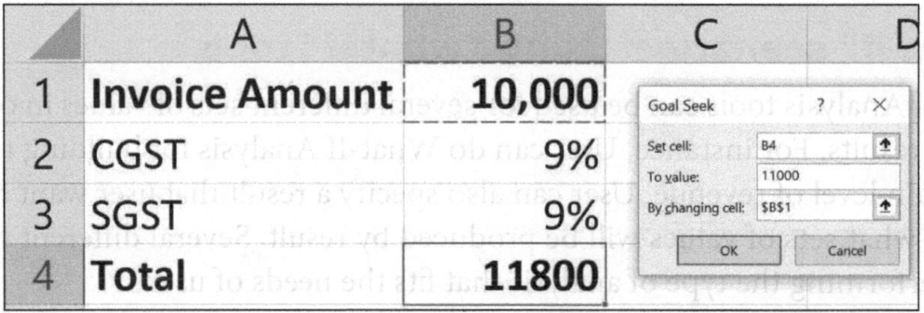

Figure 2.6: Goal Seek pop-up

The calculate will be reverse by Excel and immediately give the value of Rs. 9,322 in which +18% is equals to exactly Rs. 11,000.

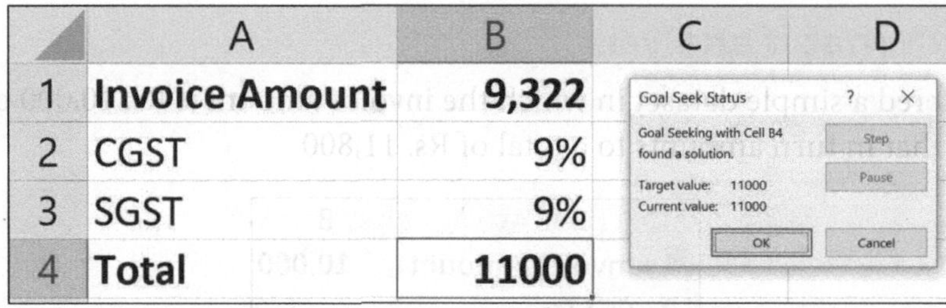

Figure 2.7: Changes in the Excel

This was a simple example of using Goal Seek in What-If analysis. The Goal Seek can be used for more complex models.

Summary

- A worksheet / spreadsheet, is an electronic sheet which is made up of rows and columns.
- Excel is a spreadsheet program that allows you to store, organize, and analyze information.
- Spreadsheet application accepts the data values and makes relationships among the data values in a tabular format which consist of rows and columns.
- Excel have feature through which user can merge and summarize the values from multiple worksheets.

- In Excel, the What-If Analysis tools can be used for several different sets of values in one or more formulas for exploring all the results.

Keywords: Spreadsheet, Creating subtotals, Consolidating data, What if scenarios, Goal Seek

Self-Assessment

A. MULTIPLE CHOICE QUESTIONS

1. Spreadsheet program allows you to:
   a. Store information
   b. organize information
   c. analyze information
   d. all of these
2. Which of the following is main requirement of summarizing the data in a single sheet without sorting the data?
   a. The values you're summarizing by must be to the left of the values you're summarizing.
   b. The data range must have headings for each column.
   c. You must assign a range name to the columns you're summarizing.
   d. All of these
3. Which of the following is not a part of What-if analysis in Excel?
   a. Data Table for sensitivity analysis
   b. Goal seek for forward calculation
   c. Scenario manager for comparison of scenarios
   d. Goal seek for reverse calculation

B. FILL IN THE BLANKS

1. Table consists of ____________ and ____________.
2. The values summarized in Excel must be to the ____________ of the values users are summarizing.

C. TRUE FALSE

1. Using Excel, One can merge and summarize the values from multiple worksheets (T/F)
2. In Excel, the What-If Analysis tools can be used for several different sets of values in only one formulas for exploring all the results (T/F)

D. ANSWER THE FOLLOWING QUESTIONS:

1. Give various features of spreadsheet?
2. How to create subtotals in Excel spreadsheet using consolidating data?
3. Give the usage of What if scenarios in Excel.

E. PRACTICAL WORK

Take any complex dataset with any invoice amount and apply 12% CGST and 13%SGST on it with discount of 400. Then use goal seek in What if analysis and calculate the invoice amount.

Answers

A. Multiple choice question answers:

1. d   2. d   3. b

B. Fill in the blanks answers:

   1. Row, Column   2. Left

C. True False answers

   1. True   2. False

SESSION 2: LINK DATA AND SPREADSHEETS

The copying and pasting data from one workbook to another is a quick and easy way of gathering related data in single place but it has some limitations that come when:

- The data from the original cell changes
- The change is not reflected in the cell to which it was copied

Or it can be said that copying and pasting a contents of cell's does not create a relation between original and target cell.

2.1 Setting up multiple sheets

In every workbook, there is at least one worksheet in default. When working with a large amount of data then user can create multiple worksheets that help in organising the workbook and make it easier for finding the content. Worksheets can be group for quick addition of information to multiple worksheets at the same time.

View Multiple Worksheets:

If user wants to view multiple Excel worksheets at the same time then user must have to execute the following steps:

- Open a Workbook
- Click on New Window from View tab in Window group

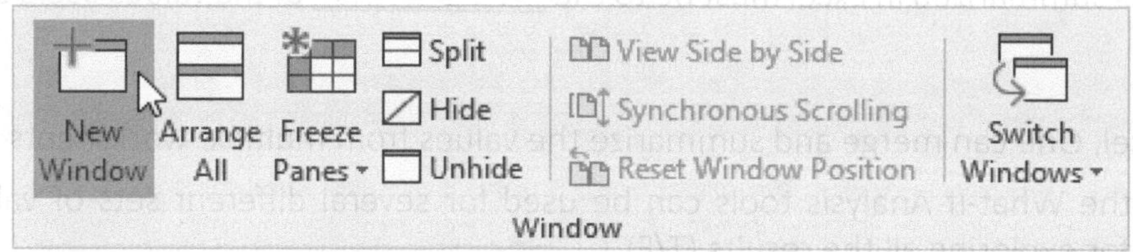

Figure 2.8: New Window Command

A new window will be pens in Excel that contain another view of the document.

- Click on Arrange All from View tab in Window group

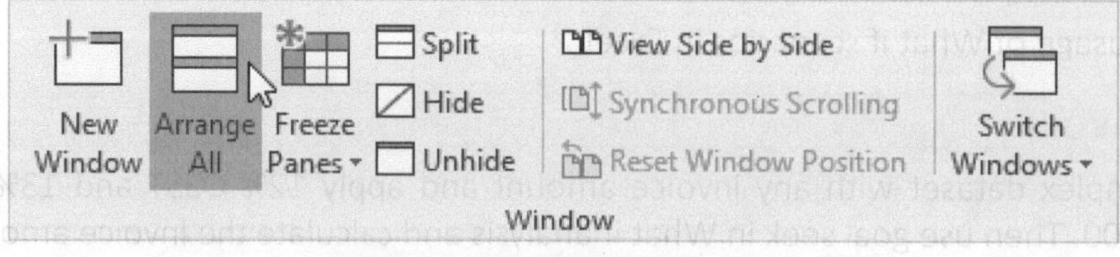

Figure 2.9: Arrange All command

✦ Select the desired arrange setting. For example, click Horizontal.

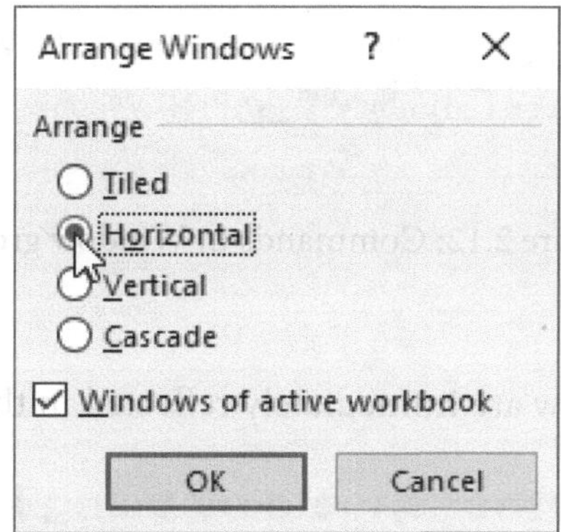

Figure 2.10: Arrange Windows pop-up

✦ Click OK button

The titles view multiple-worksheets:1 and view-multiple-worksheets:2 indicate that two windows of the same file are open.

The titles (view-multiple-worksheets:1 and view-multiple-worksheets:2) indicate that two windows of the same file are open.

✦ In the lower window, select the sheet tab of Wk2. You can now view the sales in week 1 and week 2 at the same time.

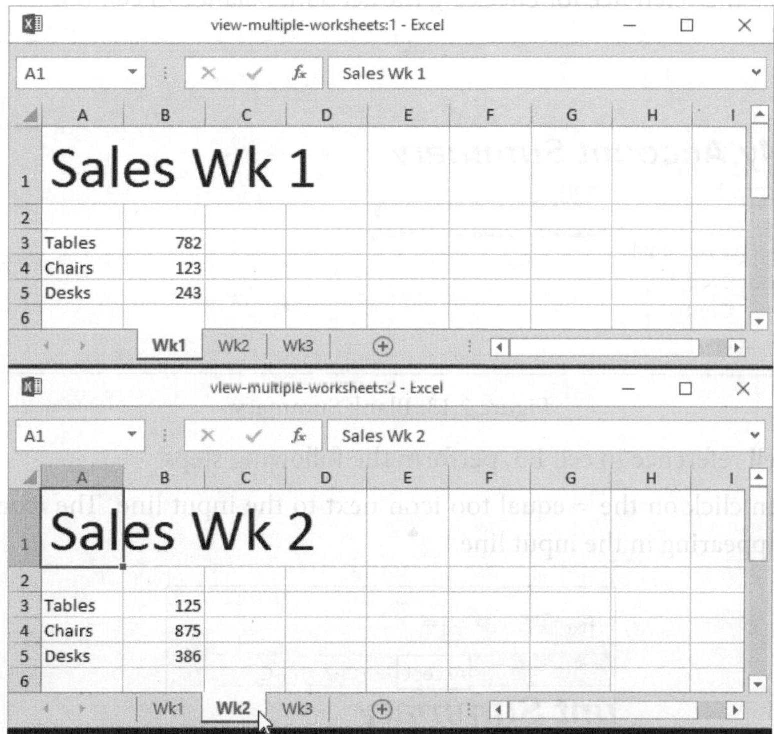

Figure 2.11: Data enter in two different worksheets

✦ Click on View Side by Side from View tab in the Window group for scrolling both worksheets at the same time. By default the Synchronous Scrolling is activated.

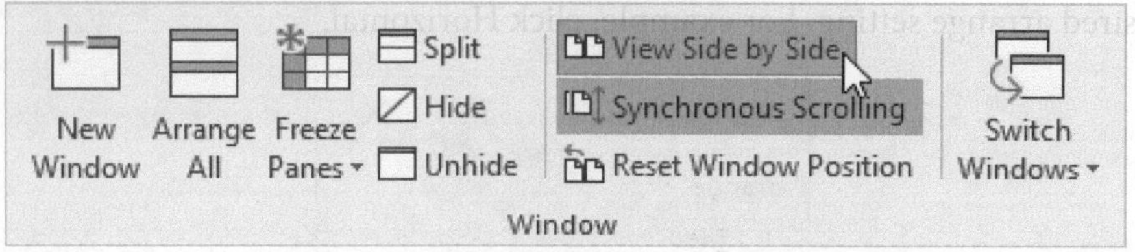

Figure 2.12: Commands in Window group

Point to remember:

Any changes you make to one window are immediately reflected in the other window.

2.2 Creating reference to other sheets by using keyboard and mouse

The balance from each of the other sheets is display on the Summary sheet. If users copy the outcomes onto each account then the current balances will be in cell F3 of each sheet.

The cells can be reference in other sheets using two ways:

- By entering formula using keyboard
- By entering formula using Mouse

By entering formula using Mouse: To use this approach, perform the following steps:

- On the Summary sheet, set up a place for all five accounts balances so that user will get to know where to put the cell reference. The Summary sheet with a blank Balance column is shown in below figure. User wants to place the reference for checking the account balance in cell B3.

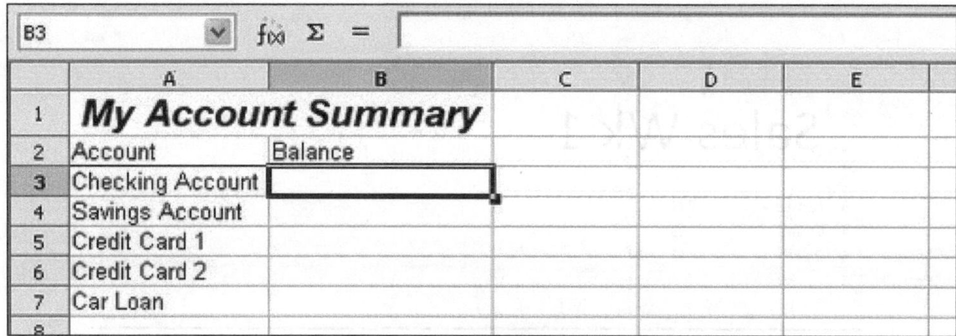

Figure 2.13: Blank Summary

- For making the cell reference in cell B3, perform the following steps:
- Select the cell then click on the = equal too icon next to the input line. The icons get change and an equals sign start appearing in the input line.

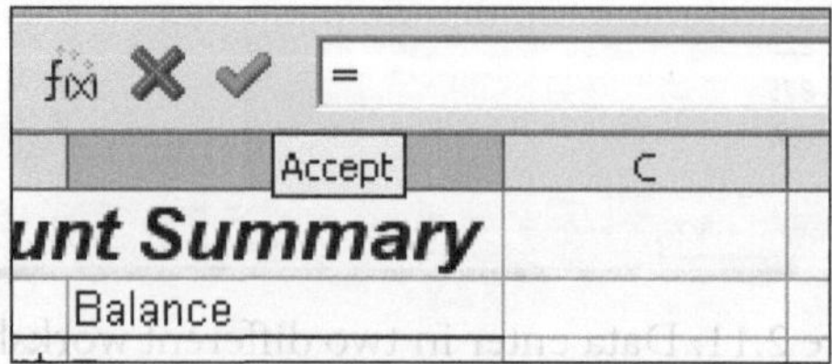

Figure 2.14: Equal Sign in input line

- After that, click on the sheet tab for the sheet consists of cell to be referenced. In our case, it is Checking Account sheet as shown in below figure.

Figure 2.15: Click on the checking account tab

- Click on cell F3 in the Checking Account sheet or any other cell if user want to see the balance in another cell.

SUM =Checking Account'.F3

	A	B	C	D	E	F
1	**Checking Account**					
2	Description	Amount	Balance			
3	Opening Balance	$75.00	$75.00		Total Balance	$380.05
4	Pay	$425.00	$500.00			
5	Groceries	-$75.00	$425.00			
6	Cable Bill	-$44.95	$380.05			
7						

Figure 2.16: Selected Call reference

- To finish, Click on green checkmark in the input line and Summary sheet will look like as shown in below figure.

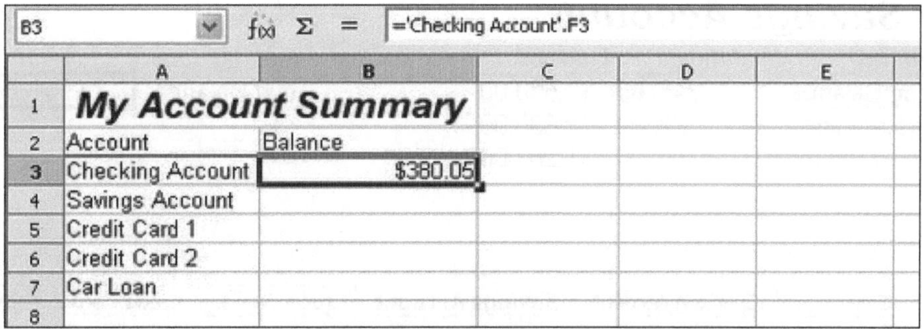

Figure 2.17: Finished checking account reference

By entering formula using Mouse: To use this approach, perform the following steps:

User can deduce how the cell reference is constructed. The reference has two parts one is sheet name that is Checking Account and other is cell reference F3. Note that they are separated by a period.

User can also fill in the Saving Account cell reference by typing it. Let assue that the balance is in the same cell in the Saving Account sheet, F3 then the cell reference will be ='Savings Account'.F3.

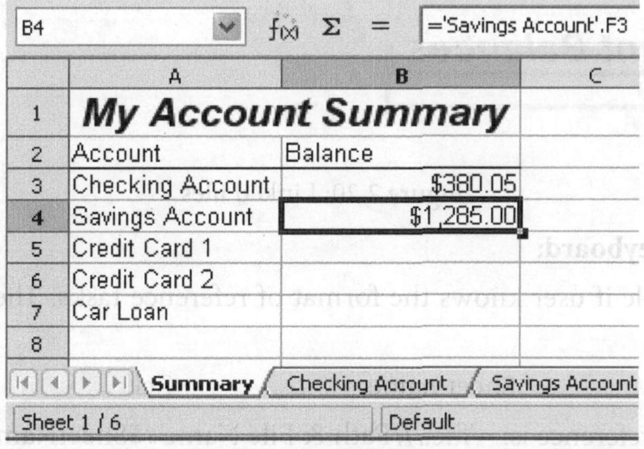

Figure 2.18: Summary of Account

Knowledge Box

The sheet name is in single quotes because it contains a space, and the mandatory period (.) always falls outside any quotes.

2.3 Creating reference to other document by using keyboard and mouse

There can be case when user want to keep their family account information in separate spreadsheet file from his own summary. In Excel, there is a feature of linking different files together. The process for this is same as used for different sheets in a single spreadsheet except some more parameter will be added to indicate which file the sheet is in.

Create the reference using Mouse: To create a reference using mouse, both spreadsheets must be open. Then select the cell in which the formula is going to be entered. Then, perform the following steps:

- Click on = icon next to the input line
- Switch to other spreadsheet > Select the sheet Savings account and then the reference cell F3

F3 | =C3+SUM(B4:B46)

	A	B	C	D	E	F
1	Savings Account					
2	Description	Amount	Balance			
3	Opening Balance	$2,500.00	$2,500.00		Total Balance	$1,285.00
4	Savings Account	$35.00	$2,535.00			
5	Car Down Payment	-$1,250.00	$1,285.00			
6						
7						
8						

Summary / Checking Account / Savings Account / Credit Card 1 / Credit Card 2 / Car Loan

Figure 2.19: Selecting the savings account reference cell

- Switch back to the original spreadsheet
- Click on the green check mark on the input line and spreadsheet will be open that look like something as shown in below figure.

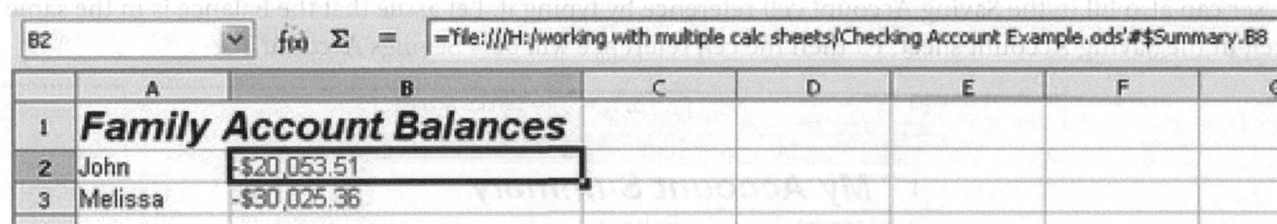

Figure 2.20: Linked files

Create a reference using keyboard:

Typing of reference is simple if user knows the format of reference tasks. The reference consists of three parts:

- Path and file name
- Sheet name
- Cell

The general format for the reference is: ='file:///Path & File Name'#$SheetName.CellName.

2.4 Relative and absolute hyperlinks

Hyperlink is a colored and underlined text or a colored and underlined graphic that user click to open any of the items given below:

- A file
- A location in a file
- A Web page on the Web
- A Web page on an intranet
- A Gopher, Telnet, or File Transfer Protocol (FTP) site

User can also click on hyperlink for viewing the newsgroups.

- Absolute hyperlink: It is a hyperlink that consists of full address of the destination file or of the Web site. For instance: http://www.microsoft.com/support
- Relative hyperlink: It is a hyperlink that consists of address that is relative to the destination file address. The hyperlink base is the address of the destination file. For instance: a document has the following hyperlink base:

  C:\Documents and Settings**Username**\My Documents

  A document that is named "Sales.doc" is located at the following file path:

  C:\Documents and Settings**Username**\My Documents\April\Sales.doc

  The relative hyperlink to this document consists of only relative address to Sales.doc. Therefore, the relative hyperlink consists of following address: April\Sales.doc

2.6 Linking to external data

User can insert tables from HTML documents and data located within named ranges from an Open Office.org Microsoft Excel Spreadsheet into a spreadsheet.

This can be done in two ways:

- Using the External Data dialog
- Using the Navigator

In case the file has named ranges or tables and user know the name of the range or table that they want to link with then use of External Data dialog is a quickest and easiest way. But, if there are number of tables in a file and user want to pick one from it then user will not be able to easily determine the exact one in these cases the use of Navigator method will be easier.

Using the External Data dialog:

- Open the Microsoft Sheet where the external data is to be inserted
- Select the cell where the upper left-hand cell of the external data is to be inserted
- Click on Insert > Link to External Data and external data dialog will appear
- Type the URL of the source document or click the [....] button for opening a file selecting dialog. Press Enter to get Excel to load the available tables list.
- In the Available tables/range list, select the named ranges or tables you want to insert. You can also specify that the ranges or tables are updated every (number of) seconds.
- Clock on Ok button to close the dialog and inserting the linked data

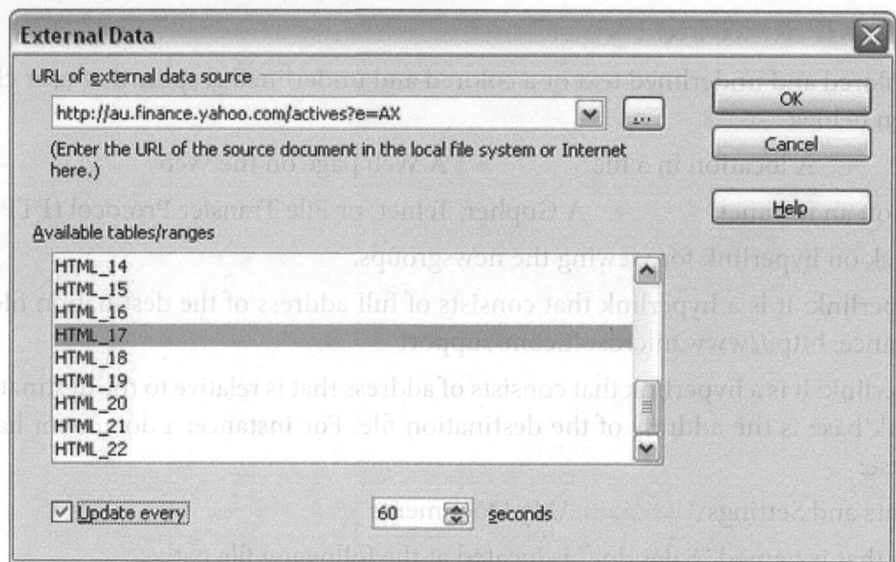

Figure 2.21: Selecting a table or range in a source document from the Web

Points to remember:

- The OK button remains unavailable (grayed out) until you select one or more tables/ranges in the list. You can hold down the Ctrl key while clicking on tables/ranges to select more than one.
- No images are imported
- The Available tables/ranges list remains empty until you press Enter after selecting the URL of the source. If you select the source document using the [...] button, then pressing Enter is not required.

Using the Navigator:

- Open the spreadsheet in which the external data is to be inserted
- Open the document from which the external data is to be taken. Choose the Web Page Quesry in case if source document is a Web page

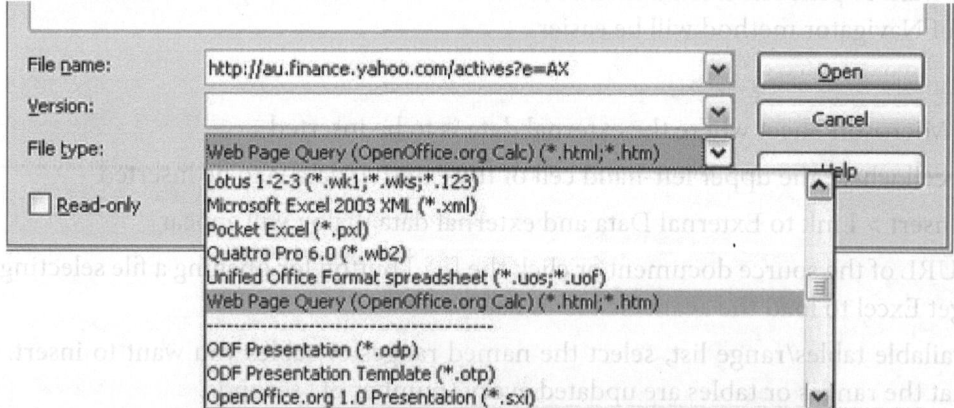

Figure 2.22: Opening a file using the Web Page Query filter

- Press F5 to open the Navigator in target document
- Select the source document in the bottom of the Navigator. The range of names or the tables containing in the source document are start showing in the Navigator.

- Click on the + next to Range names for displaying the list.
- In the Navigator, select the Insert as Link drag mode

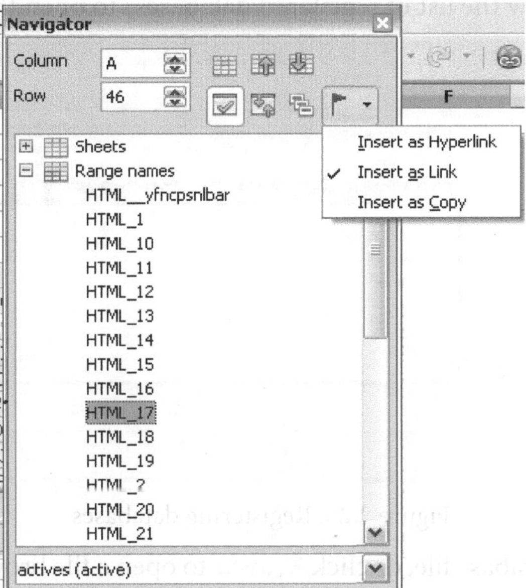

Figure 2.23: Selecting a data range in a source document, to be inserted as a link

- Select the required range or table and drag it from the Navigator into the target document, to the cell where you want the upper left-hand cell of the data range to be.
- In the target document, check the Navigator. Instead of a + by Range names, it shows a + by Linked areas. Click the + to see the same range name.

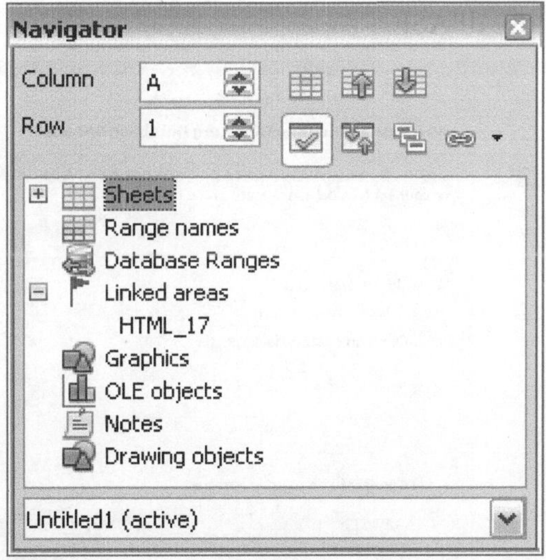

Figure 2.24: Linked areas in target spreadsheet

2.7 Linking to registered data sources

Variety of databases and other sources can be access and linked into Excel documents. Firstly there is need to find the data source with OpenOffice.org. There are various ways based on whether the data source is a database or in *.odb format.

For registering a data source that is in *.odb format, perform the following steps:

- Choose Tools > Options > OpenOffice.org Base > Databases.
- Click the New button (below the list of registered databases) to open the Create Database Link dialog.

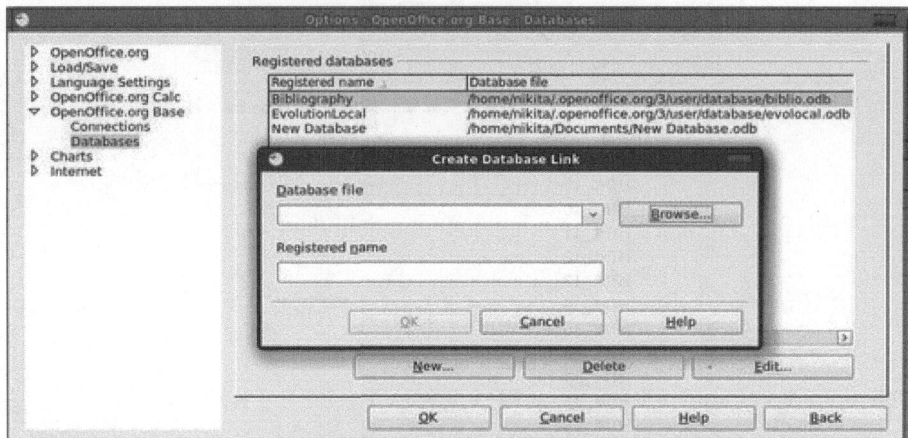

Figure 2.25: Registering databases

- Enter the location of the database file, or click **Browse** to open a file browser and select the database file.
- Type a name to use as the registered name for the database and click **OK**. The database is added to the list of registered databases. The **OK** button is enabled only when both fields are filled in.

For registering a data source that is in *.odb format, perform the following steps:

- Choose File > New > Database to open the Database Wizard.
- Select Connect to an existing database. The choices for database type depend on your operating system. For example, Microsoft Access and other Microsoft products are not among the choices if you are using Linux. In our example, we chose dBASE.

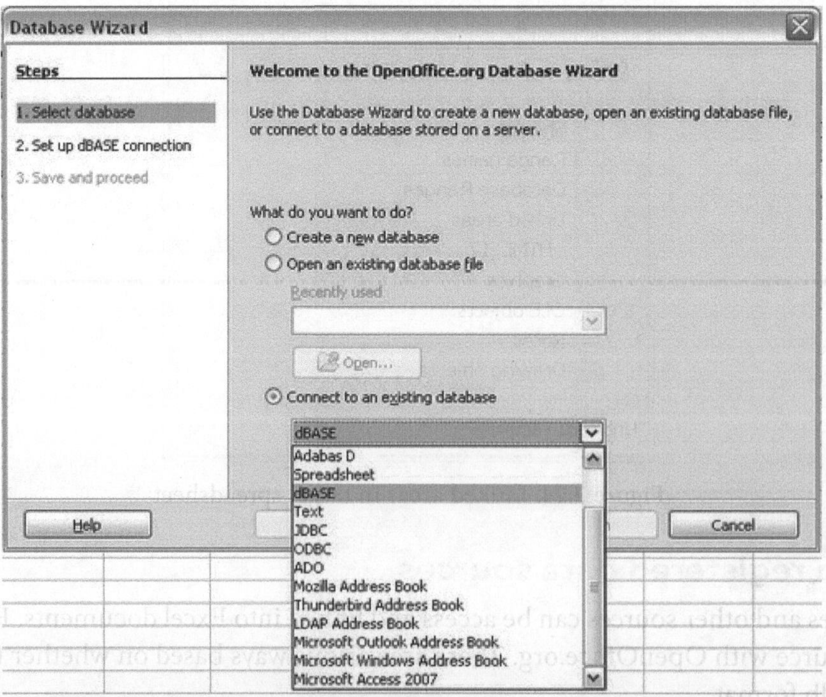

Figure 2.26: Registering a database using the Database Wizard

- Click on Next > Type the path to the database file or click Browse and use the Open dialog to navigate to and select the database file before clicking Open.
- Click Next > Select Yes, register the database for me, but clear the checkbox marked Open the database for editing.
- Click Finish > Name and save the database in the location of your choice.

Knowledge Box

changes made to the *.odb do not affect the original dBASE file.

Summary

- The copying and pasting data from one workbook to another is a quick and easy way of gathering related data in single place.
- In every workbook, there is at least one worksheet in default. When working with a large amount of data then user can create multiple worksheets that help in organising the workbook and make it easier for finding the content.
- If user wants to view multiple Excel worksheets at the same time then user must have to execute the following steps, Open a Workbook, Click on New Window from View tab in Window group.
- The balance from each of the other sheets is display on the Summary sheet. If users copy the outcomes onto each account then the current balances will be in cell F3 of each sheet.
- The cells can be reference in other sheets either by entering formula using keyboard or Entering formula using Mouse.
- User can deduce how the cell reference is constructed. The reference has two parts one is sheet name that is Checking Account and other is cell reference.
- In Excel, there is a feature if linking different files together.
- Hyperlink is a colored and underlined text or a colored and underlined graphic that user click to open any items that can be file, Web Page on the Web, Web page on an intranet and Gopher, Telnet or File Transfer Protocol Site.
- User can insert tables from HTML documents and data located within named ranges from an Open Office.org Microsoft Excel Spreadsheet into a spreadsheet.
- In case the file has named ranges or tables and user know the name of the range or table that they want to link with then use of External Data dialog is a quickest and easiest way.
- Variety of databases and other sources can be access and linked into Excel documents.

Keywords: Linking data, copying data, pasting data, entering formula, Creating reference, Relative hyperlinks, Absolute hyperlinks, External data, Navigator, Registered data sources

Self-Assessment

A. MULTIPLE CHOICE QUESTIONS.

1. Which of the following is not a part of reference?
   a. Sheet name   b. Cell   c. Row number   d. Path and file name
2. Which contains multiple tabs:
   a. Workbook   b. Ribbon   c. Worksheet   d. Template

3. Which of the following way cannot be used by user for linking sheet to external data?

    a. Navigator   b. Mouse   c. External data dialog   d. None of the above

B. FILL IN THE BLANKS

1. In every workbook, there is at least ____________ worksheet in default.
2. To create reference using, both spreadsheets must be ____________.
3. The format of reference of the sheet contains three parts: Path and file name, ____________ and Cell.
4. ____________ is a hyperlink that consists of full address of the destination file or of the Web site.
5. ____________ is used for using data using multiple sheets.

C. TRUE FALSE

1. The sheet name for entering formula using cell reference to other sheets must be in double quotes (T/F)
2. In Excel, user can link different worksheet, workbook or files together (T/F)
3. 'C:\Documents and Settings\Username\My Documents' the link given in single quotes is a relative hyperlink.

D. ANSWER THE FOLLOWING QUESTIONS:

1. Write down the steps to create reference to other sheets using mouse?
2. How to select multiple Worksheets?
3. Is it possible to create reference to other document? If yes, then give various ways of create it.

E. PRACTICAL WORK

Enter data across various workbooks and link any particular cells from that workbook so that they all start appearing in a single worksheet and get updated by doing change in it.

Create a HTML document and save it in your system. Then, Link the data of HTML into Excel spreadsheet using Navigator.

Answers

A. Multiple choice question answers:

    1. c   2. b   3. b

B. Fill in the blanks answers:

    1. One   2. Open   3. Sheet name   4. Absolute   5. Linking

C. True False answers

    1. False   2. True   3. True

SESSION 3: SHARE AND REVIEW A SPREADSHEET

User can share a workbook in Excel 2016 and can work on those file with other people on the same workbook at the same time. The workbook should be saved to a network location where other people can open it. User can also keep track of the changes done by other people while making, accepting and rejecting those changes.

3.1 Setting up a spreadsheet for sharing

Spreadsheets are an essential of an office and used for organising the data and making reports. There is need of sharing spreadsheet reports of your managers and team then it can be done using standard Microsoft Excel or Internet based spreadsheet program. In most of the spreadsheet programs there is built in feature that help in creating a spreadsheet for use by many people as long as user are using a shared server or have an Internet connection.

To share an Excel file 2016, perform the following steps:

- Open the Review tab in Changes group then click on Share Workbook button and Share Workbook dialog box will open

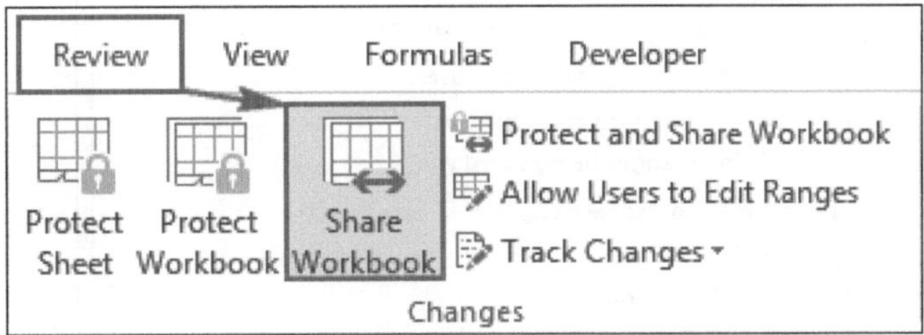

Figure 2.27: Commands in Changes group of Review Tab

- Select the Allow changes by more than one user at the same time. This allow workbook merging check box on the Editing tab

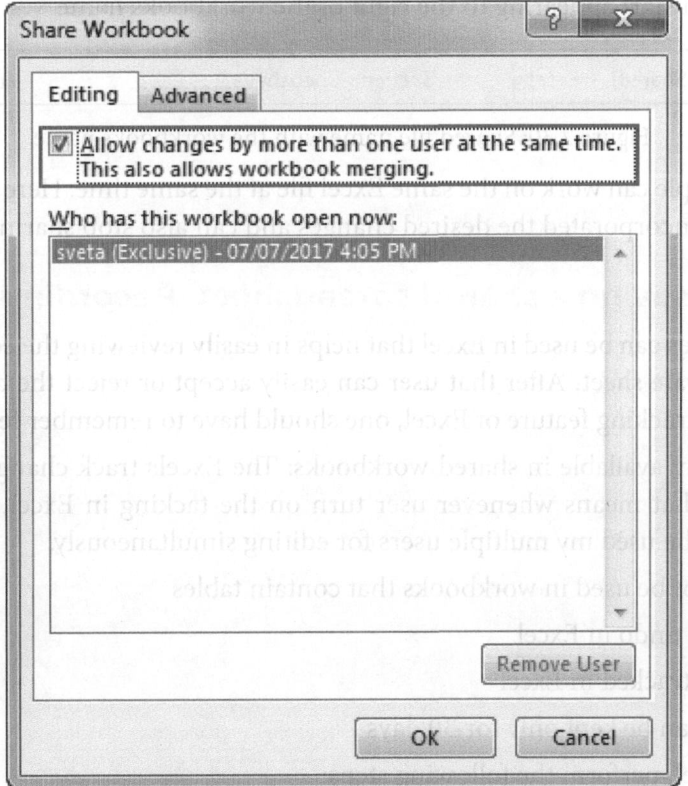

Figure 2.28: Share Workbook Window

✦ Switch to the Advanced tab > Select the desired settings for tracking changes and click on Ok button

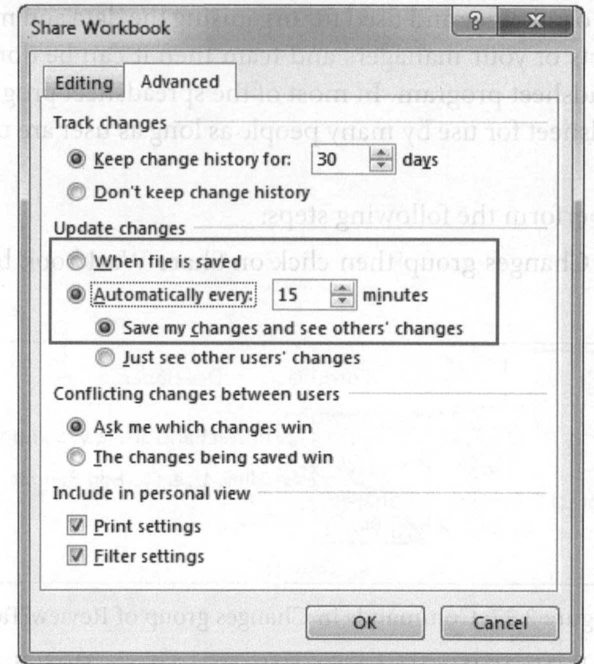

Figure 2.29: Advanced tab of Share Workbook Window

✦ Save Excel file to a network location where other people can access it or Press Ctrl + S

✦ The word shared will start appearing to the right of the workbooks name

Figure 2.30: Shared file name with the workbooks name

Now more than two people can work on the same Excel file at the same time. Here, user can accept or reject their changes and after incorporated the desired changes and can also stop sharing the workbook.

3.2 Opening and saving a shared spreadsheet. Recording changes

The built-in track changes can be used in Excel that helps in easily reviewing the edits directly in the edited worksheet or on a separate sheet. After that user can easily accept or reject the changes individually and at a time. For using the tracking feature of Excel, one should have to remember few points as given below:

✦ Track changes is only available in shared workbooks: The Excels track changes works only appear in shared workbooks that means whenever user turn on the tacking in Excel, the workbook becomes shared or can it can be used my multiple users for editing simultaneously.

✦ Track changes cannot be used in workbooks that contain tables

✦ The changes can't be undo in Excel

✦ All changes can't be tracked in Excel

✦ History of changes can be kept only for 30 days

To track changes in Excel, perform the following steps:

✦ In Change group Review tab click on Track Changes button > Select Highlight changes

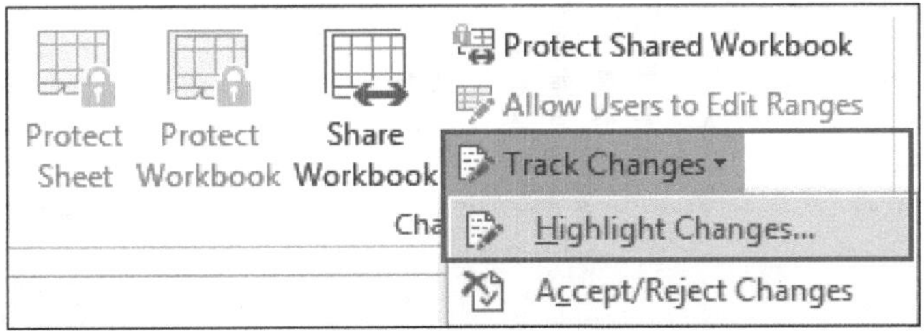

Figure 2.31: Highlight Changes command

- In Highlight Changes dialog box, Check the Track changes while editing
- Select the desired period of time in the When box under Highlight and Who box which changes
- Select the Highlight changes on screen option
- Click Ok button

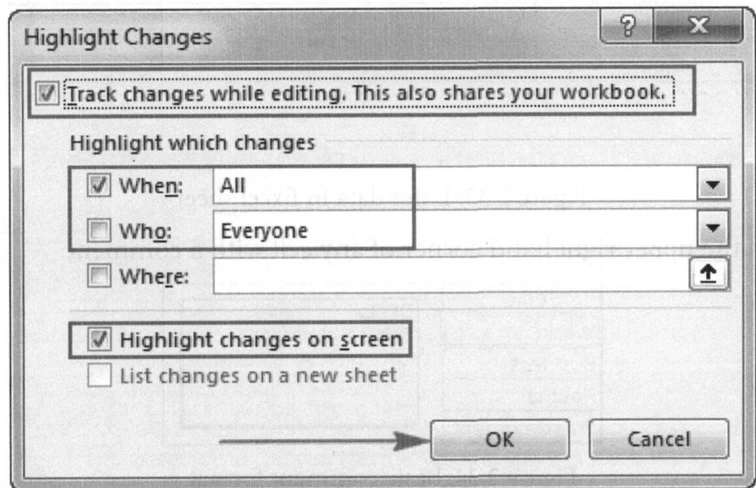

Figure 2.32: Highlight Changes Window

Now the edits done by different users are highlighted in Excel

If prompted, allow Excel to save your workbook, and you are done!

Point to remember:

If you are enabling Excel Track Changes in a shared workbook (which is indicated by the word [Shared] appended to the workbook name), the *List changes on a new sheet* will also be available. You can select this box too to view full details about each change on a separate sheet.

3.3 Add, Edit and Format the comments

In Excel, user can add a comment to any cell that could be a note to user or a reminder, correction or question of anything that is useful. The use of Excel comments are useful for workbooks for sharing information and collaborating on projects. To add a basic comment, perform the following steps:

- Right click on the cell user want to comment on
- Select comment on the menu
- Enter the comment in the comment box and comment will become a part of the cell

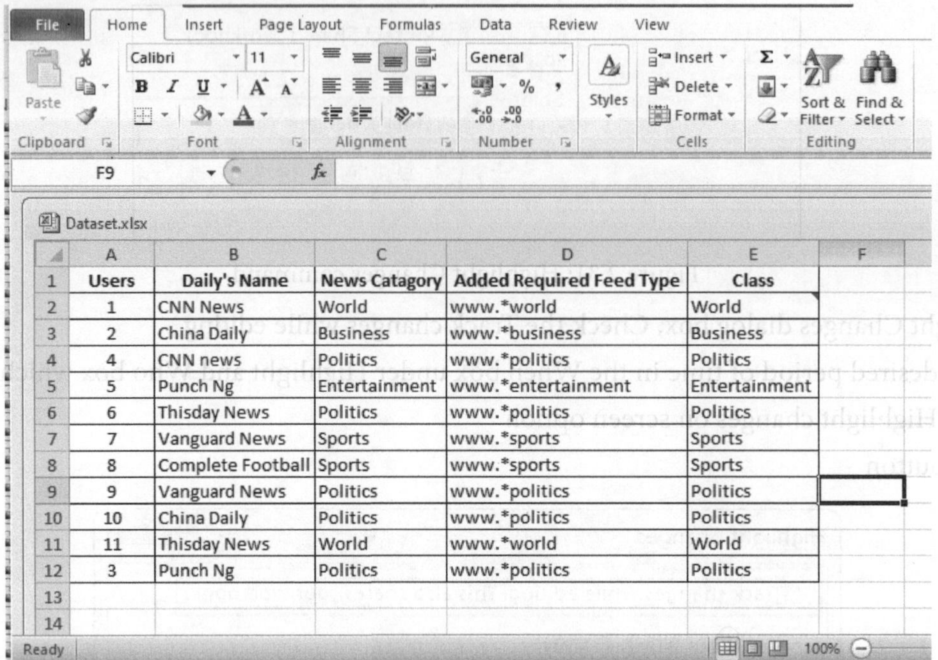

	A	B	C	D	E
1	Users	Daily's Name	News Catagory	Added Required Feed Type	Class
2	1	CNN News	World	www.*world	World
3	2	China Daily	Business	www.*business	Business
4	4	CNN news	Politics	www.*politics	Politics
5	5	Punch Ng	Entertainment	www.*entertainment	Entertainment
6	6	Thisday News	Politics	www.*politics	Politics
7	7	Vanguard News	Sports	www.*sports	Sports
8	8	Complete Football	Sports	www.*sports	Sports
9	9	Vanguard News	Politics	www.*politics	Politics
10	10	China Daily	Politics	www.*politics	Politics
11	11	Thisday News	World	www.*world	World
12	3	Punch Ng	Politics	www.*politics	Politics

Figure 2.33: Enter data in Excel sheet

There is red triangle in the upper right hand corner of any cell with a comment

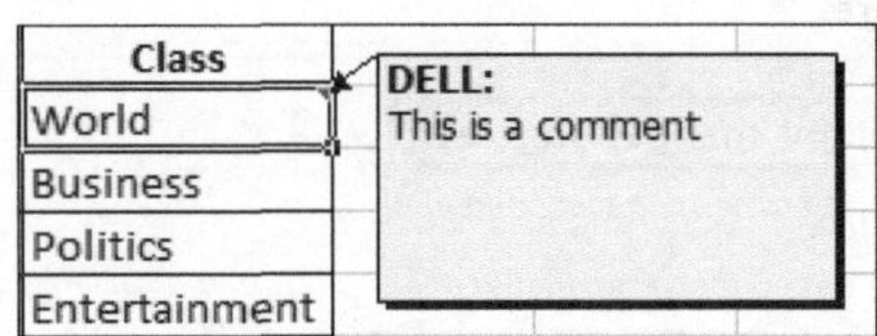

Figure 2.34: basic comment format

Formatting Comments

In Excel, user can also format the comment from its default format. To open editing for comment, perform the following steps:

- Either create a new comment or click on Edit Comment in the menu
- Once the comment box is open, right click on outer edge of the box
- Select Format Comment

Once you've open the format comment dialogue box, you have several options:

From there, you can make whatever changes you see fit

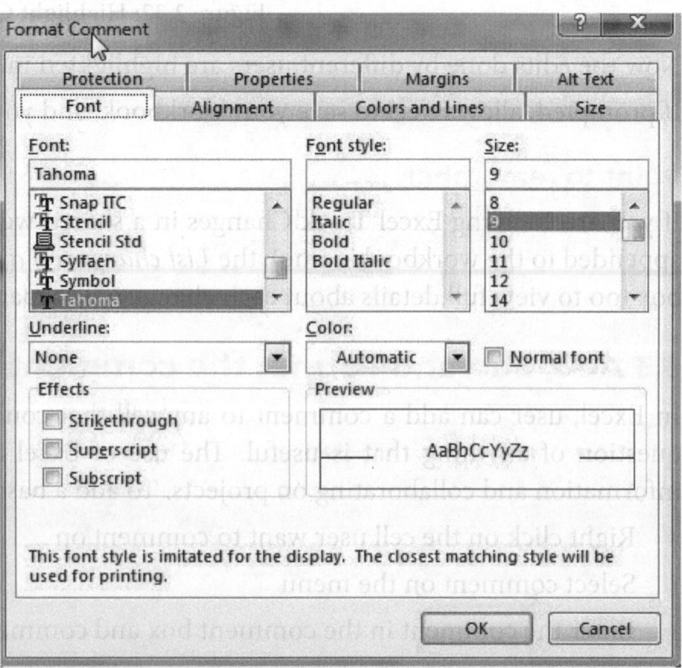

Figure 2.35: Format Comment window

3.4 Reviewing changes: accept or reject changes

To accept or reject the changes made by various users, perform the following steps:

- Go to the Review tab in Changes group > Click on Track Changes > Accept/Reject Changes

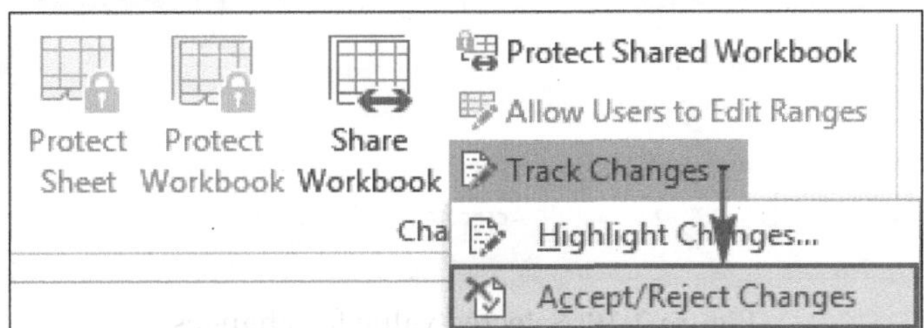

Figure 2.36: Accept/Reject Changes command

In open dialog box of Select Changes, configure the following options > Click on Ok button

- Then, choose either Not yet reviewed or Since date in the When list
- Then, select the user whose changes user want to review in the Who list
- Clear the Where box

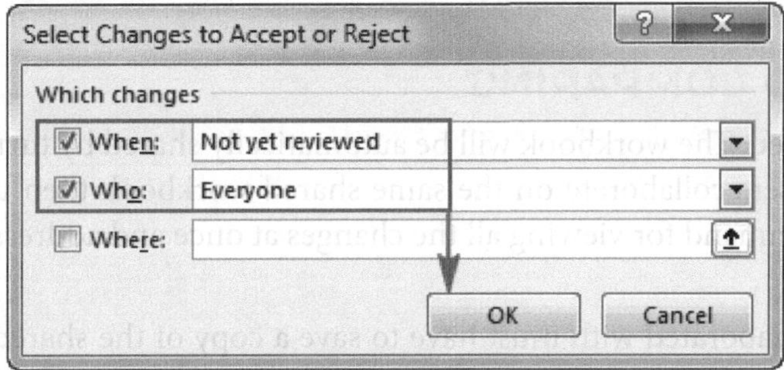

Figure 2.37: Select Changes to Accept or Reject window

Now the changes will start appearing in Excel one by one and user can click Accept or Reject to keep or cancel those changes.

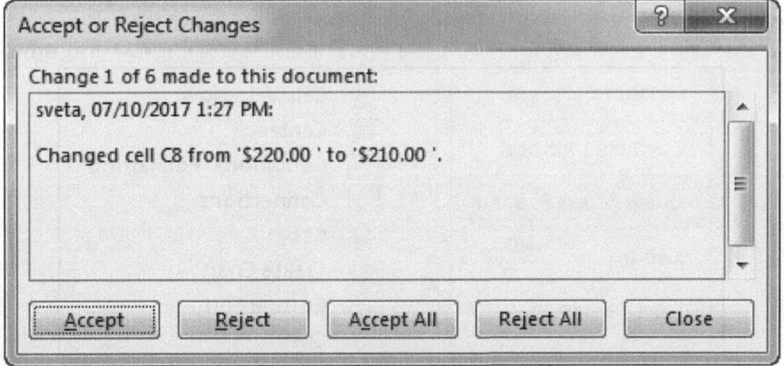

Figure 2.38: Accept or Reject Changes window

- If more than one edits were made to a given cell then user will be asked for which of the changes they want to keep:

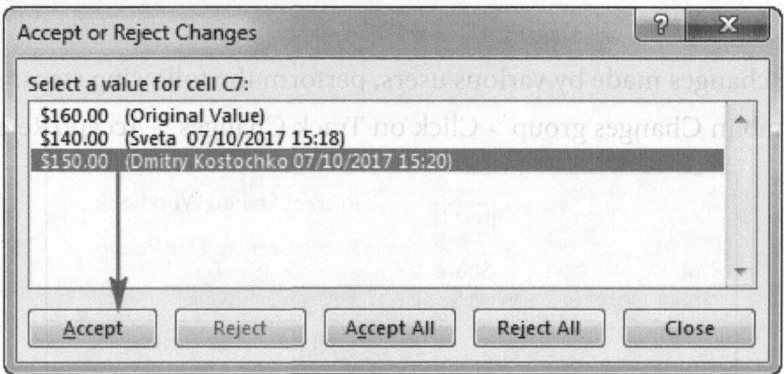

Figure 2.39: Selected value for changes

- User can also click on Accept All or Reject All for approving or cancelling all the changes in one go.

MEMORY BOX

Even after accepting or rejecting the tracked changes, they will still be highlighted in your workbook. To remove them completely, turn off Track Changes in Excel.

3.5 MERGING AND COMPARING

Shared books can be merged. The workbook will be automatically shared by turning on the Track changes feature. When multiple users collaborate on the same shared workbook then user can use the Compare and Merge workbooks command for viewing all the changes at once and address them by either accepting or rejecting it.

Each person who have collaborated with must have to save a copy of the shared workbook by unique file name that is different from the original. To add the Compare and Merge workbooks command in quick access toolbar, perform the following steps:

- Click on File tab
- Choose options and Excel options dialog box will start appearing
- Select Quick Access toolbar

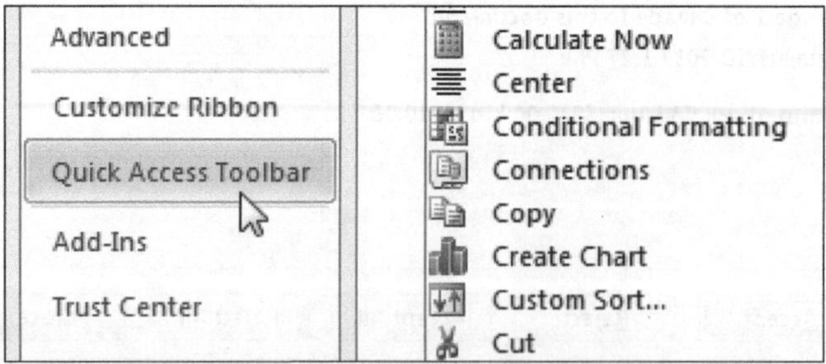

Figure 2.40: Quick Access Toolbar

- Click on drop-down menu under Choose commands from option > Select All Commands
- Find and select the Compare and Merge Workbooks command
- Click on Add for adding it to the Quick Access toolbar

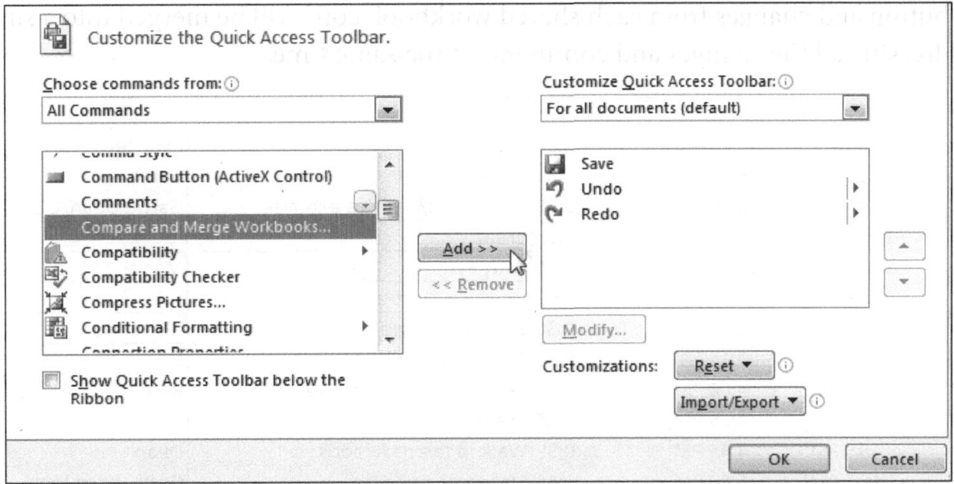

Figure 2.41: Customize the Quick Access Toolbar Window

Click on OK button and Compare and Merge Workbooks command will be added to the Quick Access toolbar

Perform the following steps to compare and merge workbooks:

- Open a copy of the shared workbook
- Click on Compare and Merge Workbooks command on the Quick Access toolbar

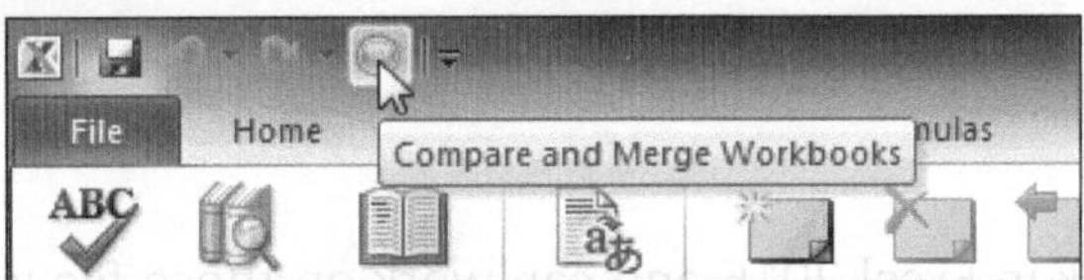

Figure 2.42: Compare and Merge Workbooks

- Allow Excel to save your workbook and Select Files to Merge into Current Workbook dialog box will start appearing.
- Select another copy of the same shared workbook that user want to merge by holding Ctrl or Shift on keyboard while clicking on file names

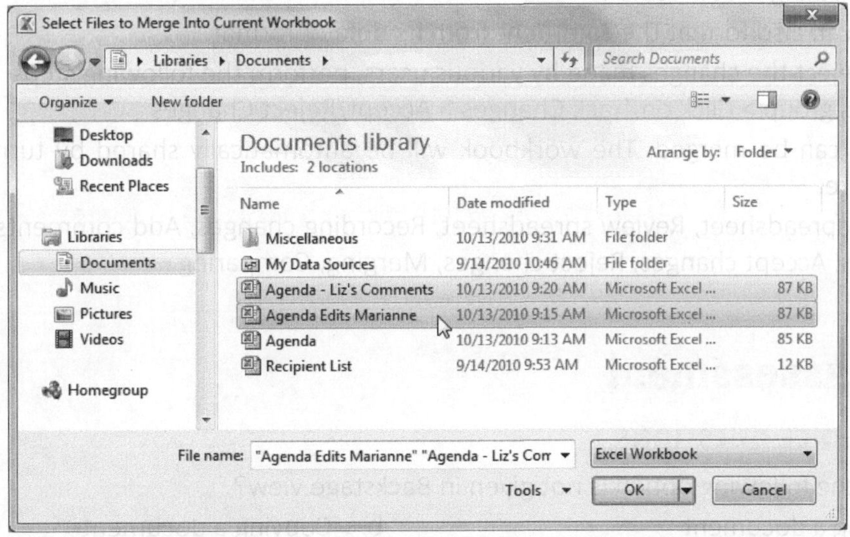

Figure 2.43: Window to select Files to Merge Into Current workbook

- Click **OK** button and changes from each shared workbook copy will be merged into a single copy. This help in addressing all the changes and comments at the same time.

6	Start	End	Time	Item	Facilitator
7	8:00 AM	9:00 AM	1:00	Breakfast, welcome	Exec team
8	9:00 AM	9:30 AM	0:30	Introduction	Garth
9	9:30 AM	10:30 AM	1:00	Work relationships exercise	Garth, Dean, Liz
10	10:30 AM	10:45 AM	0:15	Break	
11	10:45 AM	12:45 PM	2:00	Cady Falls hike (strategy game)	Marianne, Liz
12	12:45 PM	1:45 PM	1:00	Lunch (with strategy game team)	
13	1:45 PM	2:15 PM	0:30	Strategy debrief	Marianne
14	2:15 PM	3:15 PM	1:00	Get to know your team	Liz
15	3:15 PM	4:00 PM	0:45	Team building exercise	Rick
16	4:00 PM	4:15 PM	0:15	Break	
17	4:15 PM	4:45 PM	0:30	Walk in the redwoods	Dean
18	4:45 PM	6:00 PM	1:15	Strengths exercise	Garth, exec team
19	6:00 PM	8:00 PM	2:00	Dinner	

Figure 2.44: Merge workbook

The changes done by different user is represented by different color that helps in finding the changes made by which user.

Knowledge Box

User can only merge copies of the same shared workbook. All of the copies you plan to merge should be located in the same folder.

Summary

- User can share a workbook in Excel 2016 and can work on those file with other people on the same workbook at the same time.
- Spreadsheets are an essential of an office and used for organising the data and making reports.
- The built-in track changes can be used in Excel that helps in easily reviewing the edits directly in the edited worksheet or on a separate sheet.
- In Excel, user can add a comment to any cell that could be a note to user or a reminder, correction or question of anything that is useful.
- In Excel, user can also format the comment from its default format.
- To accept or reject the changes made by various users, perform the following steps: Go to the Review tab in Changes group > Click on Track Changes > Accept/Reject Changes
- Shared books can be merged. The workbook will be automatically shared by turning on the Track changes feature.

Keywords: Share spreadsheet, Review spreadsheet, Recording changes, Add comments, Edit comments, Format comments, Accept changes, Reject changes, Merging, Comparing

Self-Assessment

A. MULTIPLE CHOICE QUESTIONS.

1. Which of the following option is not given in Backstage view?

   a. Printing a document   b. Copying a document

   c. Sharing a document   d. Saving a document

2. When multiple users collaborate on the same shared workbook then user can use the ____________ workbooks command for viewing all the changes at once and address them by either accepting or rejecting it.

   a. Save   b. Compare and Merge   c. Track   d. Edit

B. FILL IN THE BLANKS

1. ____________ changes can be used in Excel that helps in easily reviewing the edits directly in the edited worksheet or on a separate sheet.
2. Accept/Reject Changes command is available in Track Changes Tab in ____________ group..
3. The workbook will be automatically shared by turning on the ____________ feature.

C. TRUE FALSE

1. The built-in track changes can be used in Excel that helps in easily reviewing the edits directly in the edited worksheet or on a separate sheet (T/F)
2. Track changes can also be used in workbooks that contain tables (T/F)
3. In Excel, use cannot format the comment from its default format (T/F)

D. ANSWER THE FOLLOWING QUESTIONS:

1. Define the term merge in excel spreadsheet? What is the purpose of using merge command in it?
2. How to add comments in Excel spreadsheet?
3. Write a note of review changes in spreadsheet?

E. PRACTICAL WORK

Draw up a spreadsheet by entering some data related to student's names and their scores in previous exam. Now, share the workbook and allow changes by various users on it. Add any 3 name of the students on shared workbook and repeat it for different students.

Answers

A. Multiple choice question answers:
   1. c   2. b

B. Fill in the blanks answers:
   1. Built-in track   2. Change   3. Track Changes

C. True False answers
   1. True   2. False   3. True

SESSION 4: CREATE AND USE MACROS IN SPREADSHEET

Macros are code for automating the work in a program that enable the user to add their own features and enhancement for getting exactly what user need to do quickly by just clicking on a button. In Excel like spreadsheets the Macros can be powerful. The macros replace the action that is done manually by users from formatting cells, copying values to calculating tools. So, by just some clicks user will be able to quickly replace the repetitive tasks.

4.1 Using the macro recorder

Macro reader is a very useful tools in Excel VBA that records every tasks performed by user with Excel. All user have to do is record a specific task then execute it over and over with the click of a button. This also help when user don't know about the program of a specific task in Excel VBA. In those cases, open the visual basic editor after recording all the tasks to check how it can be programmed. Also, there are number of things that cant be done with Macro Recorder.

For instance, user cannot loop through a range of data with the Macro Recorder and numbers of codes are used in Macro recorder than another feature is required that slow down the process.

4.2 Creating a simple macro

By using Macro in Excel VBA, user can automate the tasks. To create a simple macro, firstly turn on the Developer tab by performing the following steps:

- Right click anywhere in the ribbon > Click on Customize the Ribbon

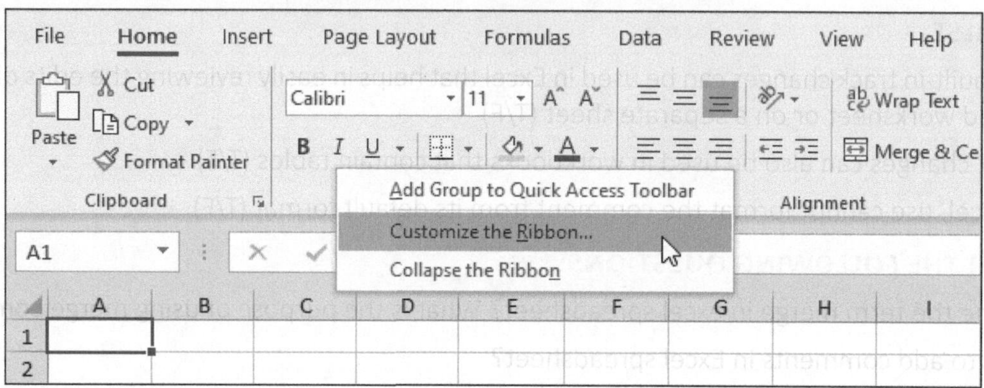

Figure 2.45: Customize the Ribbon Command

- On right side of the dialog box under Customize the Ribbon, select the Main tabs then check the developer check box

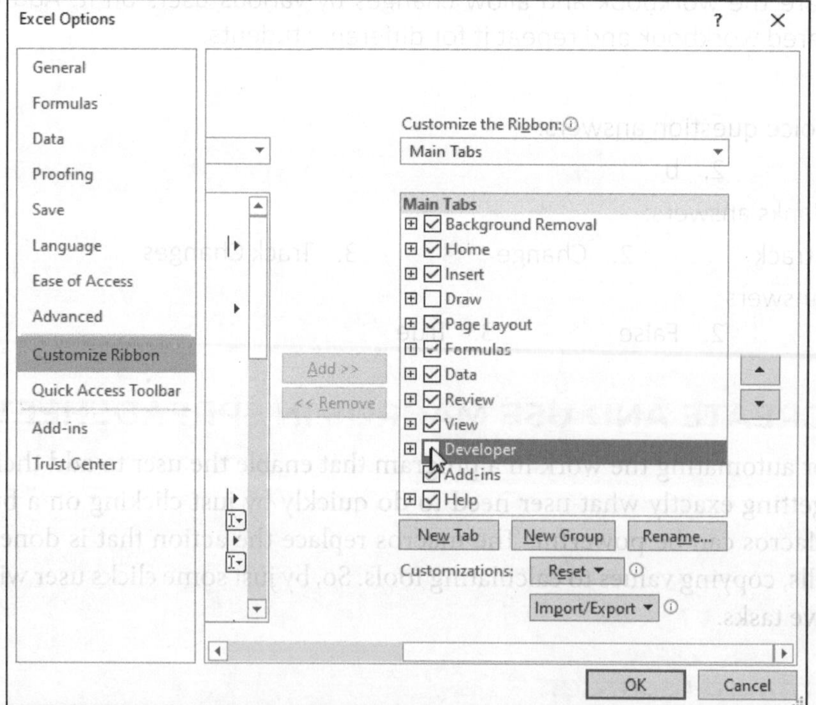

Figure 2.46: Excel Options

✦ Click OK button and user will find the Developer tab next to the View tab

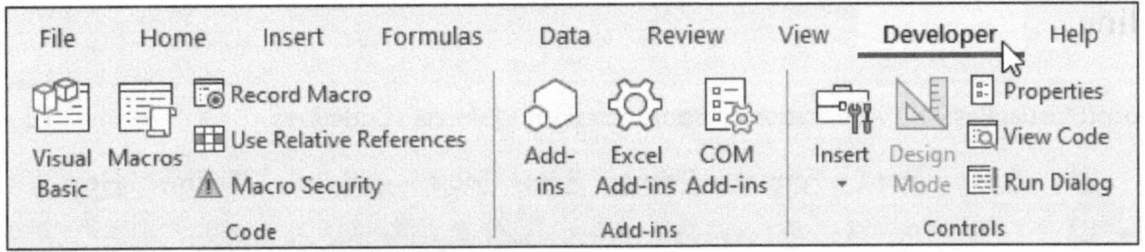

Figure 2.47: Developer Tab

Command Button

To place the command button on worksheet, perform the following steps:

✦ Click Insert present on the Developer tab

✦ Click on Command button in the ActiveX Controls group

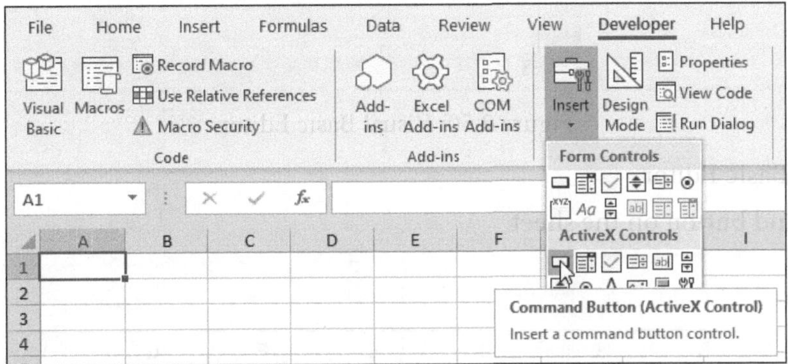

Figure 2.48: Insert Command

✦ Drag a command button on worksheet

Assign a Macro

To assign a macro to the command button, perform the following steps:

✦ Right click on Command Button 1

✦ Click on View Code and Visual Basic Editor will start appearing

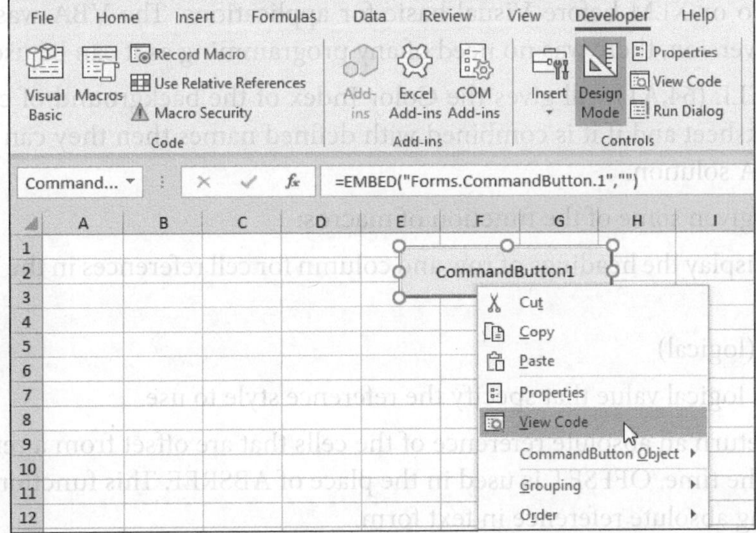

Figure 2.49: View Code command

- Place the cursor between Private Sub Command Button1 and Click () and End sub
- Add the code line

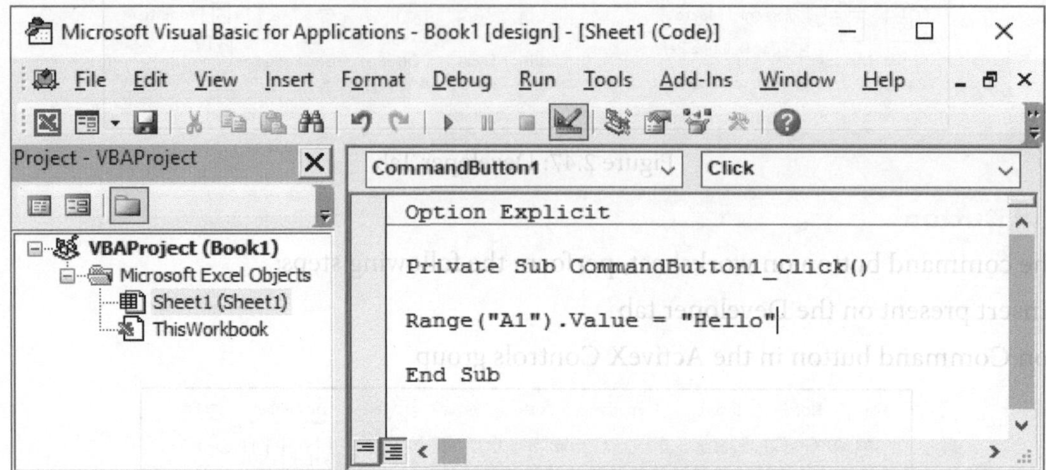

Figure 2.50: Visual Basic Editor

- Close the Visual Basic Editor.
- Click the command button on the sheet

Result:

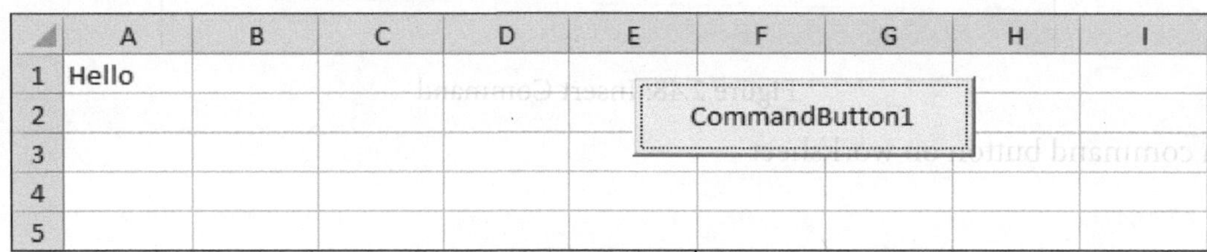

Figure 2.51:Result worksheet

4.3 Using a macro as a function

There was Excel micro or XLM before Visual basic for applications. The VBA was introduced in Excel version 5. Before this version, there was no need of any programming as it can be use like a function.

For instance: GET CELL (64,A1) will gives the Color Index of the background of cell A1. But user, cant stick it into their worksheet and if it is combined with defined names then they can be useful and can do things that need a VBA solution.

In this section, I have given some of the function of macros:

- **A1 R1 C1:** it will display the headings of row and column for cell references in the R1C1 or A1 reference style.

  Syntax: A1 R1 C1(logical)

  Where, logical is a logical value that specify the reference style to use

- **ABSREF:** It will return an absolute reference of the cells that are offset from a reference by a specified amount. Most of the time, OFFSET is used in the place of ABSREF. This function is provided by users in case of supplying absolute reference in text form.

Syntax: ABSREF(ref_text, reference)

Where, ref_text specify a position of relative reference

- **ACTIVATE:** It switches to a window if more than one window or pane of a window is open. If window is split then its panes are not frozen and switching to a pane is useful with functions such as HSCROLL, GOTO and VSCROLL that operate in active pane.

  Syntax: ACTIVATE(window_text, pane?_num)

  Where, window_text is a text specify the name of a window to switch to.

There are also other functions such as ACTIVATE.NEXT, ACTIVATE.PREV, ACTIVATE.CELL and many more that can be used in macros.

4.4 Passing arguments to a macro

For passing arguments to a macro, firstly create a Macro to accept the value. For this, user have to type a name for that value between the parenthesis at the top of the macro.

Example: Select All

```
Sub show_msg(message)
'output message that is given to this macro
MsgBox message
End Sub
```

This macro will accepts a value in the message variable and then outputs it into a message box pop-up.

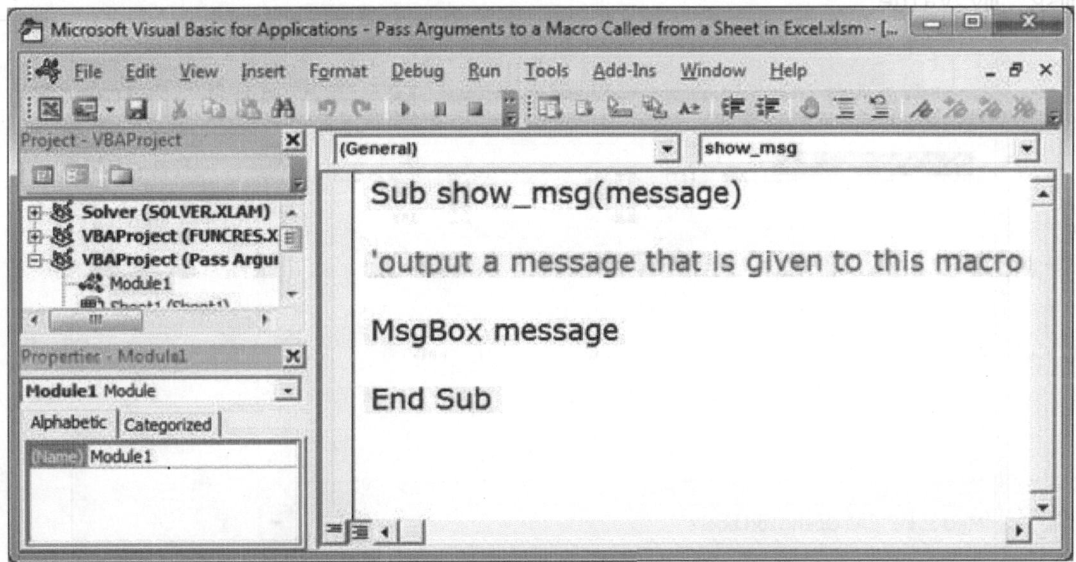

Figure 2.52: Microsoft Visual Basic for Applications

To pass a text value to the Macro:

- To get a Run Macro window, press Alt+ F8.

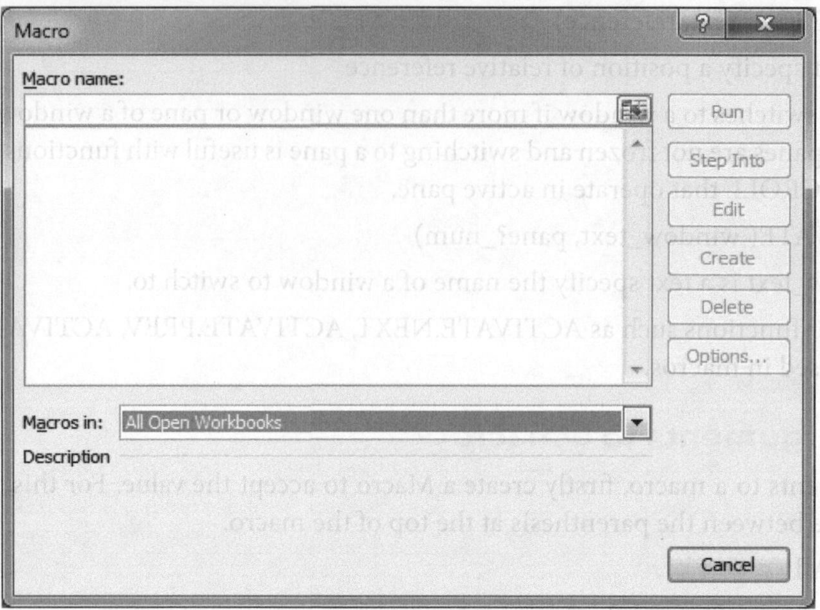

Figure 2.53: Macro Window

Here, user must type in the name of macro then argument value. For this, type in the name of the macro then add a space and value that user want to send to the macro.

```
Select All
'show_msg "my value"'
```

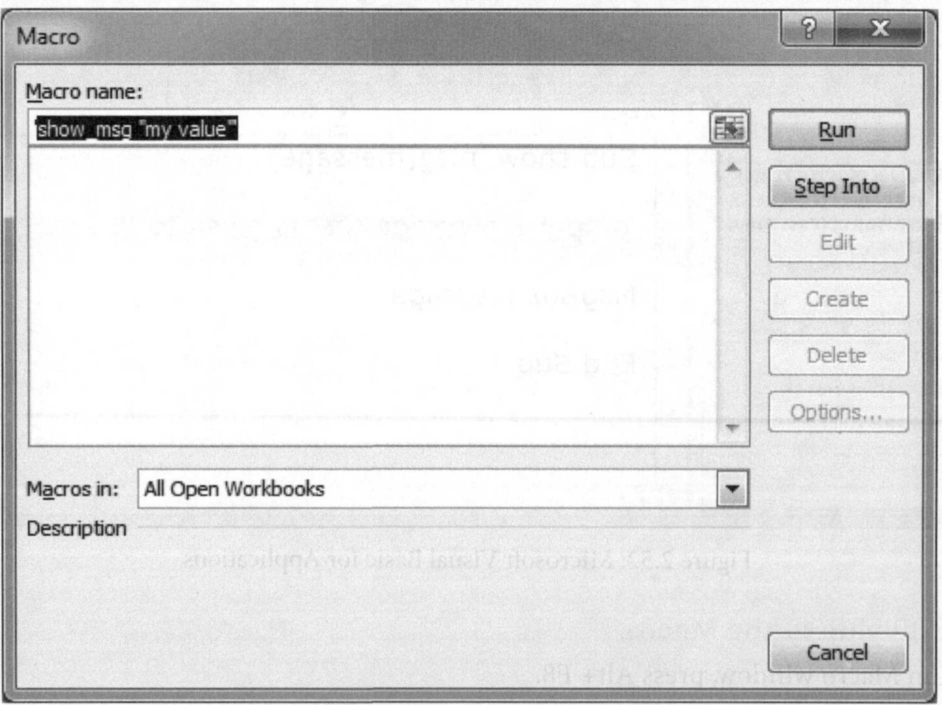

Figure 2.54: Macro name enter by user

- Click Run and once user is done

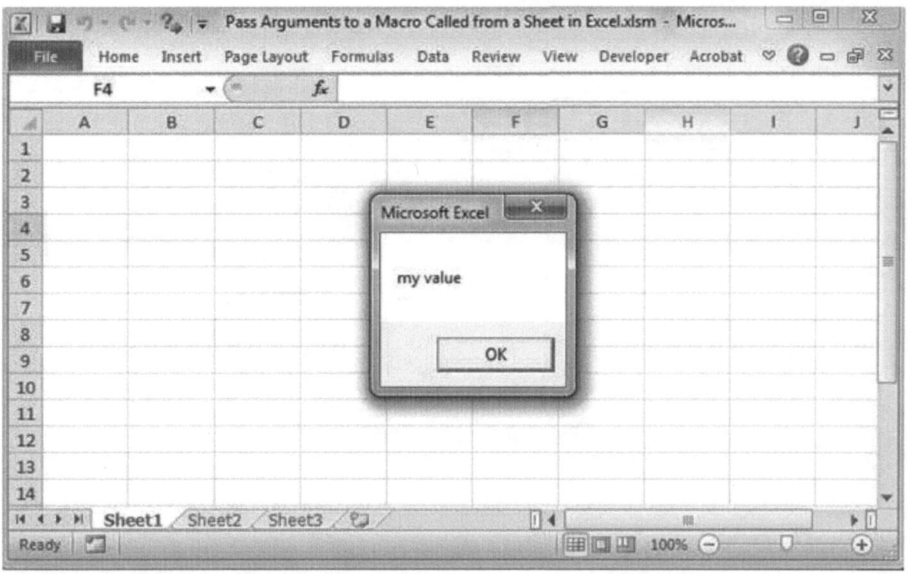

Figure 2.55: Display Macro message

To Pass a Numeric Value to the Macro:

- To run the macro press Alt + F8
- The macro name will not appear in the window that's why it must be type in under the Macro name.

Select All
'show_msg 5'

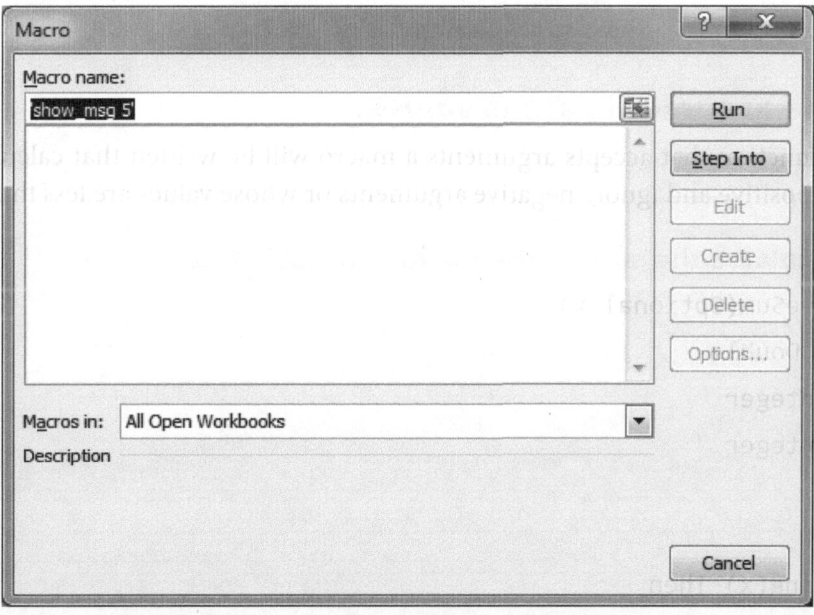

Figure 2.56: Another name enter in the Macro

- Notice the 5 after the Macro name. So, numeric argument can be passed to the Macro by simply adding space after the macro name and type the number.
- Run the macro and you will see the result

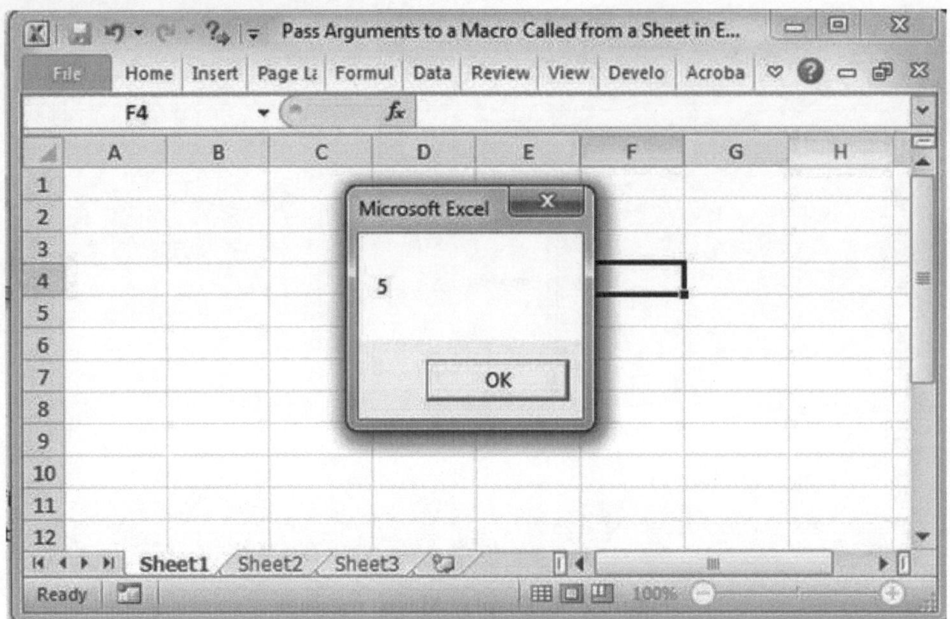

Figure 2.57: Display name in new pop-up window

Note:

- **The text is surrounded by double quotation marks and then the entire thing is surrounded by single quotation marks.**
- **The name of the macro and the argument must be surrounded by single quotation marks. Look closely in the above code and you will see this. However, the number does not have to be surrounded by double quotation marks like if you were inputting text for the argument.**

4.5 Passing the arguments areas values.

For illustration of function that accepts arguments a macro will be written that calculates the sum of its arguments that are positive and ignore negative arguments or whose values are less than zero.

PositiveSum calculates the sum of the positive arguments:

```
Function PositiveSum(Optional x)
  Dim TheSum As Double
  Dim iRow As Integer
  Dim iCol As Integer

  TheSum = 0.0
  If NOT IsMissing(x) Then
    If NOT IsArray(x) Then
      If x > 0 Then TheSum = x
    Else
      For iRow = LBound(x, 1) To UBound(x, 1)
```

```
        For iCol = LBound(x, 2) To UBound(x, 2)
          If x(iRow, iCol) > 0 Then TheSum = TheSum + x(iRow, iCol)
        Next
      Next
    End If
  End If
  PositiveSum = TheSum
End Function
```

The macro program illustrates some important techniques:

- First is the argument x is optional. In case the arguments is not optional then it is known as without and argument. Everytime when the macro is called a warning message is printed by OOo.
- Before using argument whether the argument is passed or not is check by IsMissing function
- If the argument have single value or array is check by IsArray function.
- A 2-D array of values is passes for a passing a range of value to the function.

Passing of one argument is easier than passing of two argument.

Arguments are separated by semicolon for calling a function with two arguments. For instance: TestMax(3; -4)

TestMax accepts two arguments and returns the larger of the two:

```
Function TestMax(x, y)
  If x >= y Then
    TestMax = x
  Else
    TestMax = y
  End If
End Function
```

Arguments are passed as values

Arguments passed to a macro from Excel can be values. In this, it is not possible to know about the cells if any are used.

For instance: =PositiveSum(A2) it passes the value of cell A2 and PositiveSum has no way of knowing that cell A2 was used. If you must know which cells are referenced rather than the values in the cells, pass the range as a string, parse the string, and obtain the values in the referenced cells.

4.7 Accessing cells directly

There is neither cell object nor a collection of cells. Individual cells are treated as Range objects that refer to one cell.

Cell Contents: The easy way of finding the cell contents are is to use the Visual Basic TypeName function.

```
Range("A1").Value = 100
Range("B1").Value = VBA.TypeName(Range("A1").Value)  = "Double"
```

```
Range("A2").Value = #1/1/2006#
Range("B2").Value = VBA.TypeName(Range("A2").Value)  = "Date"
Range("A3").Value = "some text"
Range("B3").Value = VBA.TypeName(Range("A3").Value)  = "String"
Range("A4").Formula = "=A1"
Range("B4").Value = VBA.TypeName(Range("A4").Value)  = "Double"
```

Text Property: User can assign a value to a cell by using its Value Property. The NumberFormat property is used for giving a cell a number format. The formatted appearance of the cell contents can be return using Text property.

```
Range("A1").Text = "$12,345.00"
```

Range Object: It contains individual or groups of cells. In this, the complete row or column can be considered as a range. Although Excel can work with three dimensional formulas the Range object in VBA is limited to a range of cells on a single worksheet. The range can be edited either using a Range object directly. For instance: Range("A1").BackColor

Cells Property: The same object is returned by applying a cells property to a range of object.

```
Application.Cells
ActiveSheet.Cells
ActiveCell
Cells
```

- Range.Cells.Count - The total number of cells in the range.
- Range.Cells(**row**, **column**) - To refer to a specific cell within a range.

```
ActiveSheet.Cells(2,2) = ActiveSheet.Range("B2")
```

- To loop through a range of cells

```
For irow = 1 to 4
    For icolumn = 1 to 4
        ActiveSheet.Cells(irow,icolumn).Value = 10
    Next icolumn
Next irow
```

```
Dim objRange As Range
Set objRange = ActiveSheet.Range(ActiveSheet.Cells(1,4), ActiveSheet.Cells(2,6))
```

Cells automatically refer to the active worksheet.

If you want to access cells on another worksheet then the correct code is:

```
Range( Worksheets(n).Cells(""), Worksheets(n).Cells("") )
```

Total number of populated cells

```
iTotal = Application.CountA(ActiveSheet.Cells)
```

4.8 Sorting the columns using macro

The spreadsheets are used for organising the data to make an intelligent calculation on it. Sorting is one of the most convenient methods of sorting the data. When user say sorting columns or column sorting then two ideas comes from it, first is sorting full columns (Rows 1 to 65,000) and sorting a range using a column as a key.

Sort Function: Sort is a function or a method in VBA. In below given syntax of sorting a columns, there is no need to mention all the parameters.

```
Columns.Sort
```

Sort(**[Key1]**, *[Order1 As XlSortOrder = xlAscending]*, *[Key2]*, *[Type]*, *[Order2 As XlSortOrder = xlAscending]*, *[Key3]*, *[Order3 As XlSortOrder = xlAscending]*, *[Header As XlYesNoGuess = xlNo]*, *[OrderCustom]*, *[MatchCase]*, *[Orientation As XlSortOrientation = xlSortRows]*, *[SortMethod As XlSortMethod = xlPinYin]*, *[DataOption1 As XlSortDataOption = xlSortNormal]*, *[DataOption2 As XlSortDataOption = xlSortNormal]*, *[DataOption3 As XlSortDataOption = xlSortNormal]*, *[SubField1]*)

Some of the important parameters are:

- Keys: it contain the data to sort
- Order: It can be ascending or descending
- Header: It can be included or excluded
- OrderCustom: It is used to separate data structure for storing user own sort criteria
- Orientation: By default the orientation is Rows that means the rows will move up and down. By setting to xlSortColumn the column will start moving to left and right.
- SortMethod: It is applicable to Chinese characters.
- DataOptions: It correspond to the respective keys and by default it treat text and numeric data separately. To mix both data use xlSortTextAsNumbers

Summary

- Macros are code for automating the work in a program that enable the user to add their own features and enhancement for getting exactly what user need to do quickly by just clicking on a button.
- Macro reader is a very useful tools in Excel VBA that records every tasks performed by user with Excel.
- By using Macro in Excel VBA, user can automate the tasks.
- There was Excel micro or XLM before Visual basic for applications. The VBA was introduced in Excel version 5.
- The A1 R1 C1 function of macros it will display the headings of row and column for cell references in the R1C1 or A1 reference style.
- ABSREF function of macros It will return an absolute reference of the cells that are offset from a reference by a specified amount. Most of the time, OFFSET is used in the place of ABSREF. This function is provided by users in case of supplying absolute reference in text form.
- Activate function of macros switches to a window if more than one window or pane of a window is open. If window is split then its panes are not frozen and switching to a pane is useful with functions such as HSCROLL, GOTO and VSCROLL that operate in active pane.
- For passing arguments to a macro, firstly create a Macro to accept the value. For this, user have to type a name for that value between the parenthesis at the top of the macro.
- For illustration of function that accepts arguments a macro will be written that calculates the sum of its arguments that are positive and ignore negative arguments or whose values are less than zero.

- Arguments passed to a macro from Excel can be values. In this, it is not possible to know about the cells if any are used.
- There is neither cell object nor a collection of cells. Individual cells are treated as Range objects that refer to one cell.
- User can assign a value to a cell by using its Value Property. The NumberFormat property is used for giving a cell a number format. The formatted appearance of the cell contents can be return using Text property.
- Range Object contains individual or groups of cells. In this, the complete row or column can be considered as a range. Although Excel can work with three dimensional formulas the Range object in VBA is limited to a range of cells on a single worksheet.
- The spreadsheets are used for organising the data to make an intelligent calculation on it. Sorting is one of the most convenient methods of sorting the data.

Keywords: Macros, Create macros, Macro recorder, Creating simple macro, Command Button, Visual basic editor, Macro as a function, Activate, ABSREF, Passing arguments, Passing Numeric value, Passing arguments areas values, Accessing cells, Sorting columns

Self-Assessment

A. MULTIPLE CHOICE QUESTIONS.

1. What is the purpose of A1 R1 C1 function of macros?
   a. Return an absolute reference of the cells
   b. Display the headings of row and column for cell references
   c. Switches window if more than one window is open
   d. None of these
2. Which of the following contains the button related to create, run and edit macros:
   a. file tab b. Developer tab c. Insert tab d. Home tab
3. What operation is done using TestMax command?
   a. It accepts two arguments and return the smaller of the two
   b. It accepts single arguments only
   c. It accepts two arguments and return the larger of the two
   d. It accepts more than two arguments and return the largest

B. FILL IN THE BLANKS

1. The __________ feature in Excel VBA can replace the action that is done manually by users from formatting cells, copying values to calculating tools.
2. The VBA was introduced in ____________ version of Excel.
3. For passing arguments to a macro, firstly create a __________ to accept the value.

C. TRUE FALSE

1. User can loop through a range of data with the Macro Recorder (T/F)
2. GET CELL (64,A1) will gives the Color Index of the background of cell A1 (T/F)

3. Arguments are separated by colon for calling a function with two arguments.

D. ANSWER THE FOLLOWING QUESTIONS:

1. Write down the steps of creating a simple macro?
2. Define various functions of Macros?
3. How to access the cells directly?

E. PRACTICAL WORK

Automate the task of performing different calculations in Excel VBA using Macro.

Practically try the following functions using macro:

- A1 R1 C1 (logical)
- ABSREF (ref_text, reference)
- ACTIVATE (window_text, pane?_num) and other functions linked with ACTIVATE such as ACTIVATENEXT, ACTIVATE.PREV and many more

Answers

A. Multiple choice question answers:

1. b 2. b 3. c

B. Fill in the blanks answers:

1. Macros 2. Fifth or five or 5 3. Macro

C. True False answers

1. False 2. True 3. False

A. MULTIPLE CHOICE QUESTIONS

1. Extension of MS Excel file is:

   a. .xcl b. .doc c. .xlxs d. .xlsx

2. What is the shortcut key to create a new workbook:

   a. Ctrl + C b. Ctrl + N c. Ctrl + P d. Ctrl + W

3. Shortcut key to save the file?

   a. Ctrl + A b. Ctrl + C c. Ctrl + S d. Ctrl + N

4. In order to arrange the class students mark those with highest marks to those with the lowest, you need to sort on the marks field in:

   a. Alphabetic order b. Ascending order c. Random order d. Descending order

5. Which of the following references represents linking between workbooks?

   a. Sum(Sheet1!B2, Sheet2!B2, Sheet3!B2) b. =Sum(Sheet1!B2, Sheet2!B2, Sheet3!B2)

   c. =Sum([Book1.xlsx]Sheet1!$B$2:$C$2) d. Both (a) and (b)

6. Various options of tracking and updating the worksheet are available in ______ tab of Share Workbook dialog box

   a. Editing   b. Advanced   c. Both (a) and (b)   d. None of these

Answers

1. d   2. b   3. c   4. d   5. b   6. b

B. SOLVED VERY SHORT AND SHORT QUESTION AND ANSWERS:

1. What do you mean by spreadsheet?

Ans. A spreadsheet or worksheet is a file made of rows and columns that help sort data, arrange data easily, and calculate numerical data. What makes a spreadsheet software program unique is its ability to calculate values using mathematical formulas and the data in cells.

2. Define MS Excel?

Ans. MS Excel is the spreadsheet component of Microsoft Office. Spreadsheets allow us to organize, analyze and store data in tabular form. Furthermore in a spreadsheet we can manipulate this data to produce certain results

3. What kind of command contain under Quick access toolbar?

Ans. The frequently used common buttons are present on it. We can remove or add another button through the drop-down arrow present on it.

4. Define Row?

Ans. In Excel rows are a horizontal arrangement of cells, and it is numbered in numerical digit start from 1, 2, 3, 4,5, and so on.

5. Define Column?

Ans. In Excel, columns are aligned vertically, and alphabets are assigned to it start from A, B, C, and so on.

6. Which key one can use to select more than one range of cells in a worksheet?

Ans. The control or Ctrl key

7. Define Relative referencing in Excel?

Ans. By default, all the cell references are relative references in which the formula gets copied in the new cell when you select any formula and drag it to a new cell. There are changes in the formula on the basis of the relative position of rows and columns.

8. What is Absolute referencing?

Ans. There are cases when you don't want a cell reference to change when copied to other cells, as happens in relative referencing. In those cases, absolute referencing is used as it will not change when copied and filled in another cell. In case of absolute referencing, a $ symbol is used before the column name and row number that make it constant for any formula.

9. What do you mean by mixed type of referencing in Excel?

Ans. It is the combination of relative and absolute referencing. It is used when we have to make some row number and column name constant, and some had to vary accordingly. In order to make the row number and column name constant, there is need to use a $ sign is before row number and column name.

10. Give various parts of What-if analysis in Excel?

Ans. Various parts of What-if analysis in Excel:

- Goal Seek for reverse calculation
- Data Table for Sensitivity analysis
- Scenario Manager for comparison of scenarios

11. What is the need of multiple sheets?

Ans. In every workbook, there is at least one worksheet in default. When working with a large amount of data then user can create multiple worksheets that help in organising the workbook and make it easier for finding the content. Worksheets can be group for quick addition of information to multiple worksheets at the same time.

12. Define linking to external data? Also give various ways of linking.

Ans. User can insert tables from HTML documents and data located within named ranges from an Open Office.org Microsoft Excel Spreadsheet into a spreadsheet.

This can be done in two ways:

- Using the External Data dialog
- Using the Navigator

13. Give the purpose of sharing a spreadsheet?

Ans. User can share a workbook in Excel 2016 and can work on those file with other people on the same workbook at the same time. The workbook should be saved to a network location where other people can open it. User can also keep track of the changes done by other people while making, accepting and rejecting those changes.

14. Give various tasks that can be perform on comments in Excel? Give steps to add basic comment.

Ans. In Excel, user can add a comment to any cell that could be a note to user or a reminder, correction or question of anything that is useful. The use of Excel comments are useful for workbooks for sharing information and collaborating on projects. To add a basic comment, perform the following steps:

- Right click on the cell user want to comment on
- Select comment on the menu
- Enter the comment in the comment box and comment will become a part of the cell

15. Define Macros in spreadsheet?

Ans. Macros are code for automating the work in a program that enable the user to add their own features and enhancement for getting exactly what user need to do quickly by just clicking on a button. In Excel like spreadsheets the Macros can be powerful.

16. Write down the steps to create simple macro?

Ans. By using Macro in Excel VBA, user can automate the tasks. To create a simple macro, firstly turn on the Developer tab by performing the following steps:

- Right click anywhere in the ribbon > Click on Customize the Ribbon
- On right side of the dialog box under Customize the Ribbon, select the Main tabs then check the developer check box
- Click OK button and user will find the Developer tab next to the View tab

17. Define Range object in Accessing cells directly?

Ans. Range Object: It contains individual or groups of cells. In this, the complete row or column can be considered as a range. Although Excel can work with three dimensional formulas the Range object in VBA is limited to a range of cells on a single worksheet. The range can be edited either using a Range object directly. For instance: Range("A1").BackColor

C. LONG SOLVED QUESTION AND ANSWERS:

1. Write a note on formatting a range of cell to be seen as labels.

Ans. There are some cases in which there is a need to format a range of cells to be seen as labels. These cases can come in telephone numbers in which every country STD code starts with 0. But when you enter the telephone number in a spreadsheet with prefix as 0, then the "0" will disappears from the telephone number because, in a spreadsheet, it stores as a numeric value that does not have a preceding 0 or zero.

But to take 0 as a prefix in the spreadsheet, we take numeric values as text. To format the selected range of cells that consist ofa telephone number as text, perform the following steps:

- Select the range of cells and click on the Format tab menu bar. Click on the cell, and Format Cells dialog box will open
- Click on Numbers tab and select Text and click OK button
- Now you can enter the numbers in a spreadsheet with prefix 0.

2. How to create a reference to other sheets by using keyboard and mouse?

Ans. The balance from each of the other sheets is display on the Summary sheet. If users copy the outcomes onto each account then the current balances will be in cell F3 of each sheet.

The cells can be reference in other sheets using two ways:

- By entering formula using keyboard
- By entering formula using Mouse

By entering formula using Mouse: To use this approach, perform the following steps:

- On the Summary sheet, set up a place for all five accounts balances so that user will get to know where to put the cell reference. The Summary sheet with a blank Balance column is shown in below figure. User wants to place the reference for checking the account balance in cell B3.
- For making the cell reference in cell B3, perform the following steps:
- Select the cell then click on the = equal too icon next to the input line. The icons get change and an equals sign start appearing in the input line.
- After that, click on the sheet tab for the sheet consists of cell to be referenced. In our case, it is Checking Account sheet as shown in below figure.
- Click on cell F3 in the Checking Account sheet or any other cell if user want to see the balance in another cell.
- To finish, Click on green checkmark in the input line and Summary sheet will look like as shown in below figure.

By entering formula using Mouse: To use this approach, perform the following steps:

User can deduce how the cell reference is constructed. The reference has two parts one is sheet name that is Checking Account and other is cell reference F3. Note that they are separated by a period.

User can also fill in the Saving Account cell reference by typing it. Let assume that the balance is in the same cell in the Saving Account sheet, F3 then the cell reference will be ='Savings Account'.F3.

3. Give in brief the ways of linking to external data in spreadsheet?

Ans. User can insert tables from HTML documents and data located within named ranges from an Open Office.org Microsoft Excel Spreadsheet into a spreadsheet.

This can be done in two ways:

- Using the External Data dialog
- Using the Navigator

In case the file has named ranges or tables and user know the name of the range or table that they want to link with then use of External Data dialog is a quickest and easiest way. But, if there are number of tables in a file and user want to pick one from it then user will not be able to easily determine the exact one in these cases the use of Navigator method will be easier.

Using the External Data dialog:

- Open the Microsoft Sheet where the external data is to be inserted
- Select the cell where the upper left-hand cell of the external data is to be inserted
- Click on Insert > Link to External Data and external data dialog will appear
- Type the URL of the source document or click the [....] button for opening a file selecting dialog. Press Enter to get Excel to load the available tables list.
- In the Available tables/range list, select the named ranges or tables you want to insert. You can also specify that the ranges or tables are updated every (number of) seconds.
- Clock on Ok button to close the dialog and inserting the linked data

Using the Navigator:

- Open the spreadsheet in which the external data is to be inserted
- Open the document from which the external data is to be taken. Choose the Web Page Quesry in case if source document is a Web page
- Press F5 to open the Navigator in target document
- Select the source document in the bottom of the Navigator. The range of names or the tables containing in the source document are start showing in the Navigator.
- Click on the + next to Range names for displaying the list.
- In the Navigator, select the Insert as Link drag mode
- Select the required range or table and drag it from the Navigator into the target document, to the cell where you want the upper left-hand cell of the data range to be.
- In the target document, check the Navigator. Instead of a + by Range names, it shows a + by Linked areas. Click the + to see the same range name.

4. How to open and save a shared spreadsheet or record changes in it.

Ans. The built-in track changes can be used in Excel that helps in easily reviewing the edits directly in the edited worksheet or on a separate sheet. After that user can easily accept or reject the changes individually and at a time. For using the tracking feature of Excel, one should have to remember few points as given below:

- Track changes is only available in shared workbooks: The Excels track changes works only appear in shared workbooks that means whenever user turn on the tacking in Excel, the workbook becomes shared or can it can be used my multiple users for editing simultaneously.
- Track changes cannot be used in workbooks that contain tables
- The changes can't be undo in Excel
- All changes can't be tracked in Excel
- History of changes can be kept only for 30 days

To track changes in Excel, perform the following steps:

- In Change group Review tab click on Track Changes button > Select Highlight changes
- In Highlight Changes dialog box, Check the Track changes while editing
- Select the desired period of time in the When box under Highlight and Who box which changes
- Select the Highlight changes on screen option
- Click Ok button

Now the edits done by different users are highlighted in Excel

If prompted, allow Excel to save your workbook, and you are done!

5. Give in detail the various function of macro?

Ans. Some of the functions of macros are:

- **A1 R1 C1:** it will display the headings of row and column for cell references in the R1C1 or A1 reference style.

  Syntax: A1 R1 C1(logical)

  Where, logical is a logical value that specify the reference style to use
- **ABSREF:** It will return an absolute reference of the cells that are offset from a reference by a specified amount. Most of the time, OFFSET is used in the place of ABSREF. This function is provided by users in case of supplying absolute reference in text form.

  Syntax: ABSREF(ref_text, reference)

  Where, ref_text specify a position of relative reference
- **ACTIVATE:** It switches to a window if more than one window or pane of a window is open. If window is split then its panes are not frozen and switching to a pane is useful with functions such as HSCROLL, GOTO and VSCROLL that operate in active pane.

  Syntax: ACTIVATE(window_text, pane?_num)

Where, window_text is a text specify the name of a window to switch to.

There are also other functions such as ACTIVATE.NEXT, ACTIVATE.PREV, ACTIVATE.CELL and many more that can be used in macros.

6. Define sort function in spreadsheet? Also, give some of the important parameters related to it.

Ans. Sort is a function or a method in VBA. In below given syntax of sorting a columns, there is no need to mention all the parameters.

Some of the important parameters are:

- Keys: it contain the data to sort
- Order: It can be ascending or descending
- Header: It can be included or excluded
- OrderCustom: It is used to separate data structure for storing user own sort criteria
- Orientation: By default the orientation is Rows that means the rows will move up and down. By setting to xlSortColumn the column will start moving to left and right.
- SortMethod: It is applicable to Chinese characters.
- DataOptions: It correspond to the respective keys and by default it treat text and numeric data separately. To mix both data use xlSortTextAsNumbers

Exercise for Assessment

A. MULTIPLE CHOICE QUESTIONS

1. By default, workbook opens with how many worksheets:
   a. one   b. two   c. three   d. four
2. Which contains the button related to data analysis:
   a. File tab   b. View tab   c. Data tab   d. insert tab
3. Split bar will split the sheet __________ when you double click it:
   a. Vertically   b. horizontally   c. both of these   d. none of these
4. Which of the following contains the button related to create, run and edit macros:
   a. file tab   b. Developer tab   c. Insert tab   d. Home tab
5. Excel documents are called:
   a. Worksheets   b. Workbooks   c. Both a and b   d. Neither a nor b
6. When you've entered numbers in your sheet, you might want to add them up. A fast way to do that is by using:
   a. Template   b. Worksheet   c. Auto sum   d. All of these
7. Which let you total your numbers quickly:
   a. QAT   b. Auto sum   c. Scrolling bar   d. Number format
8. Functions are predefined formulas that perform calculations by using specific values, called:
   a. Formulas   b. Argument
   c. Number orientation   d. number group
9. Which is a tooltip with the syntax and arguments appears as you type the function:
   a. argument   b. argument tooltip   c. developer tab   d. Insert tab
10. A mixed reference has:
    a. an absolute column and relative row   b. absolute row and relative column
    c. either a or b   d. neither a nor b

B. VERY SHORT QUESTION AND ANSWER

1. Define worksheet?
2. Give any three features of spreadsheet in Excel.
3. Name various parts of What-if analysis in Excel.
4. What is the need of setting multiple worksheets in Excel?
5. Define Relative hyperlink?
6. What is the purpose of sharing a workbook in Excel 2016?
7. Define the term merge in Excel?
8. What do you mean by macro? Also, give its usage in Excel spreadsheet.

C. SHORT QUESTION AND ANSWERS

1. How user can use merge and summarize function of Excel for quickly summarizing the data in a single sheet without sorting the data.
2. Write the steps to perform subtotal of values?
3. How someone can view multiple worksheet in Excel?
4. Write down the note on creating a reference to other sheets using keyboard.
5. What is hyperlink? Give and define various types of hyperlink in Excel.
6. Give steps of linking to registered data sources.
7. How to set up a spreadsheet for sharing.
8. Write a note on merging and comparing function in Excel?
9. Give steps of creating a simple macro.

D. LONG QUESTION AND ANSWERS

1. Briefly explain the "What if" scenarios in Excel.
2. Write down the steps to create a reference to other documents using both methods.
3. How linking to external data can be done in Excel 2016?
4. Give the way of opening and saving a shared spreadsheet in Excel. Also, how to record changes?
5. How to add, remove and format comments in spreadsheet.
6. How to use macro as a function? Give and explain various functions of macros.
7. Write a note on passing arguments to a macro?
8. What is the need of sorting in Excel? Give various sort functions of sorting a columns using factors.

E. APPLICATION BASED QUESTIONS:

1. Your father wants to check their datasheet of previous 5 years. To compare it, he want all should be on single one. Suggest him, how he can do it.
2. Office HR wants to send file to new employee of his company. To let, the employee understand about the content of Excel sheet what can be added by HR.
3. There is HTML documents and you want to locate data within named ranges from an Open Office. org Microsoft Excel spreadsheet into a spreadsheet using External Data dialog.
4. To perform the type of analysis that fits the needs of user, which two tools can be provided by Excel.

PROJECT WORK

1. Write down the names of students along with their marks in English subject in one worksheet and marks of subject Hindi in another worksheet. Repeat the same for rest of the subjects. Then use consolidating data to create subtotals in single sheet.
2. Use Data table of What-if analysis. Suppose you want to know the 10%, 20%, 30%, 40% and 50% of 5000 similarly, find the percentages for 6000, 7000, 8000, 9000 and 10000.

3. Enter the data into the worksheet for the master sheet > Insert new worksheet and move to next to the master sheet rename it as Data Entry. Now point the cursor in the cell where you need the cell value.
4. Make random list of participants with their role and roll numbers. Then, sort the columns using macro in Excel VBA.
5. Create a Macro to accept the value then pass arguments between the parenthesis at the top of the macro.

TEACHER NOTES:

1. Arrange a special session for students to understand the use of What-If analysis tool.
2. Introduce Excel VBA that records every tasks performed by user with Excel.

EXAM TIPS:

1. Practically try using Goal seek or What if scenarios for analysis of data
2. Create a reference to other sheets/document by using keyboard and mouse
3. Perform basic steps to create a simple macro
4. Do changes in the existing file and then review it by either accepting or rejecting
5. Try to link any database into Excel document.

3 Database Management System

Learning Outcomes

After this chapter, you will have the knowledge of:

- Concept of Database management system
- Concept and examples of data and information
- Features of database
- Concept of relational database management system
- Concept of various keys
- Create and edit tables using wizard and SQL commands
- Database objects
- Setting primary key table data
- DDL Commands
- Inserting, editing, deleting and sorting data in the table
- Perform operations on table
- Creating and editing relationships
- Database query, defining, editing and creating query using wizard or design view
- Applying criteria in query
- Performing calculations
- Grouping data
- Introduction to Structured Query Language (SQL)
- Creating forms and reports using wizard
- Enter or remove data or records from forms or modifying form, searching records

INTRODUCTION

A DATABASE MANAGEMENT SYSTEM makes it possible for end users to create, read, update and delete data in a database. The DBMS essentially serves as an interface between the database and end users or application programs, ensuring that data is consistently organized and remains easily accessible.

The DBMS manages three important things: the data, the database engine that allows data to be accessed, locked and modified; and the database schema, which defines the database's logical structure. These three foundational elements help provide concurrency, security, data integrity and uniform administration procedures. Typical database administration tasks supported by the DBMS include change management, performance monitoring/tuning and backup and recovery. Many database management systems are also responsible for automated rollbacks, restarts and recovery as well as the logging and auditing of activity.

SESSION 1: APPRECIATE THE CONCEPT OF DATABASE MANAGEMENT SYSTEM

The DBMS is perhaps most useful for providing a centralized view of data that can be accessed by multiple users, from multiple locations, in a controlled manner. A DBMS can limit what data the end user sees, as well as how that end user can view the data, providing many views of a single database schema. End users and software programs are free from having to understand where the data is physically located or on what type of storage media it resides because the DBMS handles all requests.

The DBMS can offer both logical and physical data independence. That means it can protect users and applications from needing to know where data is stored or having to be concerned about changes to the physical structure of data (storage and hardware). As long as programs use the application programming interface (API) for the database that is provided by the DBMS, developers won't have to modify programs just because changes have been made to the database.

1.1 Concept and examples of data and information

Microsoft Access is a database creation and management program. A database is a collection of data that is stored in a computer system. Databases allow their users to enter, access, and analyse their data quickly and easily. They're such a useful tool that you see them all the time. Ever waited while a doctor's receptionist entered your personal information into a computer, or watched a store employee use a computer to see whether an item was in stock? If so, then you've seen a database in action.

The easiest way to understand a database is to think of it as a collection of lists; Like, the database of patient information at a doctor's office. Lists contained a list of patients' names, list of past appointments, a list with medical history for each patient, a list of contact information, and etc.

This is true of all databases, from the simplest to the most complex. For instance, if you like to bake you might decide to keep a database containing the types of cookies you know how to make and the friends you give these cookies to. This is one of the simplest databases imaginable. It contains two lists: a list of your friends, and a list of cookies.

However, if you were a professional baker, you would have many more lists to keep track of: a list of customers, a list of products sold, a list of prices, a list of orders, and so on. The more lists you add, the more complex the database will be.

Figure 3.1: List of People and Cookies

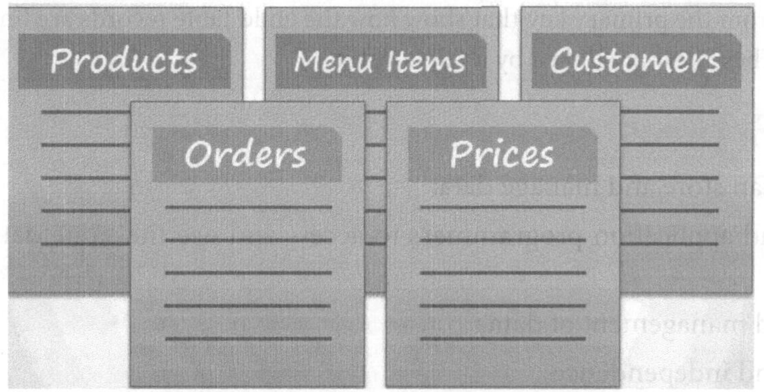

Figure 3.2: Other lists can be added in the database

In Access, lists are a little more complex than the ones you write on paper. Access stores its lists of data in tables, which allow you to store even more detailed information. In the figure below, the People list in the amateur baker's database has been expanded to include other relevant information on the baker's friends.

ID	Name	Cell Phone	Birthday	Nut Allergy?
1	Dad	555-0404	June 3	Yes
2	Aunt Aida	555-9890	July 8	No
3	Joakim	555-0462	September 19	No
4	Dwane	555-9975	January 5	No
5	Allegra	555-0099	January 14	Yes

Figure 3.3: Database

If you are familiar with other programs in the Microsoft Office suite, this might remind you of Excel, which allows you to organize data in a similar way. In fact, you could build a similar table in Excel.

1.2 Concept of database

A database is an organized collection of data. Thus, it is a collection of information organized and presented to serve an assigned purpose. Example of databases, is may be a dictionary where words are arranged alphabetically.

To design a useful database, you create tables that focus on one subject. In your tables, you capture all the data needed for that subject in fields, which hold the smallest possible unit of data.

Relational databases	A database in which data is divided into tables, which are kind of like spreadsheets. Each table has just one subject, such as customers (one table) or products (another table).
Records and fields	Storage for the discrete data in a table. Rows (or records) store each unique data point, such as the name of a customer. Columns (or fields) isolate the information being captured about each data point into the smallest possible unit—first name might be one column and last name might be another.
Primary key	A value that ensures each record is unique. For example, there might be two customers with the same name, Elizabeth Andersen. But one of the Elizabeth Andersen records has the number 12 as its primary key and the other has a primary key of 58.
Parent-child relationships	Common relationships between tables. For example, a single customer may have multiple orders. Parent tables have primary keys. Child tables have foreign keys, which are values from the primary key that show how the child table records are linked to the parent table. These keys are linked by a relationship.

1.3 Advantages of DBMS

- Using DBMS one can store and manage data.
- It lets end users and application programmers to access and use the same data while managing data integrity
- Central storage and management of data.
- Data abstraction and independence
- Data security
- A locking mechanism for concurrent access
- An efficient handler to balance the needs of multiple applications using the same data
- The ability to swiftly recover from crashes and errors, including restart ability and recoverability
- Robust data integrity capabilities
- Logging and auditing of activity

1.4 Features of database

Various features of database for managing data are:

- **Tables:** It is the building block of any relational database model in which all the actual data is entered and defined. A database contains various tables that consist of cells at the records intersection named rows and fields named columns. It is also known as field.
- **Field (Data item):** It is an area in the record that is reserved for specific piece of data. It is the individual sub-component of one record that contains set of characters such as customer name, state, current address, number, state, city and many more. It is also known as column.

- **Record:** It is the collection of data items of all the fields pertaining to one entity or complete unit of information such as company, transition, person and many more. It is also known as tuple, entity and row.
- **Queries:** It is an inquiry into the database using the SELECT statement that give filtered data on the basis of your specifications and conditions indicating the summaries, records and fields. These are what user wants to fetch from a database. It enable the extraction of information from database on the basis of conditions defined in query.
- **Forms:** It is a window or a screen in database that consists of various fields to enter data. It can be used for viewing or editing your data. In a specified interface, it is an user interface.

1.5 Concept and examples of Relational database

Relational database is a management system database that is based on relational model. It is a relational model of a database in which all the data is represented in terms of tables or grouped interrelations and rows or tuples. The relational model organized database is a relational database. It is powerful that creates a need of some assumptions about the relation of data and how it is extracted from the database. An important feature of relational database system is that a single database can be spread across various tables. Some of the examples of RDBMS are Oracle, ASE, Access, Sybase, DB2, Informix and SAP.

In this the relations are the files or tables with the data and columns are referred to fields or attributes.

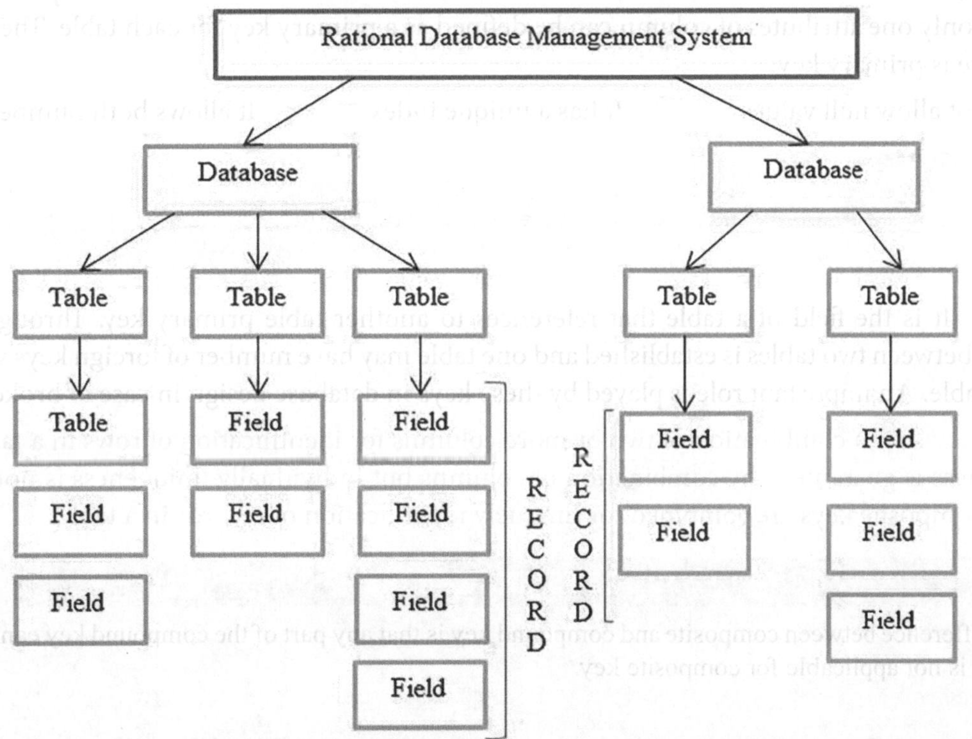

Figure 3.4: Rational Database Management System

1.7 Concept and examples of Primary key, composite primary key, foreign key

To read data from several tables and combine it in a meaningful way, you can include the primary key fields in other tables to refer back to the table that is the source of the primary key. In those other tables, the fields are called foreign keys. For example, a Customer ID field in the Customers table might also appear in the Orders table. In the Customers table, it is the primary key. In the Orders table it is called a foreign key. A foreign key, simply stated, is another table's primary key.

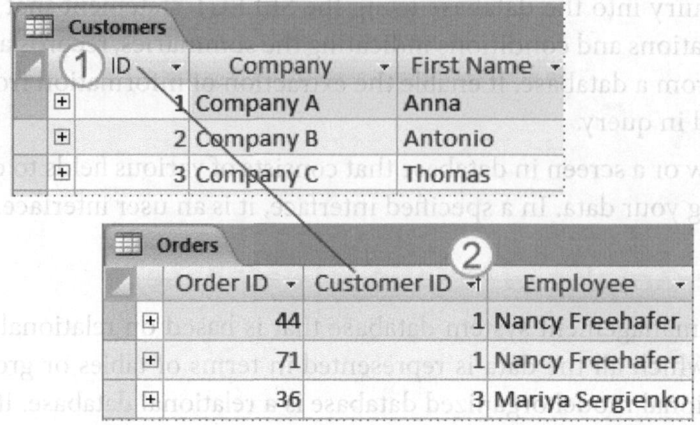

Figure 3.5: Various types of keys

1. Primary key
2. Foreign key
3. Composite key

Primary Key: A field or set of fields that identify each record uniquely in a table is known as primary key. For each row, there is at least one column in each relation for which there must be unique value for each row. In this, only one attributes of column can be defined as a primary key for each table. These properties must be there is primary key:

- It does not allow null values
- It has a unique index
- It allows both numbers and text

Knowledge Box

For instance: In the student table, the primary key will be student Id because it consists of unique Ids for each student.

Foreign key: It is the field of a table that references to another table primary key. Through this key, a relationship between two tables is established and one table may have number of foreign keys with different referenced table. An important role is played by these keys in database design in case of broken tables.

Composite key: It is a combination of two or more columns for identification of rows in a table uniquely. The uniqueness is guaranteed by combination of columns but individually uniqueness is not guaranteed. Therefore, Composite keys are combined for uniquely identification of records in a table.

LETS KNOW MORE

The main difference between composite and compound key is that any part of the compound key can be a foreign key but this is not applicable for composite key.

1.8 Relational Data base management system (RDBMS) software

A database in which data is divided into tables which are kind of like spreadsheets. Each table has just one subject, such as customers (one table) or products (another table).

However, the thing that really sets databases apart from any other way of storing data is **connectivity**. We call a database like the ones you'll work with in Access a **relational database**. A relational database is able to understand how lists and the objects within them **relate** to one another. To explore this idea, let›s go back to the simple database with two lists: names of your friends, and the types of cookies you know how to make. You decide to create a third list to keep track of the batches of cookies you make and who they're for. Because you›re only making cookies you know the recipe for and you›re only going to give them to your friends, this new list will get all of its information from the lists you made earlier.

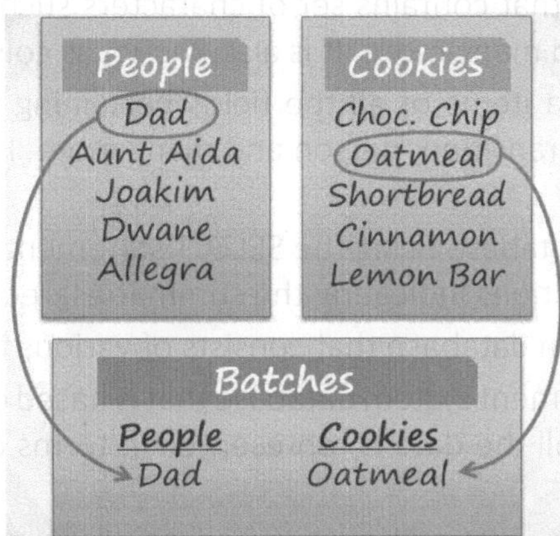

Figure 3.6: Relational Data base Management System (RDBMS)

See how the third list uses words that appeared in the first two lists? A database is capable of understanding that the **Dad** and **Oatmeal** cookies in the **Batches** list are the same things as the **Dad** and **Oatmeal** cookies in the first two lists. This relationship seems obvious, and a person would understand it right away; however, an Excel workbook wouldn't.

Excel would treat all of these things as distinct and unrelated pieces of information. In Excel, you'd have to enter every single piece of information about a person or type of cookie each time you mentioned it because that database wouldn't be **relational** like an Access database. Simply put, relational databases can recognize what a human can: If the same words appear in multiple lists, they **refer** to the same thing.

The fact that relational databases can handle information this way allows you to **enter, search for,** and **analyse** data in more than one table at a time. All of these things would be difficult to accomplish in Excel, but in Access even complicated tasks can be simplified and made fairly user friendly.

Summary

- DATABASE MANAGEMENT SYSTEM makes it possible for end users to create, read, update and delete data in a database.
- Microsoft Access is a database creation and management program. A database is a collection of data that is stored in a computer system.
- The easiest way to understand a database is to think of it as a collection of lists; Like, the database of patient information at a doctor's office.
- Lists contained a list of patients' names, list of past appointments, a list with medical history for each patient, a list of contact information, and etc.
- A database is an organized collection of data. Thus, it is a collection of information organized and presented to serve an assigned purpose.
- In Relational databases data is divided into tables, which are kind of like spreadsheets. Each table has just one subject, such as customers (one table) or products (another table).
- A field or set of fields that identify each record uniquely in a table is known as primary key.
- Foreign key is the field of a table that references to another table primary key.

- Tables is the building block of any relational database model in which all the actual data is entered and defined. A database contains various tables that consist of cells at the records intersection named rows and fields named columns. It is also known as field.
- Field or Data item is an area in the record that is reserved for specific piece of data. It is the individual sub-component of one record that contains set of characters such as customer name, state, current address, number, state, city and many more. It is also known as column.
- Record is the collection of data items of all the fields pertaining to one entity or complete unit of information such as company, transition, person and many more. It is also known as tuple, entity and row.
- Queries is an inquiry into the database using the SELECT statement that give filtered data on the basis of your specifications and conditions indicating the summaries, records and fields.
- Forms is a window or a screen in database that consists of various fields to enter data.
- Relational database is a management system database that is based on relational model. It is a relational model of a database in which all the data is represented in terms of tables or grouped interrelations and rows or tuples.
- To read data from several tables and combine it in a meaningful way. You can include the primary key fields in other tables to refer back to the table that is the source of the primary key.
- Composite key is a combination of two or more columns for identification of rows in a table uniquely.

Keywords: DBMS, Data, Information, database, customers, Relational databases, Tables, Records, Queries, Forms, advantages, features, Primary key, Foreign key, Composite key, RDBMS

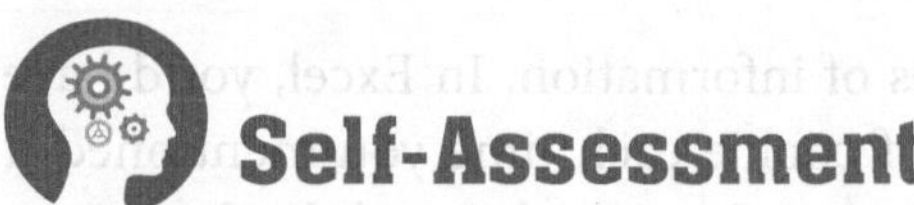

A. MULTIPLE CHOICE QUESTIONS.

1. DBMS stands for ____________.

   a. Data management system b. Data Basic management system

   c. Database management system d. Database manipulation system

2. A ______________ is an organized collection of data.

   a. Information b. Data case

   c. Database d. Both b nor c

B. FILL IN THE BLANKS

1. ______________ is a database creation and management program.
2. ______________ is an organized collection of data
3. ______________ is an area in the record that is reserved for specific piece of data
4. ______________ is the field of a table that references to another table primary key

C. TRUE FALSE

1. DBMS stands for Database managing system (T/F)
2. In Relational databases data is divided into tables, which are kind of like spreadsheets (T/F)

3. Oracle, ASE, SAP, Informix and Access are some of the examples of RDBMS (T/F)
4. Composite key is a combination of two or more rows for identification of columns in a table uniquely (T/F)

D. ANSWER THE FOLLOWING QUESTIONS:

1. What is the purpose of DBMS?
2. Write a note of concept of database?
3. Give any four main features of database

E. PRACTICAL WORK

Practically work on database and try to identify data, information, field, record and table in database.

Answers

A. Multiple choice question answers:

1. c 2. c

B. Fill in the blanks answers:

1. Microsoft Access 2. Database 3. Field 4. Foreign Key

C. True False answers

1. False 2. True 3. True 4. False

SESSION 2: CREATE AND EDIT TABLES USING WIZARD AND SQL COMMANDS

A database stores information in an organised way that makes it easy to get information in an effective way. In MS-Access, you can create various elements for database operations.

2.1 Introduction to a RDBMS

RDBMS is stands for Relational Database Management System in which data is structured in database records, fields and tables. Each RDBMS table contain various database table rows. Further, each row of database table contains one or more fields of database table. In this, data is stored in group of tables related to common columns or fields. The relational operator is also provided by RDBMS for manipulation of stored data into the database tables. In most of the RDBMS a SQL is used as database query language. Most popular RDBMS are DB2, MySQL, MS SQL Server and Oracle.

2.2 Database objects – tables, queries, forms, and reports of the database

There is tab on the top of window screen that helps in creating command for providing access to forms, queries, tables and reports in the database.

Forms: It is used for entering, Viewing and modifying the records. In various occasions such as applying for a job, registration for school and visiting to doctors office you fill out the forms. The reason behind using forms so often is due to easiness of guiding society toward entering data in correct way.

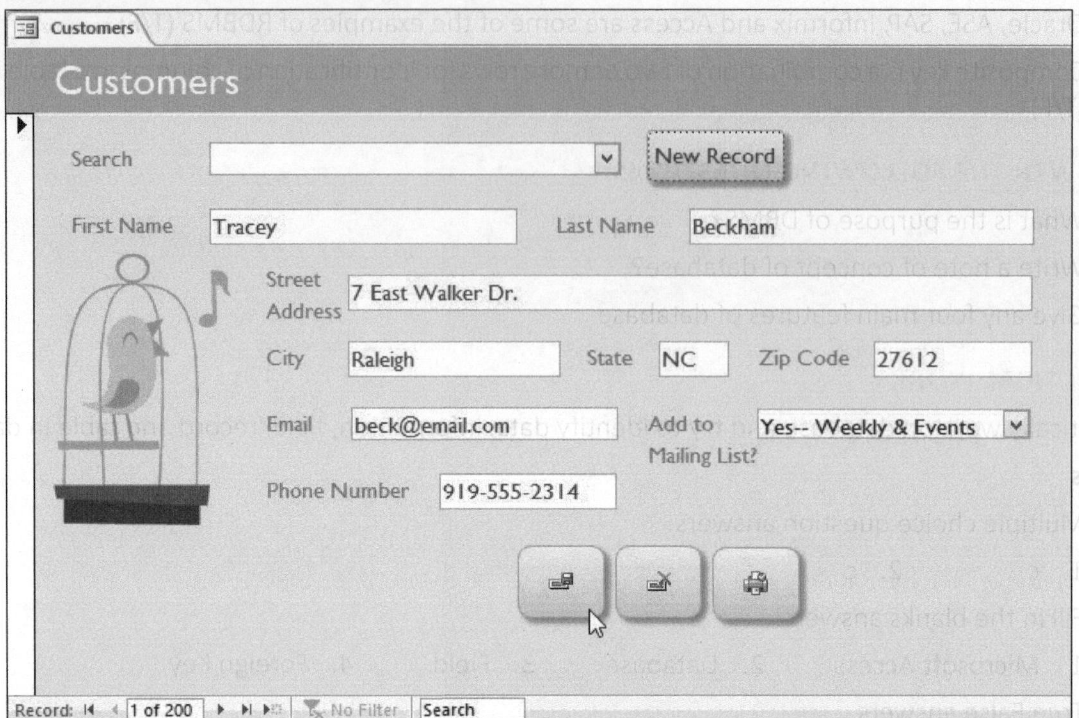

Figure 3.7: Form

Queries: It is the way of compiling and searching data from one or more tables. Asking a detailed question of your database is like running a query and when query is built in Access, it is just as defining specific search conditions for finding the exact data. As compared to simple search in a table, queries found as more powerful (figure 3.8).

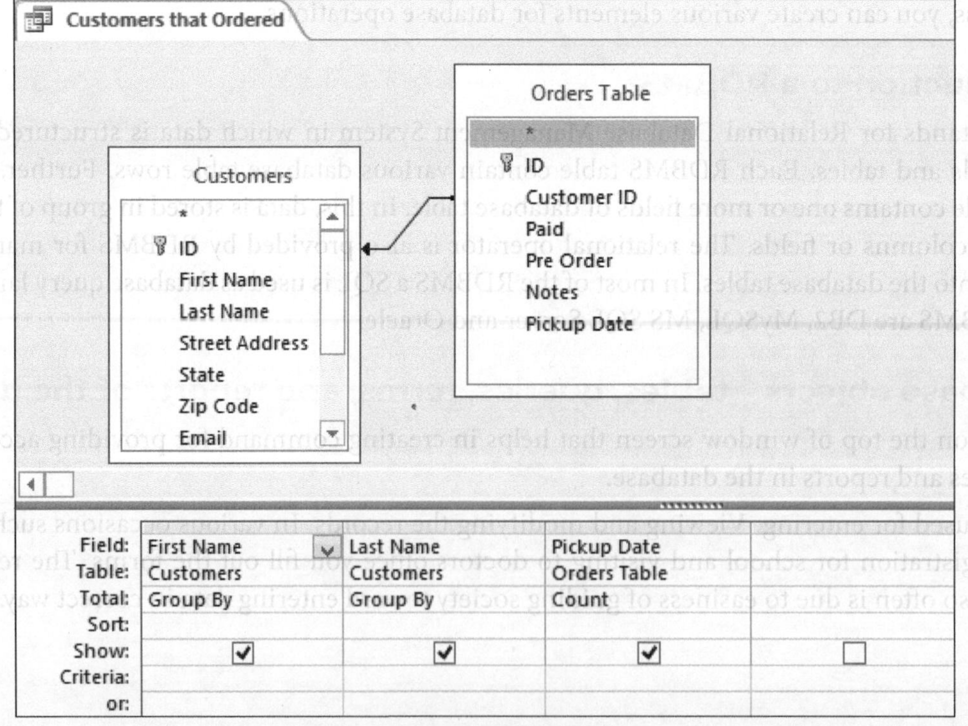

Figure 3.8: Queries

Reports: It gives the ability of presenting data in print. A database report is seen when someone has received a computer printout of a class schedule or a purchase printed invoice. It is useful due to its ability of giving access to present database components in an easy to read format. The appearance of reports can be customizing for visually appealing. In Access, there is feature of creating a report from any query or table (figure 3.9).

December Orders

Orders

First Name	Last Name	Phone Number		Pickup Date
Andrzej	Wujek	919-555-0450		12/4/2010
Dick	Whitman	919-555-5042		12/4/2010
Xy'nya	Bell	919-555-0758		12/9/2010
Xiaoxi	Zheng	919-555-2786		12/10/2010
Hakim	Auden	919-555-0045		12/14/2010
Zoey	Altman	919-555-6688		12/15/2010
Raphaelle	Duvalier	919-555-1547		12/15/2010
Zoey	Altman	919-555-6688		12/16/2010

Figure 3.9: Reports

Tables: It store data without any formatting, sorting, calculation, storing and sorting it. The most fundamental task of a database is storing data for easy management and retrieval. The appearance of tables in Excel is same as in Access. It is just like Excel spreadsheet.

Suppliers

Supplier ID	Company Name	Contact Name	Contact T
1	Exotic Liquids	Charlotte Cooper	Purchasing Ma
2	New Orleans Cajun Delights	Shelley Burke	Order Adminis
3	Grandma Kelly's Homestead	Regina Murphy	Sales Represe
4	Tokyo Traders	Yoshi Nagase	Marketing Mar
5	Cooperativa de Quesos 'Las Cabras'	Antonio del Valle Saavedra	Export Adminis
6	Mayumi's	Mayumi Ohno	Marketing Rep
7	Pavlova, Ltd.	Ian Devling	Marketing Mar
8	Specialty Biscuits, Ltd.	Peter Wilson	Sales Represe
9	PB Knäckebröd AB	Lars Peterson	Sales Agent
10	Refrescos Americanas LTDA	Carlos Diaz	Marketing Mar
11	Heli Süßwaren GmbH & Co. KG	Petra Winkler	Sales Manager
12	Plutzer Lebensmittelgroßmärkte AG	Martin Bein	International M
13	Nord-Ost-Fisch Handelsgesellschaft mb	Sven Petersen	Coordinator Fo
14	Formaggi Fortini s.r.l.	Elio Rossi	Sales Represen

Figure 3.10: Tables

Forms: It makes data available on the screen. With form, one can view and edit the data and also display it, sort, add and delete it. It enables the working with data without holding any data. It is just a tool used for viewing the data in your table. The change in form is just change in your table.

2.3 Terms in database – table, field, record

In MS-Access, tables are used for storing the data. It is used for presenting data in tabular format such as in records in rows and fields in columns. In the same ways, there is field and a record that is briefly explains in this section.

Tables: A table in database is made up of fields and records that hold data. Tables are also known as datasheets and each table in a database contains data about different and related subject (figure 3.11).

Complaints : Table

Log ID	Operator	Resolved	Duration
1201037	CS1	☑	553
1201242	CS2	☑	524
1201247	CS1	☑	581
1201220	CS4	☐	876
1221037	CS1	☑	421

Record: 5 of 5

Figure 3.11: Database Table

Records: Data is stored in records that is made up of fields and contains all the data about particular person, company, or item in a database. In database, records consists of data for one customer support incident report and it appear as rows in a database table (figure 3.12).

Complaints : Table

Log ID	Operator	Resolved	Duration
1201037	CS1	☑	553
1201242	CS2	☑	524
1201247	CS1	☑	581
1201220	CS4	☐	876
1221037	CS1	☑	421

Record: 5 of 5

Figure 3.12: Records appear as rows in a database table.

Fields: It is a part of a record consists of single piece of data for the subject of the record. There are mainly four fields in each record of database.

Log ID	**A number assigned to this customer support incident for identification purposes**
Operator	The code for the customer support operator who handled this incident
Resolved	A check box to indicate whether the incident was resolved
Duration	The time in seconds the operator spent on this incident

Fields come as columns in a database table (figure 3.13).

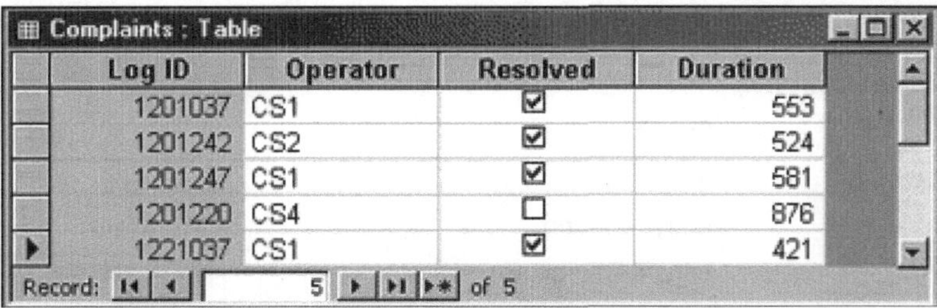

Complaints : Table

Log ID	Operator	Resolved	Duration
1201037	CS1	☑	553
1201242	CS2	☑	524
1201247	CS1	☑	581
1201220	CS4	☐	876
1221037	CS1	☑	421

Record: 5 of 5

Figure 3.13: Fields appear as columns in a database table.

2.4 Steps to create a table using table wizard, Data types in Base

To work with tables, perform the following steps:

- Click on Tables icon in the Database list or use Alt + a
- There comes three tasks that can be perform on a table

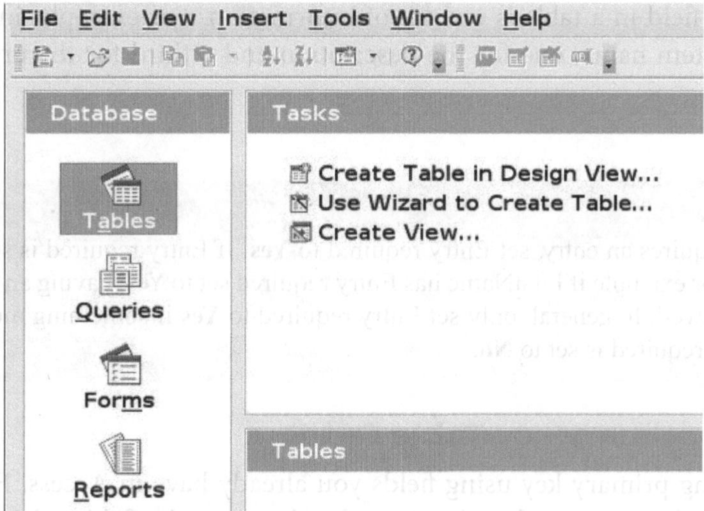

Figure 3.14: Creating Tables

Using the Wizard to create a table:

There is need of primary key field in every table that is used to number the entries and let that number to increase automatically by adding each entry. The wizard allows the table fields to come from more than one suggested table. Steps to create a table using Wizard are:

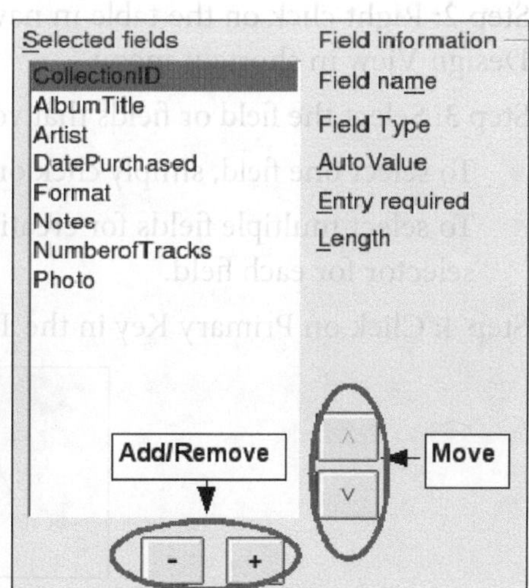

Figure 3.15: Order of fields

Step 1: Select Fields: There are two categories of tables named business and personal. User can choose one from it and each category consists of their own suggested tables. In each tables, there is list of available fields and CD-Collection Sample table can be used in the personal category for selecting the fields needed for table (figure 3.15).

Step 2: Set field types and formats: In this step the properties is given for each fields. By clicking on field, the information on the right get changed and one can also make changes according to their needs (figure 3.16).

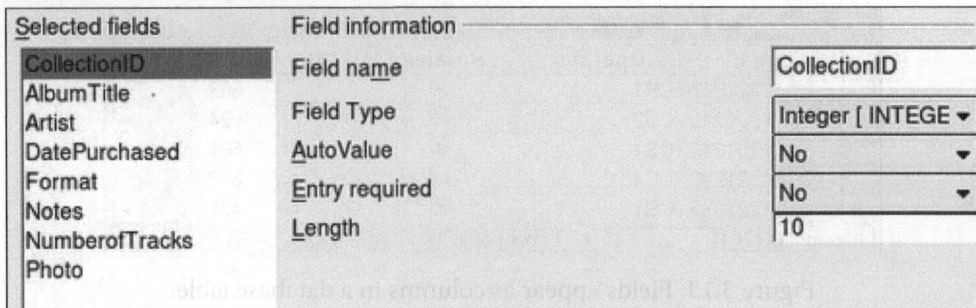

Figure 3.16: Changing field types

Step 3: Set primary key: In this step, the created primary key are checked by selecting the option of use an existing field as a primary key and select the required fields.

Step 4: Create the table: The name of table is default but user can change it in this step. Then click on finish for completing the table wizard.

Point to remember: A field in a table is one bit of information. For example, in a price list table, there might be one field for item name, one for the description and a third for the price. More fields may be added as needed.

MEMORY BOX

If any of these fields requires an entry, set Entry required to **Yes**. If Entry required is set to Yes, this field must have something in it. For example if FirstName has Entry required set to Yes, having an entry with the first name missing will not be allowed. In general, only set Entry required to **Yes** if something must always be put in that field. By default, Entry required is set to **No**.

2.5 Option to set primary key Table Data

There is option of setting primary key using fields you already have in Access. For working properly in primary key, there is need to unique identification of each row in the field and it never contain empty or null value change very rarely. Perform the following steps for setting the primary key:

Step 1: Open the database you want to modify

Step 2: Right click on the table in navigation pane in which you want to set the primary key and click on Design View in shortcut menu.

Step 3: Select the field or fields that you want to use as the primary key.

- To select one field, simply click on row selector for the field you want to add.
- To select multiple fields for creating a composite key, hold down the CTRL key and then click on row selector for each field.

Step 4: Click on Primary Key in the Tools group of Design tab (figure 3.17)

Figure 3.17: Primary key command in Tools group

In left side of the field, a key indicator is added to the left that is specify as primary key by user.

Knowledge box: If you don't see the Navigation Pane, press F11 to display it.

2.6 DDL Commands

DDL stands for Data Definition Language that helps in defining the database structure. There are mainly five main commands of DDL as given below:

CREATE: This statement is used for defining the database structure.

Syntax: CREATE TABLE TABLE_NAME (COLUMN_NAME DATATYPES[......]);

Example: Create Table students;

DROP: This commands is used to remove the tables and databases from RDBMS.

Syntax: DROP TABLE;

Example: Drop table student;

ALTER: This command enable the user to alter the structure of the database.

Syntax: ALTER TABLE table_name ADD column_name COLUMN definition;

Example: Alter table komal_data;

TRUNCATE: This command is used for deleting all the rows from the table and frees the space in the table.

Syntax: TRUNCATE TABLE table_name;

Example: TRUNCATE table students;

Summary

- RDBMS is stands for Relational Database Management System in which data is structured in database records, fields and tables.
- Forms is used for entering, Viewing and modifying the records.
- Queries is the way of compiling and searching data from one or more tables.
- Reports gives the ability of presenting data in print. A database report is seen when someone has received a computer printout of a class schedule or a purchase printed invoice.
- Tables store data without any formatting, sorting, calculation, storing and sorting it.
- Fields is a part of a record consists of single piece of data for the subject of the record.
- There is need of primary key field in every table that is used to number the entries and let that number to increase automatically by adding each entry.
- There is option of setting primary key using fields you already have in Access.
- DDL stands for Data Definition Language that helps in defining the database structure.
- Four main commands of DLL are Create, Drop, Alter and Truncate

Keywords: RDBMS, Tables, Queries, Forms, Reports, Database, Field, Record, Create table, Table wizards, Primary key, Table data, DDL Commands

Self-Assessment

A. MULTIPLE CHOICE QUESTIONS.

1. RDBMS stands for ____________.
   a. Relation Data management system   b. Relational Data Basic management system
   c. Relational Database management system   d. Relation Database management system
2. ____________ in database helps in defining the database structure..
   a. Table   b. DDL commands   c. Data commands   d. All of these
3. Which of the following is not a command of DDL?
   a. CREATE   b. DROP   c. SET   d. TRUNCATE

B. FILL IN THE BLANKS

1. ____________ database object is used for entering, Viewing and modifying the records.
2. ____________ type of database object store data without any formatting, sorting, calculation, storing and sorting it.
3. Primary key is used to ____________ identify the records in a table.
4. ____________ is the smallest part of table in which one data item can be kept.

C. TRUE FALSE

1. Queries is the way of compiling and searching data from one or more tables (T/F)
2. Data is stored in forms that is made up of fields and contains all the data about particular person, company, or item in a database (T/F).
3. A database can have only one table (T/F)
4. A table is a database may have multiple primary keys (T/F)

D. ANSWER THE FOLLOWING QUESTIONS:

1. Write a note of RDBMS?
2. Name and explain various terms related to database.
3. Write down the steps of creating a table using Wizard, Data types in Base.

E. PRACTICAL WORK

Open RDBMS and identify various database objects and then create a sample table in any category using wizard.

Create a table and then assign data types in design view and enter the data in the fields.

Answers

A. Multiple choice question answers:

1. c   2. b   3. c

B. Fill in the blanks answers:

1. Forms   2. Tables   3. Uniquely   4. Field

C. True False answers

1. True   2. False   3. False   4. False

SESSION 3: PERFORM OPERATIONS ON TABLE

3.1 Inserting data in the table

The insert statement is used for inserting or adding a row of data into the table. To insert records into a table, perform the following steps:

Enter the key words insert into followed by the table name > Open parenthesis > List of column names separated by commas > Closing parenthesis > Keyword values > List of values enclosed in parenthesis

The enter values will be seized in the rows and match up with the column names specified by user.

Example: insert into employee (first, last, age, address, city, state) values ('Luke', 'Duke', 45, '2130 Boars Nest', 'Hazard Co', 'Georgia');

In the above example, the column name first will match up with the value ‹Luke›, and the column name state will match up with the value ‹Georgia›.

Knowledge Box

The strings should be enclosed in single quotes and numbers without quotes.

3.2 Editing records in the table

Access gives feature of controlling one text for use with Short and Long Text that is also known as Memo fields. By the size of control one will be able to tell whether the size of underlying field is long or short text that tells about the size need for the underlying field of table. Around 255 characters can be stored in Short Text field and 64,000 characters in Long Text field.

Steps to edit records in the table are:

1. Open the query or table in Datasheet view
2. Click on the field and navigate the field using TAB or arrow keys > Press F2 key. The field can be selected by clicking near the left border of the field when + plus sign comes near to mouse pointer.
3. Place the cursor for entering information
4. Enter or update the text

Memory Box

1. To insert a new line in a text field, press Ctrl+Enter.
2. To insert the default value for a field, press Ctrl+Alt+Spacebar.
3. To insert the current date in a field, press CTRL+SEMICOLON.
4. To insert the current time, press CTRL+SHIFT+COLON ().
5. To check spelling, press F7.
6. To reuse similar values of a previous record, move to the corresponding field in the previous record, and then press CTRL+' (apostrophe).
7. To explicitly save your changes, press Shift+Enter.

3.3 Deleting records from the table

The process of deleting records from the table is very simple except for record related to other data and resides on the one side of a one to many relationships. For maintaining the data integrity an access does not let the deleting of related data. The steps to delete data are:

1. Open the table in either Datasheet or Form view

2. Select the record that you want to delete. Click on record selector next to the record in case of availability of record selector
3. Press delete key or select Home > Records > Delete

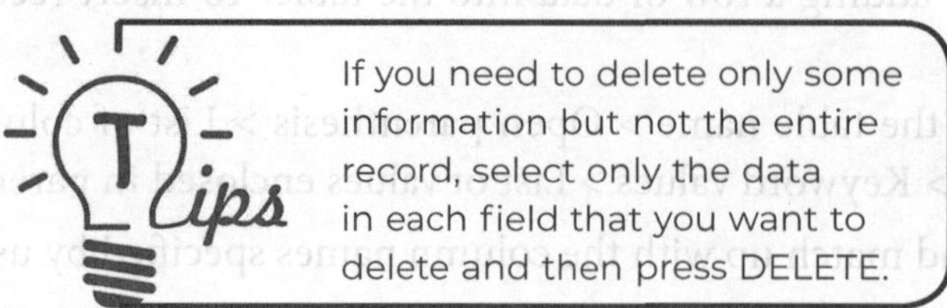

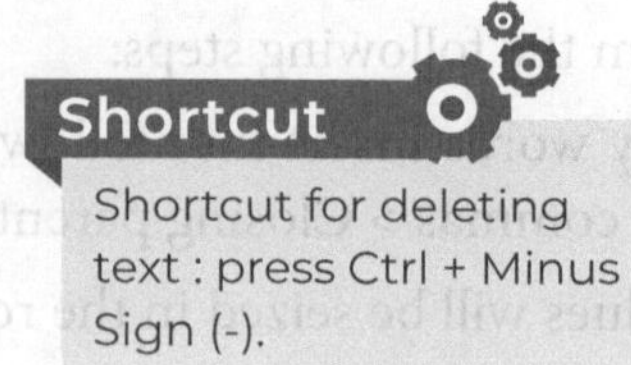

3.4 Sorting data in the table, Referential integrity

By sorting data, user can put a column of information in different orders such as numerical, alphabetical or data order. One can also insert in ascending order or descending order for both alphabets and numbers. User can also sort within a sort.

For instance, User can sort by state and then within each state by city.

While sorting within a sort, the innermost sort is performed firstly. For instance, for sorting by state and then city, user first have to sort by city then by state.

To add sort, perform the following steps (figure 3.18):

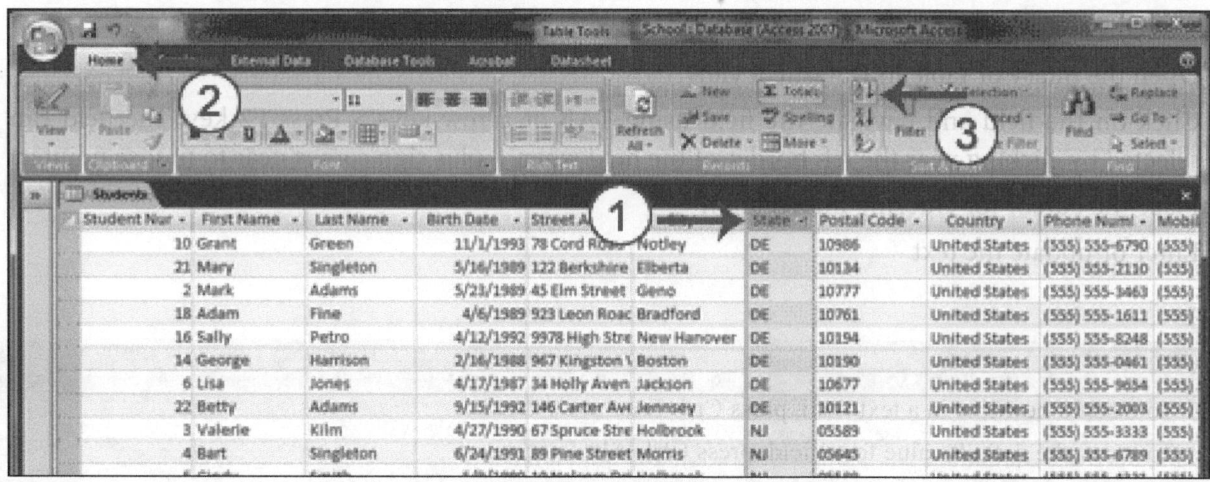

Figure 3.18: Sorting data in the table

1. Click on column label for the column you want to sort
2. Activate the Home tab
3. Click on either ascending or descending button in the Sort and Filter group. Access sorts the column in any of the order

Referential Integrity

It is a concept of database for building and maintaining logical relation between tables and avoiding the logical corruption of data. In RDBMS it is very useful and important. Usually, it is made up of both primary and foreign key.

Mainly it does not allow the addition of any record in a table consist of foreign key unless there is corresponding primary key in reference table. If in reference table, any record is deleted then all the corresponding records in referencing table will be deleted for the referential integrity.

3.5 Creating and editing relationships – one to one, one to many, many to many

In Access, data can be stored in multiple tables and then relationships are used for joining the tables. After creating relationships the data can be used from all of the related tables in report, form and query. There are three types of relationships between tables:

One to one relationship: Let user have two tables A and B. In case of one to one relationship, each record in Table A can only have one matching record in Table B and vice a versa. This type of relationships is very less because the data is stored in single table in case of one to one relationship. This relationship is created for both the related columns are primary keys or have unique constraints (figure 3.19).

Customer

customer-id	customer-name	city
C001	Rahim	Dhaka
C002	Karim	Pabna
C003	Salam	Dhaka
C004	Rafiq	Comilla
C005	Qader	Sylhet

Account

account-no.	balance
A001	200
A002	100
A003	350
A004	700
A005	1200

Figure 3.19: One to one relationship

In the above example one customer should have only one account number and each account no can be associated only with one customer ID.

One-to-Many Relationship: This is most common type of relationship in which record in Table A can have number of matching in records of Table B but Table B can only have one matching record in Table A. In case of this relationship, the primary table is the one which have one value and related table is with many values. The validity of the relationship between two tables gets ensured by referential integrity (figure 3.20).

Customer

customer-id	customer-name	city
C001	Rahim	Dhaka
C002	Karim	Pabna
C003	Salam	Dhaka
C004	Rafiq	Comilla
C005	Qader	Sylhet

Account

account-no.	balance
A001	200
A002	100
A003	350
A004	700
A005	1200

customer-id	account-no.
C001	A001
C002	A002
C003	A003
C004	A004
C005	A005

Figure 3.20: One to Many relationship

Many to Many Relationship: In this case, Table A record can have number of matching records in Table B and vice a versa. This type of relationship become possible by defining the third table named junction table whose primary key contains two fields named foreign keys from both Tables A and B. It is just like two one to many relationships with third table (figure 3.21).

Customer				Account	
customer-id	customer-name	city		account-no.	balance
C001	Rahim	Dhaka		A001	200
C002	Karim	Pabna		A002	100
C003	Salam	Dhaka		A003	350
C004	Rafiq	Comilla		A004	700
C005	Qader	Sylhet		A005	1200

Figure 3.21: Many to Many relationship

3.6 Field properties

After creating a field and setting its data type other additional properties of field can be set. The data type of field determines the other properties that can be set. For instance, the size of a Text field can be controlled by setting the properties of Field Size. There are number of field properties that can be customized and set in the panel of Field Properties.

Common properties of field are:

Along with setting up individual field properties, one can also use common fields menu for setting all the properties at once for common fields such as Address, Price, Name and Date. For accessing this menu, click on the star next to the field name (figure 3.22):

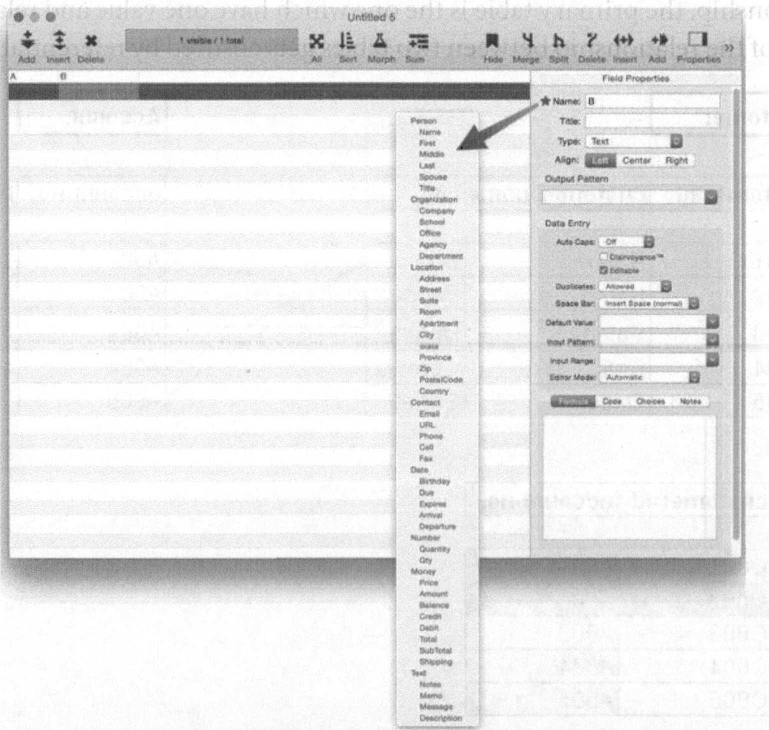

Figure 3.22: Common properties of field

By choosing name from this menu, Panorama sets up all the attributes including alignment, automatic capitalization, type, output patterns and other data entry options (figure 3.23).

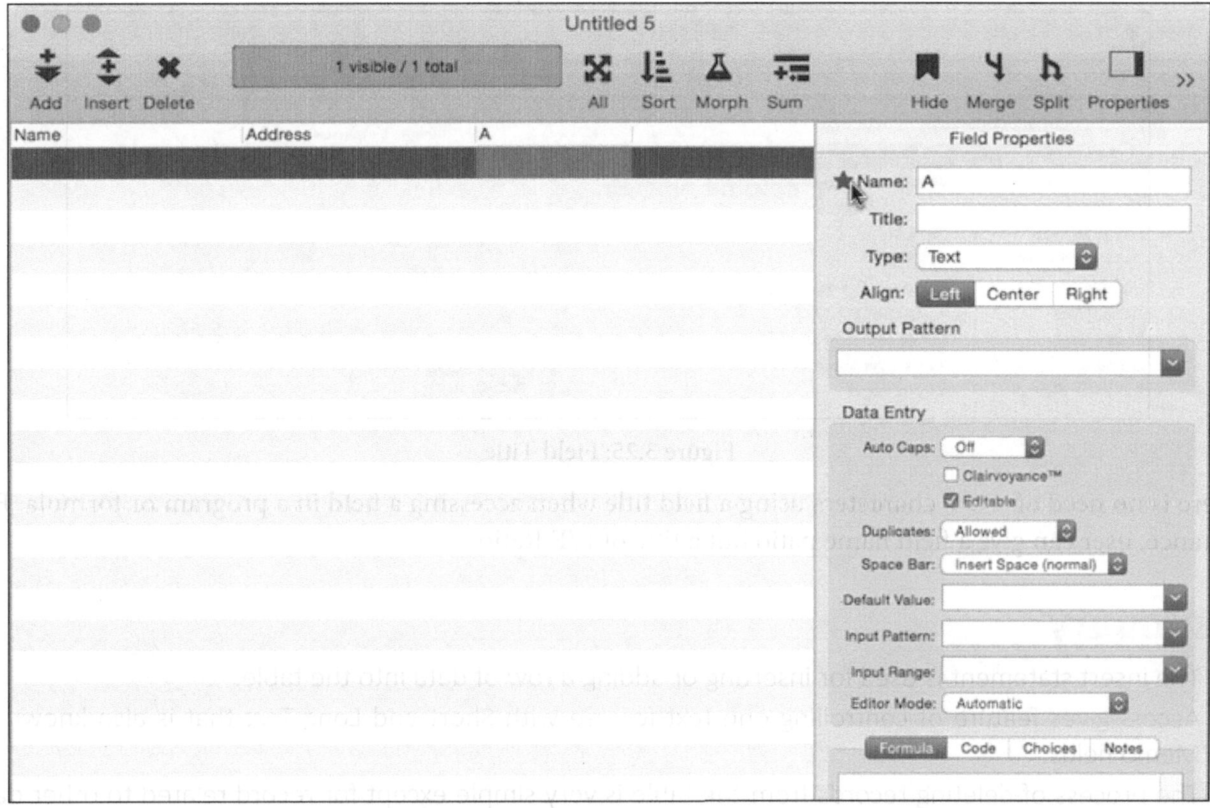

Figure 3.23: Selecting field properties

The attributes of current field normally gets changed by Common fields menu but by right clicking on start, Panorama will add a new field with specified attributes and name. A new field can be inserted by right clicking and holding the Shift key.

Field Name: In Panorama database, each field is identified by a field name. Several purposes are served by field names such as they remind you the usage of field for instance the Dates field probably contains dates and Name field contains names. They appear at the top of each column in the datasheet and used for identification of fields in procedures and formulas (figure 3.24).

Figure 3.24: Field Name

No restrictions come on the field names by Panorama and it may be long or short as per user requirements. It may also contain any character types from the keyboard. User can also have more than one fields with same name.

Field Title: The field can also be serves as title. This title will be displayed at the top of the column in data sheet (figure 3.25).

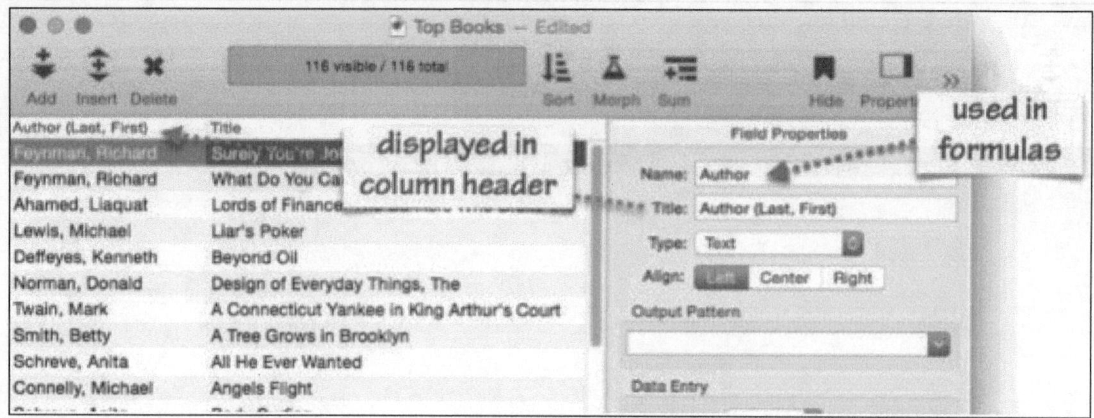

Figure 3.25: Field Title

There is no need of <<>> characters using a field title when accessing a field in a program or formula. For instance, user can give a field name patio but a title of P/E Ratio.

Summary

- The insert statement is used for inserting or adding a row of data into the table.
- Access gives feature of controlling one text for use with Short and Long Text that is also known as Memo fields.
- The process of deleting records from the table is very simple except for record related to other data and resides on the one side of a one to many relationships.
- By sorting data, user can put a column of information in different orders such as numerical, alphabetical or data order.
- Referential Integrity is a concept of database for building and maintaining logical relation between tables and avoiding the logical corruption of data.
- In Access, data can be stored in multiple tables and then relationships are used for joining the tables.
- One to Many Relationship is most common type of relationship in which record in Table A can have number of matching in records of Table B but Table B can only have one matching record in Table A.
- In case of Many to Many relationship, Table A record can have number of matching records in Table B and vice a versa.
- The data type of field determines the other properties that can be set.
- In Panorama database, each field is identified by a field name. Several purposes are served by field names such as they remind you the usage of field for instance the Dates field probably contains dates and Name field contains names.
- The field can also be serves as title. This title will be displayed at the top of the column in data sheet.

Keywords: Inserting data, Editing records, Deleting records, Table, Sorting data, Referential integrity, Creating Relationship, Editing relationship, Field properties

Self-Assessment

A. MULTIPLE CHOICE QUESTIONS.

1. Give the count of characters can be stored in Short Text field.

   a. 64 b. 365 c. 255 d. 64,000

2. What is the shortcut key to insert a new line in a text fields?

   a. Ctrl + A b. Ctrl + Enter c. Ctrl + Tab d. Ctrl + V

3. Let user have two tables A and B. In case of ____________ type of creating and editing relationships, each record in Table A can only have one matching record in Table B and vice a versa

   a. One to one relationship b. One to many relationship
   c. Many to many relationship d. Many to one relationship

4. Which of the following is not a datatype?

   a. Date/Time b. Picture c. Number d. Text

B. FILL IN THE BLANKS

1. ____________ statement in the database is used for inserting or adding a row of data into the table.
2. A record in a table is also known as ____________.
3. ____________ count of characters can be stored in Short Text field table.
4. ____________ is a concept of database for building and maintaining logical relation between tables and avoiding the logical corruption of data.
5. In ____________ database, each field is identified by a field name.

C. TRUE FALSE

1. Collection of records is called a Data redundancy (T/F)
2. User can stored only 64,000 characters in Lonf Term field table (T/F)
3. CTRL_SHIFT +COLON () is the shortcut key to insert the current time in the table (T/F)

D. ANSWER THE FOLLOWING QUESTIONS:

1. How to insert a data in table? Explain with example.
2. Give steps to edit records in the table.
3. Is it possible to sort data in the table? If yes, then give various steps involved in it.
4. Define any two from one to one, one to many and many to many way of editing relationships.

E. PRACTICAL WORK

Insert data in the table then edit records, Delete it and sort data in the table

Enter different field properties in the table and observe it

Answers

A. Multiple choice question answers:

1. a 2. b 3. a 4. b

B. Fill in the blanks answers:

1. Insert 2. Row 3. 255 4. Referential Integrity 5. Panorama

C. True False answers

1. False 2. True 3. True

SESSION 4: RETRIEVE DATA USING QUERY

We query data on daily basis from Google searches by asking Siri for a funny joke and many more. Queries are just simple questions against a set of data that can become complex by involvement of multiple tables and millions of records. But its basic concept is straight forward and not very complex.

4.1 Database query

Query is a way of requesting information from the database. Database query can be either a select query or an action query. Select query is a query for retrieving data while an action query requests additional actions to be performed on the data such as deletion, insertion and updating.

A query database is a request for data from a database. The request is to retrieve data however data can also be manipulated using queries. The data can come from one or more tables. For instance, manager can perform a query for selecting the employees who were hired 5 months ago. The results could be the base for creating evaluations of performance.

4.2 Defining query

Query is a SQL SELECT statement created in the Query painter and saved with a name so that it can be repeatedly used as the source data for a report. It saves time because there is need to specify the requirements of data just once. For instance, Columns can be specified along with which rows to retrieve and sorting order in a query. Now, there is need to only specify the query as the data source whenever someone wants to create a report using that data.

4.3 Query creation using wizard

The query can be created using Microsoft Access Query wizards. There are two query wizards that are used for maintaining a database named Find Duplicate Query Wizard that work on a single table and Find Unmatched Query Wizard that compares records in one table with records in another. All these query wizards along with Crosstab wizard is listed when choose a New Query (figure 3.26).

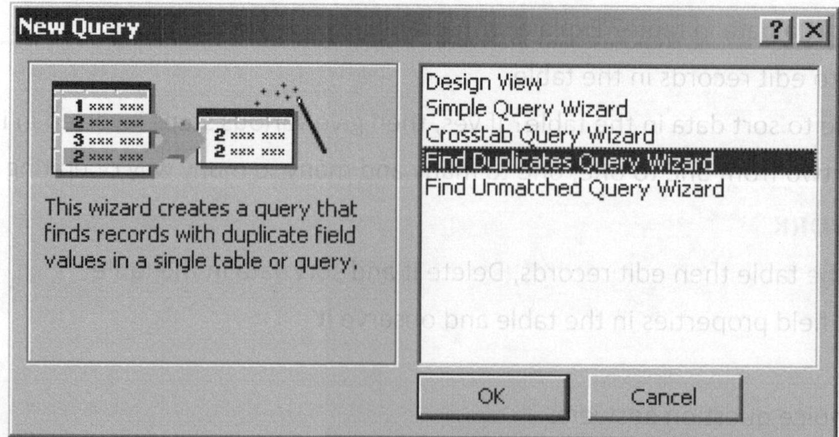

Figure 3.26: New Query

Steps to create a query using wizard are:

1. Display the create tab on the Ribbon and click the Query Wizard button
2. Select Simple Query Wizard from the New Query dialog box then click on Ok button.
3. Choose the first table or query using Tables/Queries list box then fields start appearing from that object appear in the available fields list box
4. Move the fields that you want to use in the query from the Available fields list to the selected fields list by double clicking a file name
5. The step 2 and 3 will be repeated if you are using fields from more than one table or query for adding fields from the additional tables or queries to the selected fields list and then click next.
6. Choose the type of query
7. Choose the summarization of data and click OK to close dialog box > Click Next for checking the next window of the wizard. In this check boxes are used for indicating the new fields you want to Access to create
8. Type a name for the query in the box at the top of window.
9. Click on Finish button to view the query.

4.4 Creation of query using design view

From all the available methods of creating a query, Design view is the fastest and easiest way. The steps to create a query using Design view are:

- Open the database
- Click on Queries icon in the Database window of Objects bar > Double click on it to create a query in Design view and Table dialog box will open.
- Select the query or table user want to use (figure 3.27)

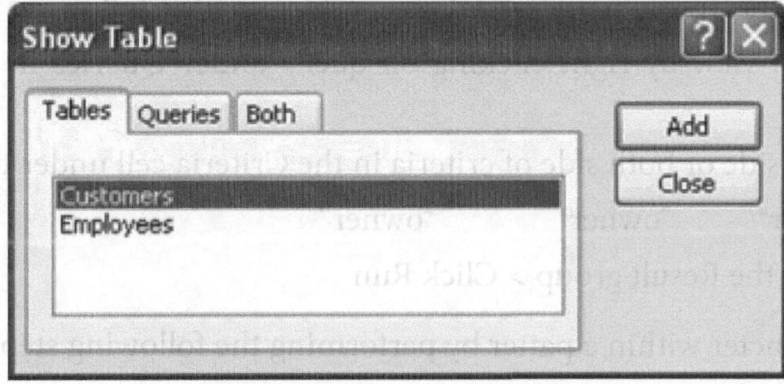

Figure 3.27: Show Table dialog box

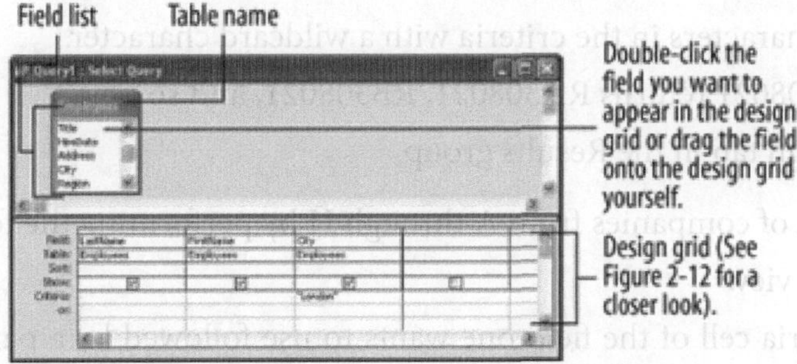

Figure 3.28: Query window in Design view

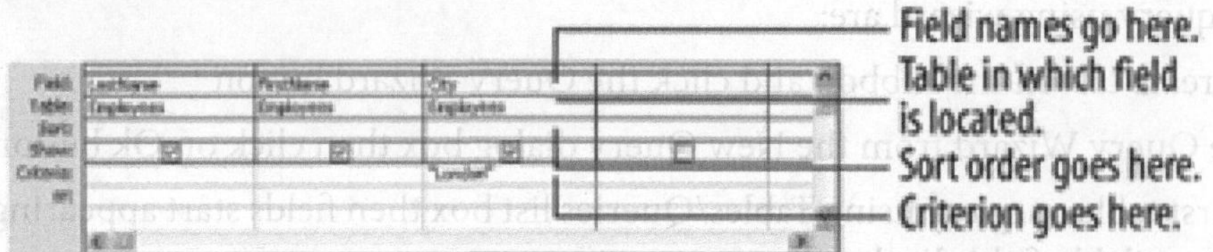

Figure 3.29: Design Grid

- Click on Employees and then Add
- Close the Show Table dialog box after finishing with adding the queries or tables
- Click Close and query window will start appearing in Design view

4.5 Editing a query

Existing queries can be edited and then save in the Personal Queries folder. One can also edit the queries in the Public Queries folder. Perform the below given steps to edit a query:

- Right click on the query in Navigation view > Click on Edit
- Select the fields to use as query filters and Edit Query Wizard page will appear.
- To filter the results of query, add and remove fields. By grouping filters in the Filters pane, create expressions of complex filter > Click Next
- Specify the values for the filters on the Define query filters page > Click Next
- Select the fields to display on the Define display fields page for formatting the query results > Click Finish

Point to remember: One can also edit the filter field and display field settings individually

4.6 Applying criteria in query – single field, multiple fields, using wildcard

One can match all characters anywhere in the data by performing the following steps:

- Open query in Design view by right clicking on query under Queries in Navigation pane > Click Design view
- Add asterisk on either side or both side of criteria in the Criteria cell under the field one want to use
- For instance: "*owner*" "owner*" "*owner"
- Click on Design tab in the Result group > Click Run

One can also match a character within a patter by performing the following steps:

- Open query in Design view
- Type operator in criteria cell of the field
- Replace one of more characters in the criteria with a wildcard character.
- For instance: Like R?308021 returns RA308021, RB308021, and so on.
- Click Run on the Design tab in the Results group

One can also retrieve a list of companies from A through H by performing the following steps:

- Open query in Design view
- Enter Like in the criteria cell of the field one wants to use followed by a pair of quotes. For instance: Like "".

- In double quotes, add a pair of square brackets with the range of characters one want to find. Such as: Like "[a-h]"
- Wildcards can be used outside the brackets. For instance: Like "[a-h]*"

Table of wildcard characters

This table lists and describes the wildcard characters you can use in an Access query.

Symbol	Description	Example
*	Matches zero or more characters. It can be used as the first or last character in the character string.	wh* finds wh, what, white, and why
?	Matches any single alphabetic character.	b?ll finds ball, bell, and bill
[ ]	Matches any single character within the brackets.	b[ae]ll finds ball and bell but not bill
!	Matches any character not in the brackets.	b[!ae]ll finds bill and bull but not ball or bell
-	Matches any one of a range of characters. You must specify the range in ascending order (A to Z, not Z to A).	b[a-c]d finds bad, bbd, and bcd
#	Matches any single numeric character.	1#3 finds 103, 113, and 123

Examples of using wildcards

Situation	Example
Your data lists some people as "owner" and others as "owner/operator".	Like "owner*" or Like "*owner*"
You want to use wildcards with a parameter query.	Like "*" & [parameter] & "*" *For example:* Like "*" & [fish] & "*" Returns all recipes containing "fish", such as fish & chips, rockfish, and so on.
Someone misspelled a name when they entered data, such as "Adrien" instead of "Adrian".	Like "Adri?n"
You want to find customers whose last name starts with A through H — for use in a bulk mailing, for example.	Like "[a-h]*"
You want to find part numbers that have all but the second and third digit in common.	Like "R??083930"
You want to send out invitations for a block party on the 1000 block of Park Street.	Like "1### Park Street"

Character	Required Syntax
Asterisk *	[*]
Question mark ?	[?]
Number sign #	[#]
Hyphen -	[-]
Set of opening and closing brackets together []	[[]]
Opening bracket [	[[]
Closing bracket]	No special treatment needed
Exclamation point !	No special treatment needed

4.7 Performing calculations

One can also perform simple calculations in Access queries. For this, one can use expressions in queries and an expression is just a formula that produce a result in the context of the running query. Expressions for this can be a simple mathematical calculation.

The simplest query with a calculation is (figure 3.30):

- SELECT 1+1

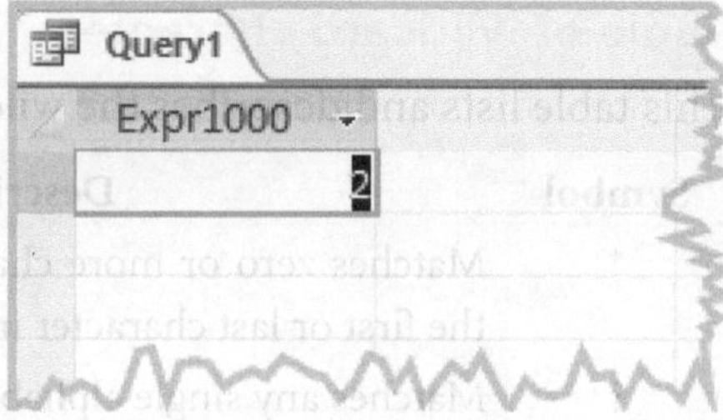

Figure 3.30: Query

This query can only be written and executed in SQL View of a query. There is need of at least one table as data source for query in graphical query designer. Usually most of the calculation is based on the data in a table. One of the realistic simple calculations is the calculation of a gross price on the basis of net price stored in a table.

The NetPrice is the name given to relevant column in demo table. This column name can be used for referring the column in an Expression.

Formula for determining the gross price is:

[NetPrice] + [NetPrice] / 100*20

20 is the current VAT rate. This same formula can be used as an expression for a calculated field in an Access query.

4.8 Grouping of data

In Microsoft Access Report data can be grouped. In this section, we will explains the way of creating a report that allows us to group the data on non-standard numeric ranges. If we use the Microsoft Access Report Wizard, when working through the stages and selecting fields to Group the report on, we can choose Group Intervals. If the grouping field is numeric, the following choices will be presented to group on (figure 3.31):

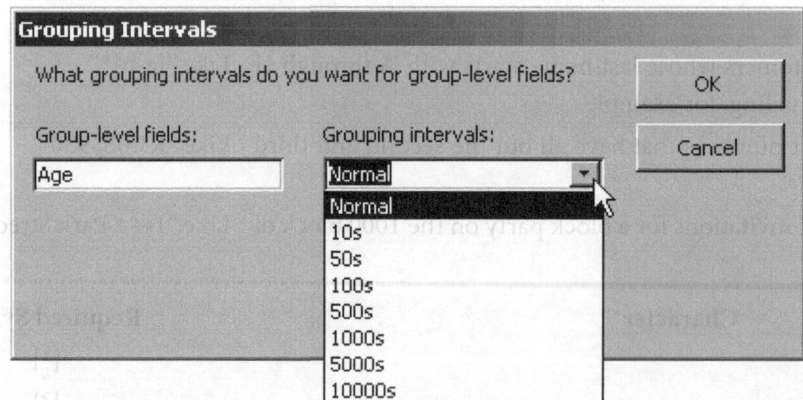

Figure 3.31: Microsoft Access Report wizard screen, showing the Grouping Intervals available for numeric data

4.9 Structured Query Language (SQL)

SQL is a standard database language used for creating, maintaining and retrieving the relational database. Some of the important facts related to SQL are:

- SQL is case insensitive but it is recommended practice to use keywords such as CREATE, UPDATE, SELECT and many more in capital letters along with user defined things such as column name, table name and many more in small letters.

- In SQL comments can be written using "--" double hyphen at the starting of any line.
- It is a programming language for relational databases such as Oracle, Postgre, MySQL, SQL server, Sybase and many more. Other non-relational or NoSQL databases are DynamoDB, MongoDB in which SQL is not used.
- There is no ISO standard for SQL this cause a very slight difference in syntax of implementations. So, there can be cases in which some queries that work well in SQL server does not work in MySQL.

Summary

- Queries are just simple questions against a set of data that can become complex by involvement of multiple tables and millions of records.
- Query is a SQL SELECT statement created in the Query painter and saved with a name so that it can be repeatedly used as the source data for a report.
- The query can be created using Microsoft Access Query wizards.
- To create a query using design view, Open the database, Click on Queries icon in the Database window of Objects bar > Double click on it to create a query in Design view and Table dialog box will open > Select the query or table user want to use.
- Existing queries can be edited and then save in the Personal Queries folder.
- One can also perform simple calculations in Access queries. For this, one can use expressions in queries and an expression is just a formula that produce a result in the context of the running query.
- In Microsoft Access Report data can be grouped
- SQL is a standard database language used for creating, maintaining and retrieving the relational database.

Keywords: Retrieve data, Database query, Defining query, Query creation, Design view, Editing query, Applying criteria, Single field, Multiple field, Wildcard characters, Calculations, Grouping data, Structured Query Language

Self-Assessment

A. MULTIPLE CHOICE QUESTIONS.

1. _____________ is a way of requesting information from the database.

   a. Retrieving   b. Query   c. Swapping   d. Editing

2. SQL stands for:

   a. Structured Quiz language   b. Structure Query language
   c. Structured Query Language   d. Structure Quiz Language

3. A _____________ retrieve records from one or many tables and then displays the result in a formatted readbale form.

   a. Forms   b. Tables   c. Queries   d. Report

B. FILL IN THE BLANKS

1. You can get information from database using _____________.
2. Query is a _____________ statement created in the Query painter and saved with a name so that it can be repeatedly used as the source data for a report.

3. __________ symbol in wildcard characters matches any single character within the brackets.
4. __________ is a standard database language used for creating, maintaining and retrieving the relational database.

C. TRUE FALSE

1. Select query is a query for retrieving data while an action query requests additional actions to be performed on the data such as deletion, insertion and updating (T/F)
2. Existing queries cannot be edited (T/F)
3. # symbol in wildcard query matches any single numeric character (T/F)

D. ANSWER THE FOLLOWING QUESTIONS:

1. Define Query?
2. How to create a query using Wizard?
3. How to group the data in Microsoft Access Report?

E. PRACTICAL WORK

Given a database table:

Customer	Title	Forename	Surname	House Number	Place	Occupation
101	Miss	Komal	Kaur	112	Patiala	IT Engineer
102	Mr	Yogesh	Kumar	23	Mohali	Lecturer
103	Mrs	Harsaroop	Chadha	123	Seattle	IT Engineer
104	Mr	Simran	Sethi	1162	Canada	Business
105	Mr	Devinder	Singh	143	Chandigarh	IT Engineer

- Create a query that lists the customers having Occupation as IT Engineer.
- Also, create a query that lists customers with customer No. <104, sorted as per their Forname

Answers

A. Multiple choice question answers:

1. b   2. c   3. c

B. Fill in the blanks answers:

1. Query   2. SQL SELECT   3. [ ]   4. SQL or Structured Query Language

C. True False answers

1. True   2. False   3. True

SESSION 5: CREATE FORMS AND REPORTS USING WIZARD

5.1 Forms in Base

Databases are used for storing data and forms are the means of putting data into the database. In terms of databases, forms are a front end for editing and entering data. In simple form there is a field from a table as shown in below figure 3.32. The complex forms can consist of more data. These can consists of graphics, selection boxes, additional text and many other elements.

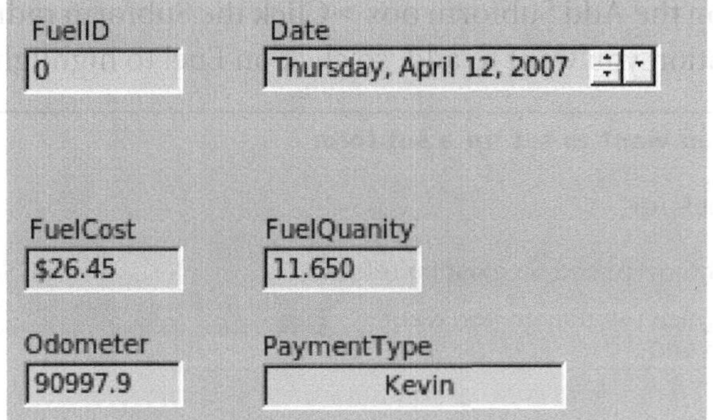

Figure 3.32: Fields of a simple form

5.2 Creating form using wizard

Wizard can also be used for creating a form. In this section, I will use the Wizard for creating two forms:

- Fuel
- Vacations

The Fuel form will be simple one and vacations form contains a form and a sub form. The vacations form will be created with its subform and enable the modification in Fuel form using the same process.

To create a form, you need to perform the following steps that may vary for simple and complex forms:

- Double click on Use Wizard to Create Form that will open a wizard.
- Select fields:

Under queries or Tables, select Vacations as the table > The field will shows the fields for Vacations table

Click on right double arrow for moving all of these fields to the Fields in the form list > Click Next (figure 3.33)

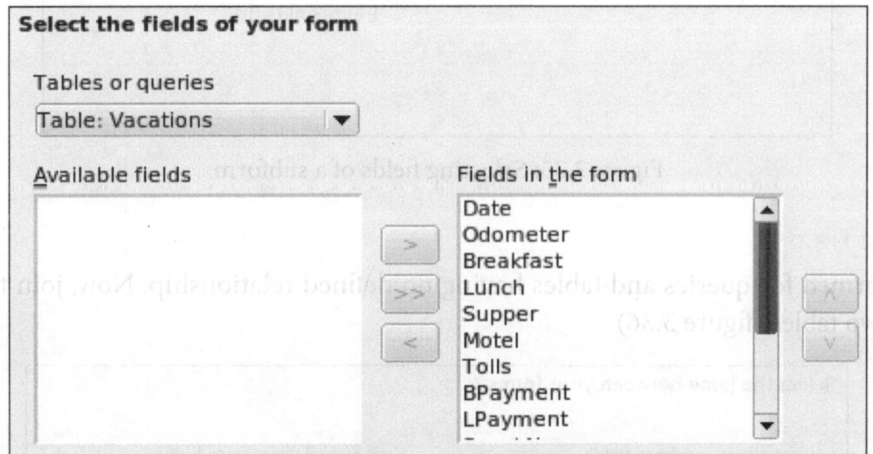

Figure 3.33: Form Wizard steps

Set up Sub-Forms

The relationship between fuel and vacations tables has been created now it will be used.

Or

Create a relation by clicking on the Add Subform box > Click the Subform radio button based upon existing relation > Fuel is listed as relation you want to add, so click on Fuel to highlight it > Click Next (figure 3.34)

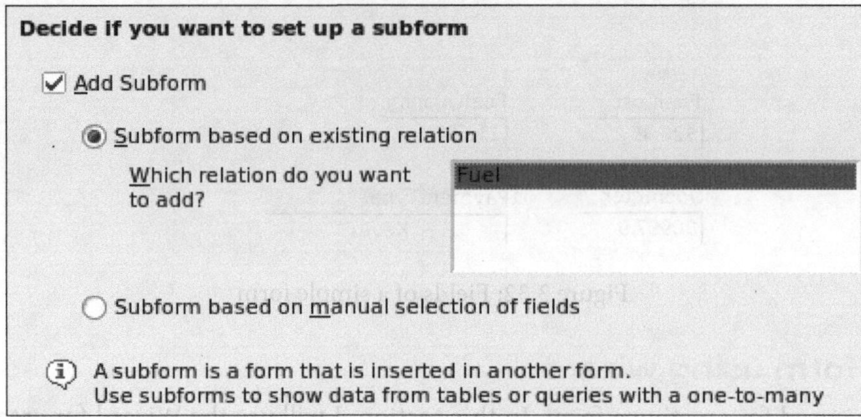

Figure 3.34: Adding a subform

Add fields for subform:

This step is same as step 1 (figure 3.35)

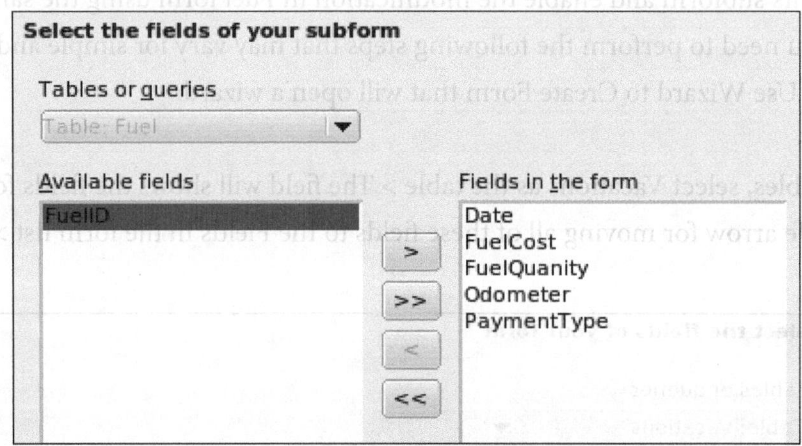

Figure 3.35: Selecting fields of a subform

Getting Joined fields

This step is performed for queries and tables having no defined relationship. Now, join the Date fields of the mentioned two tables (figure 3.36)

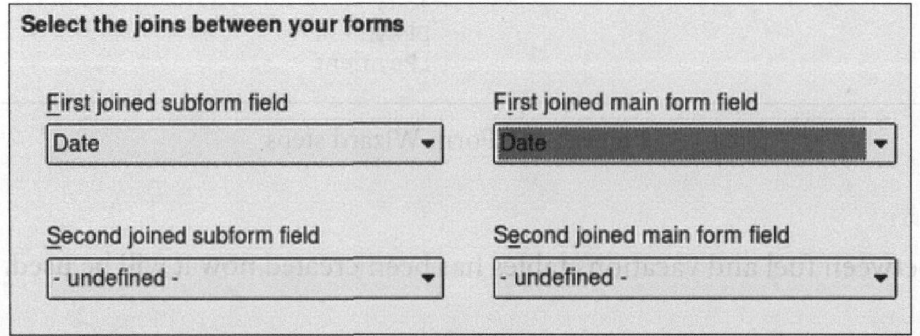

Figure 3.36: Selection of joined subform and main form fields

Arrange Controls:

Arrangement of the main form will be done by clicking on Columnar Labels on top

Arrangement of subform will be done by clicking on As Data Sheet > Click Next (figure 3.37)

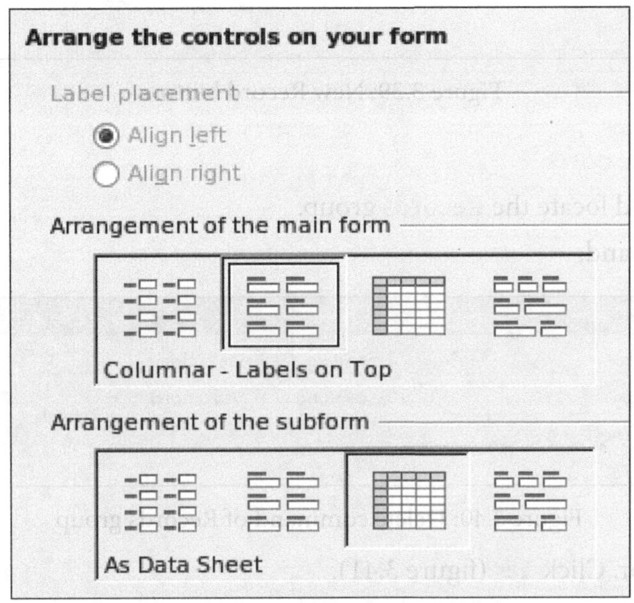

Figure 3.37: Control arrangements

Set data entry

- Apply Styles: In this, you can select the color you want in the Apply Styles list, Field border > Click Next
- Set name: Enter the name for the form > Click the circle in form of Modify the form > Click Next

Knowledge Box

Each control in a form consists of two parts: label and field. This step in creating the form determine where a control's label and field are placed in relationship with each other.

5.4 Options to enter or remove data from forms

One can enter data from the forms along with that one can also remove it.

On the basis of used database, the forms consists of various special tools and features for performing common tasks with one click of a button.

To add a new record:

There are two ways to add a new record to a form:

- In the Records group on the Home tab of the Ribbon > click the New command (figure 3.38).

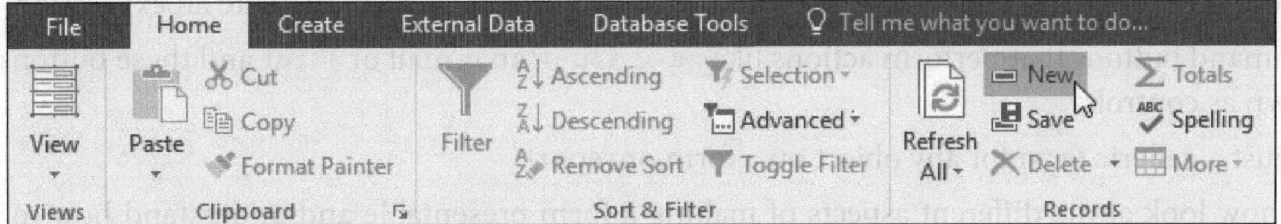

Figure 3.38: New command of Records group

✦ On the Record Navigation bar at the bottom of the window, click the New Record button (figure 3.39).

Figure 3.39: New Record buttons

To delete the current record:

✦ Select the **Home** tab and locate the **Records** group.

✦ Click the **Delete** command.

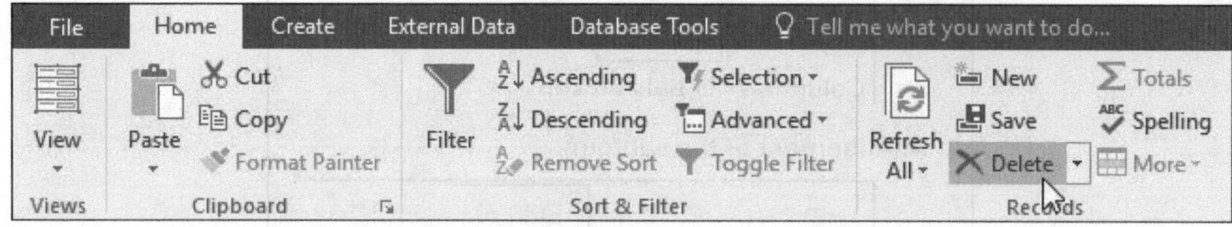

Figure 3.40: Delete command of Records group

✦ A dialog box will appear. Click **Yes** (figure 3.41).

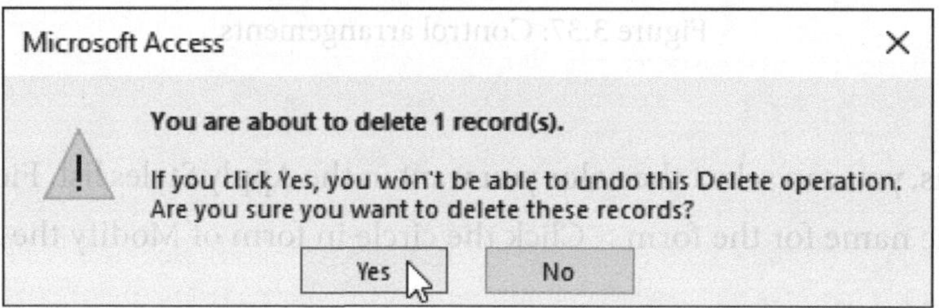

Figure 3.41: Microsoft Access pop-up

✦ The record will be permanently deleted.

5.5 Modifying form

The forms can be modifying by changing its size and other features related to it. For this, there is need to add or remove a control.

Controls: It is merely a generic term used to describe any object on a form or report that displays data, performs actions or items used for decorations such as a line. In other words, a control is just about anything that is placed on a form or report.

The following can be considered as controls:

✦ Objects such as labels.

✦ Unbound or bound text boxes that you can use to add or edit or even calculate an expression.

✦ Command buttons that perform actions like **Save**, **Open** an e-mail or **Print** and these buttons are also known as controls.

✦ It is just a generic term for any object on a form or report.

We will now look at the different aspects of making a form presentable and understand how to edit and modify a form. Let us now open our Multiple Items form which lists out all employees from **tnlEmployees.**

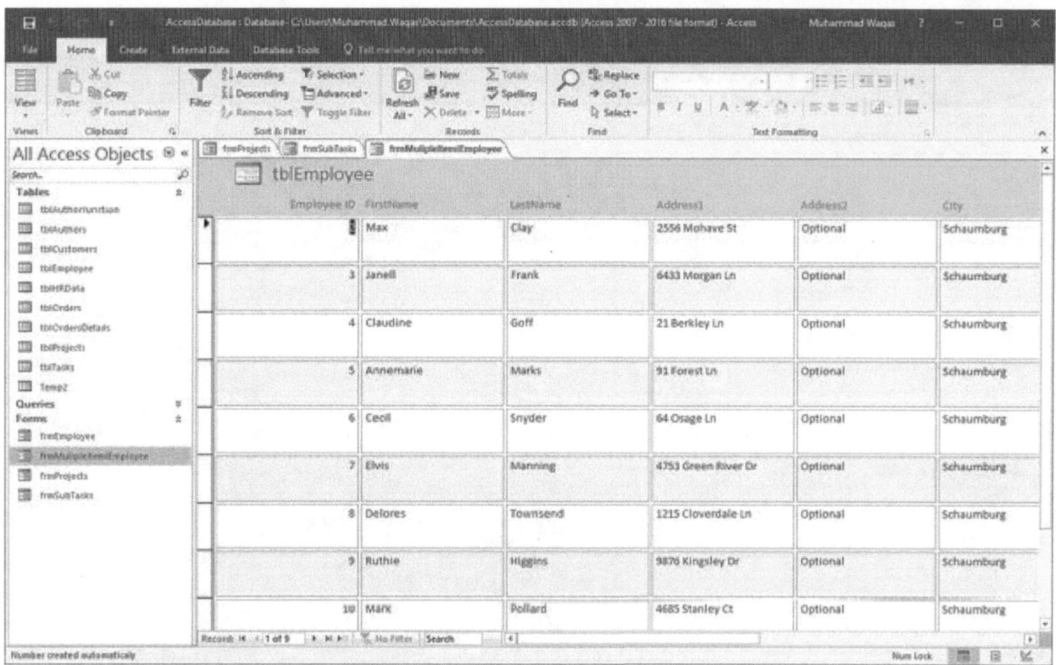

Figure 3.42: Multiple Items form

As you can see a list of employees, but doesn't really look like a very user friendly list. Our controls are oversized. They are too big, spaced apart and do not provide a very useful list view.

To edit the appearance of your controls on this form, you have two form views that you can use. In the Home tab, click the **View** drop-down.

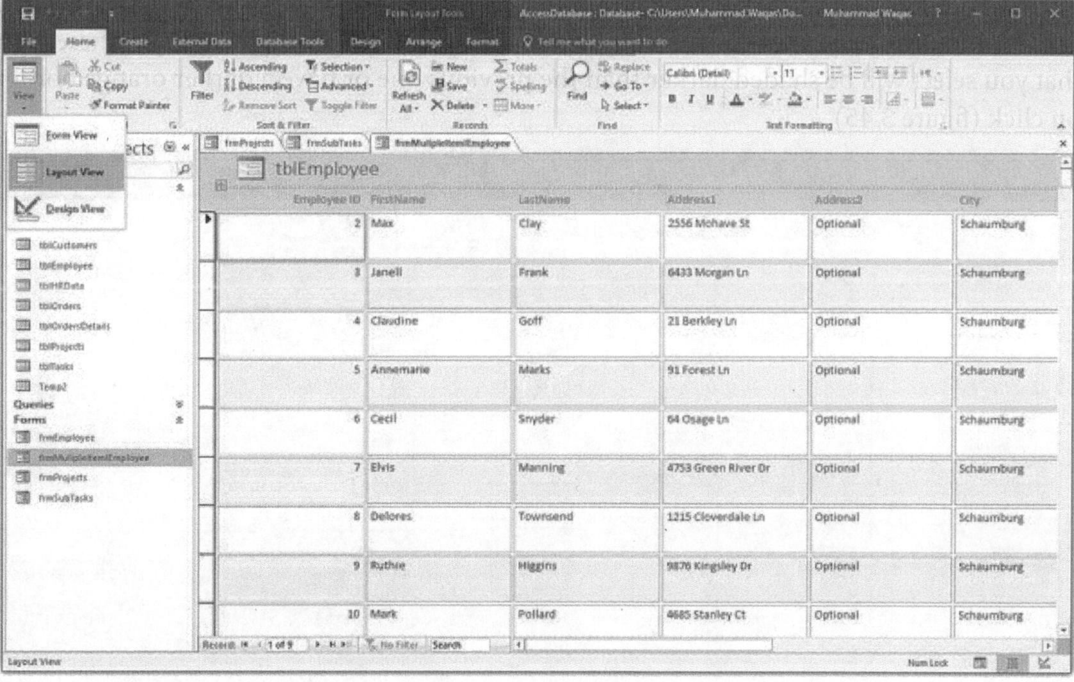

Figure 3.43: Edit the appearance of the form

You have the Layout View or the Design View, and both of these views are used to edit your form. The Form View opens up by default; this is the view you will use to interact with or edit the underlying data source.

To edit the appearance of the form itself, we need to go to the Layout View first (figure 3.44).

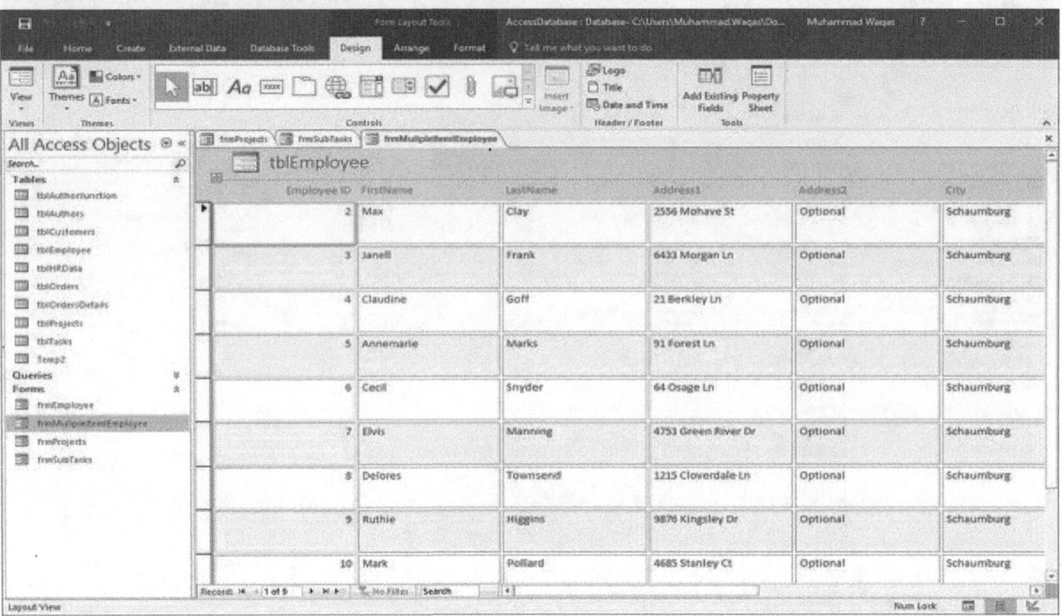

Figure 3.44: Layout View

When you switch to the Layout View, you will see a series of contextual tabs appear.

At the top of Access, you will see an area marked **Form Layout Tools** with three tabs — Design tab, an Arrange tab, and a Format tab and each of these tabs have different options for formatting the look or appearance of the form.

When you take your mouse and click on any one of these controls, you will notice that Access will highlight a given area of that form and all controls within that area are shaded a light orange whereas the actual control that you select will be shaded darker than the previous one or have a darker orange border around where you click (figure 3.45).

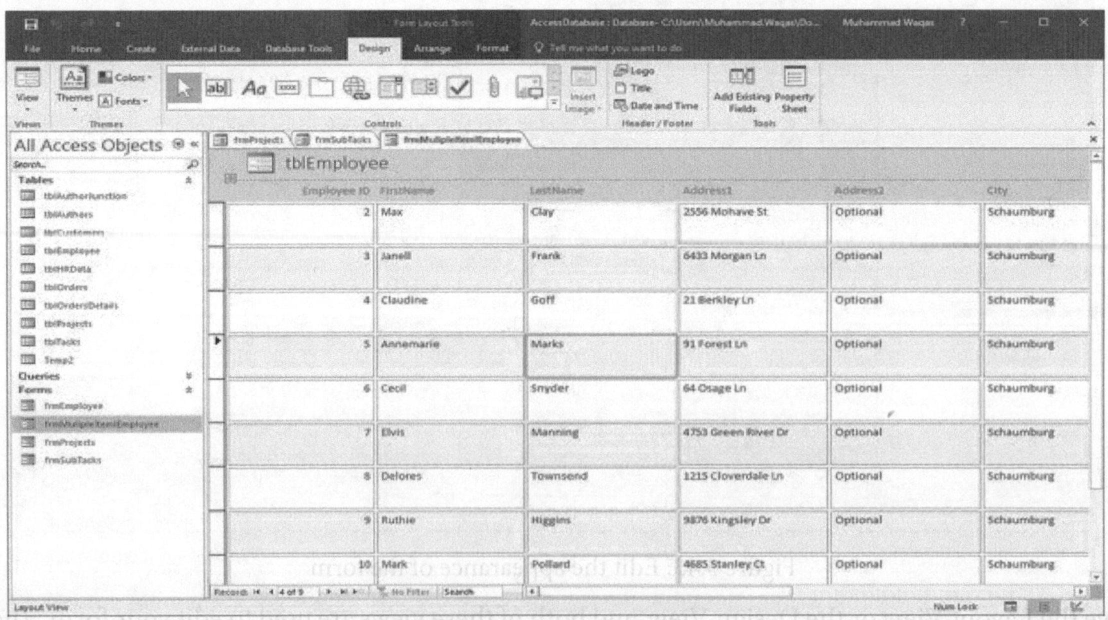

Figure 3.45: Various Controls

Here you can resize your controls as you want by clicking and dragging your mouse to resize the height or width or both of that one control (figure 3.46).

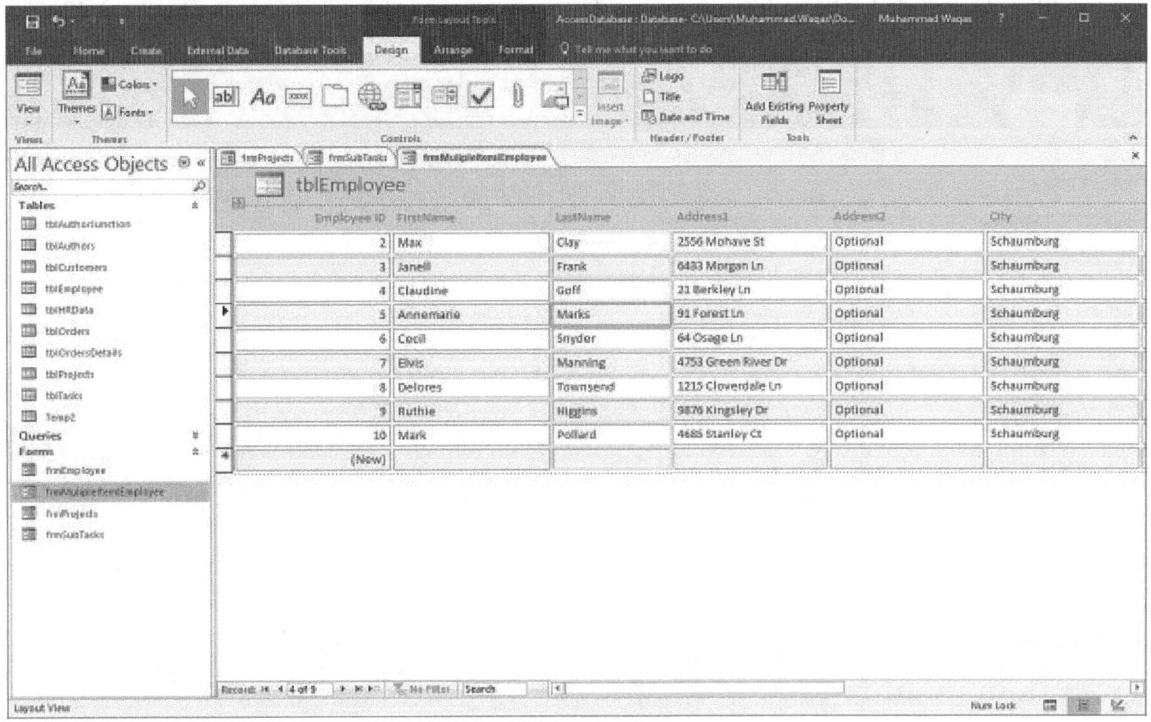

Figure 3.46: Resize controls

On this particular form, when you resize any single control, you also change the size of the rest of your controls on your form, this is because of how these controls are grouped. Let us now adjust all the fields the way you want by using the click and drag function of the mouse (figure 3.47).

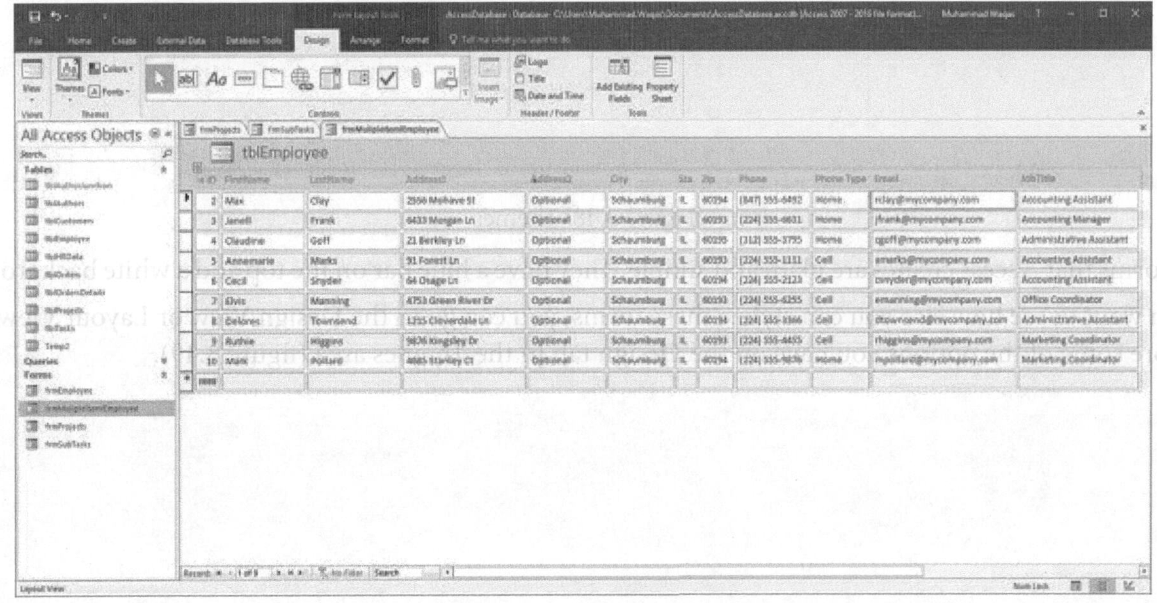

Figure 3.47: Drag function

That is one quick way of editing the height and width of controls in your form from this Layout View.

Themes

In Access, there are some basic ways to format your forms by using built-in themes, colors, and font styles, customizing fill colors and shading alternate rows. Let us now open **frmEmployees** (figure 3.48).

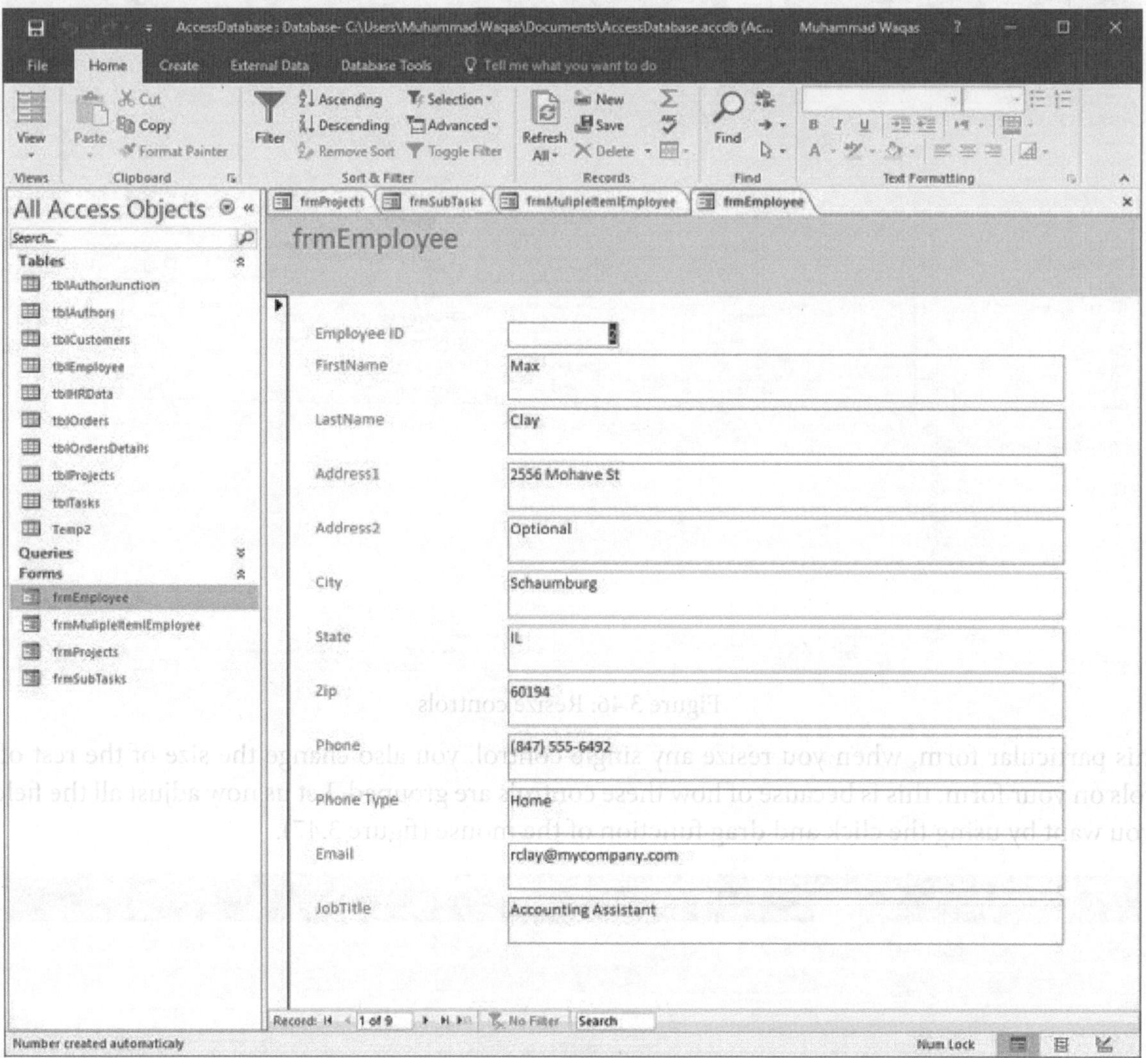

Figure 3.48: Themes

The forms that Access creates are plain and simple. They have a blue bar on the top and a white background. If you want to see how else you can stylize these forms, you can go to the Design View or Layout View and explore some of the options you have on the Design tab in the Themes area (figure 3.49).

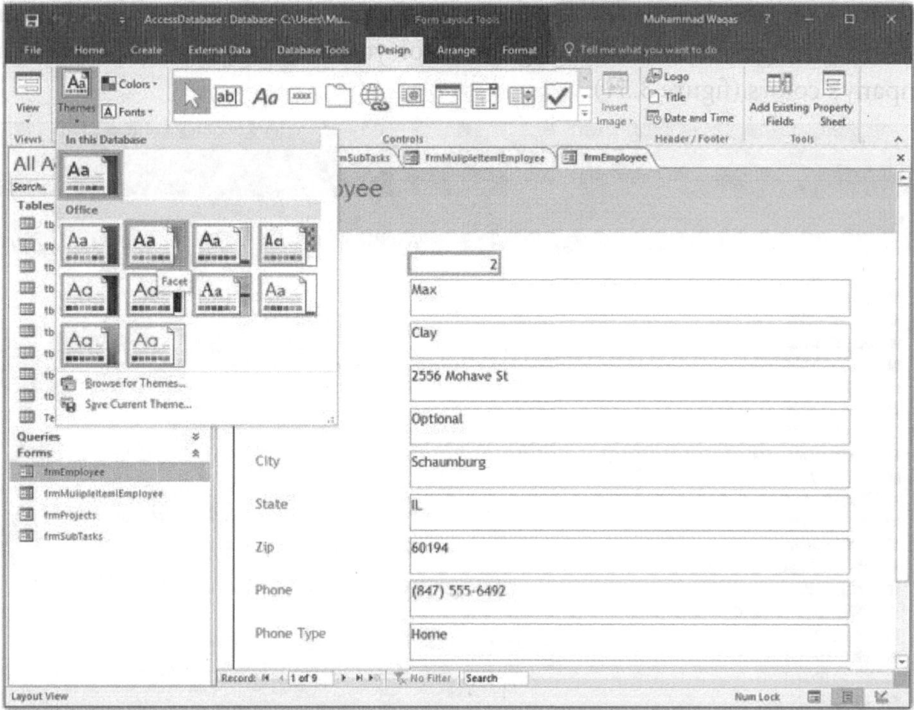

Figure 3.49: Design tab in themes command

If you click on the Themes' drop-down gallery, you have many pre-created themes to try out from. Hovering your mouse over any one of them will give you a preview of changing things like colors and font sizes and the actual font used. To apply a particular style, simply click your mouse on it and you can see what that looks like (figure 3.50).

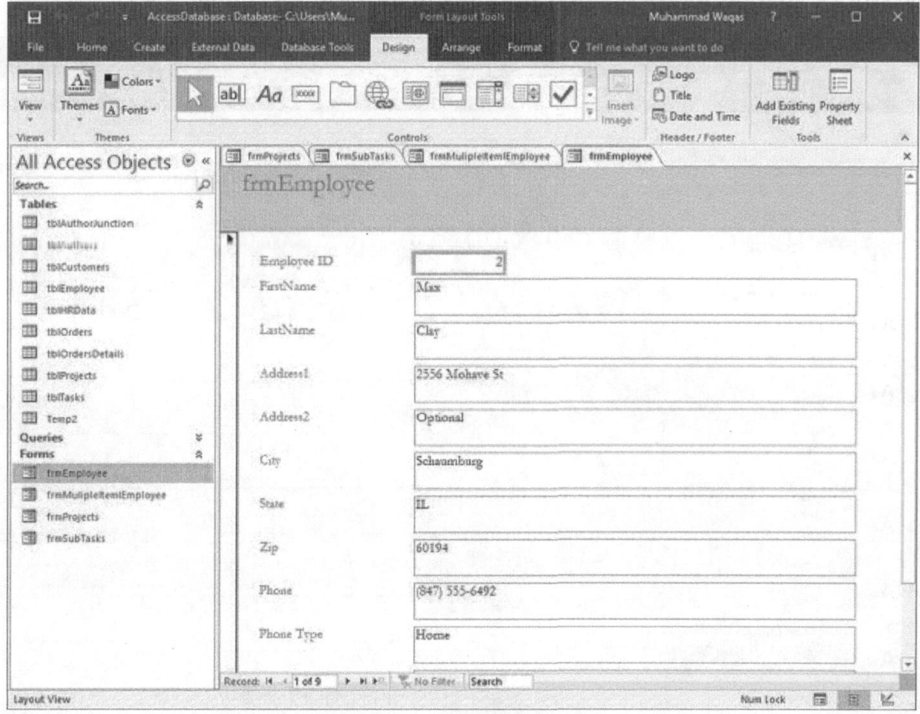

Figure 3.50: Design Tab

If you like the theme but you want to change the colors, you can adjust the colors by going back to the Themes group on the Design tab and choosing the color you like. You can also create custom colors to match your company's colors (figure 3.51).

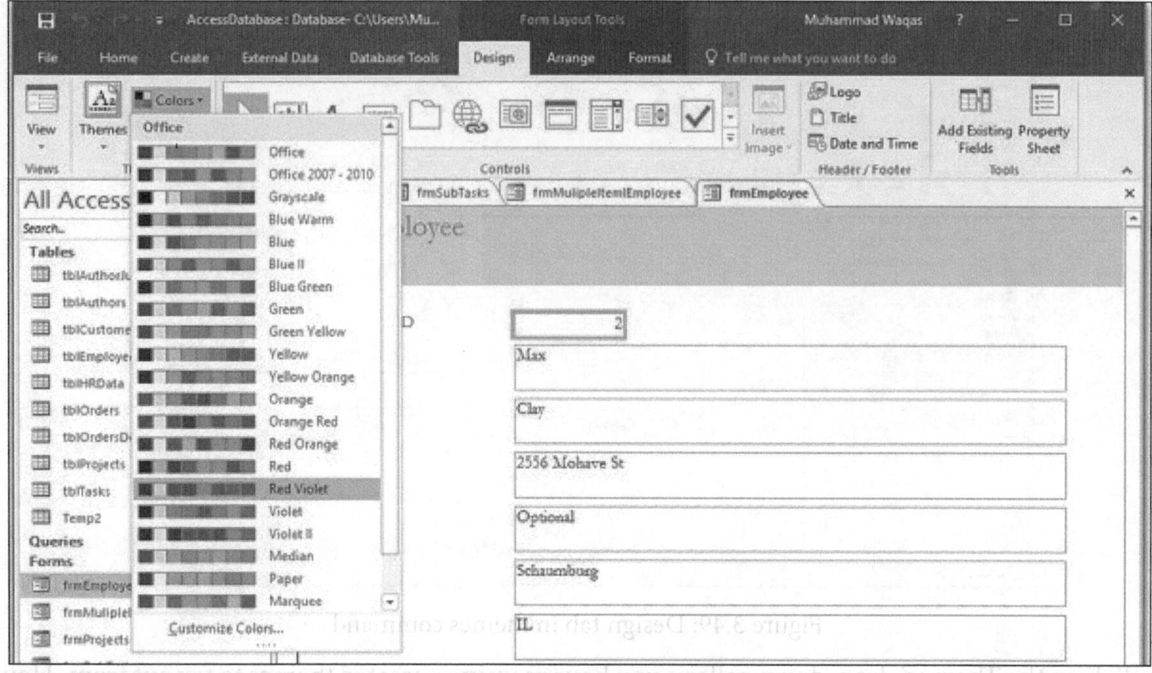

Figure 3.51: Change colors

Similarly, you also have a series of font styles to choose from. You can choose one from the many that come prebuilt with the Office Suite or you can customize those fonts, choosing a specific heading font, a body font and even creating a custom name for that font group and saving (figure 3.52).

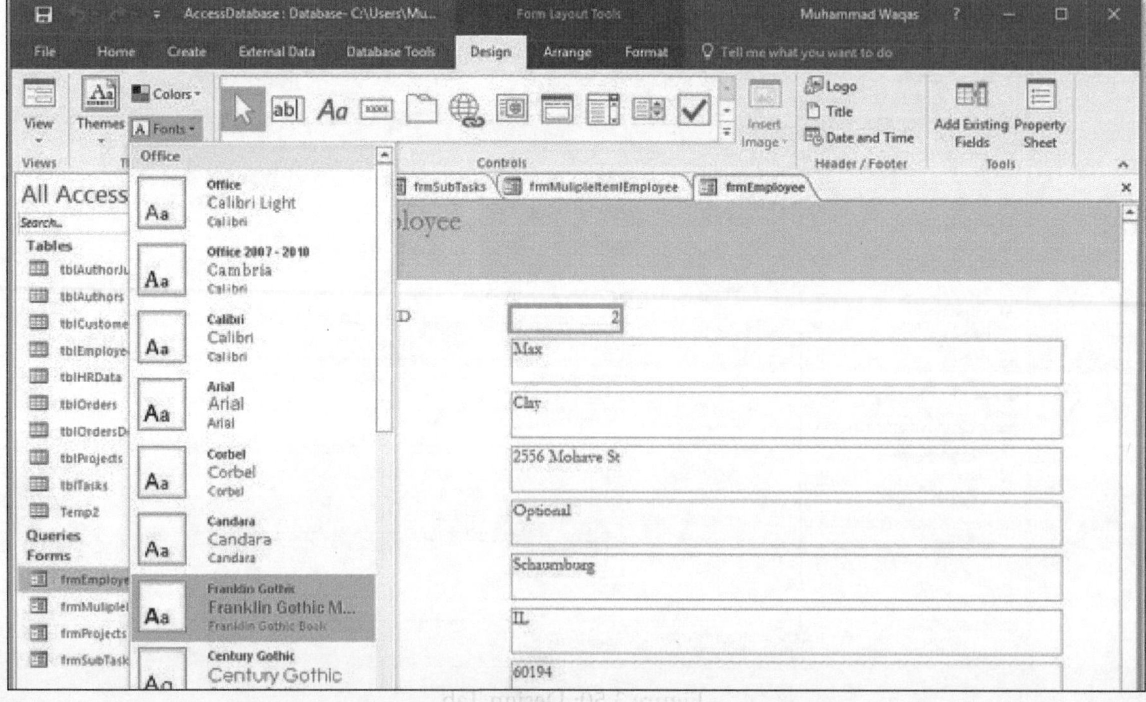

Figure 3.52: Series of font styles

Let us go back to **frmEmployees**. In this form, you will see that every alternate row is shaded light gray.

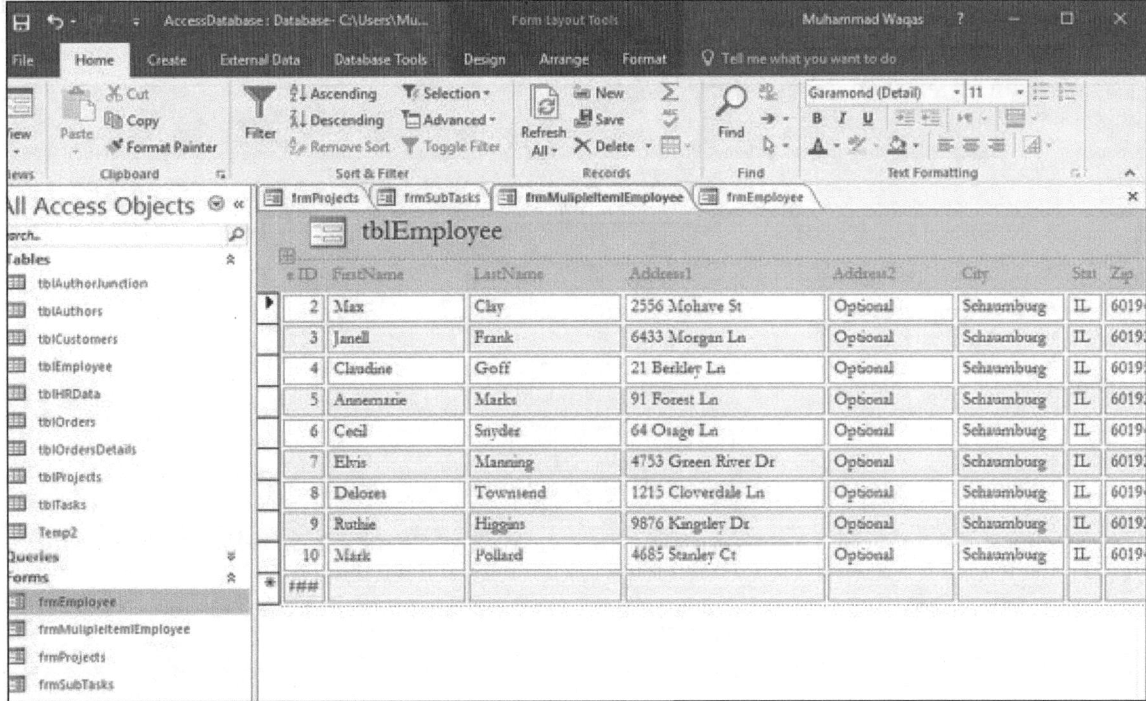

Figure 3.53: Shaded alternate Row

The formatting option is referred to as **Alternate Row Color** and if you want to adjust that in a multiple form, go to the **Design View** (figure 3.54).

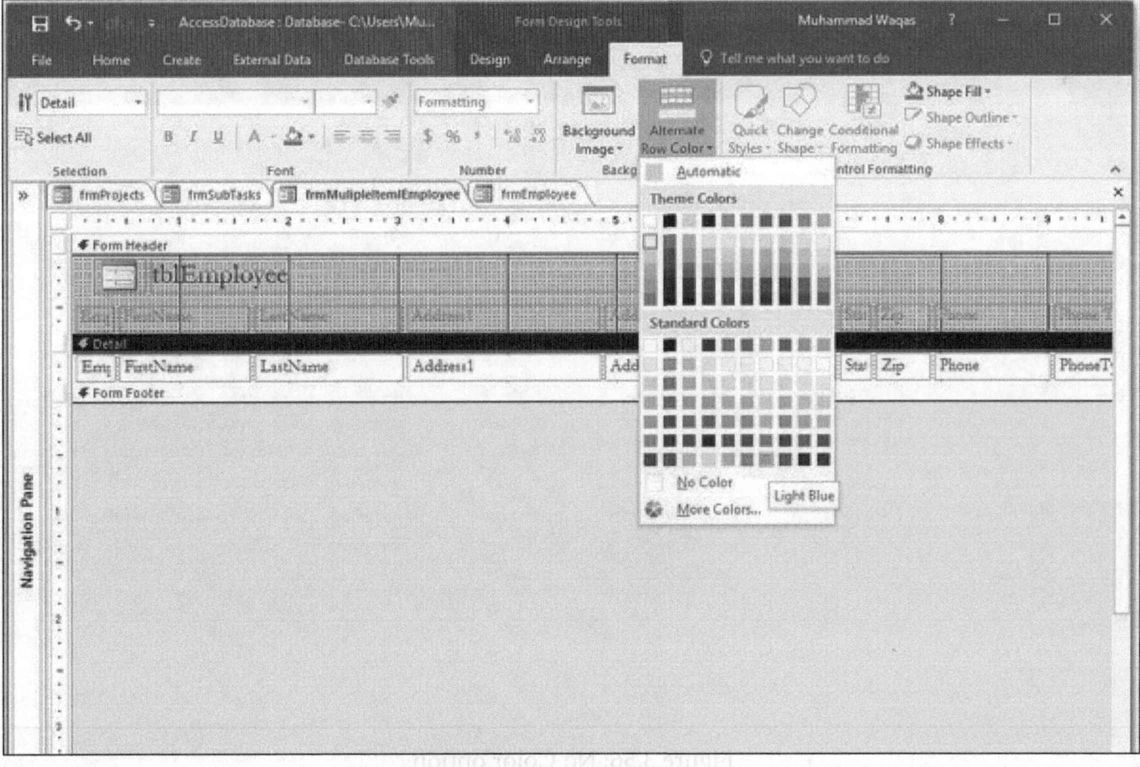

Figure 3.54: Format tab

Select that detail section and then go to the Format tab and in background group you should see an option for **Alternate Row Color**. You can change the colors for alternate rows. To see what that looks like, simply go to the Form View or the Layout View (figure 3.55).

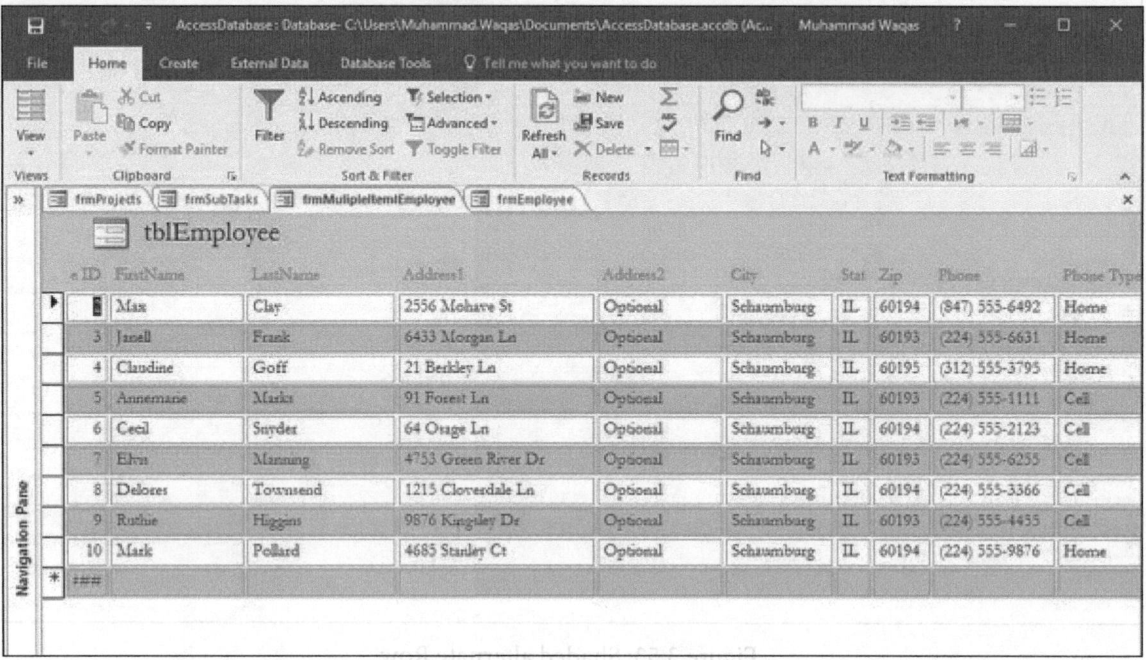

Figure 3.55: Layout View

If you don't want any shading at all, you can choose **No Color** as your **Alternate Row Color** and that is more the traditional look from earlier versions of Access.

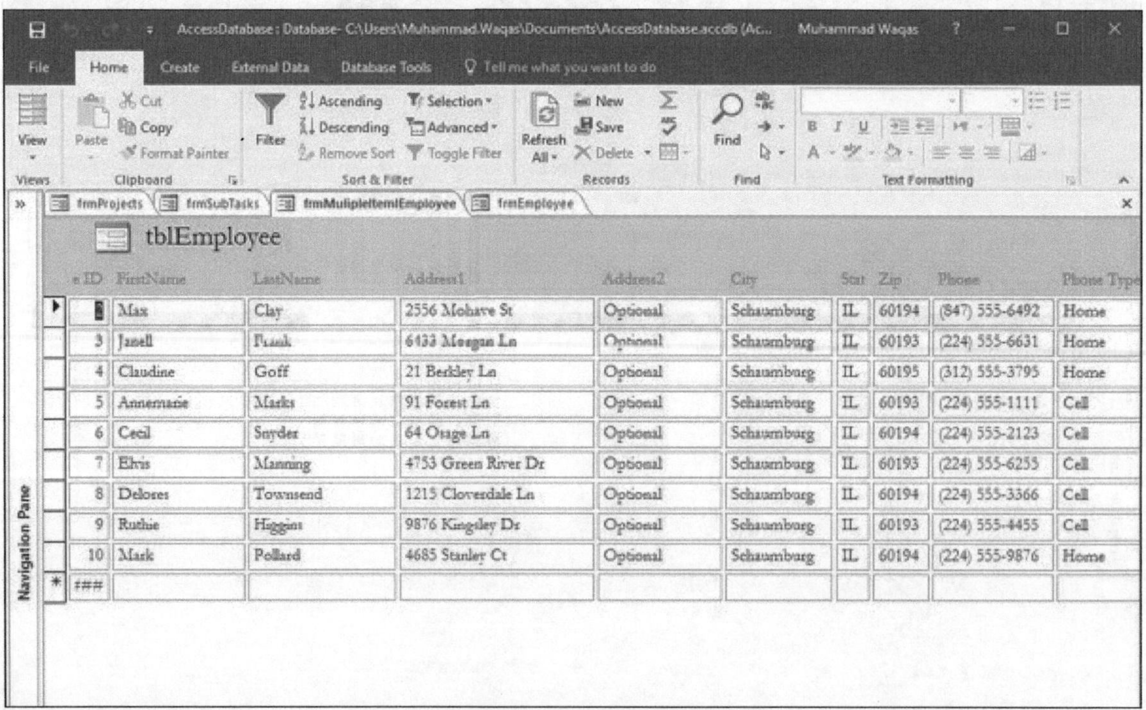

Figure 3.56: No Color option

5.7 Searching record using Form

By increase in the size of database, locating specific records will need more than a quick look at a datasheet. The fives ways of locating the specific records on the basis of one's needs are:

- Browse through all records
- Go to a specific record
- Search for a specific record
- Filter to see a limited number of records
- Create a query to find a specific record

Browse through all records:

You can browse through records by using the TAB key when you want to move through one record at a time, in order, to locate a specific record. You can also browse through records in a table in Datasheet view using the record navigation buttons. The record navigation buttons are available at the bottom of the table or form.

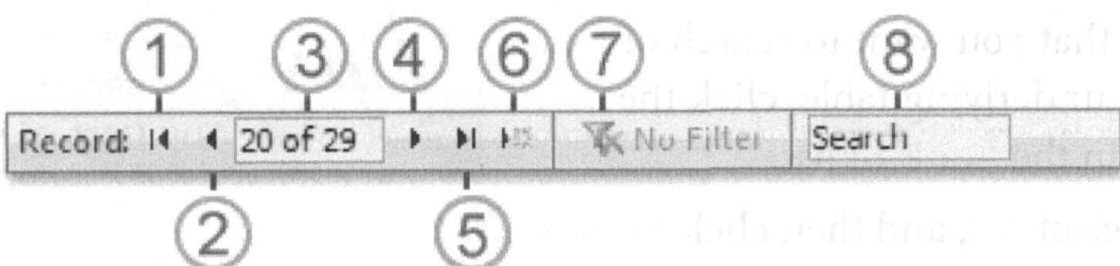

Figure 3.57: Navigation buttons

- Go to the first record
- Go to the previous record
- Current Record box
- Go to the next record
- Go to the last record
- Open a new (blank) record
- Filter indicator
- Search box

Note:

- When you click in the Current Record box, you can type a record number, and then press ENTER to navigate to that record. The record number is counted sequentially from the start of the form or datasheet. It does not correspond to any field value.
- To know if a filter has been applied, see the filter indicator button. If there is no filter applied or all the filters have been cleared, it displays No filter. When it displays Filtered, you can click this button to remove the filter. Similarly, when it displays Unfiltered, you can click this button to apply the last filter that you used, if any.
- When you enter text in the **Search** box, the first matching value is highlighted in real time as you enter each character. You can use this feature to quickly search for a record with a matching value.

Top of Page: The steps are:

- Go to a specific record: You can go to a specific record in Access when you know which record one wants to find out. > Go to box will allow user to choose a particular record from a drop-down list and it will be added to forms

- To navigate to a specific record, click the arrow to the right of the Go to box > select a record from the drop-down list.

Note: If you know the first few characters of the record to which you want to navigate, you can type those characters in the **Go to** box to help you quickly find that record.

The **Go to** box displays only enough data to uniquely identify each record. When you select a record from the list, Access displays the rest of that record›s data in the main area of the form.

Top of Page: User can search for a specific record in a table or form using the Find tab in the Find and Replace dialog box. This is an effective option for locating a specific record. In this user have to used contains or equals like comparison operators.

Note: You can only use the **Find and Replace** dialog box if the table or form currently displays data. This is true even if there are no visible records because a filter has been applied.

- Open the table or form, and then click the field that you want to search.
- On the **Home** tab, in the **Find** group, click **Find**, or press CTRL+F.
- The **Find and Replace** dialog box appears, with the **Find** tab selected.
- In the **Find What** box, type the value for which you want to search.
- To change the field that you want to search or to search the entire underlying table, click the appropriate option in the **Look In** list.

The **Match** list represents your comparison operator (such as "equals" or "contains"). To broaden your search, in the **Match** list, click **Any Part of Field**.

- In the **Search** list, select **All**, and then click **Find Next**.
- When the item for which you are searching is highlighted, click **Cancel** in the **Find and Replace** dialog box to close the dialog box. Records that match your conditions are highlighted

Filter to see a limited number of records: User can also see the limited number of records using filter. This is used in case of seeing only the records that satisfy comparison operators and specific criteria. Steps to use it are:

- To apply a filter that is based on a selection, open a table or form.
- To make sure that the table or form is not already filtered, on the **Home** tab, in the **Sort & Filter** group, click **Advanced**, and then click **Clear All Filters**, if that command is available.
- Navigate to the record that contains the value that you want to use as part of the filter, and then click inside the column (in Datasheet view) or control (in Form, Report, or Layout view). To filter based on a partial selection, select just the characters that you want.
- On the **Home** tab, in the **Sort & Filter** group, click **Selection**, and then click the filter you want to apply.
- To filter other fields based on a selection, repeat steps 3 and 4.

Create a query to find a specific record: The use of filter records technique is very useful for finding the specific records but there can be cases when you want to perform the same filter and search operation on daily basis. So, in these cases user can create a query instead of reproducing a set of filters and search steps.

You can create a query that displays issues whose status is closed by following these steps:

- On the **Create** tab, in the **Queries** group, click **Query Design**.
- In the **Show Table** dialog box, double-click **Issues**, and then click **Close**.
- In the query designer, double-click the asterisk (*) in the **Issues** table. This helps make sure that the query will display all the fields from the records it returns.
- **Issues.*** appears in the first column of the design grid, in the **Field** row. This indicates that all the fields from the Issues table should be returned.
- In the query designer, double-click **Status** on the **Issues** table.

- **Status** appears in the second column in the design grid, in the **Field** row.
- In the second column of the design grid, clear the check box in the **Show** row. This helps make sure that the query does not display the Status field.
- If you do not clear the **Show** check box in the Status column, the Status field will be displayed two times in the query results.
- In the second column of the design grid, in the **Criteria** row, type ="**Closed**". This is your search criterion. This is how you make sure that the query will return only those records where the value of **Status** is «Closed.»

Note: In this example, only one search criterion is used. You can use many search criteria for any given search by adding criteria to more fields, and by using the or row and the additional rows below

Your query is ready to run, and looks something like this (figure 3.58):

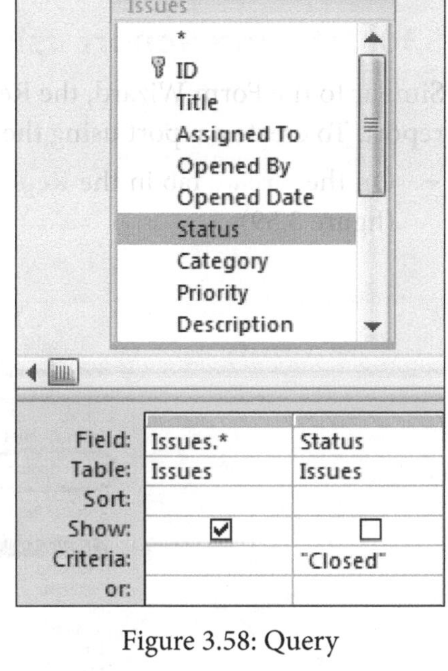

Figure 3.58: Query

5.8 Inserting and deleting record using Form View,

To insert a record to a table or form, perform the following steps:

- Open the table in **Datasheet View** or the form in **Form View**.
- On the **Home** tab, in the **Records** group, click **New**, or click **New (blank) record**, or press Ctrl+Plus Sign (+).
- Find the record with an asterisk in the record selector, and enter your new information.
- Click or otherwise place the focus on the first field that you want to use, and then enter your data.
- To move to the next field in the same row, press TAB, use the Right or Left arrow keys, or click the cell in the next field.
- In a table, to move to the next cell in a column, use the Up or Down arrow keys, or click the cell you want.
- When you view another record or close the table or form, Access saves the new record that you added. To explicitly save changes to the current record, press Shift+Enter.

To delete a record, perform the following steps: The process of deletion is very simple except when the records are related to other data and resides in one to much relationship.

- Open the table in **Datasheet View** or form in **Form View**.
- Select the record or records that you want to delete.
- To select a record, click the record selector next to the record, if the record selector is available.
- To extend or reduce the selection, drag the record selector (if it is available), or press SHIFT+DOWN ARROW or SHIFT+UP ARROW.
- Press DELETE, select **Home > Records > Delete**, or press Ctrl+Minus Sign (-).

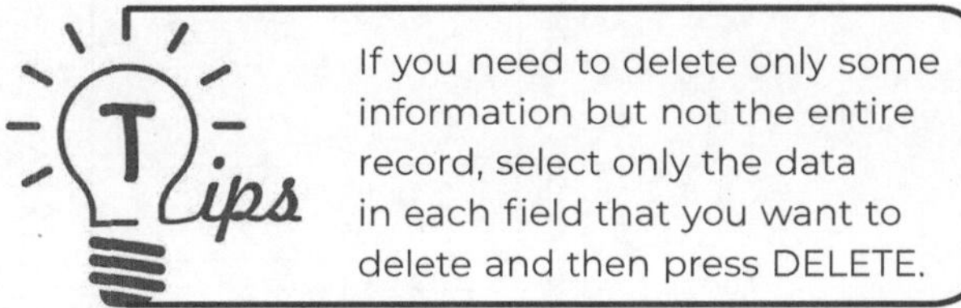

5.9 Concept of Report in Base

Reports offer a way of viewing, formatting and summarizing the information in Microsoft Access database.

For instance: User can create a simple report consists of phone numbers for all their contacts or a summary report on the total sales across different time periods and regions.

5.10 Creating Report using wizard

Similar to the Form Wizard, the Report Wizard walks you through a series of decisions in order to build a report. To create a report using the Report Wizard, follow the steps below.

- On the **Create** tab in the **Reports** group, click **Report Wizard.** The wizard starts window will appear (figure 3.59).

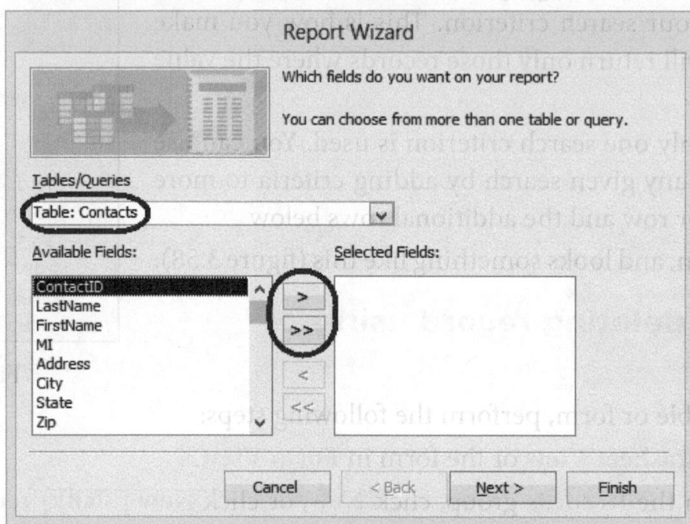

Figure 3.59: Report Wizard

- From the **Tables/Queries** drop-down list, select the table (or query) to base the report on. The fields for the selected table load in the **Available Fields** list box.
- Move the fields to include on the report from the **Available Fields** list box to the **Selected Fields** list box. To do so, double-click a field name to move it or highlight the field name and click >. To move all fields at once, click >> (figure 3.60).

Figure 3.60: Click on double greater than button

✦ Click **Next** > (figure 3.61).

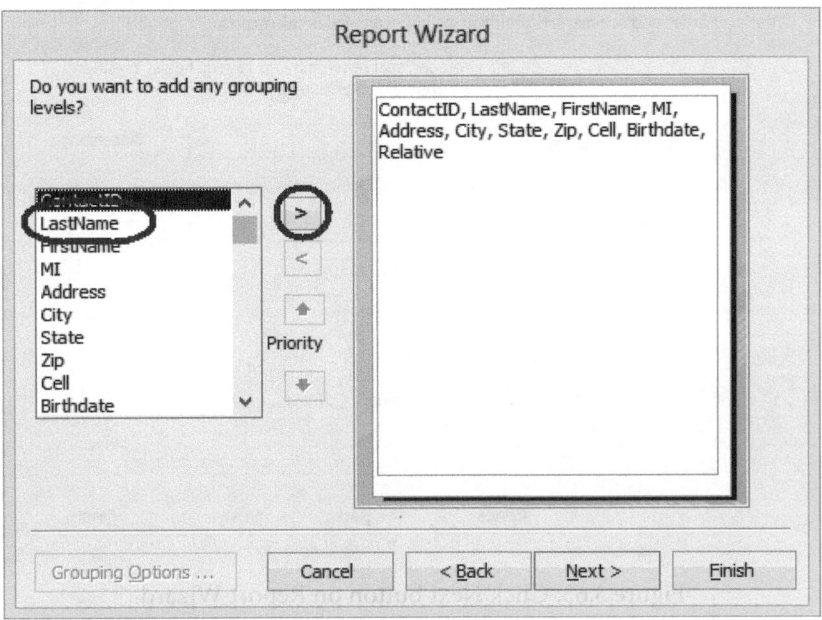

Figure 3.61: Click on Next button on Report Wizard

✦ To group records on the report by a particular field, highlight the field in the list box and click > (figure 3.62).

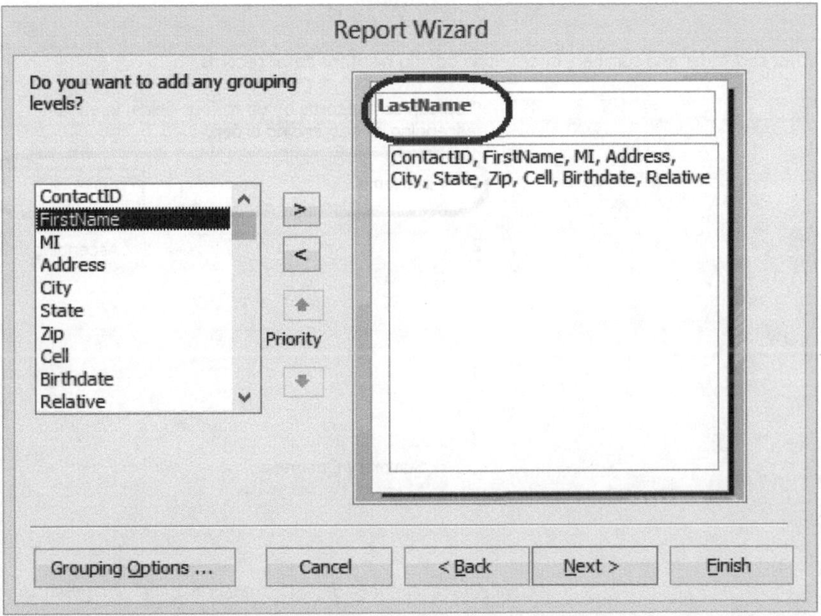

Figure 3.62: Group records

✦ Add more grouping levels if desired. You can use the arrows to change the order of the grouping levels if needed.

✦ When you finish defining how you want records grouped, click **Next** > (figure 3.63).

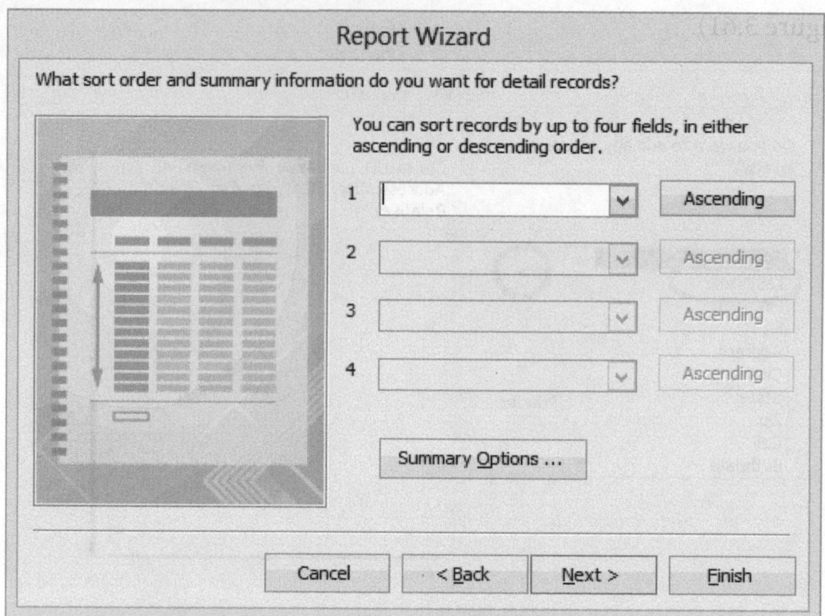

Figure 3.63: Click Next button on Report Wizard

- In the first drop-down list, select the field to sort records by. By default, records will be sorted in ascending order by the field you select. If you want to sort in descending order, click the **Ascending** button to change its label to «Descending» (figure 3.64).

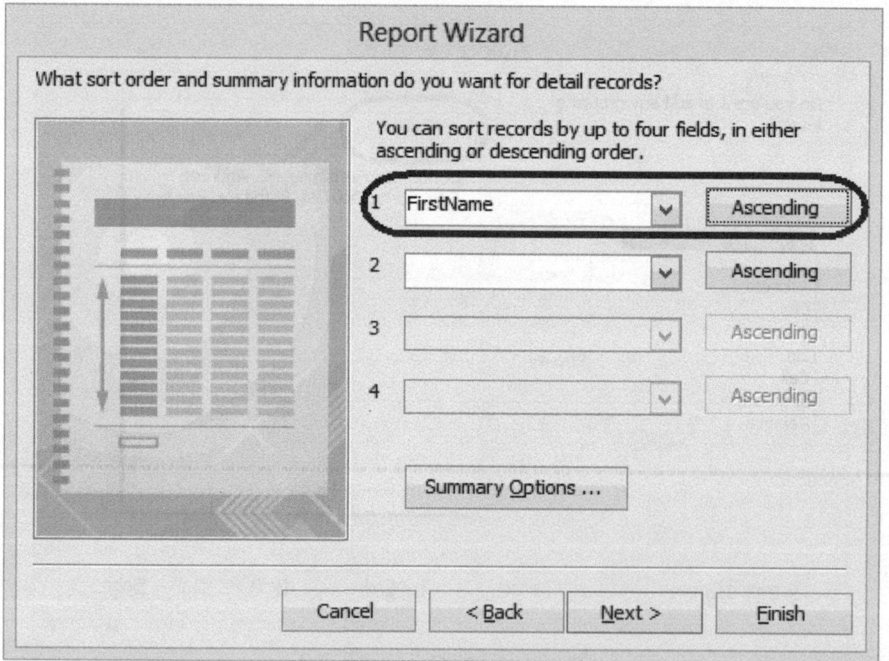

Figure 3.64: Sort records

- You can specify up to four levels of sorting. When you finish specifying sorting options, click **Next >** (figure 3.65).

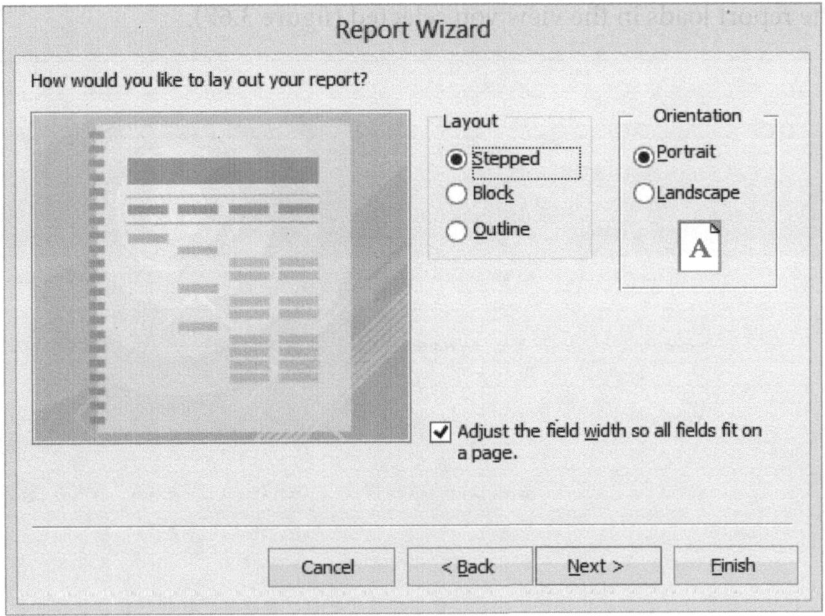

Figure 3.65: Specify the layout and orientation

- In the **Layout** field, select the format of the report. Your options are «Stepped», «Block», and «Outline». (Try the options to see a preview of the report layouts.)
- In the **Orientation** field, select whether to lay out the report in portrait or landscape mode.
- If you want all fields to fit on a single page, ensure the Adjust the field width so all fields fit on a page check box is marked.
- Click Next > (figure 3.66)

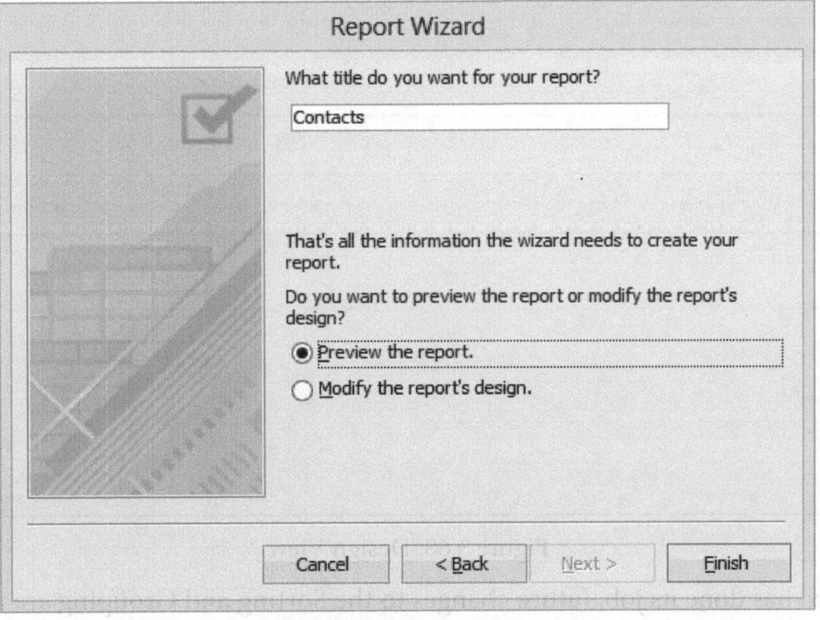

Figure 3.66: Adjust field width

- Enter a title for the report.
- Select an option for the view you want to open the report in. Your options are:

- Click Finish. The report loads in the view you selected (figure 3.67).

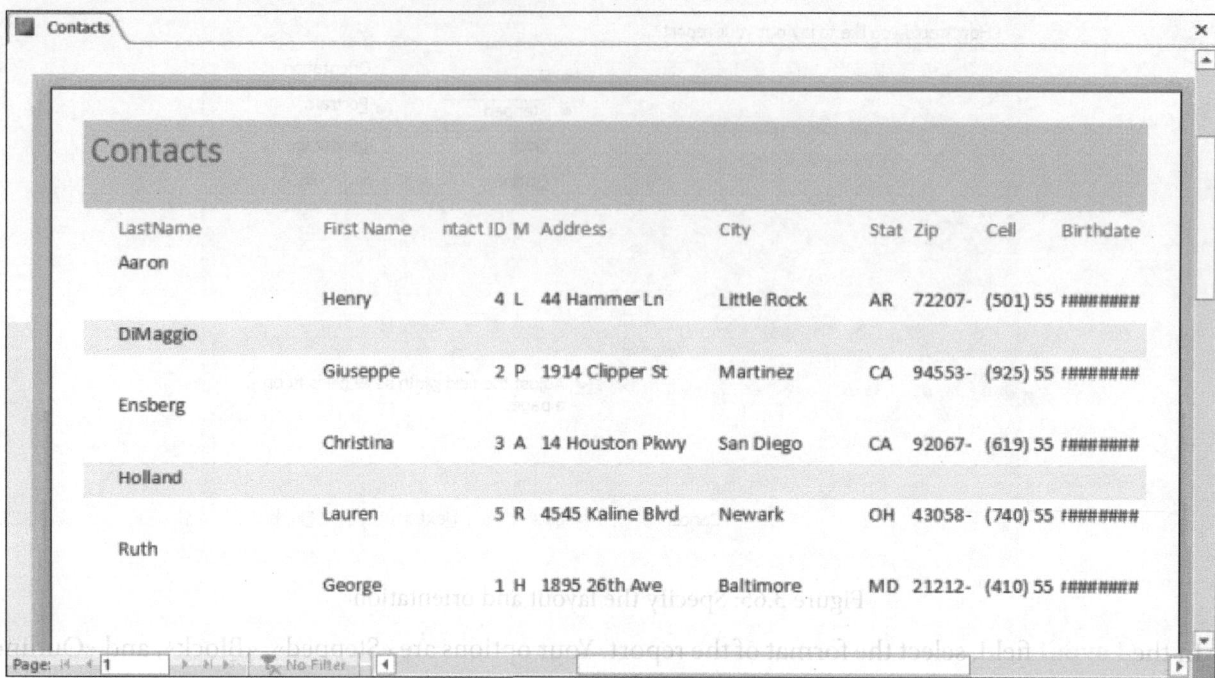

Figure 3.67: Print Preview

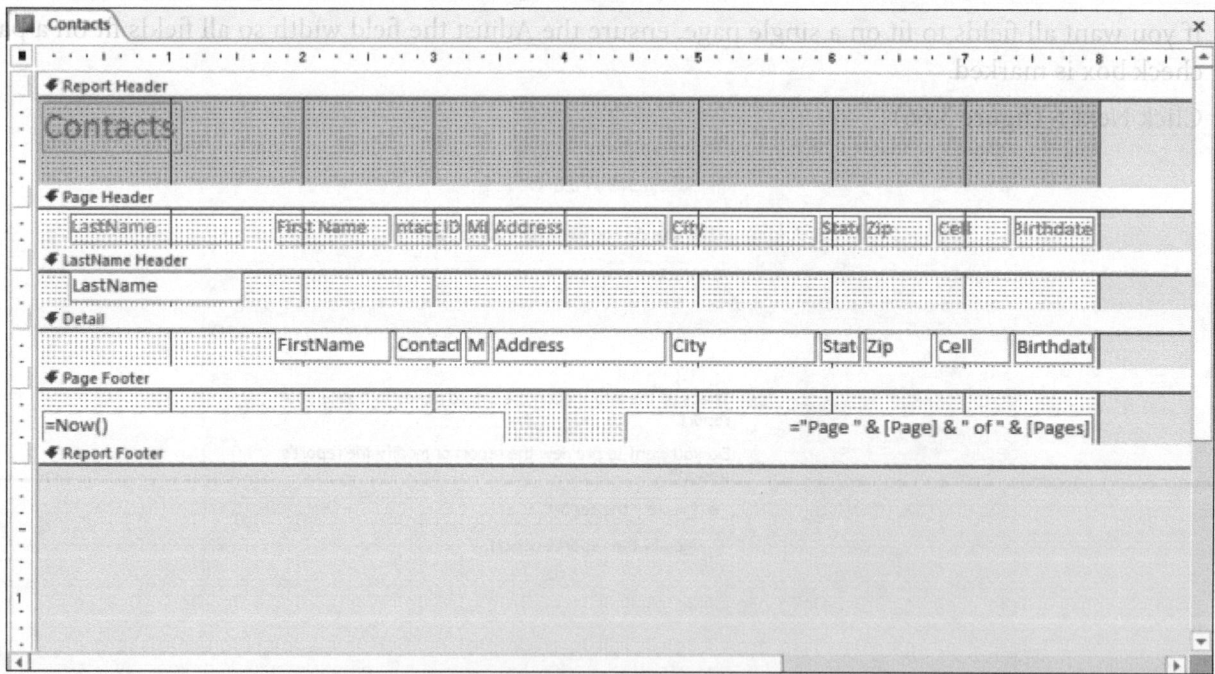

Figure 3.68: Design View

- Once the wizard has done its job, future changes to the Sorting and Grouping are made in the Group, Sort, and Total area: Design > Group & Sort. You may change the order of, remove, or edit any existing items. You may also add a group and a sort as well (figure 3.69).

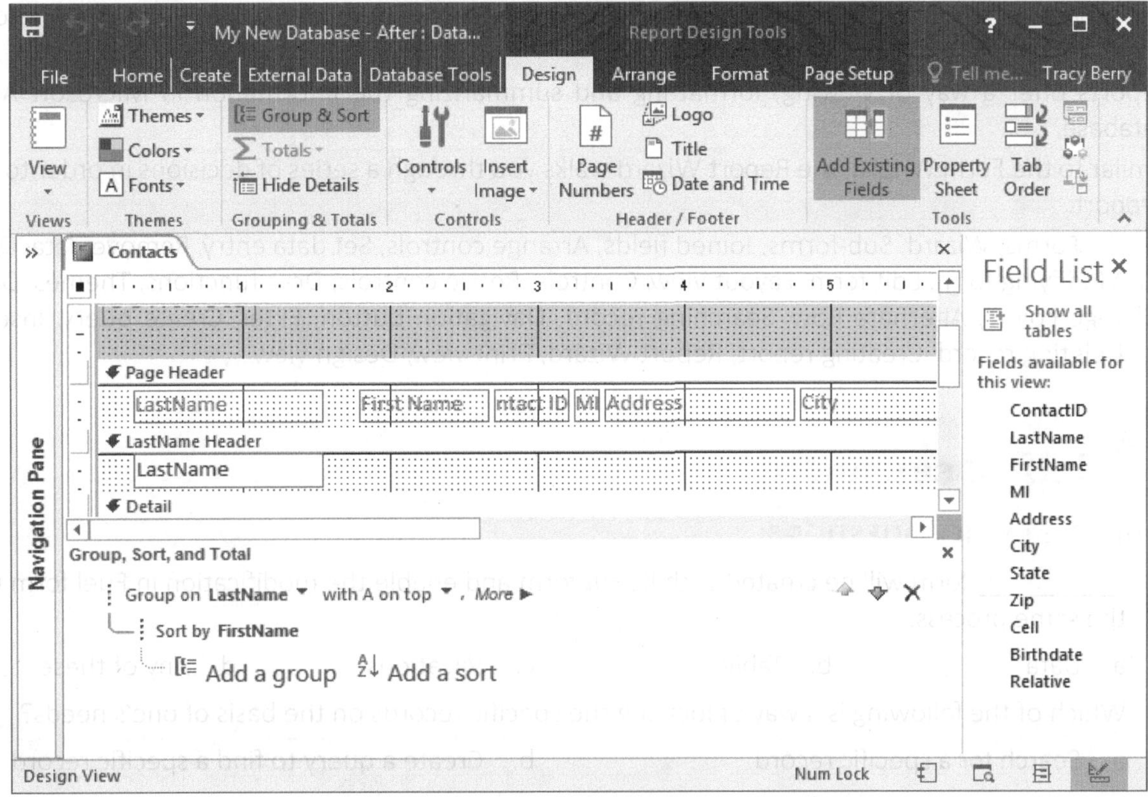

Figure 3.69: Design tab to edit existing items

Summary

- Databases are used for storing data and forms are the means of putting data into the database.
- The Fuel form will be simple one and vacations form contains a form and a sub form.
- The vacations form will be created with its subform and enable the modification in Fuel form using the same process.
- On the basis of used database, the forms consists of various special tools and features for performing common tasks with one click of a button.
- The forms can be modifying by changing its size and other features related to it by adding or removing a control.
- Controls is merely a generic term used to describe any object on a form or report that displays data, performs actions or items used for decorations such as a line.
- By increase in the size of database, locating specific records will need more than a quick look at a datasheet.
- You can browse through records by using the TAB key when you want to move through one record at a time, in order, to locate a specific record.
- User can search for a specific record in a table or form using the Find tab in the Find and Replace dialog box.
- User can also see the limited number of records using filter. This is used in case of seeing only the records that satisfy comparison operators and specific criteria.
- The use of filter records technique is very useful for finding the specific records but there can be cases when you want to perform the same filter and search operation on daily basis.

- The process of deletion is very simple except when the records are related to other data and resides in one to much relationship.
- Reports offer a way of viewing, formatting and summarizing the information in Microsoft Access database.
- Similar to the Form Wizard, the Report Wizard walks you through a series of decisions in order to build a report.

Keywords: Forms, Wizard, Sub-forms, Joined fields, Arrange controls, Set data entry, Remove data, Delete record, Modifying form, Edit form, Layout view, Controls, Resize controls, Drag functions, Themes, Design tab, Change colors, Alternate Row, Searching record, Navigation button, Filter, Create query, Inserting record, Deleting record, Creating report, Report Wizard, Print view, Design view

Self-Assessment

A. MULTIPLE CHOICE QUESTIONS.

1. __________ form will be created with its subform and enable the modification in Fuel form using the same process.

   a. Data   b. Table   c. Vacations   d. Any of these

2. Which of the following is a way of locating the specific records on the basis of one's needs?

   a. Search for a specific record   b. Create a query to find a specific record

   c. Go to a specific record   d. All of these

B. FILL IN THE BLANKS

1. __________ are easier way to get data from user and store in tables.
2. __________ are an easy way to represent data in a formatted way.

C. TRUE FALSE

1. A form has one or more tables linked with it (T/F)
2. You can create reports from one or more tables (T/F)
3. Ctrl _- or minus sign shortcut key can be used to insert a record (T/F).

D. ANSWER THE FOLLOWING QUESTIONS:

1. What do you mean by Forms in Base?
2. Write down the steps to enter or remove data from forms?
3. How to search record using Form?
4. Define the concept of Report in Base?

E. PRACTICAL WORK

Perform the various steps for creating form using Form wizard and then try to enter or remove data from forms, modify forms and change label and background of form.

Answers

A. Multiple choice question answers:

   1. c   2. d

B. Fill in the blanks answers:

1. Form 2. Reports

C. True False answers

1. True 2. True 3. False

Solved Exercise

A. MULTIPLE CHOICE QUESTIONS

1. A relational database consists of a collection of

   a. Tables b. Fields c. Records d. Keys

2. A __________ in a table represents a relationship among a set of values.

   a. Column b. Key c. Row d. Entry

3. The term __________ is used to refer to a row.

   a. Attribute b. Tuple c. Field d. Instance

4. The term attribute refers to a __________ of a table.

   a. Record b. Column c. Tuple d. Key

5. For each attribute of a relation, there is a set of permitted values, called the __________ of that attribute.

   a. Domain b. Relation c. Set d. Schema

6. A __________ is a property of the entire relation, rather than of the individual tuples in which each tuple is unique.

   a. Rows b. Key c. Attribute d. Fields

7. Which one of the following attribute can be taken as a primary key ?

   a. Name b. Street c. Id d. Department

8. Query design window has two parts. The upper part shows

   a. Name of fields, field type and size

   b. Tables with fields and relationships between tables

   c. Criteria

   d. Sorting check boxes

9. To create a new table, in which method you don't need to specify the field type and size?

   a. Create table in Design View b. Create Table using wizard

   c. Create Table by Entering data d. All of above

10. A database language concerned with the definition of the whole database structure and schema is __________.

    a. DCL b. DML c. DDL d. All of above

Answers

1. a 2. c 3. b 4. b 5. a

6. b 7. c 8. b 9. c 10. c

B. SOLVED VERY SHORT AND SHORT QUESTION AND ANSWERS:

1. Give various advantages of DBMS?

Ans. Various advantages of DBMS are:

- Using DBMS one can store and manage data.
- It lets end users and application programmers to access and use the same data while managing data integrity
- Central storage and management of data.
- Data abstraction and independence
- Data security
- A locking mechanism for concurrent access
- An efficient handler to balance the needs of multiple applications using the same data
- The ability to swiftly recover from crashes and errors, including restart ability and recoverability
- Robust data integrity capabilities
- Logging and auditing of activity

2. Define relational database?

Ans. Relational database is a management system database that is based on relational model. It is a relational model of a database in which all the data is represented in terms of tables or grouped interrelations and rows or tuples. The relational model organized database is a relational database. It is powerful that creates a need of some assumptions about the relation of data and how it is extracted from the database.

3. What is the full form of RDBMS?

Ans. RDBMS is stands for Relational Database Management System

4. What is the purpose of forms in database?

Ans. It is used for entering, Viewing and modifying the records. In various occasions such as applying for a job, registration for school and visiting to doctors office you fill out the forms.

5. Define the usage of Reports in database?

Ans. It gives the ability of presenting data in print. A database report is seen when someone has received a computer printout of a class schedule or a purchase printed invoice.

6. What are the DDL commands in database? Explain any four with syntax and example.

Ans. DDL stands for Data Definition Language that helps in defining the database structure. There are mainly four main commands of DDL as given below:

CREATE: This statement is used for defining the database structure.

Syntax: CREATE TABLE TABLE_NAME (COLUMN_NAME DATATYPES[......]);

Example: Create Table students;

DROP: This commands is used to remove the tables and databases from RDBMS.

Syntax: DROP TABLE;

Example: Drop table student;

ALTER: This command enable the user to alter the structure of the database.

Syntax: ALTER TABLE table_name ADD column_name COLUMN-definition;

Example: Alter table komal_data;

TRUNCATE: This command is used for deleting all the rows from the table and frees the space in the table.

Syntax: TRUNCATE TABLE table_name;

Example: TRUNCATE table students;

7. How to delete records from the table.

Ans. The process of deleting records from the table is very simple except for record related to other data and resides on the one side of a one to many relationships. For maintaining the data integrity an access does not let the deleting of related data. The steps to delete data are:

4. Open the table in either Datasheet or Form view
5. Select the record that you want to delete. Click on record selector next to the record in case of availability of record selector
6. Press delete key or select Home > Records > Delete

8. Define database query with example?

Ans. A query database is a request for data from a database. The request is to retrieve data however data can also be manipulated using queries.

Example: manager can perform a query for selecting the employees who were hired 5 months ago. The results could be the base for creating evaluations of performance.

9. Name any five ways of locating the specific records using Form?

Ans. By increase in the size of database, locating specific records will need more than a quick look at a datasheet. The fives ways of locating the specific records on the basis of one's needs are:

- Browse through all records
- Go to a specific record
- Search for a specific record
- Filter to see a limited number of records
- Create a query to find a specific record

C. LONG SOLVED QUESTION AND ANSWERS:

1. Give in detail various features of database?

Ans. Various features of database for managing data are:

- **Tables:** It is the building block of any relational database model in which all the actual data is entered and defined. A database contains various tables that consist of cells at the records intersection named rows and fields named columns. It is also known as field.
- **Field (Data item):** It is an area in the record that is reserved for specific piece of data. It is the individual sub-component of one record that contains set of characters such as customer name, state, current address, number, state, city and many more. It is also known as column.
- **Record:** It is the collection of data items of all the fields pertaining to one entity or complete unit of information such as company, transition, person and many more. It is also known as tuple, entity and row.
- **Queries:** It is an inquiry into the database using the SELECT statement that give filtered data on the basis of your specifications and conditions indicating the summaries, records and fields. These are what user wants to fetch from a database. It enable the extraction of information from database on the basis of conditions defined in query.
- **Forms:** It is a window or a screen in database that consists of various fields to enter data. It can be used for viewing or editing your data. In a specified interface, it is an user interface.

2. Write down the steps to create table using Wizard?

Ans. There is need of primary key field in every table that is used to number the entries and let that number to increase automatically by adding each entry. The wizard allows the table fields to come from more than one suggested table. Steps to create a table using Wizard are:

Step 1: Select Fields: There are two categories of tables named business and personal. User can choose one from it and each category consists of their own suggested tables. In each tables, there is list of available fields and CD-Collection Sample table can be used in the personal category for selecting the fields needed for table.

Step 2: Set field types and formats: In this step the properties is given for each fields. By clicking on field, the information on the right get changed and one can also make changes according to their needs.

Step 3: Set primary key: In this step, the created primary key are checked by selecting the option of use an existing field as a primary key and select the required fields.

Step 4: Create the table: The name of table is default but user can change it in this step. Then click on finish for completing the table wizard.

3. Write a note on create and edit relationships: one to one, one to many and many to many?

Ans. In Access, data can be stored in multiple tables and then relationships are used for joining the tables. After creating relationships the data can be used from all of the related tables in report, form and query. There are three types of relationships between tables:

One to one relationship: Let user have two tables A and B. In case of one to one relationship, each record in Table A can only have one matching record in Table B and vice a versa. This type of relationships is very less because the data is stored in single table in case of one to one relationship. This relationship is created for both the related columns are primary keys or have unique constraints.

Customer				**Account**	
customer-id	**customer-name**	**city**		**account-no.**	**balance**
C001	Rahim	Dhaka		A001	200
C002	Karim	Pabna		A002	100
C003	Salam	Dhaka		A003	350
C004	Rafiq	Comilla		A004	700
C005	Qader	Sylhet		A005	1200

In the above example one customer should have only one account number and each account no can be associated only with one customer ID.

One-to-Many Relationship: This is most common type of relationship in which record in Table A can have number of matching in records of Table B but Table B can only have one matching record in Table A. In case of this relationship, the primary table is the one which have one value and related table is with many values. The validity of the relationship between two tables gets ensured by referential integrity.

Customer

customer-id	customer-name	city
C001	Rahim	Dhaka
C002	Karim	Pabna
C003	Salam	Dhaka
C004	Rafiq	Comilla
C005	Qader	Sylhet

Account

account-no.	balance
A001	200
A002	100
A003	350
A004	700
A005	1200

customer-id	account-no.
C001	A001
C002	A002
C003	A003
C004	A004
C005	A005

Many to Many Relationship: In this case, Table A record can have number of matching records in Table B and vice a versa. This type of relationship become possible by defining the third table named junction table whose primary key contains two fields named foreign keys from both Tables A and B. It is just like two one to many relationships with third table.

Customer

customer-id	customer-name	city
C001	Rahim	Dhaka
C002	Karim	Pabna
C003	Salam	Dhaka
C004	Rafiq	Comilla
C005	Qader	Sylhet

Account

account-no.	balance
A001	200
A002	100
A003	350
A004	700
A005	1200

7. Write down the steps of creating Query using design view?

Ans. From all the available methods of creating a query, Design view is the fastest and easiest way. The steps to create a query using Design view are:

- Open the database
- Click on Queries icon in the Database window of Objects bar > Double click on it to create a query in Design view and Table dialog box will open.
- Select the query or table user want to use
- Click on Employees and then Add
- Close the Show Table dialog box after finishing with adding the queries or tables
- Click Close and query window will start appearing in Design view

8. How to create a query to find a specific record?

Ans. The use of filter records technique is very useful for finding the specific records but there can be cases when you want to perform the same filter and search operation on daily basis. So, in these cases user can create a query instead of reproducing a set of filters and search steps.

You can create a query that displays issues whose status is closed by following these steps:

- On the **Create** tab, in the **Queries** group, click **Query Design**.
- In the **Show Table** dialog box, double-click **Issues**, and then click **Close**.
- In the query designer, double-click the asterisk (*) in the **Issues** table. This helps make sure that the query will display all the fields from the records it returns.
- **Issues.*** appears in the first column of the design grid, in the **Field** row. This indicates that all the fields from the Issues table should be returned.
- In the query designer, double-click **Status** on the **Issues** table.
- **Status** appears in the second column in the design grid, in the **Field** row.
- In the second column of the design grid, clear the check box in the **Show** row. This helps make sure that the query does not display the Status field.
- If you do not clear the **Show** check box in the Status column, the Status field will be displayed two times in the query results.
- In the second column of the design grid, in the **Criteria** row, type **="Closed"**. This is your search criterion. This is how you make sure that the query will return only those records where the value of **Status** is «Closed.»

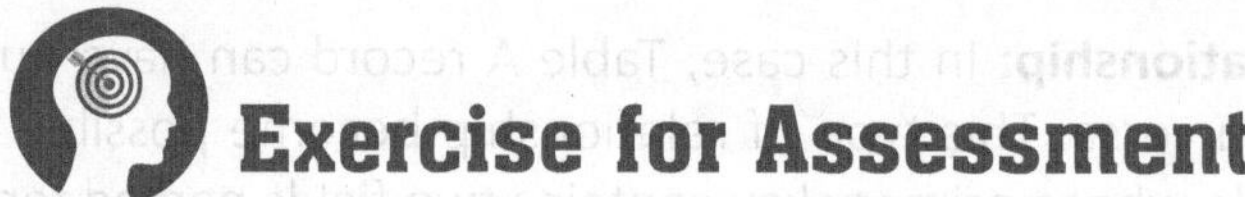

A. MULTIPLE CHOICE QUESTIONS

1. For each attribute of a relation, there is a set of permitted values, called the ____________ of that attribute.

   a. Domain   b. Relation   c. Set   d. Schema

2. The tuples of the relations can be of ____________ order.

   a. Any   b. Same   c. Sorted,   d. Constant

3. Which one of the following cannot be taken as a primary key ?

   a. Id   b. Register number   c. Dept_id   d. Street

4. In one-to-many relationship the table in 'one' side is called ____________ and on 'many' side is called ____________

   a. Child , Parent   b. Parent , Child   c. Brother , Sister   d. Father , Son

5. To create relationship between two tables

   a. drag the primary key of a table into foreign key of another table
   b. drag the foreign key of a table into the primary key of another table
   c. drag any field from parent table and drop on child table
   d. Any of above can be done to create relationship

6. In table design view what are the first column of buttons used for

   a. Indicate Primary Key   b. Indicate Current Row
   c. Both of above   d. None of above

7. Which of the following is not a type of relationship that can be applied in Access database

   a. One to One   b. One to Many
   c. Many to Many   d. All of above can be applied

8. The subset of super key is a candidate key under what condition ?
   a. No proper subset is a super key
   b. All subsets are super keys
   c. Subset is a super key
   d. Each subset is a super key
9. A attribute in a relation is a foreign key if the ____________ key from one relation is used as an attribute in that relation .
   a. Candidate
   b. Primary
   c. Super
   d. Sub

B. VERY SHORT QUESTION AND ANSWER

1. Define Referential Integrity?
2. Write down the steps of inserting data in the table.
3. What is database?
4. Define database management system.
5. Define Table?
6. What is primary key
7. What do you mean by data field?
8. What are records?
9. What does the term field means?

C. SHORT QUESTION AND ANSWERS

1. Write the difference between records and fields.
2. What are the advantages and disadvantages of DBMS?
3. What is good database design?
4. Why data base is needed.
5. Write the steps to create a database.
6. How to open an existing database.
7. What are the different types of datatypes?
8. What makes a good primary key?
9. How primary key is used.
10. Write steps to open an existing table.

D. LONG QUESTION AND ANSWERS

1. Briefly explain the primary, foreign and Composite key in database?
2. Write a note on RDBMS Software?
3. Write a note on Field properties in MS Access?
4. How to edit a query? Explain with various steps associated with it.
5. Explain the applying criteria in query: Single field and multiple fields using wildcard.
6. Define Forms? How to create a forms using Wizard?
7. Write down the various features involved in modifying form?
8. Give various steps of inserting and deleting record using Form view?
9. How to create a report using Wizard?

E. APPLICATION BASED QUESTIONS:

1. Help Arushi to know about various features of database that make it easy for her to create a database and understanding any existing database.

2. To uniquely identify a records in a table which type of key should be used by Komal.
3. Rahul wants to create a table or report using table wizard. Help him with various steps related to it
4. How user can set a primary key in the table with large list of data.
5. Jasspreet has create a record in the table in his previous class. Now, he wants to edit it. Help him with performing various steps related to it.

PROJECT WORK

1. Create a database name class 10th with following specifications:

Field Name	Data Type
Roll no.	Number
Name	Character
Age	Number
DOB	Date
Address	Text
City	Text

Then, specify Roll no. as primary key and save the table as Student list.

2. Make a table and assign primary key to the field, composite key and foreign key
3. Use DDL commands for creating and editing a table in design view also assign data types of field.
4. Insert a data in the table and created and edit relationships one to one, one to many and many to many.
5. Prepare a query for finding particular type of data in large table by adding some condition on it using design view and also perform some calculations using query in Base.
6. Perform various steps to create form and also search record using form. Along with uut, perform various steps to create Report using Report Wizard.

TEACHER NOTES:

1. Arrange a special session for creating table with some standard fields and assign primary key in front of students
2. Perform all the basic editing tasks of query in Computer lab and also demonstrate to apply various criteria in query such as single field and multiple fields using wild card

EXAM TIPS:

1. Identify the field, record, table in the database along with its purpose
2. Check the purpose of various types of keys.
3. Perform various steps to start RDBMS and observe various parts of main window and also assign data of different datatypes.
4. Prepare queries using both wizard and design view and then try to edit it.

4 Web Applications and Security

Learning Outcomes

After this chapter, you will have the knowledge of:

- Web Applications
- Impact of various impairment that impact computer usage
- Launching Accessibility options
- Keyboard Tabs
- Understanding Network fundamental
- Peer-to-Peer Architecture
- Client-Server architecture
- Types of Networks
- Internet, World Wide Web
- Benefits of Networking
- Getting Access to the Internet
- Commonly used Internet Connectivity options
- Data transfer on the Internet
- Introduction to Instant Messaging
- Launching and chatting with a contact Google Talk
- General rules and etiquettes of chatting
- Chatting on various types of messengers
- Creating and Publishing Web pages- Blog
- Set up title and other parameters in a blog posting comments
- Offline blog editor
- Online transaction: Concept of e-commerce
- Internet security, Cyber threats
- Practices for internet security and secure passwords
- Concept of backup and antivirus
- Maintain Workplace safety
- Basic safety rules at workplace
- Prevent accidents and Emergencies
- Types and handling of Accidents and Emergencies
- Protect Health and Safety at work
- General evacuation procedures
- Healthy living

INTRODUCTION

Web applications come from web system and web sites. Tim Berners-Lee have created the first Web sites and formed a distributed hypermedia system that enables researchers in having access of information and documents published by peoples directly through their computers or laptops. The documents were viewed and accessed with browser a software application runs on client system. The computer system with an internet connection help in performing various activities such as reviewing newspapers, listening to music, shopping online, receiving and sending emails, playing games and many more.

SESSION 1:

1.1 Understanding various types of impairment that impact computer usage

Accessibility is a word that is defined as services for people with some disabilities so that they can perform their work without any problem.

In the same way, computer accessibility is defined as the customizing the functioning of computer system. This enable disable person to use a computer. Various types of disabilities that affect the computer usage are color blindness or other eye related problem, speech impairment, paralysis or injured arm, leg or hands and hearing problem.

1.2 Launching Accessibility Options

To launch the option of accessibility, perform the following steps:

Click Start > Control Panel > Ease of access

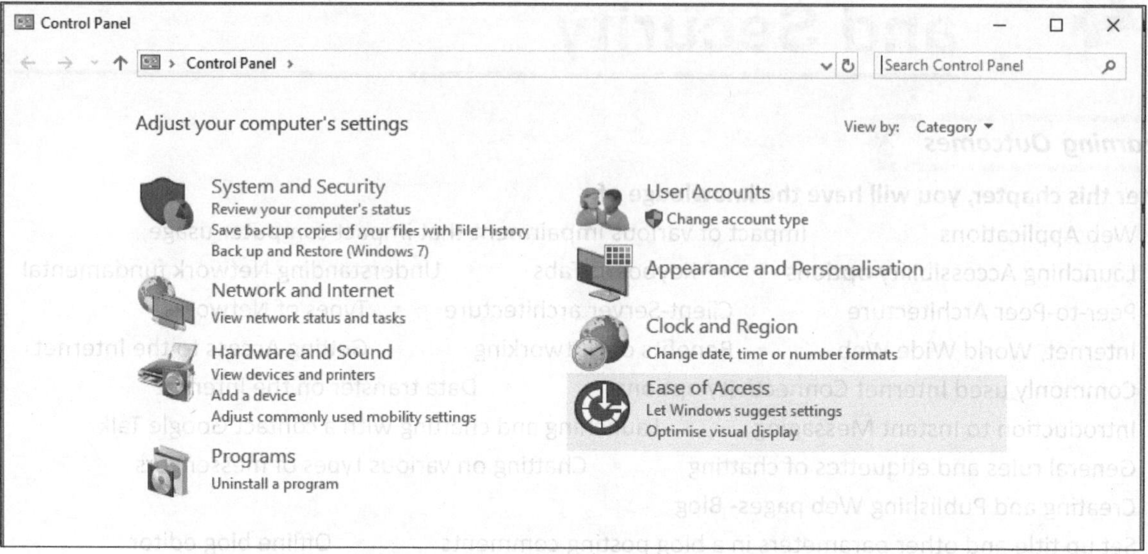

Figure 4.1: Window of Control Panel

Clicking on Ease of Access will further give various options come under it.

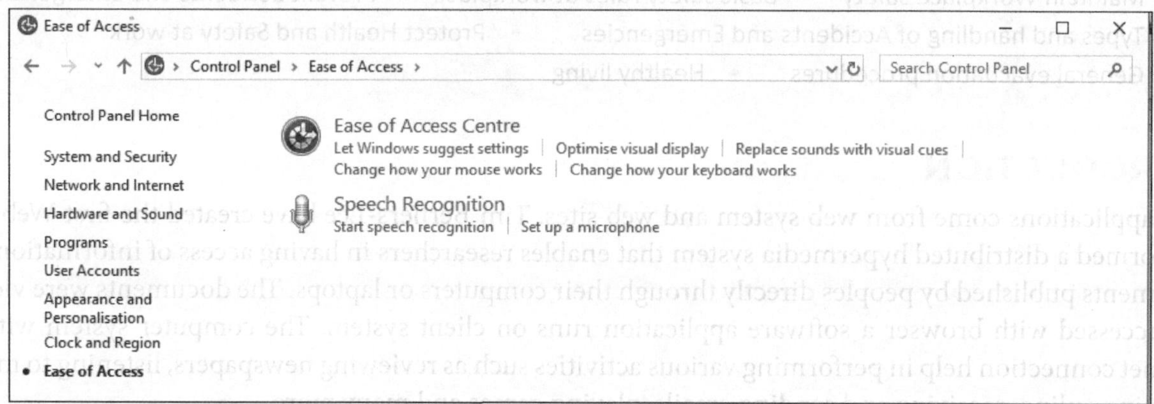

Figure 4.2: Window of Ease of Access Centre

Knowledge Box

The ease of access to the market results in its oversupply, and this in turn weakens the position of employees.

1.3 Keyboard Tab

- Sticky Keys: It is an access feature that helps computer users who have physical disabilities along with by people who want to reduce their repetitive strain.
- Filter Keys: It is Microsoft Windows feature and function of accessibility that tells keyboard about ignoring repeated keystrokes that make typing easy for people have trembles hand.
- Toggle Keys: It is Microsoft Windows feature and function of accessibility that is designed for users suffering from cognitive disabilities or vision impairment. By enabling the Toggle Keys the computer

start emitting sound cues while pressing Scroll Lock, Num Lock and Caps Lock like locking keys. In case of turning on the key a low sound comes from keys and vice a versa for turning it on.

Sound Tab: A window with options to configure accessibility options for sound is displayed. Other things included in it are:

- Sound Sentry: It is used for helping people having auditory injuries. By this tab a visual warning will be generated for instance a sound is generated by computer on blinking of title bar.
- Slow Sounds: It help in instructing application for conveying information by sound and visually information is also provided by it through a captions of text or informative icons.

Display Tab: By selecting a display Tab a window will pop up that consists of various options of configuring the accessibility options. Such options are:

- High Contrast: It is features of accessibility that assist user have impairment related to vision. Through this for ease of viewing user can change the colour or size of fonts and background.
- Cursor Options: It is features of accessibility that assist user have impairment related to vision via changing the width and blink rate of the cursor.

Mouse Tab: Various keys come under it are:

- Mouse Keys: It is features of accessibility that assists user having problem in using a mouse. In this option, numeric keypad or other part of keyboard are used as a pointing device.

General Tab: It enable in configuring the accessibilities options for all users. By selecting this tab a window to configure the additional accessibility options will be displayed.

- Serial Keys: It is features of accessibility that assists user have difficulty in using mouse or keyboard.

Keyboard shortcut of Ease of Access:

Opening the Ease of Access Centre: Windows logo key + U

Turn filter keys on and off: Right shift for eight second

Turn high contrast on and off: Left Alt + Left Shift + Print Scress

Turn Mouse keys on or off: Left Alt + Left Shift+ Num Lock

Turn Toggle keys on or off: Num Lock for 5 seconds

Summary

- Web applications come from web system and web sites.
- Accessibility is a word that is defined as services for people with some disabilities so that they can perform their work without any problem.
- Various types of disabilities that affect the computer usage are color blindness or other eye related problem, speech impairment, paralysis or injured arm, leg or hands and hearing problem.
- To launch the option of accessibility, Click Start > Control Panel > Ease of access
- Sticky Keys is an access feature that helps computer users who have physical disabilities along with by people who want to reduce their repetitive strain.
- Filter Keys is Microsoft Windows feature and function of accessibility that tells keyboard about ignoring repeated keystrokes that make typing easy for people have trembles hand.
- Toggle keys is Microsoft Windows feature and function of accessibility that is designed for users suffering from cognitive disabilities or vision impairment.

- A window with options to configure accessibility options for sound is displayed on Sound tab.
- Sound Sentry: It is used for helping people having auditory injuries. By this tab a visual warning will be generated for instance a sound is generated by computer on blinking of title bar.
- Slow Sounds: It help in instructing application for conveying information by sound and visually information is also provided by it through a captions of text or informative icons.
- By selecting a display Tab a window will pop up that consists of various options of configuring the accessibility options
- Serial Keys: It is features of accessibility that assists user have difficulty in using mouse or keyboard.

Keywords: Web Applications, Web sites, Impairment, Accessibility options, Keyboard Tabs, Sticky keys, Filter keys, Toggle keys, Display tab, Mouse tab, Sound Tab

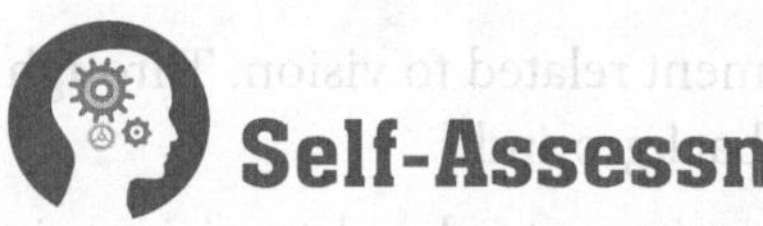

Self-Assessment

A. MULTIPLE CHOICE QUESTIONS.

1. Sticky keys are designed for users suffering from __________ disabilities.
   a. Auditory b. Vision c. Physical
2. Which of the following feature is used to assist people with vision impairment
   a. High contrast b. Sound safety c. Filter keys
3. Function of press right shift for eight seconds is __________.
   a. Turn high Contrast on or off b. Turn Toggle keys on or off
   c. Turn filter keys on or off d. Turn stricky keys on or off

B. FILL IN THE BLANKS

1. Sound Sentry help users with __________ impairments
2. By __________ option of computer, even a disabled person can use computers.
3. __________ is used for reading text on the screen that will read aloud what is on-screen
4. Shift, Ctrl and Alt keys are __________ key

C. TRUE FALSE

1. Toggle keys are designed for people with vision impairments or cognitive disabilities (T/F)
2. To turn mouse keys on or off press Left Alt + Left Shift + Print Screen (T/F)

D. ANSWER THE FOLLOWING QUESTIONS:

1. What do you mean by computer accessibility?
2. Give the usage of Toggle keys.
3. Define general tab?
4. Define sound sentry?
5. What is High contrast feature?
6. What is the uses of Sticky keys, Toggle keys and Filter keys.
7. What all options are available on Windows OS?

E. PRACTICAL WORK

Illustrate the use of various options under computer accessibility like sound, mouse, keyboard, serial keys, display settings and cursor options

Answers

A. Multiple choice question answers:

1. c   2. a   3. c

B. Fill in the blanks answers:

1. Auditory   2. Accessibility   3. Narrator   4. Modifier

C. True False answers

1. True   2. False

SESSION 2: UNDERSTAND NETWORK FUNDAMENTAL

Computer network is consist of various computers along with hardware components that are interconnected with each other through satellites or cables like communication channels that allow sharing of information and resources.

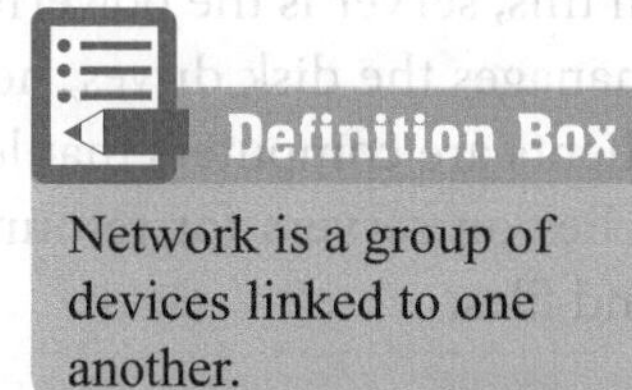

Network is a group of devices linked to one another.

2.1 Peer-to-peer (P2P) Architecture

If all computers in a network have an equal status then it is known as peer to peer networks. In such kind of network there is equally competent CPU of each terminal. That means the request can be initiated by each peer to other peers along with it can respond to incoming requests from other peers on the network.

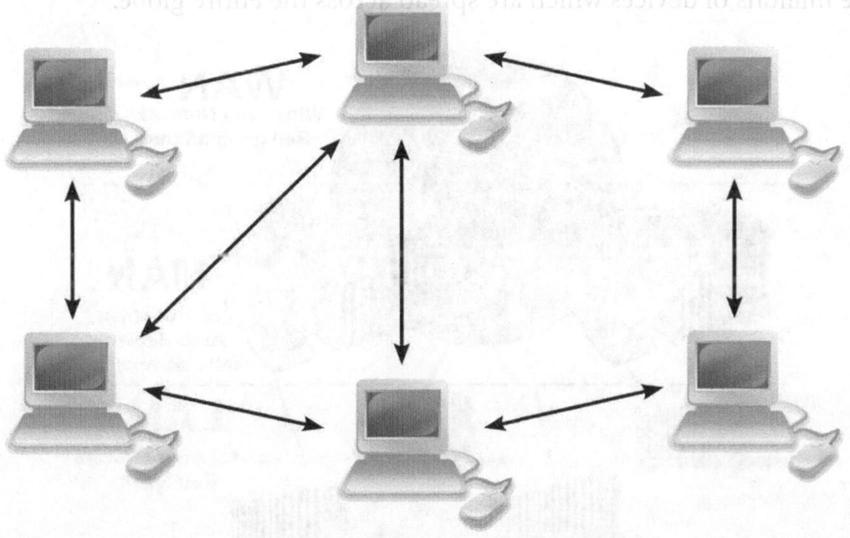

Figure 4.3: Peer to peer network

2.2 Client-Server Architecture:

If some computers in a network have dedicated tasks that provide services to rest of the computers in the network is known as client server architecture. In such kind of network, the server is the computers that provide services and clients are the one that uses these services.

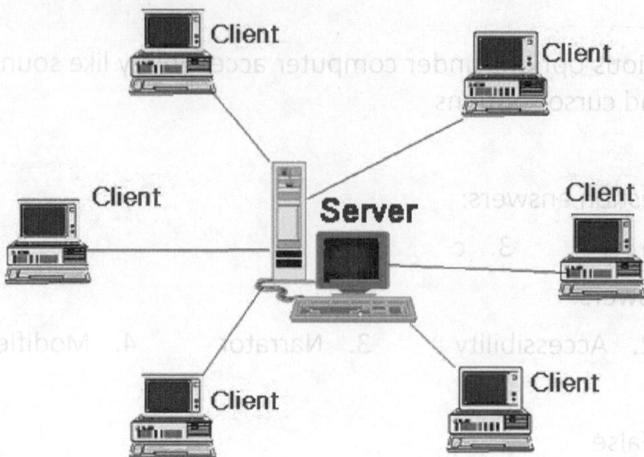

Figure 4.4: Client-Server network

In this, server is the powerful computers that store information in it. It manages the disk drives, network traffic and printers. On other hand, clients are computers that let users to access that data on the server. It relies on servers for resources that can be devices, processing power and files.

Knowledge Box

A computer that is not connected to a network is called stand alone computer.

2.3 Types of Networks

There are different types of computer networks, which can be characterized by their size and their purpose. (Figure 3) Size of a network can be expressed by the geographic area which it occupies and the number of computers which are part of the network. Networks can range from a handful of devices present within a single room to the millions of devices which are spread across the entire globe.

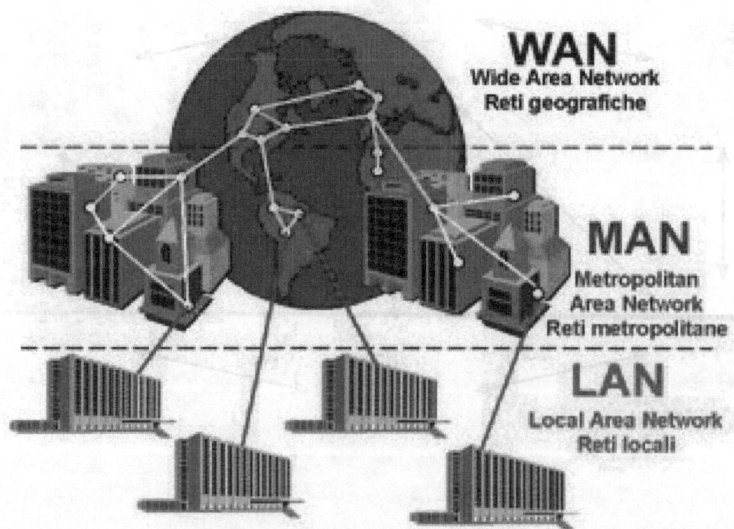

Figure 4.5: Types of network

Different networks based on size are:

- ✦ Local area network, or LAN
- ✦ Metropolitan area network, or MAN
- ✦ Wide area network, or WAN

2.3.1 LAN

LAN stands for Local area network that is a combination of computer network at a single site for instance within an office building. In this various computers are interconnected within a small area that can be building, room or campus. It is used for sharing resources, such as printer. The hardware cost is very less and by only two or thousands computers a LAN network can be establish. Mostly wired connections are used for increasing the security and speed. Even the amount of noise and errors is minimum due to short distance.

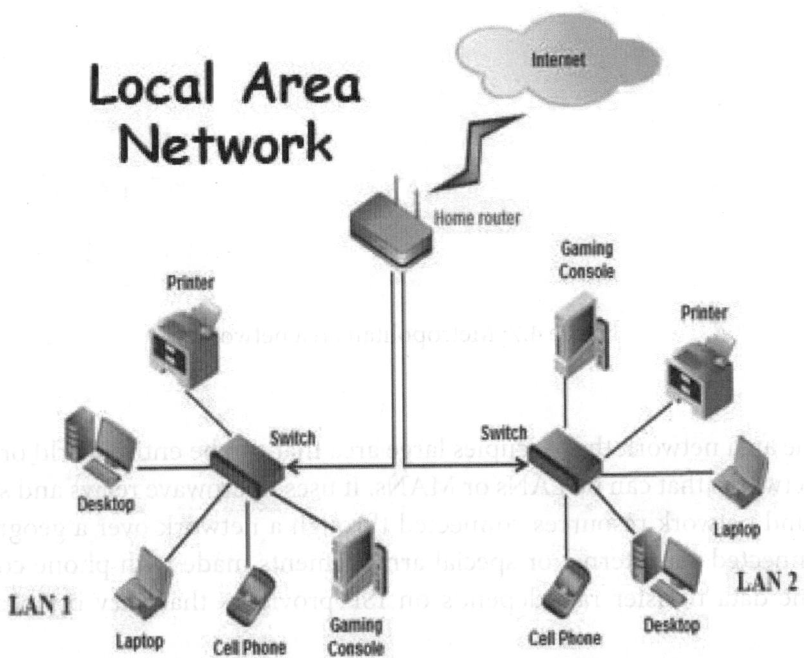

Figure 4.6: Local area network

Characteristics of LAN

- Coverage area is form 10 m to 1 km.
- Transmission rate is of 1 Mb/s to 100 Mbit / sec or higher.
- One can run the multiple devices to share a transmission medium.
- It supports a variety of communications transmission medium such as a Ethernet cable, fibre and wireless transmission.
- A LAN usually has low cost, installation, expansion and maintenance.
- LAN installation is relatively simple, good scalability.

2.3.2 MAN

MAN stands for Metropolitan area network that is a combination of computer network across small region, college campus and entire city. It is larger than LAN or often it is the connection between various LANs to form a bigger network. It is design for extending over a large area that can be up to 10 km. As compared to LAN the data rate of MAN is smaller. For instance, organization with different branches located in the city.

Characteristics of MAN

- It covered large geographical area.
- It transmission is very fast.
- It supports voice communication.
- It uses Fibre optic cable as a transmission media
- It generally covered a city or a town.

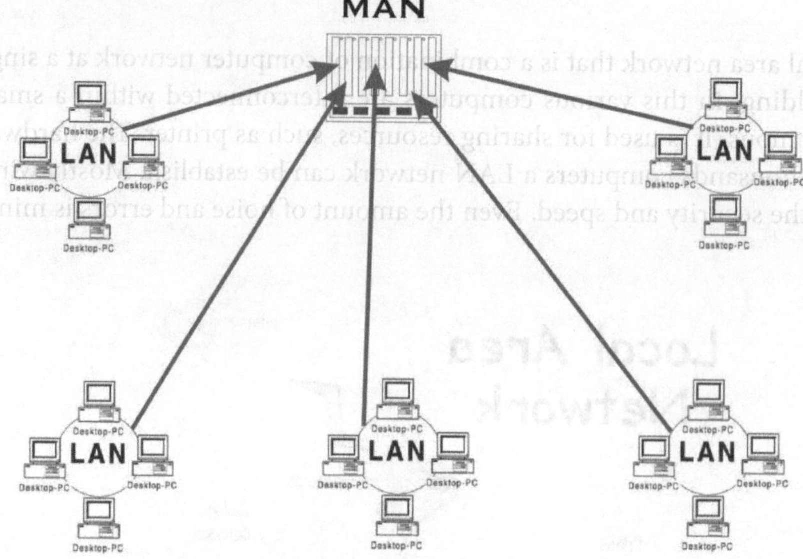

Figure 4.7: Metropolitan area network.

2.3.3 WAN

WAN stands for wide area network that occupies large area that can be entire world or country. It consists of various smaller networks that can be LANs or MANs. It uses microwave relays and satellites and consist various computers and network resources connected through a network over a geographical area. These networks can be connected via Internet or special arrangements made with phone companies or service providers. In this the data transfer rate depends on ISP providers that vary by location. For instance, Internet.

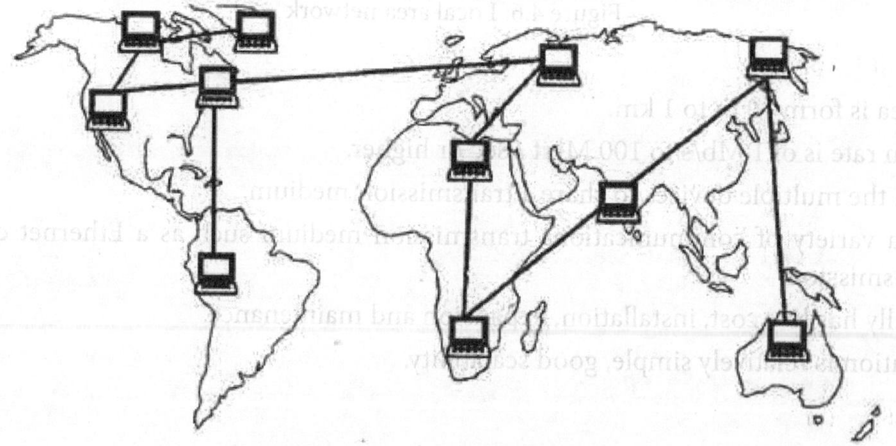

Figure 4.8: Wide area network

Features of WAN:

- Multiple computers are connected together
- It connect devices which are separated by a broader geographical area than a LAN
- A WAN usually interconnects multiple LANs
- Communication links between computers are provided by telephone networks, public data networks, satellites etc.

- Links have low data rate transfer.
- Bit error rate is higher as compared to that for a LAN.
- The typical data rates for WAN are 56kbps to 155Mbps, 622Mbps, 2.4 Gbps or higher speed WAN.

LETS KNOW MORE

LAN, MAN and WAN

Network type	Local area network (LAN)	Metropolitan area network (MAN)	Wide area network (WAN)
Coverage area	**Small**	**Medium**	**Large**
Network	single site	network designed for town.	Geographically dispersed
Coverage area	around 1 km.	Up to 10 km	Can expand most of the world.
Distance	Limited	Limited	Unlimited
Speed	High- 1000 mbps	High - 100 to 1000 mbps	Low – 10 to 100 mbps

2.3 Internet, World Wide Web

2.3.1 Internet

It is a global system of interconnected computer networks that use the standard Internet protocol suite for serving a large count of users worldwide. It consists of millions of private, business, government, academic and public networks.

Figure 4.9: Internet

Features:

- Global system of interconnected computer networks.
- Uses the standard Internet Protocol Suite (TCP/IP).
- Serve billions of users worldwide.
- It consists of millions of private, public, academic, business, and government networks.
- It carries a vast array of information resources and services.

Knowledge Box

Networking started in 1969 with the development of the first network called the ARPANET.

Definition Box

Internet is a worldwide network of computer networks.

WORLD WIDE WEB: It is abbreviated as WWW or W3 or most of the time it is known as Web. It is a system of interlinked hypertext documents that are accessed through Internet. One can view web pages containing videos, images, text and other multimedia with a Web browser and through hyperlinks it navigate between them.

Figure 4.10: World Wide Web

2.4 Benefits of networking

Various benefits associated with networking are:

- Data sharing: It allow sharing of data
- Files transfer: It enable the sending of text files, documents, audio files, presentation, spread sheets and video files to other users.
- Hardware sharing: It enable sharing of scanners, printers like hardware components.

- ✦ Internet Access Sharing: It enable the purchasing of Internet connection and sharing it with other computer systems in the network.
- ✦ Use of applications based of network: It enable the use of network based applications for instance email clients, video calling, chat applications and audio calling.

2.5 GETTING ACCESS TO THE INTERNET

There is need of internet connection for using Internet in the network. The Vodafone, Bharat Sanchar Nigam Limited (BSNL), Reliance, Airtel Jio is some of the Internet Service providers.

- ✦ **INTERNET SERVICE PROVIDER:** Internet Service provider is abbreviated as ISP that is an organization that provides access of internet through dial-up in which modem is used or using hard wired that is direct connection or wireless connection.
- ✦ **MODEM:** Modem stands for modulator and demodulator that convert the digital signals come from computer into analog signal that can be travel through phone lines. In receiver side it also re-converts the analog signals back into digital signals.

MEMORY BOX

Gateway is a device that connects dissimilar networks.

2.6 Some of the commonly used Internet Connectivity options

Some of the most commonly used Internet connectivity are broadly categorised into two technologies named wired and wireless.

Wired Technology: Dial-up: In this Public switched Telephone network (PSTN) facilities are used for establishing a internet connection through telephone lines using MODEM. By dialling a number access of internet is achieved by users. These types of connections are very slow.

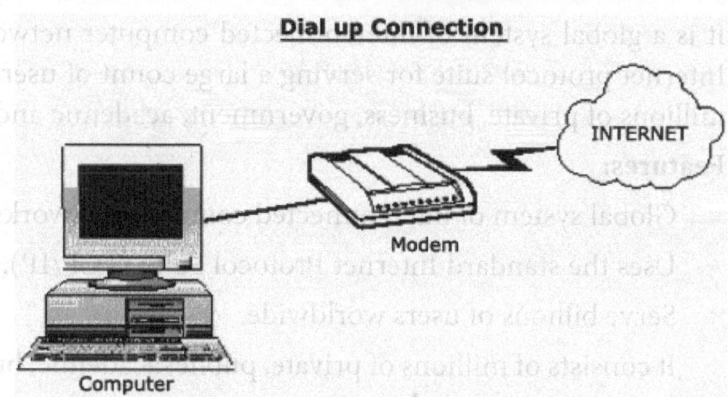

Figure 4.11: Dial-up connection

DSL: DSL stands for Digital Subscriber Line that provides internet connection by transmission of digital data over wires of local telephone network. It enables the use of Telephone and Data transmission on single line of telephone. The DSL modem and subscription is required for using DSL connection.

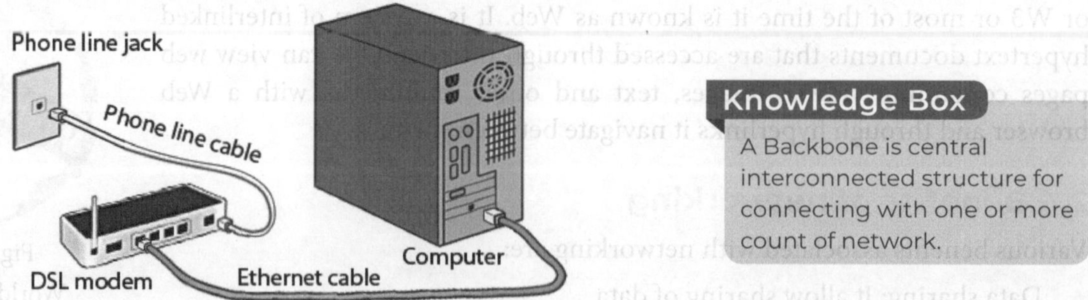

Knowledge Box

A Backbone is central interconnected structure for connecting with one or more count of network.

Figure 4.12: DSL connection

Cable Internet Access: It is one of the forms of broadband Internet access in which TV infrastructure is used. It is provided via existing networks of cable TV. It is almost same as DSL.

2.7 DATA TRANSFER ON THE INTERNET

- For transferring data on the Internet, the data is break down into various bits of same size named packets. Further, a header is added to these packets that explain the source of data and where it should end and fits in with other packets.
- Each packet is transmitted from one computer to another till that final destination is not achieved by it. In this, it's not necessary that same route will be taken by all the packets.
- In destination side, the packets are examined and in case of damage or missing of any packets a message is sent that contain acknowledgement of sending that packet again. This process repeats till that all the packets are not received.
- Now, the packets are reassembled into their original form in few seconds.

Summary

- Computer network is consist of various computers along with hardware components that are interconnected with each other through satellites or cables like communication channels that allow sharing of information and resources.
- If all computers in a network have an equal status then it is known as peer to peer networks.
- If some computers in a network have dedicated tasks that provide services to rest of the computers in the network is known as client server architecture.
- There are different types of computer networks, which can be characterized by their size and their purpose.
- Various types of network are LAN, MAN and WAN
- LAN stands for Local area network that is a combination of computer network at a single site for instance within an office building.
- MAN stands for Metropolitan area network that is a combination of computer network across small region, college campus and entire city.
- WAN stands for wide area network that occupies large area that can be entire world or country. It consists of various smaller networks that can be LANs or MANs.
- Internet is a global system of interconnected computer networks that use the standard Internet protocol suite for serving a large count of users worldwide.
- World Wide Web is abbreviated as WWW or W3 or most of the time it is known as Web. It is a system of interlinked hypertext documents that are accessed through Internet.
- Various benefits of networking are data sharing, File transfer, Hardware sharing, Internet Access Sharing, Use of applications based of network.
- Internet Service provider is abbreviated as ISP that is an organization that provides access of internet through dial-up in which modem is used or using hard wired that is direct connection or wireless connection.
- Modem stands for modulator and demodulator that convert the digital signals come from computer into analog signal that can be travel through phone lines.
- Some commonly used Internet connectivity options are Dial-up, DSL and Cable Internet Access

Keywords: Computer network, Peer-to-peer, Client-server, Services, Types of Networks, LAN, MAN, WAN, Internet, World Wide Web, Networking benefits, Data sharing, Hardware sharing, Internet service provider, Modem, Internet Connectivity options, Dial-up, Wired Technology, DSL, Cable Internet Access

Self-Assessment

A. MULTIPLE CHOICE QUESTIONS.

1. ___________ is the full form of LAN.
   a. Locate network area b. Local network of area
   c. Locate area of network d. Local area network
2. Modem stands for:
   a. Mobile device b. Mobile demodulator
   c. Modulator device d. Modulator/demodulator
3. Which of the following is not a type of network?
   a. LAN b. TAN c. MAN d. WAN
4. ___________ is the amount of data that a signal can carry.
   a. Bandwidth b. Broadband c. Cable length d. All

B. FILL IN THE BLANKS

1. In ___________ network one computer acts as server and rest as clients
2. In a Star network topology, all of the computers are connected to ___________.
3. ___________ topology transfer data in only one direction.
4. In Mesh topology there are ___________ number of physical channels to link n devices.
5. ___________ is necessary to connect Internet over a telephone line.

C. TRUE FALSE

1. PAN is a type of Networks (T/F)
2. The speed of WAN is less than LAN (T/F)
3. Tree topology is used in Wide area network (T/F)
4. Dial-up connections transmit data at a faster rate than broadband connections (T/F)

D. ANSWER THE FOLLOWING QUESTIONS:

1. Briefly explain the peer to peer network.
2. Name various types of networks.
3. Give various benefits of networking.
4. Define Internet. Also, write some of its applications.
5. Name various types of Internet Connections. Give detail explanation of any two of it.
6. Define various Network Topologies?
7. Give any 2 disadvantages of network.

E. PRACTICAL WORK

Try to know about Internet connection in your hostel and check the availability of Wi-Fi. List any three Internet service providers in your area. Collect some information like their connectivity type, speed and charges then conclude the best one with reason.

Answers

A. Multiple choice question answers:

1. d 2. d 3. b 4. a

B. Fill in the blanks answers:

1. Client Server networks 2. Hub 3. Bus 4. n(n-1)/2 5. Modem

C. True False answers

1. True 2. False 3. True 4. False

SESSION 3: INTRODUCTION TO INSTANT MESSAGING

Instant Messaging abbreviated as IM is a form of communication over the Internet that offer an instantaneous transmission of messages based on text from sender to receiver. Most of the IM software have feature of performing audio chat, sharing desktops, audio chat, dile transfers, conferencing and calling and many more.

3.1 Learn key features of instant messaging

Various key features of IM are:

- Audio calling and conferencing
- Message history that includes saving messages for future reference
- Video calling and conferencing
- As like SMS sending of text messages to one or more than one persons
- Transferring files that can be audio, spread sheets, documents and video files.

3.2 INSTANT MESSAGING SERVICES

There are two types of instant messaging software named application and web based.

- **Application based:** These software are installed after being download in users computer. For instance: Yahoo messenger, Rediff Bol, Skype, Google Talk, Window Live Messenger and many more.
- **Web Based:** These software are access through browser such as Internet Explorer, Google chrome, etc. For instance: For Web it is Yahoo Messenger, MSM Web Messenger, IMO and Meebo, etc.

3.3 CREATING AN INSTANT MESSAGING ACCOUNT

Google Hangout is developed by Google Inc and is an Instant Messaging service that allows communication through voice and text. On it, video calls can also be made but there is need of account in Google for using Google Hangouts. This Google Hangouts app can be used through Gmail account. Other instant messaging service is Google Talk that can be downloaded by searching it on Google.

Knowledge Box

You need to download and install Google Talk application from www.google.com/talk prior to this exercise.

3.4 LAUNCHING GOOGLE TALK

The steps involved to launch Google Talk are:

Click Start > Programs > Google Talk

Figure 4.13: Google Talk

Other option is double click on Google Talk icon on the desktop. For this, there is need of list of contacts for chatting. If there is no contact in the list then you can also add it through Gmail account to your contact list by sending an invite.

Knowledge Box

If you don't have a Gmail account already you have to create a new Gmail account.

Summary

- Instant Messaging abbreviated as IM is a form of communication over the Internet that offer an instantaneous transmission of messages based on text from sender to receiver.
- Various key features of IM are audio calling and conferencing, Video calling and conferencing, Transferring files, keeping message history and many more.
- There are two types of instant messaging software named application and web based.
- Google Hangout is developed by Google Inc and is an Instant Messaging service that allows communication through voice and text. On it, video calls can also be made but there is need of account in Google for using Google Hangouts.
- To launch Google Talk, Click Start > Programs > Google Talk

Keywords: Instant messaging, Services, Account, Google Talk

Self-Assessment

A. MULTIPLE CHOICE QUESTIONS.

1. Which of the following is not an application based IM services?

   a. Skype b. IMO c. Google Talk

2. To use instant messaging software there is need of valid messaging __________.

   a. Page b. Account c. Book d. Site

3. WhatsApp and WeChat are __________ type of software?

   a. Web based b. User based c. Application based d. Server based

4. Which of the following is not a instant messenger

   a. Google chrome b. LinkedIn c. WhatsApp d. Google Hangouts

B. FILL IN THE BLANKS

1. Google Talk is a __________ based software
2. Audio and __________ conferencing can be done using Google account.

C. TRUE FALSE

1. Skype is a Web based software (T/F)
2. Instant messages enables to create a chat room with friends (T/F)

D. ANSWER THE FOLLOWING QUESTIONS:

1. What do you mean by Instant messaging
2. Name various types of IM services.
3. How to launch a Google talk? Write down the steps to launch it in your system.
4. What are two main types of IM software?
5. List any 3 Application based and Web based Instant messaging software.

E. PRACTICAL WORK

Sign in into your Google Talk Account, if you don't have it then first sign up for creating an account then sign In.

Answers

A. Multiple choice question answers:

1. c   2. b   3. c   4. a

B. Fill in the blanks answers:

1. Web based   2. Video

C. True False answers

1. False   2. True

SESSION 4: CHATTING WITH A CONTACT – GOOGLE TALK

Google talk is also known as Google instant messaging network and its IM client. This can be downloaded from talk.google.com and learn more about it.

It enables the sending and receiving of voice over-IP internet phone calls and text-based instant messages. For using Google Talk as a text based IM client, you need a computer and internet connection and to use calling feature there is also need of microphone and speaker for your system.

Point to remember: To use Google Talk or Google Chat, you must have a Gmail username and password.

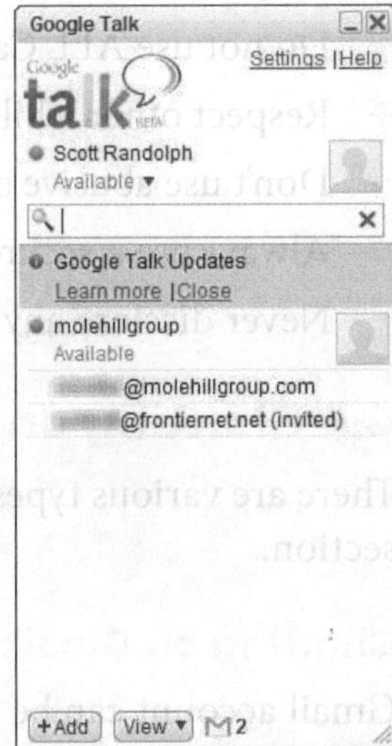

Figure 4.14: Main Window of Google Talk

4.1 Learn to chat with a contact that is already added to your contact list:

Like most of the IM clients, Google talk starts automatically by turning on the computer system. User will be impelled to sing in via their Gmail ID and Google Talk window will start appearing on it. The below figure shows the friends in your contact list and user will green circle to their names are available for chat.

To start the conversation with one of user in your fiend list, user have of just click on name of that persons. It will open a new chat window as shown in below figure 13. Now, to start chat, just enter a message in bottom text box and press Enter key.

Figure 4.15: Chat window in Google Talk

4.2 Sending text chat messages instantly on a contact

To send a direct message to someone in chat room, perform the following steps:

- Sign in to Gmail
- Click a room present on the left under Rooms
- Click on room name of view members
- Click on person name to whom user want to chat
- Enter a message
- Click on Send

LETS KNOW MORE

To start a direct message with your friend, you can also click on your friend photo.

4.3 General rules and etiquettes to be followed while chatting

Some general rules and etiquettes to be followed while chatting include:

- Use short messages
- Give time to respond to messages
- Properly end a conversation
- Do not use ALL Caps
- Respect other while chatting
- Don't use abusive or indecent language while chatting
- Always use a secure chat room
- Never disclose any personal information

4.4 Chatting on various types of messengers

There are various types of messenger available on which you can chat. Some of them are explained in this section.

Chatting on Gmail:

Gmail account can be used for chatting. After signing into account, one have to click on contact window displayed on the left side within the Gmail account page.

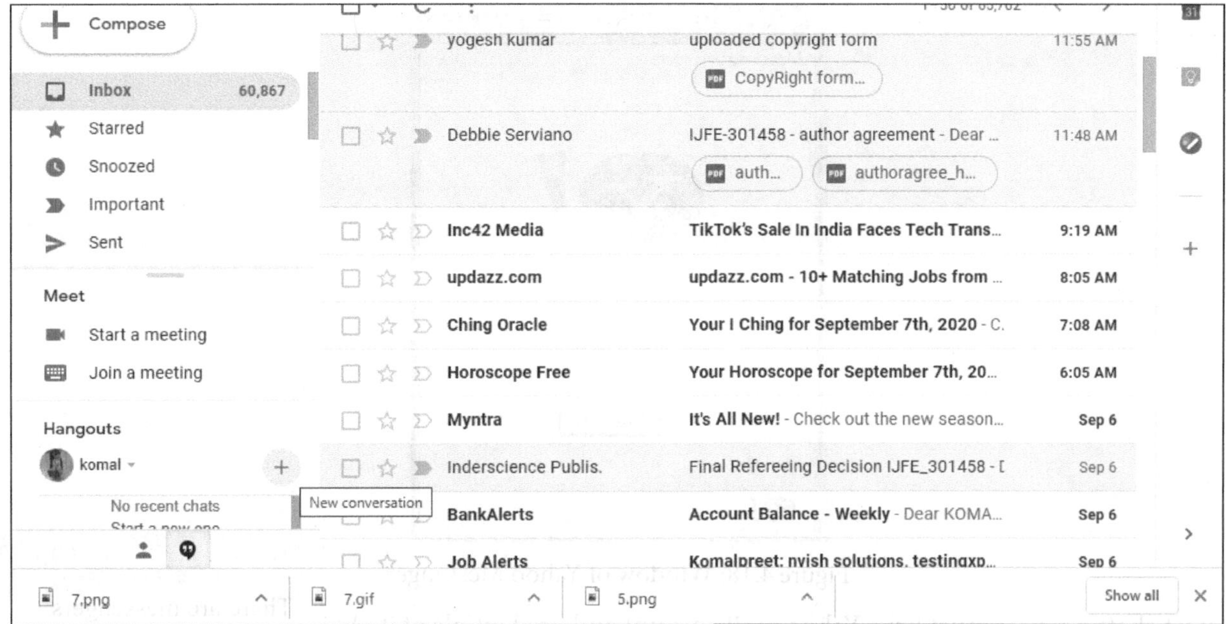

Figure 4.16: Interface window of Gmail

To start a new chat, simply click on "+" sign and pop-up window will appear as shown in below figure 4.17.

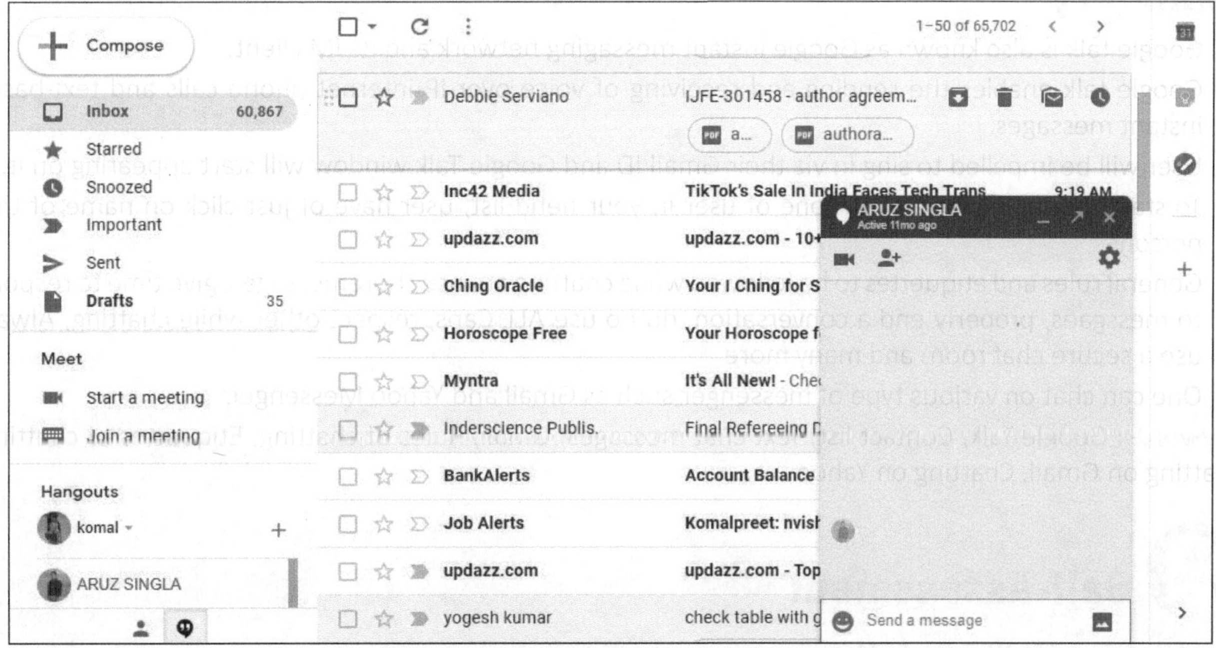

Figure 4.17: Chat window in Gmail

Chatting on Yahoo

Yahoo messenger is an IM program that helps in keeping in touch with near and dear ones. It enable the sending if messages and voice conferencing calls. To use it, download and install Yahoo! Messenger from http://in.messenger.yahoo.com/download.

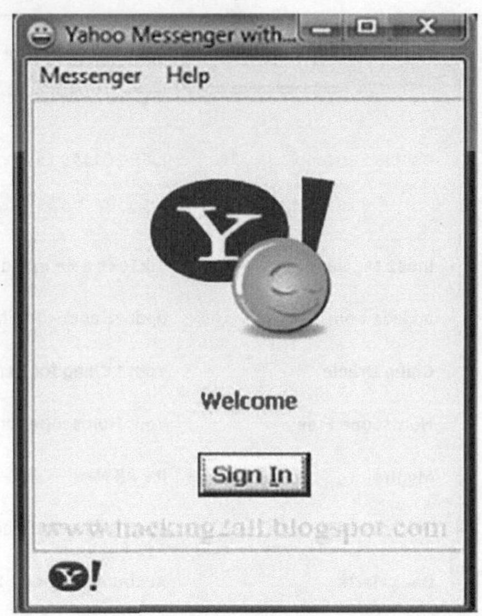

Figure 4.18: Window of Yahoo Messenger

To start chatting, user must have Yahoo mail account and credentials of it. As you sign in using these credentials a contacts list will start appearing for chat.

LETS KNOW MORE

There are messengers other than Gmail and Yahoo named Rediff, Sify, MSN and many more.

Summary

- Google talk is also known as Google instant messaging network and its IM client.
- Google talk enables the sending and receiving of voice over-IP internet phone calls and text-based instant messages.
- User will be impelled to sing in via their Gmail ID and Google Talk window will start appearing on it.
- To start the conversation with one of user in your fiend list, user have of just click on name of that persons.
- General rules and etiquettes to be followed while chatting are use short messages, give time to respond to messgaes, properly end a conversation, do no use ALL Caps, respect other while chatting, Always use a secure chat room and many more
- One can chat on various type of messenger such as Gmail and Yahoo Messenger.

Keywords: Google Talk, Contact list, Text chat messages, Gmail, Rules of chatting, Etiquettes of chatting, Chatting on Gmail, Chatting on Yahoo

Self-Assessment

A. MULTIPLE CHOICE QUESTIONS.

1. Give ___________ to respond to messages

   a. Explanation b. Time c. Feedback

2. Google Talk is also known as ___________.

   a. Application

   b. Instant messaging server

   c. Google instant messaging network

3. Avoid using __________ while chatting
   a. Lowercase
   b. Uppercase
   c. Sentence-case
   d. Both Lowercase and Uppercase
4. Use __________ messages while chatting.
   a. Very long
   b. Long
   c. Short
   d. Medium

B. FILL IN THE BLANKS

1. One can chat with their friends using Gmail and __________ messenger
2. One can open their Google Hangouts account using __________.

C. TRUE FALSE

1. Sender has to continuously send messages without waiting for receiver response (T/F)
2. It is necessary to properly end a conversation while chatting (T/F)

D. ANSWER THE FOLLOWING QUESTIONS:

1. What is Google Talk?
2. Give name of any four chat services.
3. Write down the steps to instantly send text chat messages on a contact?
4. Briefly explain the chatting in various types of messengers.

E. PRACTICAL WORK

Create an account on Gmail and Yahoo and chat with your friends.

Practically chat using various available messenger services and observe the difference

Answers

A. Multiple choice question answers:

1. b   2. c   3. b   4. c

B. Fill in the blanks answers:

1. Yahoo   2. Gmail account

C. True False answers

1. False   2. True

SESSION 5: CREATING AND PUBLISHING WEB PAGES – BLOG

Modern age is a communication age in which everyone likes to communicate in different ways all over the world. The article and dairy writing is replaced with modern tech-alternative named blogging. Blogs enable the writing of topics about which they are passionate and reach to like-minded people over the globe.

LETS KNOW MORE

Today, there are more than 600 million blogs **on the web**. The number of bloggers in the United States alone is set to reach 31.7 million users by 2020.

5.1 Learn and appreciate a blog and its creation with the help of some blog providers

A blog is a discussion style site that is used by various non-technical users for creation of personal web pages. It is same as online personal diary used by user to write their interest and knowledge about it. User can convey news, messages, announcements and events over it.

It is managed through web browser for which there is need of Internet connection. One can also create a blog through Offline Blog software and later publish it by connecting with an Internet connection. Various Websites that offer blog services are:

- www.blog.com
- www.wordpress.com
- www.weebly.com
- www.blogger.com

To create a blog, perform the following steps:

- Open a web browser on your computer system
- Type the address www.wordpress.com in the address bar and click on Get started button

Figure 4.19: Get Started button window

- A new page with different fields such as blog address, username and password will appear as shown in below figure 4.20.

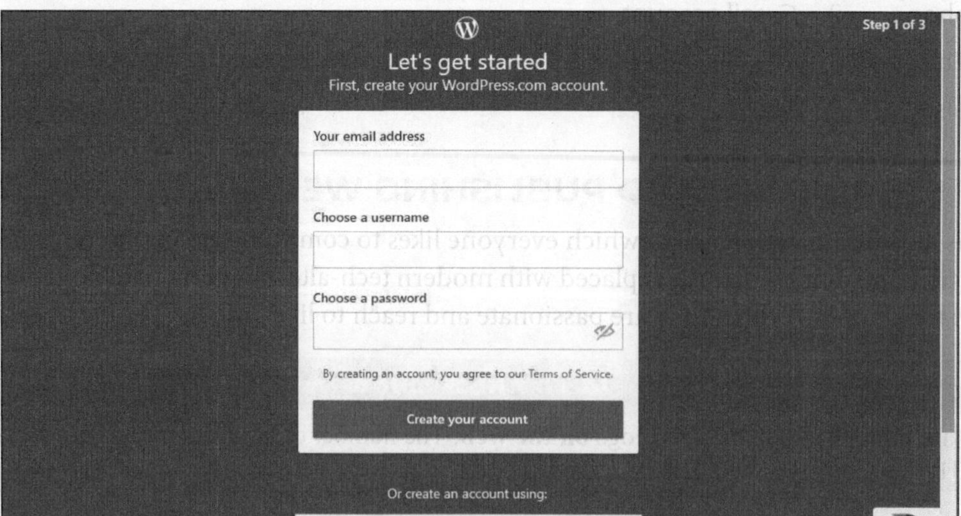

Figure 4.20: Sign up window

- Enter all the details
- Click on Create your account button
- Click on link sent to registered email for activating your blog account
- After activation, a WordPress blog account page start appearing on user scree.

Knowledge Box

Blogs are easy and quick to update or add new posts. Blogs are easy to set up and don't need much technical knowledge.

5.2 Set up title and other parameters in a blog posting comments

Once you have created a blog, your blog address will start appearing on the top of web page. Double clicking on the link will take you on the home page where you can add content to you blog. There is need to provide a unique title for you post and typing content in the text box. Once you have typed the content simply click on Publish button.

To set up a tittle and other parameters in a blog positing comments, perform the following steps:

- Click on Create a blog or New blog
- Enter a title for your blog and choose the URL or blog address

Figure 4.21: WordPress title and text window

- Type the content in text box
- Click on publish button

You can also comment on posts published by others by typing your comment in comment box located below the post named as Leave a Reply.

Figure 4.22: Window for Commenting on post

- Blog is an online journal where entries are posted
- Blogging is an act of writing posts on blogs
- Blogger is the person who does blogging

5.3 Using offline blog editors

Offline blog editor is an editor that let bloggers to create a blog posts without internet connection. It enables the creation, editing and formatting your content before uploading it on the website. Once users are done with all the updates, they can post it directly on their blog in the presence of Internet connection.

Some of the popular offline blog editors are Qumana, Microsoft Word, MarsEdit, Windows Live Writer, Bloglet and many more.

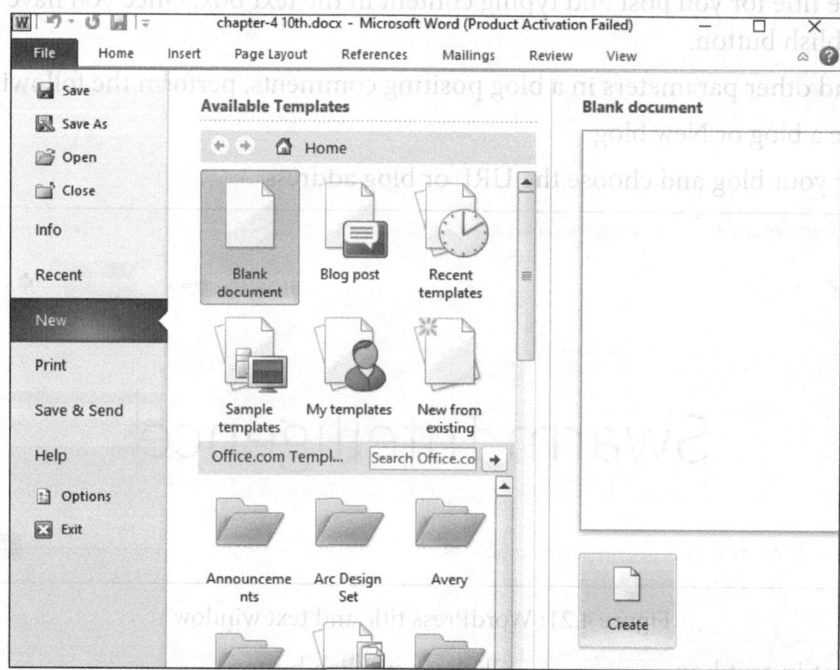

Figure 4.23: Offline Blog editor: Microsoft Word

Definition Box

Offline blog editor is an editor that lets users to create a posts without an internet connection.

Summary

- Blogs enable the writing of topics about which they are passionate and reach to like-minded people over the globe.
- One can also create a blog through Offline Blog software and later publish it by connecting with an Internet connection.
- Various websites of blog services are www.blog.com, www.weebly.com, www.wordpress.com, www.blogger.com
- Once you have created a blog, your blog address will start appearing on the top of web page.

- Offline blog editor is an editor that let bloggers to create a blog posts without internet connection. It enable the creation, editing and formatting your content before uploading it on the website.
- Some of the popular offline blog editors are Qumana, Microsoft Word, MarsEdit, Windows Live Writer, Bloglet and many more.

Keywords: Creating Blog, Publishing Various websites, Web pages, Blog posting comments, Offline blog editor

Self-Assessment

A. MULTIPLE CHOICE QUESTIONS.

1. __________ enable the writing of topics over the globe.

   a. Internet b. Dairy c. Blog

2. The act of writing posts on blogs is known as __________.

   a. Blog b. Blogger c. Blogging

3. Person who creates a blogs is known as:

   a. Blog b. Blogger c. Writer d. Blogging

4. Which of the following is not a blogging site?

   a. meblog b. WordPress c. blogsome d. blog

B. FILL IN THE BLANKS

1. A __________ is a discussion style site that is used by various non-technical users for creation of personal web pages.
2. __________ is a person who does blogging.

C. TRUE FALSE

1. Once user have created a blog, its blog address will start appearing on the top of web page (T/F)
2. Blogging is the person who writes blogs (T/F)
3. Bloggers cannot create offline blogs (T/F)

D. ANSWER THE FOLLOWING QUESTIONS:

1. Name various websites that offer blog services.
2. Write a note on offline blog editor.
3. Define the term blog and other associated terms linked to it.

E. PRACTICAL WORK

Practically create a Blog and set the various parameters associated with it.

Answers

A. Multiple choice question answers:

1. c 2. c 3. b 4. a

B. Fill in the blanks answers:

1. Blog 2. Blogger

C. True False answers

1. True 2. False 3. False

SESSION 6: ONLINE TRANSACTION

Online transaction is also known as E-payments that is a method of payment in which money is transferred online. E-payments or an electronic payment is a secure real time transfer of funds between customer and financial institution through Internet.

6.1 Concept of e-commerce

Nowadays, e-commerce has become a popular application of Internet through which users can buy or sell goods over Internet by transferring money online through their debit or credit cards. Various documents involved in e-payments are:

- Digital order: It is sent by payment client to the payment server for providing transaction information.
- Digital receipts: It is sent from payment server to payment client for indicating the outcome of transaction.
- Transaction: It is the combination of both digital order and receipt. As several transactions are issued by merchants for each order or purchase by customer.

6.2 Various online applications:

There are various online applications and some of it is covered under this section:

6.2.1 E-shopping

It is a form of electronic commerce that enables customers to buy goods from a seller on the Internet using a web browser or their applications. Further, credit or debit cards are used by customers for making payment on the Internet.

Some of the e-shopping websites are:

- www.flipkart.com
- www.snapdeal.com
- www.mantra.com
- www.amazon.com
- www.jabong.com

Figure 4.24: E-shopping

6.2.2 E-ticketing

It is the new facility of booking or cancelling tickets of flights, train and buses through Internet. This also enable user to book a tickets on IRCTR portal provided by Indian Railway. It is nothing but an electronic version of a regular paper tickets.

Figure 4.25: E-Ticketing

Summary

- Online transaction is also known as E-payments that is a method of payment in which money is transferred online.
- E-commerce has become a popular application of Internet through which users can buy or sell goods over Internet by transferring money online through their debit or credit cards.
- Various documents involved in e-payments are digital order, digital receipts and transaction.
- Various online applications are E-shopping and E-ticketing.
- E-shopping is a form of electronic commerce that enables customers to buy goods from a seller on the Internet using a web browser or their applications.
- E-ticketing is the new facility of booking or cancelling tickets of flights, train and buses through Internet.

Keywords: Concept of e-commerce, Online applications, Digital order, Digital receipts, Transaction, Online applications, E-shopping, E-ticketing

Self-Assessment

A. MULTIPLE CHOICE QUESTIONS.

1. __________ is the document sent by payment client to the payment server for providing transaction information.

   a. Digital receipts   b. Digital order   c. Transaction

2. __________ is the new facility of booking or cancelling tickets of flights, train or buses through Internet.

   a. E-shopping   b. E-commerce   c. E-ticketing

B. FILL IN THE BLANKS

1. Online transaction is also known as __________ that is a method of payment in which money is transferred online.
2. In terms of e-commerce, __________ is the combination of both digital order and receipt.
3. __________ is the new facility of booking or cancelling tickets of flights, train and buses through Internet.

C. TRUE FALSE

1. Digital order is sent by payment client to the payment server for providing transaction information (T/F)
2. www.jobang.com is one of the E-ticketing site.

D. ANSWER THE FOLLOWING QUESTIONS:

1. Define the concept of E-commerce.
2. Name various online applications.
3. Briefly explain the concept of E-ticketing?

E. PRACTICAL WORK

Demonstrate the use of passwords for securing online transactions

Answers

A. Multiple choice question answers:

1. b 2. c

B. Fill in the blanks answers:

1. E-payments 2. Transaction 3. E-ticketing

C. True and False:

1. True 2. False

SESSION 7: INTERNET SECURITY

Nowadays, Internet security has become a major concern that includes the security of browser and network. The computer systems are getting insecure due to involvement of various threats associated to it.

Figure 4.26: Internet Security

7.1 Need of internet security

In today's modern world the internet proves to be the best communication medium for everyone. Even though it has many advantages, it also has a few drawbacks which the users need to be aware of to steer clear from the online dangers. Keeping your data and your network safe is vital. Malware is more common today and comes with different tactics to achieve nefarious goals.

It's essential to understand the difference between an antivirus program and internet security software. The antivirus program scans for viruses and malware. While it is excellent for discovering malicious software that has already made it onto your computer, it will typically not offer advanced firewall management to monitor inbound and outbound web traffic feeds.

Internet security software is created to prevent hackers from accessing sensitive information through leaks in the networks. Therefore, to protect your confidential data, it monitors all accessed URLs. Phishing websites are already on its lists; consequently, the software compares the sites visited by the user to its master list of phishing websites, and immediately issues an alert to block the site should there be a match, it immediately warns the administrators through email to block the website.

7.2 Cyber threats

There are various types of cyber threats that make system insecure. Some of these threats are covered under this section:

- **Virus:** A computer virus is a kind of malware program which, when run, get replicated by inserting copies of itself into another computer programs, data files of the hard drive. When the replication process of virus get succeeds, the affected areas are called as "infected".

Figure 4.27: Computer virus

- **Spyware:** It's a malware which is installed on a computer with the aim of collecting the owner's private information. Spyware gathers the information about internet interaction, keylogging, passwords, and other valuable data, without even knowing the user of computer.

Figure 4.28: Spyware

Figure 4.29: Malware

- **Malware:** It's a piece of software which is inserted into an information system to cause harm to that or some other systems. Malware can gain remote access to an information system, record and sent data to third party without the user permission or knowledge.
- **Trojan:** It is a malicious computer program which misrepresents itself to appear useful or interesting just to persuade a victim to install it. Typically, an individual e-mails you a Trojan in the form of a joke program, which appears to be useful but that actually does damage.
- **Spamming:** It is an approach of flooding the Internet with various copies of same messages comes in the form of commercial achievements sent to users as unwanted emails.

Figure 4.30: Spamming

- **Snooping:** It is a way of unauthorized access of computer data of another person's. It may include casual observance of an email appears on screen of other person computer and enable them to watch what user is typing.
- **Phishing:** It is used for gaining personal information for identification of theft using fraud email messages comes from genuine users. This is done for gaining personal information of user such as their account numbers and passwords, Adhar card number and credit cards credentials.

Figure 4.31: Phishing attack

7.3 Best practices for internet security and secure passwords

Security is the freedom from risk or danger. It is the prevention of accessing of information by unauthorised persons and unauthorised destruction intentionally.

The safety of information can be ensured by following the below given measures:

Proper use of Passwords: Password is an important form of protecting your data online. As you will be able to login in your account only if you have correct credentials such as Id and password. The password gives the access to online account so it is necessary to keep it secure. This help user in online protection .

Figure 4.32: Secure password

A strong password helps in:

- Keeping your personal information safe and secure
- Protecting your files, emails and other important contents
- Preventing someone from hacking your account

7.4 Concept of backup and antivirus

Anti-Virus Software: It is sometimes also known as anti-malware software, is computer software used to prevent, detect and remove malicious software. Antivirus software was originally developed to detect and remove computer viruses, hence the name. However, with the proliferation of other kinds of malware, antivirus software started to provide protection from other computer threats. In particular, modern antivirus software can protect from:

- Malicious browser helper objects (BHOs)
- Browser hijackers
- Ransomware
- Keyloggers
- Backdoors
- Rootkits
- Trojan horses
- Worms
- Adware
- Spyware

Figure 4.33: Anti-Virus

Some products also include protection from other computer threats, such as infected and malicious URLs, spam, scam and phishing attacks, online identity (privacy), online banking attacks, social engineering techniques, advanced persistent threat (APT) and botnet DDoS attacks.

Data Backup: In information technology, a backup, or the process of backing up, refers to the copying and archiving of computer data so it may be used to restore the original after a data loss event. The verb form is to back up in two words, whereas the noun is backup. Backups have two distinct purposes:

- The primary purpose is to recover data after its loss, be it by data deletion or corruption. Data loss can be a common experience of computer users.
- The secondary purpose of backups is to recover data from an earlier time, according to a user-defined data retention policy, typically configured within a backup application for how long copies of data are required.

Though backups represent a simple form of disaster recovery, and should be part of any disaster recovery plan, backups by themselves should not be considered a complete disaster recovery plan. One reason for this is that not all backup systems are able to reconstitute a computer system or other complex configuration such as a computer cluster, active directory server, or database server by simply restoring data from a backup.

Figure 4.34: Data Backup

Summary

- Internet security has become a major concern that includes the security of browser and network.
- The antivirus program scans for viruses and malware.
- A computer virus is a kind of malware program which, when run, get replicated by inserting copies of itself into another computer programs, data files of the hard drive.
- Spyware is a malware which is installed on a computer with the aim of collecting the owner's private information.
- Malware is a piece of software which is inserted into an information system to cause harm to that or some other systems.
- Trojan is a malicious computer program which misrepresents itself to appear useful or interesting just to persuade a victim to install it.
- Spamming is an approach of flooding the Internet with various copies of same messages comes in the form of commercial achievements sent to users as an unwanted emails.
- Phishing is used for gaining personal information for identification of theft using fraud email messages comes from genuine users.
- Security is the freedom from risk or danger. It is the prevention of accessing of information by unauthorised persons and unauthorised destruction intentionally.
- Anti-virus is sometimes also known as anti-malware software, is computer software used to prevent, detect and remove malicious software.
- In information technology, a backup, or the process of backing up, refers to the copying and archiving of computer data so it may be used to restore the original after a data loss event.

Keywords: Internet security, Need of Internet security, Cyber threats, Virus, Spyware, Malware, Trojan, Spamming, Snooping, Phishing, Internet security, Secure passwords, Anti-virus software, Data Backup

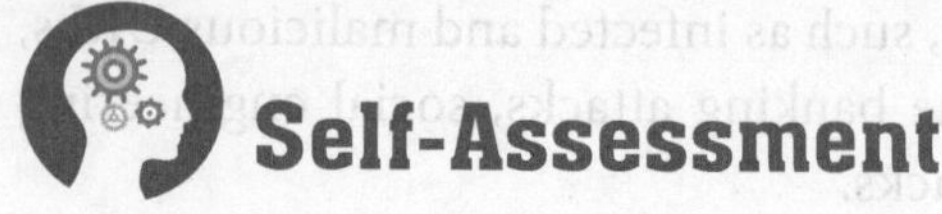

A. MULTIPLE CHOICE QUESTIONS.

1. __________ is one of the purpose of recovering data from an earlier time according to a user-defined data retention policy.

   a. Communication b. Backups c. Removing data

2. __________ is a way of unauthorized access of computer data of another person's.

   a. Phishing b. Malware c. Snooping

3. Which of the following is not a type of Virus:

   a. Boot Sector virus b. Residential Virus c. Direct action Virus d. Overwrite virus

4. What software is used for avoiding viruses?

   a. Disk Cleanup software b. Firewall

   c. Anti-virus software d. Safety software

5. Which of the following is not a antivirus software?

   a. Quick Heal b. Avira c. Norton d. Kasberry

B. FILL IN THE BLANKS

1. The copy of data used to restore and recover the data is known as __________.
2. Always keep your __________ secret.

C. TRUE FALSE

1. You should keep your password same for your all online accounts (T/F)
2. You should download software from any sources without verifying it (T/F)

D. ANSWER THE FOLLOWING QUESTIONS:

1. Define Internet Security.
2. What is the need of Internet security?
3. Explain the term Spyware.
4. Name various threats involved in a system?
5. Give the purpose of data backup.
6. Define these terms:
   - Malware
   - Adware
   - Spamming
   - Phishing
   - Snooping
   - Eavesdropping
7. What is antivirus software?

E. PRACTICAL WORK

Clear a data stored in browser applications

Illustrate the internet security threats through various ways

Check whether Windows firewall is ON in your school computer systems and also install any Antivirus on it.

Answers

A. Multiple choice question answers:

1. b   2. c   3. b   4. c   5. d

B. Fill in the blanks answers:

1. Backup   2. Password

C. True False answers

1. False   2. False

SESSION 8: MAINTAIN WORKPLACE SAFETY

Nowadays, every industry has different type of tools, machinery and equipment to protect their employees from various hazards that can take place while operating machines. The hazard can be electrical, psychological, biological or physical. It is very important for all the employees to be aware about the various risk hazards associated with their work. And safety instructions should be followed by them while handling all the machines and tools. For this, there is need to give a special training to employees so that every precautions should be taken by them while guarding against accidents and hazards related work.

Figure 4.35: Workplace Safety

8.1 Basic safety rules to follow at workplace

The basic safety rules to follow at workplace are:

- Fire escape plans must be installed at proper levels
- Maintain all the safety equipment on regular basis
- Conduct regular drills
- Improper working of smoke or fire alarm bells in industries
- Presence of smoke or fire alarm system
- Proper maintenance of emergency staircase or fire exits
- Proper route of exit or emergency staircase for reaching the place of safety

8.2 Falls and slips, Electrical safety

Various falls and slips, electricity safety rules are:

- The workplace must be properly ventilated
- Oil spills, dust must be cleaned immediately
- Floors must be dry and clean
- Take care that the circuits and outlets must be not overloaded
- Recognised organisation must approve the electrical equipment's.

These are mostly common in textile industry as machines; fabrics and fire-prone equipment are being dealt with. It is more dangerous when employees or worker creates an electrical contact with keyed up equipment or a conductor. The electrical accidents occur when individuals work around the electrical apparatus which is live but they think it is dead. The accidents can also be caused by use of faulty and wrong use of equipment. Other reason can be working on near the electric equipment without appropriate equipment and adequate training. The permanent and brutal injuries can take place by shocks from faulty equipment.

8.3 Use of first aid

The A.B.C of first aid is refer to the three critical things needed to look for as a first aider. Its description is given below:

A stands for airway: To check whether the person have an unobstructed airway or not

B stands for breathing: To check whether the person is breathing or not

C stands for circulation: To check whether the person shows a pulse at major pulse points such as on groin, carotid artery or wrist.

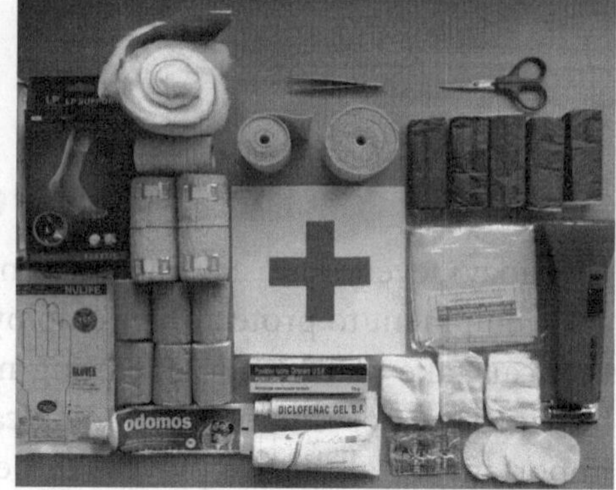

Figure 4.36: First Aid

Few important points:

- The person should avoid moving the casualty until he or she is not in immediate danger. It may make the injuries worse mainly in case of injuries linked to spinal cord.
- Next is calling for emergency services by yourself or telling someone else to call for help on early basis. Try to establish breathing in case if you are the only person on the spot and stay there for long time.
- In case of unconscious person try to shake them gently and speak with them and open their airway in case the person is still unresponsive. The airway can be opened by either jaw thrust method or head tilt or chin lift method.

Summary

- Every industry has different type of tools, machinery and equipment to protect their employees from various hazards that can take place while operating machines.
- The basic safety rules to follow at workplace are conduct regular drills, absence of smoke or fire alarm bells in the industries, maintaining all the safety equipment at proper levels, setting proper route of exit or emergency staircase and many more.
- Various falls and slips, electrical safety rules are the workplace must be properly ventilated, floors must be dry and clean, recognised organization must approve the electrical equipment's, oil spills or dust must be cleaned immediately and many more.
- The electrical risks are mostly common in textile industry as machines; fabrics and fire-prone equipment are being dealt with. It is more dangerous when employees or worker creates an electrical contact with keyed up equipment or a conductor.
- The A.B.C of first aid is refer to the three critical things needed to look for as a first aider.
- A stands for airway: To check whether the person have an unobstructed airway or not
- B stands for breathing: To check whether the person is breathing or not
- C stands for circulation: To check whether the person shows a pulse at major pulse points such as on groin, carotid artery or wrist.

Keywords: Workplace safety, Basic safety rules, Falls and slips, Electrical safety, Use of first aid

Self-Assessment

A. MULTIPLE CHOICE QUESTIONS.

1. What is A stands for in first AID?

   a. Air b. Air pass c. Airway

2. It is very important for all the employees to be aware about the various _______ hazards associated with their work.

   a. Electrical b. Risk c. Kind of

B. FILL IN THE BLANKS

1. B in A.B.C of first aid refers to _______________.

C. TRUE FALSE

1. C in A.B.C of first aid refers to Circular.
2. In case of unconscious person try to shake them gently and speak with them and open their airway in case the person is still unresponsive.

D. ANSWER THE FOLLOWING QUESTIONS:

1. Give various basic safety rules to be followed at workplace.
2. Define the term first aid?
3. What are the reasons of electrical hazard?

E. PRACTICAL WORK

Practice to follow basic safety rules at workplace to prevent accidents and protect workers – Fire safety,

Answers

A. Multiple choice question answers:

   1. c 2. b

B. Fill in the blanks answers:

   1. Breathing

C. True False answers

   1. False 2. True

SESSION 9: PREVENT ACCIDENTS AND EMERGENCIES

The construction industry often comes to mind when one thinks of on-the-job accidents, however, every industry has its risks and workers in all professions can become a victim of an accident.

9.1 Accidents and Emergency

An accident is any unforeseen or unplanned circumstance that is a mishap and has a negative outcome. While most minor accidents are not life threatening, a lot of major accidents happen around us every day.

Most common types of accidents involve:

- Automobile and road accidents
- Sports related accidents
- Fall injuries
- Fire accidents

It is important to understand the emergency services and emergency management required during an accident, for the victim.

The critical care of victims, who have suffered injuries during the accident (e.g. road accident), is handled by the accident and emergency department (A&E department) of the hospital. Paramedics who work in the accident and emergency department are deployed to help the victim at the site of accident. They provide the accident victims with emergency medical services, ambulance services and provide transport to the emergency room.

9.2 Types of Accidents

There are various types of accidents and few of them are covered under this section.

- **Motor Vehicle Accidents:** People who drive as part of their jobs are exposed to negligent drivers, family automotive equipment and inclement weather. All of these factors can cause a car, bus or truck accidents. Workers who spend their days around moving vehicles also face a high risk of getting hurt in a collision. For examples, a worker at a construction site could get hit by a tractor, or a worker in a factory or warehouse could collide with a forklift.

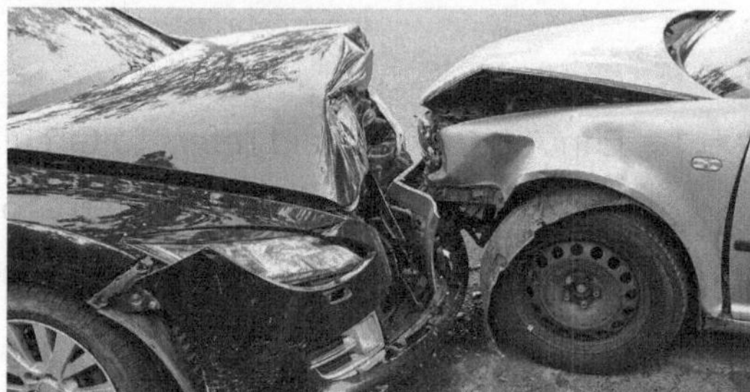

Figure 4.37: Motor Vehicle Accidents

Figure 4.38: Slip and Falls

- **Slip and Falls:** In a workplace there are various different factors that can cause a slip and fall including wet floors or icy surfaces scattered debris and cords uneven or unstable walking surfaces and poor lighting. A fall can lead to sever injuries including broken on bones, traumatic brain injury, spinal cord injury and soft tissue damage.

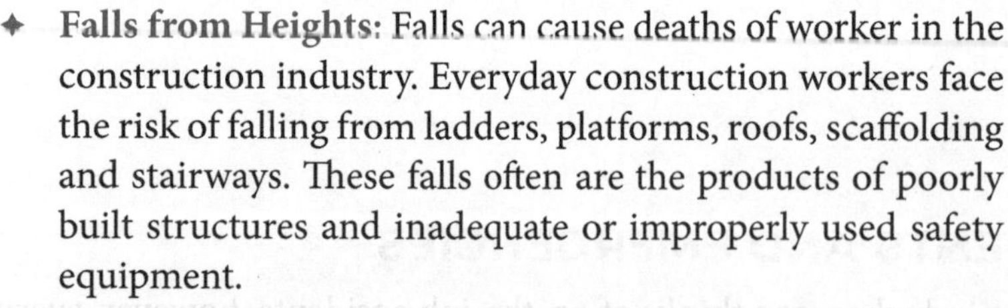

- **Falls from Heights:** Falls can cause deaths of worker in the construction industry. Everyday construction workers face the risk of falling from ladders, platforms, roofs, scaffolding and stairways. These falls often are the products of poorly built structures and inadequate or improperly used safety equipment.

Figure 4.39: Falls from Heights

- **Electrocution:** Electrocution related injuries can cause from working around exposed cords or wires. Harm can also be caused by faulty electrical outlets. In some cases, workers may suffer electrocution from working around power lines or hitting underground cables as they dig. Employers should make sure that all electrical hazards are identified and give their workers a proper warming.

- **Overexertion:** Pushing, carrying, lifting, pulling and throwing activities are most common cause of injuries related to job. These injuries may occur in a single incident that can be cumulative and result in years of engaging in the same strenuous activity on daily basis. The worker muscles, ligaments or tendons can also be injured who rips or slips without falling.

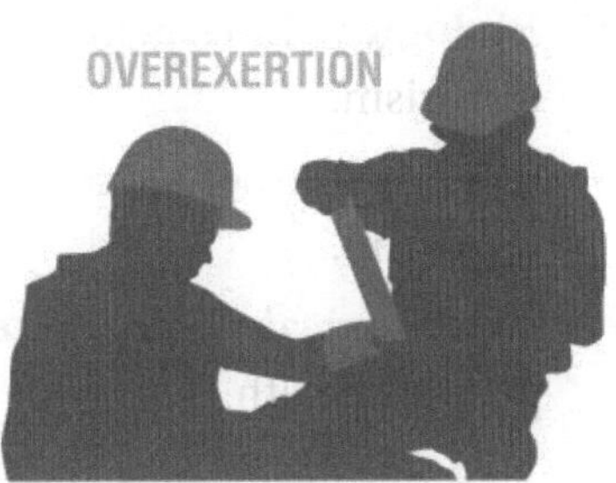

Figure 4.40: Overexertion

- **Struck by Objects:** Being hit by an object that has fallen from above or thrown by a person or machinery can also cause serious injury. Falling, flying, rolling or swinging objects can cause blunt-force trauma such as fractures, internal organ injuries, eye injuries, cuts and bruises. The most common injury from a fallen object is a head injury.

Other can be repetitive injuries, Over stuck and many more.

9.3 Handling Accidents

The best way to avoid workplace accidents is through a strategic safety plan. With proactive measures in place, you and your employees can create a culture of safety and a targeted accident prevention program.

Consider the following tips to bolster your safety efforts:

- **Promote safety awareness and education** with regular safety briefings and employee safety training.
- **Install proper lighting** to create a well-lit and visible jobsite that makes it easier for your staff to see potential risks and avoid them.
- **Communicate safety hazards with adequate signage** that clearly identifies hazardous areas and potential risks like obstacles, spills, toxic materials, or other hazards.
- **Contain spills** quickly when they happen, and remember to always have cleanup equipment readily accessible in your workplace.
- **Routinely check for safety hazards**, like spills or obstacles.
- **Install proper ventilation** to prevent toxic chemicals or other foreign particles from being inhaled by your employees.
- **Enforce proper attire** that's necessary for accident prevention, like hard hats or slip-resistant shoes.

Concepts in accident prevention

- **Primary prevention:** removal of circumstances causing injury - eg, traffic speed reduction, fitting stair gates for young children, reducing alcohol consumption.
- **Secondary prevention:** reduces severity of injury should an accident occur - eg, use child safety car seats, bicycle helmets, smoke alarms.
- **Tertiary prevention:** optimal treatment and rehabilitation following injuries - eg, effective first aid, appropriate hospital care.

9.4 Types of Emergencies

There are various types of emergencies that could affect you and your family. An emergency can happen at any time and in any place. Knowing the facts can help you be prepared for these emergencies and help you to stay safe. Various types of emergency are:

- **Biological Emergencies:** These include diseases as well as biological agents that may be used for terrorism.
- **Chemical Emergencies:** These include harmful chemical spills and chemicals that are used in acts of terrorism.
- **Radiological Emergencies:** These are emergencies involving the release of radiation that could harm people's health.
- **Weather and Home Emergencies:** These are emergencies involving potential hazards such as winter weather, extreme heat, flooding, or carbon monoxide.

Summary

- An accident is any unforeseen or unplanned circumstance that is a mishap and has a negative outcome.
- The critical care of victims, who have suffered injuries during the accident (e.g. road accident), is handled by the accident and emergency department (A&E department) of the hospital.
- Various types of accidents are motor vehicle accidents, Slip and Falls, Falls from heights, Electrocution, Overexertion, Stuck by objects, repetitive injuries and many more.
- The best way to avoid workplace accidents is through a strategic safety plan.
- Primary prevention is the removal of circumstances causing injury- eg, traffic speed reduction, fitting stair gates for young children, reducing alcohol consumption.
- Secondary prevention reduces severity of injury should an accident occur - eg, use child safety car seats, bicycle helmets, smoke alarms.
- Tertiary prevention is the optimal treatment and rehabilitation following injuries- eg, effective first aid, appropriate hospital care.
- Various types of emergency can be Biological, chemical, radiological and weather and home emergencies.

Keywords: Accidents, Emergency, Motor Vehicle Accidents, Slip and Falls, Falls from Heights, Electrocution, Overexertion, Struck by objects, Handling accidents, Accident prevention, Primary prevention, Secondary prevention, Tertiary prevention, Types of emergencies, Biological emergencies, Chemical emergencies, Radiological emergencies, Weather Emergencies, Home emergencies

Self-Assessment

A. MULTIPLE CHOICE QUESTIONS

1. An ___________ is any unforeseen or unplanned circumstance that is a mishap and has a negative outcome.

   a. Emergency b. Work c. Accident

2. Pushing, carrying, lifting, pulling and throwing activities are most common cause of injuries related to job. This comes under which type of accident?

   a. Electrocution b. Overexertion c. Slip and Falls

B. FILL IN THE BLANKS

1. ___________ is any unforeseen or unplanned circumstance that is a mishap and has a negative outcome

2. __________ related injuries can cause from working around exposed cords or wires.

3. __________ emergency involve the release of radiation that could harm people's health.

C. TRUE FALSE

1. Removal of circumstances causing injury- eg, traffic speed reduction, fitting stair gates for young children, reducing alcohol consumption is the secondary prevention of accident (T/F).
2. Biological Emergencies include diseases as well as biological agents that may be used for terrorism (T/F)

D. ANSWER THE FOLLOWING QUESTIONS:

1. Name various types of accidents.
2. What are the most common types of accidents?
3. Define stuck by objects type of accident.

E. PRACTICAL WORK

Demonstrate to follow evacuation plan and procedure in case of an emergency.

Answers

A. Multiple choice question answers:

1. c

B. Fill in the blanks answers:

1. Accident 2. Electrocution 3. Radiological

C. True False answers

1. False 2. True

SESSION 10: PROTECT HEALTH AND SAFETY AT WORK

Most manufacturing units have similar hazards in their processes and work areas. Hence, it is mandatory to have adequate equipment and facilities in the factory to Safety, Maintenance and Organisational Hazards avoid these hazards. Adequate planning, training and awareness workshops are necessary to train employees and workers, in which, the employees must be made aware of various hazards associated with its units, such as embroidery, and the precautions to be taken. Even though manufacturing units like the garment manufacturing is an organised sector in India, they usually fail to adhere to all standards and rules set down by the government. Many small units are located in residential areas which may be prone to fire and other hazards

10.1 Hazards and sources of hazards

Hazard is a potentially damaging physical event, phenomenon or human activity that may cause the loss of life or injury, property damage, social and economic disruption or environmental degradation. Hazards can include latent conditions that may represent future threats and can have different origins: natural or induced by human processes. Some of the common cause of occupational injuries and deaths in industries such as healthcare, cleaning, transportation, building, maintenance, extraction and construction are:

- **Fire Hazard:** These hazards are common in industries that use a lot of flammable material such as chemicals and cotton. It mainly occur due to improper working of fire and smoke bells in industries, absence of fire and smoke alarm systems in many industries and improper maintenance of fire exists or emergency staircase.

- **Biological hazards:** These hazards involve contagious bacteria, toxins and viruses. It can take place due to non-airy and dark rooms, bad ventilation and unhygienic conditions of washrooms. For instance, influenza affects a broad population of workers. Due to biological hazards mainly gardeners, farmers, civilian and building outdoor workers gets affected.
- **Psycho-social hazards:** These hazards are related to mental health and emotional well-being of the employees and workers in an organisation may not be normal. This may occur due to feeling of job insecurity, lack of enthusiasm towards work, frustration about not being allowed to deliver quality product due to quantitative production pressure and long working hours and many more. These aspects should be dealt with care as these are sensitive issues.
- **Electrical hazards:** These hazards are common in textile industries such as machines, fabrics and other fire-prone equipment dealt with here. It is dangerous when worker or employees creates electrical circuits with keyed up equipment or a conductor. These accidents mainly take place when the individuals are working around electrical apparatus which is live but they think it is dead.

10.2 General evacuation procedures

Some important suggestions for maintaining the health and safety of workers:

- Respiratory and hand protection
- Eye protection
- Heat stress protection
- Supply of filtered drinking water
- Setup rest or sick rooms as per the number of workers
- Set up recreation facility for the workers

In order to remove monotony from work, it is very essential to setup a recreation facility for the workers:

- Fire protection
- Finger protection
- Proper lighting
- Ergonomic design of the workstation
- Awareness towards physical and psychological health
- First aid facility
- Adequate washrooms for the workers

10.3 Healthy living

Healthy lifestyle involves a lot of things under it, including a nutritional diet, daily exercise, adequate sleep, being happy and thinking positively. When we do all the necessary elements to have a healthy lifestyle, our lives are going on the right path. Living a healthy life is vital for everyone to be happy and feel good in their present and future life. Once someone choose to live a healthy life, it lasts all your life. It not only helps in living longer but also better and less prone to sickness and diseases. A healthy living is the kind of living that everyone should strive for.

Summary

- Adequate planning, training and awareness workshops are necessary to train employees and workers, in which, the employees must be made aware of various hazards associated with its units, such as embroidery, and the precautions to be taken.
- Hazard is a potentially damaging physical event, phenomenon or human activity that may cause the loss of life or injury, property damage, social and economic disruption or environmental degradation.
- Some of the common cause of occupational injuries and deaths in industries such as healthcare, cleaning, transportation, building, maintenance, extraction and construction are Fire hazard, Biological hazard, psycho-social hazard and electrical hazard.

- Some important suggestions for maintaining the health and safety of workers are Eye protection, Heat stress protection, Set up recreation facility for the workers, supply of filtered drinking water and many more
- Healthy lifestyle involves a lot of things under it, including a nutritional diet, daily exercise, adequate sleep, being happy and thinking positively.

Keywords: Hazards, sources of hazards, Fire hazards, Biological hazards, Electrical hazards, Psycho-social hazards, General evacuation procedures, Healthy living

Self-Assessment

A. MULTIPLE CHOICE QUESTIONS.

1. __________ is a potentially damaging physical event, phenomenon or human activity that may cause the loss of life or injury, property damage, social and economic disruption or environmental degradation.

   a. Earth quake b. Hazard c. Accident

2. Which of the following hazards are common in textile industries such as machines, fabrics and other fire-prone equipment?

   a. Fire hazard b. Biological hazard c. Electrical hazard

Answers

1. b 2. c

B. ANSWER THE FOLLOWING QUESTIONS:

1. Give various types of hazards that can take place in work area.
2. What do you mean by Hazards?
3. What are the benefits of having healthy living?

C. PRACTICAL WORK

Identify the problems at workplace that could cause accidents,

Solved Exercise

A. MULTIPLE CHOICE QUESTIONS

1. The framework within which an organization strives to meet its needs for information security is codified as:

   a. security policy b. confidentiality c. CAM d. CAD

2. Which of the following are the mechanisms and techniques—administrative, procedural, and technical—that are instituted to implement a security policy:

   a. Privacy b. Integrity c. Availability d. Management control

3. ___________ is a small program which badly effects the working of the computer:

   a. worm b. Trojan c. virus d. antivirus

4. Antivirus software is:
   a. self-replicate
   b. can give fake pop ups to buy non-existent antivirus software
   c. performs scans of every file on the computer
   d. activated by creating Process
5. In keyboard tab, ___________ is an access feature that helps computer users who have physical disabilities along with by people who want to reduce their repetitive strain.
   a. Filter Keys   b. Toggle Keys   c. Sticky Keys   d. Numeric keys
6. Virus can:
   a. give fake pop ups to buy non-existent antivirus software
   b. monitor what you are doing
   c. both a and b
   d. neither a nor b
7. If some computers in a network have dedicated tasks that provide services to rest of the computers in the network is known as ___________.
   a. Peer to Peer network   b. Client-Server network
   c. LAN network   d. WAN network
8. Which of the following have datarate of 56 kbps to 155 Mbps, 622 Mbps, 2.4 Gbps and higher speed.
   a. LAN   b. MAN   c. WAN   d. None of these

Answers

1. a   2. d   3. c   4. c   5. c   6. c   7. b   8. c

B. SOLVED VERY SHORT AND SHORT QUESTION AND ANSWERS:

1. Define Accebility?

Ans. Accessibility is a word that is defined as services for people with some disabilities so that they can perform their work without any problem.

2. What is the functioning of Filter keys in Keyboard tab?

Ans. It is Microsoft Windows feature and function of accessibility that tells keyboard about ignoring repeated keystrokes that make typing easy for people have trembles hand.

3. Give the usage of Sound Sentry?

Ans. It is used for helping people having auditory injuries. By this tab a visual warning will be generated for instance a sound is generated by computer on blinking of title bar.

4. Briefly explain Client-Server network?

Ans. If some computers in a network have dedicated tasks that provide services to rest of the computers in the network is known as client server architecture. In such kind of network, the server is the computers that provide services and clients are the one that uses these services.

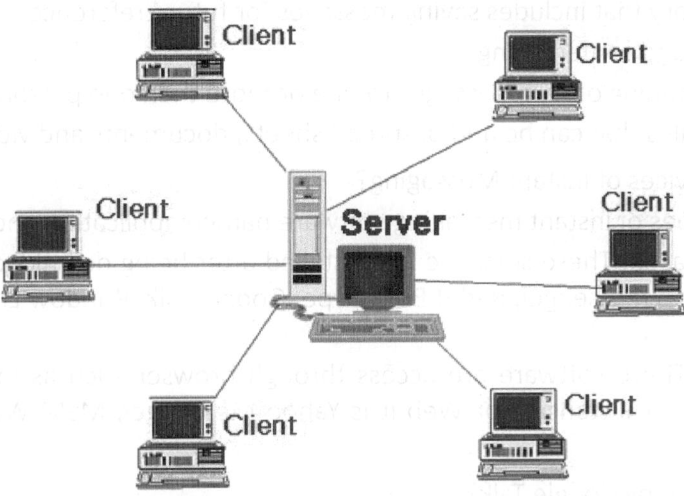

Client-Server network

In this, server is the powerful computers that store information in it. It manages the disk drives, network traffic and printers. On other hand, clients are computers that let users to access that data on the server. It relies on servers for resources that can be devices, processing power and files.

5. Give name of different networks based on size?

Ans. Different networks based on size are:

- Local area network, or LAN
- Metropolitan area network, or MAN
- Wide area network, or WAN

6. Give characteristics of MAN?

Ans. Characteristics of MAN

- It covered large geographical area.
- It uses Fibre optic cable as a transmission media
- It transmission is very fast.
- It generally covered a city or a town.
- It supports voice communication.

7. What are the various benefits of networking?

Ans. Various benefits associated with networking are:

- Data sharing: It allow sharing of data
- Files transfer: It enable the sending of text files, documents, audio files, presentation, spread sheets and video files to other users.
- Hardware sharing: It enable sharing of scanners, printers like hardware components.
- Internet Access Sharing: It enable the purchasing of Internet connection and sharing it with other computer systems in the network.
- Use of applications based of network: It enable the use of network based applications for instance email clients, video calling, chat applications and audio calling.

8. Define Cable Internet Access?

Ans. It is one of the forms of broadband Internet access in which TV infrastructure is used. It is provided via existing networks of cable TV. It is almost same as DSL.

9. Give various key features of Instant Messaging?

Ans. Various key features of IM are:

- Audio calling and conferencing

- Message history that includes saving messages for future reference
- Video calling and conferencing
- As like SMS sending of text messages to one or more than one persons
- Transferring files that can be audio, spread sheets, documents and video files.

10. What are the services of Instant Messaging?

Ans. There are two types of instant messaging software named application and web based.

- Application based: These software are installed after being download in users computer. For instance: Yahoo messenger, Rediff Bol, Skype, Google Talk, Window Live Messenger and many more.
- Web Based: These software are access through browser such as Internet Explorer, Google chrome, etc. For instance: For Web it is Yahoo Messenger, MSM Web Messenger, IMO and Meebo, etc.

11. What do you mean by Google Talk?

Ans. Google talk is also known as Google instant messaging network and its IM client. This can be downloaded from talk.google.com and learn more about it. It enables the sending and receiving of voice over-IP internet phone calls and text-based instant messages. For using Google Talk as a text based IM client, you need a computer and internet connection and to use calling feature there is also need of microphone and speaker for your system.

12. Give various rules and etiquettes that need to be followed while chatting?

Ans. Some general rules and etiquettes to be followed while chatting include:

- Use short messages
- Give time to respond to messages
- Properly end a conversation
- Do not use ALL Caps
- Respect other while chatting
- Don't use abusive or indecent language while chatting
- Always use a secure chat room
- Never disclose any personal information

13. Define Offline Blog editors?

Ans. Offline blog editor is an editor that let bloggers to create a blog posts without internet connection. It enables the creation, editing and formatting your content before uploading it on the website. Once users are done with all the updates, they can post it directly on their blog in the presence of Internet connection.

14. What is E-ticketing:

Ans. It is the new facility of booking or cancelling tickets of flights, train and buses through Internet. This also enable user to book a tickets on IRCTR portal provided by Indian Railway. It is nothing but an electronic version of a regular paper tickets.

15. Define Virus as Cyber threat?

Ans. A computer virus is a kind of malware program which, when run, get replicated by inserting copies of itself into another computer programs, data files of the hard drive. When the replication process of virus get succeeds, the affected areas are called as "infected".

16. What is spamming?

Ans. It is an approach of flooding the Internet with various copies of same messages comes in the form of commercial achievements sent to users as unwanted emails.

17. Give basic safety rules to follow at workplace?

Ans. The basic safety rules to follow at workplace are:

- Fire escape plans must be installed at proper levels

- Maintain all the safety equipment on regular basis
- Conduct regular drills
- Improper working of smoke or fire alarm bells in industries
- Presence of smoke or fire alarm system
- Proper maintenance of emergency staircase or fire exits
- Proper route of exit or emergency staircase for reaching the place of safety

18. When Overexertion take place?

Ans. Pushing, carrying, lifting, pulling and throwing activities are most common cause of injuries related to job. These injuries may occur in a single incident that can be cumulative and result in years of engaging in the same strenuous activity on daily basis. The worker muscles, ligaments or tendons can also be injured who rips or slips without falling.

C. LONG SOLVED QUESTION AND ANSWERS:

1. Define in detail the various types of keyboard Tab?

Ans. Sticky Keys: It is an access feature that helps computer users who have physical disabilities along with by people who want to reduce their repetitive strain.

- Filter Keys: It is Microsoft Windows feature and function of accessibility that tells keyboard about ignoring repeated keystrokes that make typing easy for people have trembles hand.
- Toggle Keys: It is Microsoft Windows feature and function of accessibility that is designed for users suffering from cognitive disabilities or vision impairment. By enabling the Toggle Keys the computer start emitting sound cues while pressing Scroll Lock, Num Lock and Caps Lock like locking keys. In case of turning on the key a low sound comes from keys and vice a versa for turning it on.

Sound Tab: A window with options to configure accessibility options for sound is displayed. Other things included in it are:

- Sound Sentry: It is used for helping people having auditory injuries. By this tab a visual warning will be generated for instance a sound is generated by computer on blinking of title bar.
- Slow Sounds: It help in instructing application for conveying information by sound and visually information is also provided by it through a captions of text or informative icons.

Display Tab: By selecting a display Tab a window will pop up that consists of various options of configuring the accessibility options. Such options are:

- High Contrast: It is features of accessibility that assist user have impairment related to vision. Through this for ease of viewing user can change the colour or size of fonts and background.
- Cursor Options: It is features of accessibility that assist user have impairment related to vision via changing the width and blink rate of the cursor.

Mouse Tab: Various keys come under it are:

- Mouse Keys: It is features of accessibility that assists user having problem in using a mouse. In this option, numeric keypad or other part of keyboard are used as a pointing device.

General Tab: It enable in configuring the accessibilities options for all users. By selecting this tab a window to configure the additional accessibility options will be displayed.

- Serial Keys: It is features of accessibility that assists user have difficulty in using mouse or keyboard.

2. Define Network and various types of network in Computers?

Ans. Computer network is consist of various computers along with hardware components that are interconnected with each other through satellites or cables like communication channels that allow sharing of information and resources.

Various types of computer network are:

Peer-to-peer (P2P) Architecture,

If all computers in a network have an equal status then it is known as peer to peer networks. In such kind of network there is equally competent CPU of each terminal. That means the request can be initiated by each peer to other peers along with it can respond to incoming requests from other peers on the network.

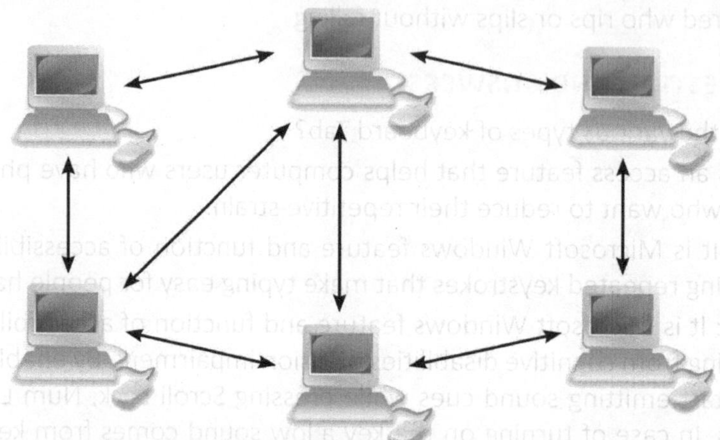

Figure 3: Peer to peer network

2.2 Client-Server Architecture:

If some computers in a network have dedicated tasks that provide services to rest of the computers in the network is known as client server architecture. In such kind of network, the server is the computers that provide services and clients are the one that uses these services.

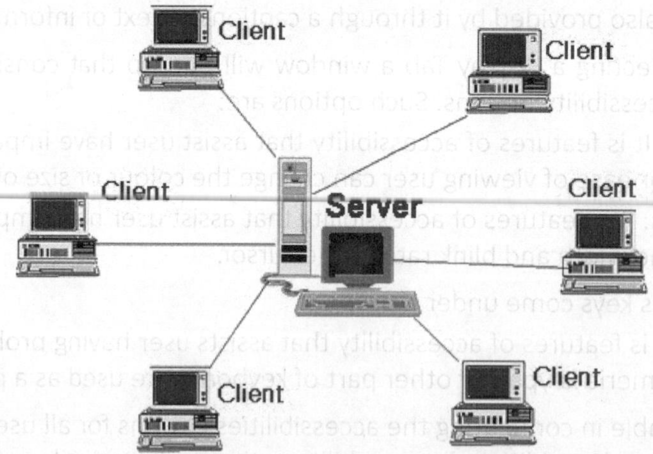

Client-Server network

In this, server is the powerful computers that store information in it. It manages the disk drives, network traffic and printers. On other hand, clients are computers that let users to access that data on the server. It relies on servers for resources that can be devices, processing power and files.

3. Write a note on Internet and World Wide Web?

Ans. Internet

It is a global system of interconnected computer networks that use the standard Internet protocol suite for serving a large count of users worldwide. It consists of millions of private, business, government, academic and public networks.

Features:

- Global system of interconnected computer networks.
- Uses the standard Internet Protocol Suite (TCP/IP).
- Serve billions of users worldwide.
- It consists of millions of private, public, academic, business, and government networks.
- It carries a vast array of information resources and services.

WORLD WIDE WEB: It is abbreviated as WWW or W3 or most of the time it is known as Web. It is a system of interlinked hypertext documents that are accessed through Internet. One can view web pages containing videos, images, text and other multimedia with a Web browser and through hyperlinks it navigate between them.

Benefits of networking

Various benefits associated with networking are:

- Data sharing: It allow sharing of data
- Files transfer: It enable the sending of text files, documents, audio files, presentation, spread sheets and video files to other users.
- Hardware sharing: It enable sharing of scanners, printers like hardware components.
- Internet Access Sharing: It enable the purchasing of Internet connection and sharing it with other computer systems in the network.

Use of applications based of network: It enable the use of network based applications

4. Give in detail about chatting on various types of network?

Ans. There are various types of messenger available on which you can chat. Some of them are explained in this section.

Chatting on Gmail:

Gmail account can be used for chatting. After signing into account, one have to click on contact window displayed on the left side within the Gmail account page.

To start a new chat, simply click on "+" sign and pop-up window will appear.

Chatting on Yahoo

Yahoo messenger is an IM program that helps in keeping in touch with near and dear ones. It enable the sending if messages and voice conferencing calls. To use it, download and install Yahoo! Messenger from http://in.messenger.yahoo.com/download.

To start chatting, user must have Yahoo mail account and credentials of it. As you sign in using these credentials a contacts list will start appearing for chat.

5. How to set up title and other parameters in a blog posting comments?

Ans. Once you have created a blog, your blog address will start appearing on the top of web page. Double clicking on the link will take you on the home page where you can add content to you blog. There is need to provide a unique title for you post and typing content in the text box. Once you have typed the content simply click on Publish button.

To set up a tittle and other parameters in a blog positing comments, perform the following steps:

- Click on Create a blog or New blog
- Enter a title for your blog and choose the URL or blog address
- Type the content in text box
- Click on publish button

You can also comment on posts published by others by typing your comment in comment box located below the post named as Leave a Reply.

6. Give detail of various online applications?

Ans. Main two online applications are:

E-shopping: It is a form of electronic commerce that enables customers to buy goods from a seller on the Internet using a web browser or their applications. Further, credit or debit cards are used by customers for making payment on the Internet.

Some of the e-shopping websites are:

- www.flipkart.com
- www.snapdeal.com
- www.mantra.com
- www.amazon.com
- www.jabong.com

E-ticketing: It is the new facility of booking or cancelling tickets of flights, train and buses through Internet. This also enable user to book a tickets on IRCTR portal provided by Indian Railway. It is nothing but an electronic version of a regular paper tickets.

7. Write a note of need of Internet Security?

Ans. In today's modern world the internet proves to be the best communication medium for everyone. Even though it has many advantages, it also has a few drawbacks which the users need to be aware of to steer clear from the online dangers. Keeping your data and your network safe is vital. Malware is more common today and comes with different tactics to achieve nefarious goals.

It's essential to understand the difference between an antivirus program and internet security software. The antivirus program scans for viruses and malware. While it is excellent for discovering malicious software that has already made it onto your computer, it will typically not offer advanced firewall management to monitor inbound and outbound web traffic feeds.

Internet security software is created to prevent hackers from accessing sensitive information through leaks in the networks. Therefore, to protect your confidential data, it monitors all accessed URLs. Phishing websites are already on its lists; consequently, the software compares the sites visited by the user to its master list of phishing websites, and immediately issues an alert to block the site should there be a match, it immediately warns the administrators through email to block the website.

8. Give various types of Cyber threats?

Ans. There are various types of cyber threats that make system insecure. Some of these threats are covered under this section:

- Virus: A computer virus is a kind of malware program which, when run, get replicated by inserting copies of itself into another computer programs, data files of the hard drive. When the replication process of virus get succeeds, the affected areas are called as "infected".
- Spyware: It's a malware which is installed on a computer with the aim of collecting the owner's private information. Spyware gathers the information about internet interaction, keylogging, passwords, and other valuable data, without even knowing the user of computer.
- Malware: It's a piece of software which is inserted into an information system to cause harm to that or some other systems. Malware can gain remote access to an information system, record and sent data to third party without the user permission or knowledge.

- Trojan: It is a malicious computer program which misrepresents itself to appear useful or interesting just to persuade a victim to install it. Typically, an individual e-mails you a Trojan in the form of a joke program, which appears to be useful but that actually does damage.
- Spamming: It is an approach of flooding the Internet with various copies of same messages comes in the form of commercial achievements sent to users as unwanted emails.
- Snooping: It is a way of unauthorized access of computer data of another person's. It may include casual observance of an email appears on screen of other person computer and enable them to watch what user is typing.
- Phishing: It is used for gaining personal information for identification of theft using fraud email messages comes from genuine users. This is done for gaining personal information of user such as their account numbers and passwords, Adhar card number and credit cards credentials.

9. Write a Note on Concept of backup and antivirus?

Ans. Anti-Virus Software: It is sometimes also known as anti-malware software, is computer software used to prevent, detect and remove malicious software. Antivirus software was originally developed to detect and remove computer viruses, hence the name. However, with the proliferation of other kinds of malware, antivirus software started to provide protection from other computer threats. In particular, modern antivirus software can protect from:

- Malicious browser helper objects (BHOs)
- Browser hijackers
- Ransomware
- Keyloggers
- Backdoors
- Rootkits
- Trojan horses
- Worms
- Adware
- Spyware

Some products also include protection from other computer threats, such as infected and malicious URLs, spam, scam and phishing attacks, online identity (privacy), online banking attacks, social engineering techniques, advanced persistent threat (APT) and botnet DDoS attacks.

Data Backup: In information technology, a backup, or the process of backing up, refers to the copying and archiving of computer data so it may be used to restore the original after a data loss event. The verb form is to back up in two words, whereas the noun is backup. Backups have two distinct purposes:

- The primary purpose is to recover data after its loss, be it by data deletion or corruption. Data loss can be a common experience of computer users.
- The secondary purpose of backups is to recover data from an earlier time, according to a user-defined data retention policy, typically configured within a backup application for how long copies of data are required.

Though backups represent a simple form of disaster recovery, and should be part of any disaster recovery plan, backups by themselves should not be considered a complete disaster recovery plan. One reason for this is that not all backup systems are able to reconstitute a computer system or other complex configuration such as a computer cluster, active directory server, or database server by simply restoring data from a backup.

10. Give various types of accidents?

Ans. Some of the accidents that take place in workplace or on road are:

- Motor Vehicle Accidents: People who drive as part of their jobs are exposed to negligent drivers, family automotive equipment and inclement weather. All of these factors can cause a car, bus or truck accidents. Workers who spend their days around moving vehicles also face a high risk of getting hurt in a collision. For examples, a worker at a construction site could get hit by a tractor, or a worker in a factory or warehouse could collide with a forklift.

- Slip and Falls: In a workplace there are various different factors that can cause a slip and fall including wet floors or icy surfaces scattered debris and cords uneven or unstable walking surfaces and poor lighting. A fall can lead to sever injuries including broken on bones, traumatic brain injury, spinal cord injury and soft tissue damage.
- Falls from Heights: Falls can cause deaths of worker in the construction industry. Everyday construction workers face the risk of falling from ladders, platforms, roofs, scaffolding and stairways. These falls often are the products of poorly built structures and inadequate or improperly used safety equipment.
- Electrocution: Electrocution related injuries can cause from working around exposed cords or wires. Harm can also be caused by faulty electrical outlets. In some cases, workers may suffer electrocution from working around power lines or hitting underground cables as they dig. Employers should make sure that all electrical hazards are identified and give their workers a proper warming.
- Overexertion: Pushing, carrying, lifting, pulling and throwing activities are most common cause of injuries related to job. These injuries may occur in a single incident that can be cumulative and result in years of engaging in the same strenuous activity on daily basis. The worker muscles, ligaments or tendons can also be injured who rips or slips without falling.
- Struck by Objects: Being hit by an object that has fallen from above or thrown by a person or machinery can also cause serious injury. Falling, flying, rolling or swinging objects can cause blunt-force trauma such as fractures, internal organ injuries, eye injuries, cuts and bruises. The most common injury from a fallen object is a head injury.

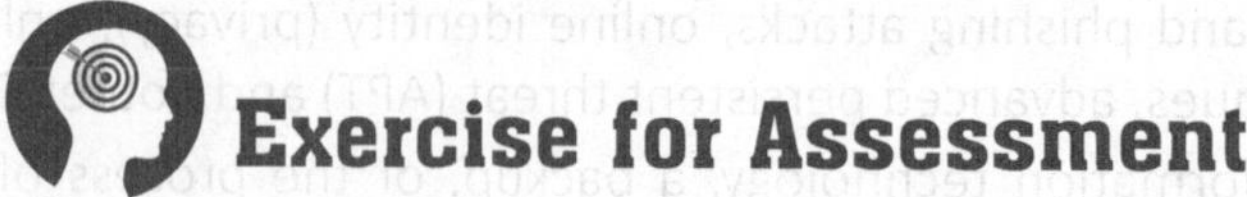

A. MULTIPLE CHOICE QUESTIONS

1. Which of the following is not a keyboard Tab?

   a. Display Tab b. Sound Tab c. Vision Tab d. Mouse Tab

2. A set of rules used for communication is known as ________.

   a. Period b. Protocol c. Process

3. Which of the following is not a free blog service website?

   a. www.blogger.com b. www.amazon.com
   c. www.wordpress.com

4. Always use ____________ password.

   a. Very short b. Short c. Strong

5. ISP is stands for:

   a. Integrated security protocol b. Integrated service provider
   c. Internet service period d. Internet service provider

6. Which of the following is the class of personal information?

   a. Online nickname b. Gender
   c. Date of birth d. Largest peak in your continent

7. Several computers connected together is known as:

   a. Hub   b. Computer network   c. Client   d. Client-server

8. Which of the following is the online portal for booking tickets?

   a. Flipkart   b. EBay   c. Amazon   d. IRCTC

9. ____________ acts as a bridge between your computer and other computers on servers.

   a. Spam   b. Hardware   c. Software   d. Firewall

10. To update your blog content, click the ____________.

    a. Browse   b. Publish Post   c. Title

B. VERY SHORT QUESTION AND ANSWER

1. Define the term Filter keys?
2. What is the full form of P2P architecture?
3. What is WWW?
4. Name various types of Instant messaging services.
5. Give various websites that offer blog services.
6. Name any two types of offline blog editor.
7. Define Spyware cyber threat.
8. Give the full form of First AID.
9. What are the various hazards that can take place in workplace?

C. SHORT QUESTION AND ANSWERS

1. How to launch an accessibility option in the system? Write down the step for the same.
2. Define the term Computer network.
3. How to perform the data transfer on the Internet?
4. The IM stands for instant messaging. What are the various features associated with it?
5. What are the various general rules and etiquettes to be followed while chatting?
6. Write down the steps to create a blog.
7. What is the need of Internet security?
8. Define the term anti-virus software.
9. Give basic safety rules that need to be follow at workplace.
10. What are the tips to bolster the safety efforts?
11. Define Biological hazard?

D. LONG QUESTION AND ANSWERS

1. Give in brief about the purpose of different keys or tab on keyboard?
2. Write a note of various types of network?
3. What do you mean by Google Talk? Also give its usage and how to use it.
4. How to set up title and other parameters in a blog posting comments?

5. Briefly define various online transaction applications?
6. Name and explain various types of cyber threats.
7. Briefly define various types of accidents?

E. APPLICATION BASED QUESTIONS:

1. In your computer lab, a network is created between various computers. Tell the type of network and architecture.
2. In case you want to do audio calling and conferencing then which application will be used for it
3. Modern age is a communication age in which everyone likes to communicate in different ways all over the world. The article and dairy writing is replaced with modern tech-alternative. Name it
4. In case user cant go out physically to buy something. Then, which of the new concept of online transaction he/she can use to buy necessary products by sitting at home.

PROJECT WORK

1. Observe the various types of network in your surrounding and make a list of two places in which LAN, MAN and WAN network is created according to its features.
2. Use Instant messaging application such as Google talk for audio chat and calling your school mate.
3. Create a new blog with any name and publish an article on it with including various pictures related to it.
4. Practically try to book a Railway ticket online for your family using various online applications available for the same.
5. Observe various hazards that have took place in your surroundings. Make a list from last five years record.

TEACHER NOTES

1. Illustrate the use of sound sentry, show sounds and toggle keys, filter keys and sticky keys.
2. Give demonstration to students on how to create blogs using a blog application offline
3. Identify the applications of Internet and compare the various technologies of Internet.

EXAM TIPS

1. Practice the general evacuation procedures in case of an emergency.
2. Illustrate the steps of creating instant messaging account
3. Illustrate chat with a contact and send messages
4. Illustration of internet security threats through various ways
5. Demonstration of strong passwords using various websites

CBSE | DEPARTMENT OF SKILL EDUCATION

INFORMATION TECHNOLOGY (SUBJECT CODE 402)

CLASS X (SESSION 2021-2022)
BLUE – PRINT FOR SAMPLE QUESTION PAPER FOR TERM – 1

Max. Time Allowed: 60 Minutes (1 Hrs.) **Max. Marks: 25**

PART A – EMPLOYABILITY SKILLS (05 MARKS):

UNIT NO.	NAME OF THE UNIT	NO. OF QUESTIONS (1 MARK EACH)
1	Communication Skills-II	2
2	Self-Management Skills-II	2
3	Information and Communication Technology Skills-II	2
TOTAL QUESTIONS		6 Questions
NO. OF QUESTIONS TO BE ANSWERED		Any 5 Questions
TOTAL MARKS		1 x 5 = 5 Marks

PART B – SUBJECT SPECIFIC SKILLS (20 MARKS):

UNIT NO.	NAME OF THE UNIT	NO. OF QUESTIONS (1 MARK EACH)
1	Digital Documentation (Advanced)	11
2	Electronic Spreadsheets (Advanced)	13
3	Database Management System	3
TOTAL QUESTIONS		27 Questions
NO. OF QUESTIONS TO BE ANSWERED		20 Questions
TOTAL MARKS		1 x 20 = 20 MARKS

CBSE | DEPARTMENT OF SKILL EDUCATION

INFORMATION TECHNOLOGY (SUBJECT CODE 402)

CLASS X (SESSION 2021-2022)
BLUE – PRINT FOR SAMPLE QUESTION PAPER FOR TERM – 1

Max. Time Allowed: 60 Minutes (1 Hrs.) **Max. Marks: 25**

General Instructions:

1. Please read the instructions carefully
2. This Question Paper is divided into 03 sections, viz., Section A, Section B and Section C.
3. Section A is of 05 marks and has 06 questions on Employability Skills.
4. Section B is of 15 marks and has 20 questions on Subject Specific Skills.
5. Section C is of 05 marks and has 07 competency-based questions.
6. Do as per the instructions given in the respective sections.
7. Marks allotted are mentioned against each section/question.
8. All questions must be attempted in the correct order

SECTION A

Answer any 5 questions out of the given 6 questions on Employability Skills **(1 x 5 = 5 marks)**

1. **__________ feedback is specific information, in the form of written comments or verbal conversations that help the learner understand what she or he needs to do in order to improve.** **1**

   a. Descriptive b. Specific c. General d. Sign

2. **__________ communication is the use of body language, gestures and facial expressions to convey information to others.** **1**

   a. Verbal b. Written c. Non-Verbal d. Visual

3. **Sonika gets up at 6 am and goes for her hobby classes. Then she comes back home and finishes her homework before going to school. She does all work by herself. No one tells her to do so. This is called __________.**

   a. Self-Awareness b. Self-Motivation c. Self-Regulation d. Discipline

4. **High expectations from self can leave one with chronic anxiety and stress, thus leading to __________ stress.** **1**

   a. Physical b. Emotional c. Mental d. Financial

5. **A __________ operating system is a computing environment that reacts to input within a specific period of time.** **1**

   a. Single User b. Multi-User c. Real Time d. Distribute

6. **Identify the measure to protect computer from threats and viruses:** 1

a. Sharing password with friends
b. Allow anyone to use your device
c. Use Antivirus
d. Leave computer without logging out

SECTION B

Answer any 15 questions out of the given 20 questions **(1 x 15 = 15 marks)**

7. **When you apply a __________, you apply a group of formatting effects together in one single step.** 1

a. Effect b. Style c. Template d. Format

8. **Which function cannot be performed through Subtotal in a Spreadsheet?** 1

a. Sum b. Product c. Average d. Percentage

9. **In a document, __________ refers to the vertical or horizontal placement of a graphic in relation to the chosen anchor point.** 1

a. Arrangement b. Anchoring c. Alignment d. Text Wrapping

10. **A __________ is a model that you use to create other documents.** 1

a. Template b. Document c. Design d. Copy Paste

11. **__________ styles in a text document affect selected text within a paragraph, such as the font and size of text, or bold and italic formats.** 1

a. Cell b. Paragraph b. Formatting d. Character

12. **To repeat the graphic across the entire background area, we need to select option in word processor.** 1

a. Tile b. Position c. Stretch d. Area

13. **Scenarios are a tool to test questions.** 1

a. Auto b. Goal Seek c. What-if d. Drop Down

14. **__________ is particularly useful when creating a watermark or when wrapping the image in the background in a document.** 1

a. Transparency b. Fill c. Filters d. Crop

15. **It refers to a cell or a range of cells on a worksheet and can be used to find the values or data that you want formula to calculate.** 1

a. Row b. Column c. Autosum d. Cell Referenc

16. **__________, totals/adds data arranged in an array—that is, a group of cells with labels for columns and/or rows Which step one must should follow before using the Subtotal option?** 1

a. Consolidate b. Rename Data c. Filter Data d. Subtotal

17. **A __________ hyperlink contains the full address of the destination file or web page.** 1

a. Relative b. Absolute c. Mixed d. Address

18. **Which of the following is more elaborate form of Goal Seek?** 1

a. Subtotal b. Scenario c. Solver d. Consolidate

19. __________ means combining data in a spreadsheet from different worksheets into master worksheet 1

a. Hyperlinks b. Consolidating c. Linking d. Filter

20. An __________ link will stop working only if the target is moved while a __________ link will stop working only if the start and target locations change relative to each other. 1

a. absolute, fixed b. Relative, Absolute

c. absolute, relative d. permanent, absolute

21. Database servers are referred to as __________. 1

a. Front-ends b. Back-ends c. Clients d. Model

22. A table is a set of data elements that is organized using a model of vertical __________ and horizontal __________. 1

a. Rows, Tables b. Columns, Rows c. Rows, Columns d. Forms, Reports

23. __________ include fonts, alignment, borders, background, number formats (for example, currency, date, number), and cell protection in document. 1

a. Cell Style b. Numbering Style c. Paragraph Style d. Character Style

24. By default, sheets tab are present at the __________ of the spreadsheet. 1

a. Top b. Bottom c. Center d. Right

25. The cell reference in a spreadsheet for cell range B2 to F15 is __________. 1

a. B2.F15 b. B2;F15 c. B2:F15 d. B2-F15

26. __________ controls how graphics are stacked upon each other or relative to the text. 1

a. Arrangement b. Alignment c. Anchoring d. Wrapping

SECTION C (COMPETENCY BASED QUESTIONS)

Answer any 5 questions out of the given 6 questions (1 x 5 = 5 marks)

27. Millennium University is organizing a reunion meet for their alumnae students. For this purpose, university wants to send the invite to all these students with their different addresses. Which feature of the Word Processor University should use to accomplish the task? 1

a. Mail Merge b. E-Mail c. Templates d. Data Source

28. Prisha is a book editor. She wants to change the indentation of all paragraphs, and change the font of all titles in the book. Which feature she should use to make the task easy? 1

a. Styles b. Templates c. Table of content d. Consolidating

29. Gaurav has inserted an image in a document. He wants to remove the unwanted area of the image. Which option of the word processor he will use to complete the task? 1

a. Clip art b. Cut c. Crop d. Contrast

30. Hema is a chartered accountant. She used to maintain the accounts in a spreadsheet on everyday basis. There are number of steps which she needs to follow every time. Can you suggest her a feature of spreadsheet through which she can perform these tasks quickly without repeating the steps every time? 1

a. Record Changes b. Track Changes c. Goal Seek d. Using Macros

31. Raj has created a worksheet where he has added all the information of his employees. He wants every employee to go through the worksheet and update their address and phone number, if required. He also would like to know the changes done by his employees. Which feature of spreadsheet he should enable to see the changes made by his employees? 1

a. Macro
b. Link Workbook
c. Change Worksheet
d. Track Changes

32. Akshat wants to store a huge amount information about his firm in a database. Which type of table organization would be most suitable for this purpose? 1

a. Relational
b. Flat File
c. Either Relational or Flat file
d. Hierarchical

33. Sunita is making a project in spreadsheets. Her friend has told her how to rename a spreadsheet as it will help her identify the worksheet data easily. She was very excited and told the same to her brother. Her brother told her that in spreadsheets (OpenOffice0, a worksheet can be renamed using __________ ways. 1

a. 2
b. 3
c. 4
d. 1

Solutions

1. a	2. c	3. b	4. c	5. c	6. c	7. b	8. d
9. a	10. a	11. d	12. a	13. c	14. a	15. d	16. d
17. b	18. c	19. b	20. c	21. b	22. b	23. a	24. b
25. c	26. a	27. a	28. z	29. c	30. d	31. d	32. c
33. b							

Notes